DESIGN TECHNICS

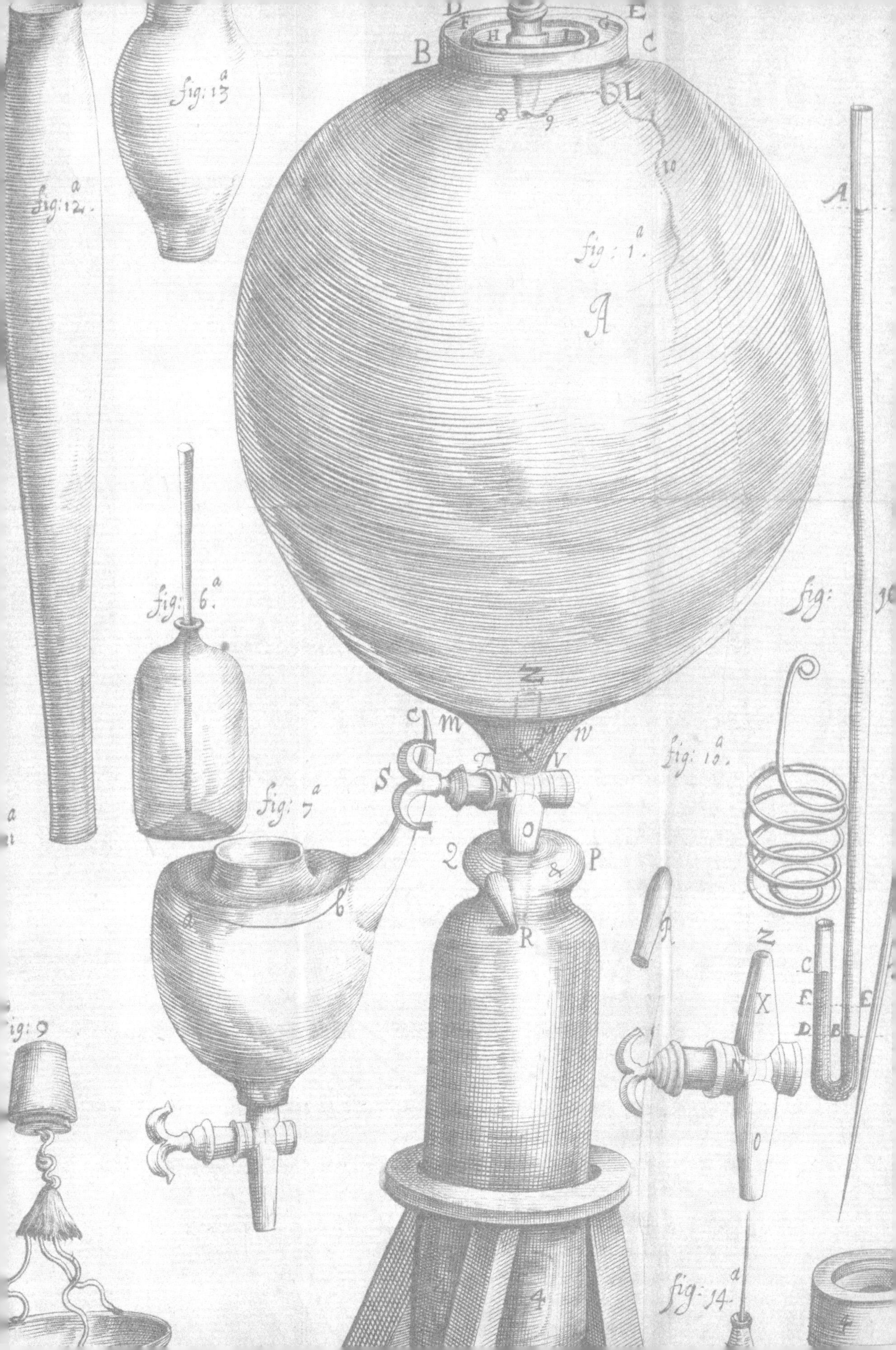

fig: 13a
fig: 12a
fig: 1a
A
B
C
D
E
L
fig: 6a
fig: 7a
fig: 10a
fig: 9
fig: 14a
S
N
O
P
R
Q
Z
X

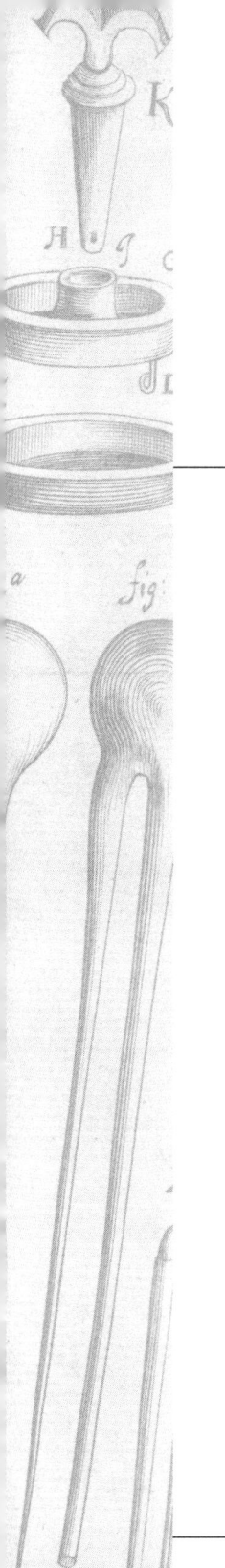

DESIGN TECHNICS

ARCHAEOLOGIES OF ARCHITECTURAL PRACTICE

Zeynep Çelik Alexander and John May, Editors

UNIVERSITY OF MINNESOTA PRESS
MINNEAPOLIS • LONDON

The University of Minnesota Press gratefully acknowledges the financial assistance provided for the publication of this book by the Department of Art History and Archaeology at Columbia University and the Harvard University Graduate School of Design.

Every effort was made to obtain permission to reproduce material in this book. If any proper acknowledgment has not been included here, we encourage copyright holders to notify the publisher.

Copyright 2020 by the Regents of the University of Minnesota.

All rights reserved. No part of this publication may be reproduced, stored in a retrieval system, or transmitted, in any form or by any means, electronic, mechanical, photocopying, recording, or otherwise, without the prior written permission of the publisher.

Published by the University of Minnesota Press
111 Third Avenue South, Suite 290
Minneapolis, MN 55401-2520
http://www.upress.umn.edu

Printed in the United States of America on acid-free paper

The University of Minnesota is an equal-opportunity educator and employer.

27 26 25 24 23 22 21 20   10 9 8 7 6 5 4 3 2 1

Library of Congress Cataloging-in-Publication Data
Names: Çelik Alexander, Zeynep, editor. | May, John (Architect), editor.
Title: Design technics : archaeologies of architectural practice / Zeynep Çelik Alexander and John May, editors.
Description: Minneapolis : University of Minnesota Press, [2020] | Includes biographical references and index.
Identifiers: LCCN 2019023248 (print) | ISBN 978-1-5179-0684-9 (hc) | ISBN 978-1-5179-0685-6 (pb)
Subjects: LCSH: Architectural design. | Architecture and technology.
Classification: LCC NA2750 .D4166 2019 (print) | DDC 720.285—dc23
LC record available at https://lccn.loc.gov/2019023248

Contents

Acknowledgments   vii

Introduction: *Architecture and Technics*   ix
ZEYNEP ÇELIK ALEXANDER

1 Rendering: *On Experience and Experiments*   1
LUCIA ALLAIS

2 Modeling: *A Secret History of Following*   45
MATTHEW C. HUNTER

3 Scanning: *A Technical History of Form*   71
ZEYNEP ÇELIK ALEXANDER

4 Equipping: *Domestic Sleights of Hand*   103
EDWARD A. EIGEN

5 Specifying: *The Generality of Clerical Labor*   129
MICHAEL OSMAN

6 Positioning: *Architecture of Logistics*   163
JOHN HARWOOD

7 Repeating: *Cybernetic Intelligence*   191
ORIT HALPERN

Afterword: *Architecture in Real Time*   219
JOHN MAY

Contributors   245

Index   247

Acknowledgments

This book is a testament to intellectual collaboration—with all its ups and downs, its thrills and inefficiencies. The inefficiencies were all of our own making, but for the thrills we are indebted, first and foremost, to the Aggregate Architectural History Collaborative. We cannot thank enough our remarkable group of most immediate collaborators in this project: Lucia Allais, Ed Eigen, Orit Halpern, John Harwood, Matthew Hunter, and Michael Osman. It has been a rare and singular pleasure to spend these past years exchanging ideas with all of them, and the impact the work has already had—even prior to this final publication—is a testament to the intellectual dynamism that fueled the project throughout.

Along its development from 2013 to 2016, this work was given an audience by other Aggregate members—Timothy Hyde, Daniel Abramson, Arindam Dutta, Pamela Karimi, Ijlal Muzafar, Jonathan Massey, and Meredith TenHoor, a group of remarkable scholars whom we are also lucky to call friends. We are ever grateful for our many conversations with them, and the work contained here belongs as much to their generous engagement with our ideas these past years.

The project that comprises not only this book but also the many conferences, symposia, and essays held in its orbit originated in a series of seminars we co-taught between 2012 and 2014 in the Daniels Faculty of Architecture, Landscape, and Design at the University of Toronto. If it is now somewhat common to find architectural history and theory seminars examining contemporary design technologies, it was far less so when we began, and we are ever grateful to Dean Richard Sommer for lending institutional support to what was, at the time, a highly unusual pedagogical experiment. We are especially grateful to the many students who participated in those classes with genuine curiosity and a willingness to probe into questions that initially must have seemed far from their design pursuits.

This work was given its most extended public treatment during a conference and exhibition at the Princeton School of Architecture in November 2014, and we would like to express gratitude to Dean Stan Allen for supporting that initiative, and to Lucia Allais for her hard work in bringing it to fruition. The insights and productive criticisms generously offered by the extraordinary conference participants—D. Graham Burnett, Jimena Canales, Fabrizio Gallanti, Matthew Jones, Alex Killian, Forrest Meggers, John Tresch, Carolyn Yerkes, and Alejandro Zaera-Polo—were pivotal in pushing our collective work into more difficult but consequential terrain.

Our home institutions have lent crucial material support during the final phases of this publication project. Our sincere thanks to Dean Mohsen Mostafavi at the Harvard University Graduate School of Design as the book moved through the production process. We were lucky to have the assistance and input of many fantastic graduate students along the course of the project's development. Among them, Ultan Bryne, Venessa Heddle, Krister Holmes, Samantha Vasseur, and especially Elliott Sturtevant lent their time and considerable energy in ways that are impossible to quantify.

The ideas in this book were developed thanks to a multiyear grant from the Social Science and Humanities Research Council of Canada. The present volume would never have made its way to our publisher's desk were it not for the many long working sessions made possible by the SSHRC's financial support.

We are tremendously grateful to Pieter Martin for his patience, and to the entire editorial and publication team at the University of Minnesota Press, including Ana Bichanich, Anne Carter, Eric Lundgren, Mike Stoffel, Neil West, and Anne Wrenn. Our thanks to Sheila McMahon and Douglas Easton for their excellent assistance in finalizing the manuscript.

And finally, to our families, we are ever grateful, as always, for their patience and support.

INTRODUCTION

Architecture and Technics

ZEYNEP ÇELIK ALEXANDER

The question of technics appears to saturate the contemporary discipline of architecture. Technical courses occupy increasingly more of the timetable in design schools; students and practitioners alike are repeatedly forced to train and retrain themselves with new software; and new degrees at architectural schools and new courses in continuing education programs stress the growing importance of technical know-how. Perhaps more importantly, the recent centrality of technics seems to be reconfiguring the evidentiary regimes used by designers: it is now routine in architecture schools, for example, for students to justify many of their design decisions, first and foremost, as *technical* solutions—to such daunting problems as rising sea levels or humanitarian emergencies—with little concern that in doing so they might receive the once-derogatory "functionalist" label. All this attention to technics, however, does not necessarily amount to critical analysis. In fact, it may be argued, the more central the role that technics have come to play in the discipline, the narrower the definition of the term has become. The stories that the discipline has been telling itself about the rise of the so-called digital are a case in point: even when they purport to historicize, these stories have foreclosed the promise of history by constructing genealogies that only reaffirm entrenched narratives.[1]

The essays in this volume take another approach. They do not only inquire into the question of technics in an adamantly historical manner but suggest that technics, in fact, might be the most promising arena for a theoretical line of inquiry in the discipline. First, they propose a more capacious meaning for the term *technics*, which is used here to denote a constellation of interrelated practical, artifactual, and procedural material conditions. Even though this publishing endeavor was at first naïvely named "Instruments Project" (a nickname that stuck even after its theoretical premise was abandoned), it quickly became clear that analyzing artifacts used by designers (from the T-square and the French curve to the various kinds of software used today) would be a strategy that would as much duplicate as invert historical sciences' tendency to rest all agency with subjects—in the case of architectural history, for example, with individual designers. Prioritizing the subject or the object conformed too readily to a master-and-slave dialectic familiar from Enlightenment discourses: if humans were the master, instruments were nothing but neutral, passive tools, applying human intentions to a compliant nature. Similarly, if instruments were to be seen as the master, they acquired godlike powers. It was in an attempt to avoid such intractable antinomies that the scholars who contributed to this volume decided to focus on the middle between the object and the subject and between the instrument and its user. That middle is impossibly amorphous, sticky, and mutable, it turns out, and therefore a much more intriguing focus of historical analysis.

As recent media theory has shown us, attending to that middle also means attending to techniques. Second, then, instead of constructing complete genealogies of architecture's relationship to technics, these essays begin with a handful of practices that today's designer undertakes in the studio: rendering, modeling, scanning, equipping, specifying, positioning, and—last but not least—repeating. The point of departure here is no different from the insight articulated by Blaise Pascal in the seventeenth century that belief does not exist as such but becomes possible only by virtue of seemingly mundane practices. "The external must be joined to the internal to obtain anything from God," Pascal wrote, "that is to say, we must kneel, pray with the lips, etc., in order that proud man, who would not submit himself to God, may be now subject to the creature."[2] According to Louis Althusser, who rephrased this passage from *Pensées* to account for the relationship between idea and ideology, this was a significant move. Once the force of such habits and rituals as kneeling down and opening one's hands in prayer is recognized, Althusser wrote, an inversion occurs that rips even religious belief of its metaphysical pretensions: belief as an idea with "ideal or spiritual existence" disappears and belief as a term with a concrete history becomes possible.

This is what Ian Hacking called "historical ontology," an act of de-ontologizing that analyzes how categories, easily mistaken to have robust, unchangeable existences, historically come into being.[3] It is also similar to the insight articulated more recently by media theorists such as Bernhard Siegert that "*man* does not exist independently of cultural techniques of hominization, *time* does not exist independently of cultural techniques for calculating and measuring time; *space* does not exist independently of cultural techniques for surveying and administering space."[4] Lewis Mumford's brilliant analysis of how the invention of glass gave rise to selfhood in the modern sense can be seen as a similar kind of exercise.

> If the outward world was changed by glass, the inner world was likewise modified. Glass had a profound effect upon the development of the personality: indeed, it helped to alter the very concept of the self. . . . For perhaps the first time, except for reflections in the water and in the dull surfaces of metal mirrors, it was possible to find an image that corresponded accurately to what others saw. Not merely in the privacy of the boudoir: in another's home, in a public gathering, the image of the ego in new and unexpected attitudes accompanied one. The most powerful prince of the seventeenth century created a vast hall of mirrors, and the mirror spread from one room to another in the bourgeois household. Self-consciousness, introspection, mirror-conversation developed with the new object itself: this preoccupation with one's image comes at the threshold of the mature personality when young Narcissus gazes long and deep into the face of the pool—and the sense of separate personality, a perception of the objective attributes of one's identity, grows out of this communion.[5]

This is not quite as radical as Michel Foucault's argument that "before the end of the eighteenth century, *man* did not exist" or as fatalistic as Friedrich Kittler's repeated derision of the "so-called man."[6] Yet the relationship between technics and the human seems to be subtly dialectical in Mumford's account of the mirror and the ego: the human appears here not simply as the master of material conditions but rather as a figure who owes its very existence to those material conditions. This way of thinking upsets the long-standing trope of defining artifactual technologies as an extension of the human body—from Marx's application of the Hegelian master and slave dialectic into the interface between machines and humans to Ernst Kapp's conceptualization of all technology as organ-projection *(Organprojektion)* and to Marshall McLuhan's formulation that media are extensions of the human sensorium.[7] By this logic, the hand does not precede the instrument that it holds but is dialectically reconfigured by it: it is material conditions—whether of the artifactual kind discussed by Mumford or the procedural kind discussed by Althusser and Siegert—that make seemingly obdurate existences possible in the first place.

This volume attempts to understand questions of technics in the discipline of architecture in a similar manner. The seven gerunds that structure the book can be seen as cultural techniques that stand in opposition to "any ontological usage of philosophical terms" that have shaped the discipline.[8] While each author undertakes their analysis in a different manner—some take a panoramic view and examine a longer historical arc while others unfold around a single historical moment—they are all thoroughly historical in their approach. How was the concept of form immanent in the practices of scanning that have been debated in aesthetic discourses since the late nineteenth century? How can modeling be understood in relation to following? What was the historical relationship between rendering and experience in Enlightenment discourses? How did practices of specifying configure the distinction between intellectual and manual labor? What would it mean to imagine the primary purpose of architecture as "positioning" as opposed to "holding"? What kind of rationality is inherent in the designer's constant clicking of the mouse in front of her screen? Each essay summons a different kind of archive and excavates it using a slightly different method, but each begins with a single technique, which is then historicized in the hopes of shedding new light on concepts and practices that are used in the design studio today.[9]

Such an effort is bedeviled with countless difficulties, which begin with the term *technics* already. In the English language at least, the word *technics* has been almost entirely eclipsed by what Leo Marx has called the "hazardous" concept of *technology*.[10] The term, Marx explains, was not only physically but also conceptually weaponized: it came to assume omnipotence as "an ostensibly discrete entity" capable of driving history, "a virtually autonomous, all-encompassing agent of change."[11] The meaning of the word *technology*, other historians tell us, underwent a twofold transformation before the twentieth century.[12] First, the English word *technology* collapsed the two possible meanings inherent in the German *Technik*, from which it was adapted: *Technik* can refer to artifacts or procedures whereas in English these two possible meanings splinter into the words *technology* and *technique*.[13] Second, as the word *technology* became more widespread in the Anglo-American world especially after the 1930s, it lost its previously arcane meanings as the rules of grammar, on the one hand, and as the field that studied what had hitherto been called useful arts, mechanical arts, or applied science, on the other.[14] Meanwhile, *technics*, once closer to the double meaning implied by *Technik*, became increasingly obsolete—except when revived by the likes of Lewis Mumford, who used it more generously to describe "that field of activity wherein, by an energetic organization of the process of work, man controls and directs the forces of nature for his own purposes"—that is, as a force that was not only symbolic but also constitutive of culture in general.[15]

Add to this the difficulty of placing the question of technics within the discipline of architecture, whose place among other disciplines at the university has historically been an uncertain proposition.[16] If *technics* has been reduced to *technology* in common parlance, the question has been made almost synonymous with *tectonics* in architectural discourses. This is in large part because historians who have written histories of architectural modernism have chosen to shape their narratives around genealogies of a "tectonic impulse."[17] Such genealogies usually start in the German-speaking world with the architect and archaeologist Karl Bötticher, who defined *Tektonik* in 1852 intriguingly as "the structural and instrument-forming labor *[Geräthebildende Werkthätigkeit]*" but quickly provided a caveat so that he would not be mistaken for a dangerous materialist: "as long as it is able to ethically penetrate its tasks arising from the needs of the spiritual or physical life, and thus not only meet the mere needs of a materially necessary body formation but also to raise the latter to an art form *[Kunstform]*."[18] Conventionally the tectonic genealogy continues with Gottfried Semper—despite the fact that in his monumental *Der Stil* the theorist did not even have the chance to get to that final volume on architecture whose four elements can be seen as a more dynamic version of Marc-Antoine Laugier's fictitious primitive hut.[19] Eugène-Emmanuel Viollet-le-Duc makes an important appearance in this narrative: the "structural rationalism" that he found in the Gothic is understood to have been informed by a tectonic sensibility according to which each component of a building was imagined to be as indispensable to the whole as a bone would be to an animal.[20]

The work of these important theorists notwithstanding, for the likes of Sigfried Giedion writing in the early twentieth century, the previous century had failed to produce a robust tectonic sensibility—beyond a "tectonic unconscious" that was discernible in the infrastructural work of engineers.[21] Yet, Giedion argued, the repressed would ultimately return: the architects of the Modern Movement would heroically retrieve this implicit tectonic impulse, making technics a "conscious" centerpiece of architectural modernity. Given the influence of this narrative, it is no surprise that in historiography, architects who chose to design *tectonic expressivity* (think of Ludwig Mies van der Rohe's adamant articulation of the steel I-beam column in the corner of his skyscrapers even when the steel element did not reach the ground) won over those who chose to design *tectonic process* (think of Louis Sullivan's ingenious turn to factory-produced terracotta in the midst of strikes that disrupted the work of masons on the construction site).[22] So influential proved the tectonic teleology that even narratives written against it have ended up utilizing its powerful rhetoric. The rich historiography on ornament—structure's "other" in modernist discourses—that has developed within the last two decades could be seen in this light.[23] As the reappearance of ornament in the work of historians coincided with the reinvention of a new ornamental sensibility by contemporary designers, the narrative about modern architecture's tectonic trajectory has only become stronger.[24] Far from challenging the tectonic narrative, then, talk of ornament has strengthened it.

Paradoxically, Giedion, the most effective proselytizer of the tectonic trajectory, was also among the first to identify "a new constellation" in architectural modernism's vexed relationship to technics.[25] In his monumental *Mechanization Takes Command* of 1948, the émigré examined the copious documentation that he found in the patent office of his newly adopted country and wrote an anonymous history of "tools and objects." This was a history of such "humble" things as locks, chairs, bathtubs, and bread, and such processes as the assembly line, regeneration, and, most crucially, mechanization, all of which, Giedion claimed, had "shaken our mode of living to its roots."[26] These humble things might have taken center stage in *Mechanization Takes Command,* but the human agents who made them did not disappear altogether either: a patent, after all, is a recording of authorship. It would fall to Reyner Banham to pick up where Giedion had left things off. Relentlessly critiquing architectural modernism's tendency to demarcate technics into structures and mechanical systems to the detriment of the latter, Banham brilliantly proclaimed another meaning of technics for architecture and yet another return of the repressed. In 1969 he rewrote the history of modern architecture from the perspective of environments created by mechanical equipment as opposed to spaces created by tectonics.[27] "Ask a historian of modern architecture who invented the *piloti,* and he can tell you," Banham sneered, but "ask him who invented the (equally consequential) revolving door, and he cannot."[28] Modernists had for too long designed buildings that *looked like* machines; Banham longed for a modern architecture that *worked like* machines.

Against historians who pointed out that the tall austere massing of the Larkin Administration Building was indebted to grain silos, Banham extolled the building in *The Architecture of the Well-Tempered Environment* for being among the first to employ mechanical systems that provided air-conditioning in the modern sense. Yet this radicality was temperate at best. A decade after the appearance of that book, when Banham returned to the Larkin Administration Building to discuss in more detail how the mechanical systems moved the air in the building, he penned a missive directed at architectural historians on the pages of the field's journal of record.[29] The brief text owed its rhetorical power to a rather dry set of engineering drawings that demonstrated the workings of ductwork—drawings that were not nearly as attractive as the axonometric drawings that had been made by Mary Banham for the book. While these drawings were meant to open up a new archive for modern architecture, however, they foreclosed the possibility of another kind. Banham, attentive to the mechanical systems of the building, was oblivious to another technical ingenuity of the building: its ability to accommodate the bureaucracy that made the company's success possible in the first place.[30] The building had been designed, after all, to process massive quantities of information—a fact that Banham, in his obsession with the machine, failed to take note. In Banham's world, *artifactual* technics trumped *procedural* ones: one could say that he ultimately fell prey to the machine aesthetic that he criticized so vehemently throughout his career.[31] It is the contention of this volume that procedural technics—seven of which are examined in more detail here—deserve critical attention as well.

If historians of the Modern Movement simplified the myriad meanings of technics, the discipline of architecture today is unwittingly performing another theoretical flattening by trying to understand architecture's relationship to technics under the misleading rubric of the *digital*.[32] It is argued that because there is not a scale (building, urban, or regional) or a stage of the building process (design, construction, or maintenance) that is not affected by it, the digital is the primary category through which to understand the central questions of the discipline today. Subtle and thoughtful historical analyses are few and far between while there is no shortage of declarations about the transformative role that new computational technics will play.[33] One textbook on the topic begins with a juxtaposition of the Crystal Palace and the Eiffel Tower—two favorites of the "tectonic unconscious," according to the likes of Giedion—with an image of a wireframe model of Frank Gehry's Bilbao Museum.[34] The consequences of the new computational tools for the building industry, the introduction of the book claims, "are likely to be on a scale similar to those of the industrial revolution: the Information Age, just like the Industrial Age before, is challenging not only how we design buildings, but also how we manufacture and construct them."[35] The conclusions drawn from such historical comparisons are not modest: what unites designers today is "the use of digital technology as an enabling apparatus that directly integrates conception and production in ways that are unprecedented since the medieval times of master builders."[36] According to this line of thinking, the history of architecture now has to be reimagined around a digital trajectory. This volume is an attempt to complicate such narratives before they ossify into a genealogy as persistent as that of the tectonic.

The essays in this volume take an unabashedly historical and, it should be stressed, theoretical approach to understanding the question of technics and its instrumentalities. This, in itself, may seem like a provocative position after the alleged death of architectural theory, a variant of critical theory that was considered the lingua franca of the humanities for decades. During the reign of architectural theory, the discipline of architecture drew on such fields as philosophy, literary criticism, or comparative literature and stayed as clear of the question of technics as of the specter of instrumentalizing knowledge. These days, by contrast, the discipline's focus seems to be on the other side of the humanities divide—that is, on biology, ecology, neuroscience, computer science, and other fields of knowledge whose disciplinary projects are informed by the model of the natural sciences and quantitative data. This development, however, cannot simply be explained away as indicative of a new "instrumental" sensibility that seeks immediate results within research universities. Unlike the previous generation of architectural historians and theorists, in fact, the contributors to this volume are not afflicted with anxieties about the instrumentalization of knowledge. Instead, they start with the assumption that all knowledge is always already instrumentalized and pose questions about the historical conditions that make that instrumentalization possible in the first place: How? Why? Under what institutional conditions? To what ends? It seems important to note, for example, that if the position of architecture within the disciplinary landscape of the university was always up for debate, now—that is, after the triumph of the neo-Kantian position in the early twentieth century; after the positivism controversy at midcentury; after postmodernism, science wars, and the postcritical debate—it seems even more controversial.[37] The status of theory within architecture should be understood, then, not as a vulgar turn away from experimental speculation toward technical solutions that seek to monetize knowledge but rather as part of larger changes in the epistemological landscape of the university. This volume's call to constructing a new archive for technics in the discipline of architecture, then, is also a call for understanding architecture's position within these new arrangements of knowledge. How the discipline understands technics will have implications for how it situates itself within other disciplines at the university. It will also determine how it might "theorize" its own epistemological agenda.

The contributors to this collection share a few assumptions about how this disciplinary reconstruction might be carried out. First, they all argue, history or, more precisely, historical ontology is crucial to this attempt. This volume does so for a number of concepts that have come to play crucial roles in architecture's understanding of its own disciplinary history. Lucia Allais offers an architectural history of the concept of *experience,* that contested term of modernity; Zeynep Çelik Alexander proposes a history of *form,* an abstraction that acquired salience in aesthetic discourses only in the late nineteenth century; and Michael Osman argues that it was the architectural specification that has sustained what might otherwise be taken to be the long-standing dichotomy between *intellectual* and *manual labor* in the discipline. Such histories have been attempted before, but what these essays offer are "technical" accounts of these histories—that is, histories that weave lofty intellectual concepts into concrete artifacts, practices, habits, and rituals on the ground.

Second, the essays collected here operate with the assumption that architecture is ultimately an epistemic enterprise. John May suggests in the essay that serves as an afterword to this volume that the gerunds under examination here are not "the minor expressions of technical systems external to thought, or instrumentalizable techniques with known or controllable affects" but are far more consequentially "the gestural basis of an entire consciousness." Following a similar logic, Matthew C. Hunter proposes modeling as a mode of reasoning in its own right that he compares to children's games; Allais suggests that an act as seemingly simple as drawing a line is an epistemic gesture that organizes experience in particular ways; and John Harwood imagines the possibility of another way of conceptualizing architecture's epistemic jurisdiction by reading into such seemingly mundane details as those of the third rail in the Grand Central Terminal in Manhattan. Most alarmingly, Orit Halpern warns that the cybernetic logic underlying the repetitious operations of a designer today may belong to a form of rationality that is ultimately irrational (design students repeating the same commands on their computers all day may empathize with the poor porpoise that loses her mind in Halpern's story!) while Edward A. Eigen narrates another story of insanity about subjects trapped at home between control and comfort provided by the home's equipment.

Third, these essays insist not on historical breaks and paradigm shifts, as so much literature on the technical developments of the last few decades tends to do, but rather on historical continuities. They do this despite their reliance on an archaeological rather than genealogical approach—that is, their rejection of complete lineages and insistence on partial, necessarily incomplete excavations.[38] If there are any "revolutions" to speak of here, they are revolutions in the sense of celestial bodies returning to the same position while they move in their orbits. Or, to adapt the historian G. M. Trevelyan's famous phrase for nineteenth-century revolutions, the contemporary might simply be "the turning point at which history fails to turn."[39] According to Osman's account, modern standards do not emerge out of technological developments as countless modernists have fantasized; Allais traces early modern debates about experience and experiment all the way up to the present preoccupations with rendering; and in Çelik Alexander's history of form, the nineteenth-century distinction between morphology and dissection survives not only far longer than expected but also in the most unlikely places.

Finally, one of the most surprising outcomes of this volume must be the relationship of technics to the figure of the human. However much the narratives by Mumford, Banham, and even Giedion of *Mechanization Takes Command* may seem like compelling alternatives to the tectonic trajectory, at a moment when the centrality of the human is being questioned as the distinguishing mark of a problematically reflexive modernity, it is also hard to stomach these texts' overtly humanist undertones.[40] Despite his stated goal to write an anonymous history (akin to his mentor Heinrich Wölfflin's "art history without names"), Giedion's agenda was to "reinstate human values."[41] The book, after all, was published three years after the end of World War II, during which the "mechanization of death" occurred not only in the slaughterhouses discussed in the book but also in concentration camps.[42] For Mumford, too, understanding the machine was the prerequisite to "reconquer[ing]" and to "re-orient[ing]" human civilization.[43] Both texts, in fact, can be said to be guilty of psychologizing the effects of mechanization: Giedion for his long-standing belief that modernity resulted in a cognitive dissonance and Mumford for attributing the modern feeling of alienation to the machine.[44] As for Banham, however central the concept of environment might have been to his project of reestablishing a new technics in architecture, that conception of the environment was shaped resolutely around the human and its comfort.[45]

The human appears in an altogether different guise in this volume. The domestic technologies discussed in Eigen's story attempt to transform machines into humans while they transform humans into machines; the neural nets in Halpern's account are understood as the limit condition of human reason. In the cases of Çelik Alexander and Allais, the human, far from preceding the technologies under examination, is made and remade through them. Time and again these technics end up stabilizing the otherwise impossibly unstable category of the human. Indeed, as May argues, it is precisely the recognition of this ontological codependency between the technical and the human that defines technics as a philosophical category.

This is not to say that the goal of this volume is to jettison altogether concepts—experience, image, form, and even the category of the human—whose histories are paratactically attempted herein. Instead the essays collected here implicitly ask: How can central concepts of the discipline be reconfigured through a new theoretical engagement with technics? Can a reexamination of the question of technics become the beginning of a new architectural theory? As the discipline of architecture absorbs dramatic epistemological changes and keeps reconstructing its agenda, it seems more productive to be epistemologically modest. And lest such a reconstruction effort turn to a foundationalist epistemology, it is useful to keep in mind the metaphor of the raft famously used by the philosopher Otto Neurath.

> We are like sailors who on the open sea must reconstruct their ship but are never able to start afresh at the bottom. Where a beam is taken away a new one must at once be put there, and for this the rest of the ship is used as support. In this way, by

using the old beams and driftwood, the ship can be shaped entirely anew, but only by gradual reconstruction.[46]

NOTES

1. See, for example, the exhibition and publication undertaken by the Canadian Centre for Architecture that ultimately constructs a genealogy of the digital around such figures as Peter Eisenman and Frank Gehry: Greg Lynn, ed., *Archaeology of the Digital: Peter Eisenman, Frank Gehry, Chuck Hoberman, Shoei Yoh* (Montreal: Canadian Centre for Architecture; Berlin: Sternberg, 2013).

2. Blaise Pascal, *Pensées* (1670; repr., London: Routledge and Kegan Paul, 1950), section 250. The phrase is, in fact, Althusser's paraphrasing of Pascal in Louis Althusser, "Ideology and Ideological State Apparatuses (Notes towards an Investigation)," in *Lenin and Philosophy and Other Essays* (New York: Monthly Review Press, 1971), 127–86.

3. See Ian Hacking, *Historical Ontology* (Cambridge, Mass.: Harvard University Press, 2002).

4. Bernhard Siegert, "Cacography or Communication? Cultural Techniques in German Media Studies," trans. Geoffrey Winthrop-Young, *Grey Room*, no. 29 (Fall 2007): 30.

5. Lewis Mumford, *Technics and Civilization* (1934; repr., Chicago: University of Chicago Press, 2010), 128–29.

6. Michel Foucault, *The Order of Things: An Archaeology of the Human Sciences* (1966; repr., New York: Vintage, 1994), 308; Friedrich Kittler, *Gramophone, Film, Typewriter*, trans. Geoffrey Winthrop-Young and Michael Wutz (Stanford: Stanford University Press, 1999). Kittler's book abounds with references to the "so-called man."

7. Karl Marx, *Capital: A Critique of Political Economy*, vol. 1, ed. Ernest Mandel (London: Penguin, 1981); Ernst Kapp, *Grundlinien einer Philosophie der Technik* (Braunschweig: George Westermann, 1877), translated by Lauren K. Wolfe as *Elements of a Philosophy of Technology: On the Evolutionary History of Culture*, ed. Jeffrey West Kirkwood and Leif Weatherby (Minneapolis: University of Minnesota Press, 2018); Marshall McLuhan, *Understanding Media: Extensions of Man* (New York: McGraw-Hill, 1964).

8. Siegert, "Cacography or Communication?," 30. See also Lorenz Engell and Bernhard Siegert, eds., *Zeitschrift für Medien- und Kulturforschung, Schwerpunkt Kulturtechnik* 1 (2010); Bernhard Siegert, *Cultural Techniques: Grids, Filters, Doors, and Other Articulations of the Real*, trans. Geoffrey Winthrop-Young (New York: Fordham University Press, 2015).

9. This is not to argue that the design studio is the only site for these techniques but to limit the scope of what is addressed in this volume. Future work on architectural techniques beyond the design studio is sorely needed in the discipline.

10. Leo Marx, "Technology: The Emergence of a Hazardous Concept," *Technology and Culture* 51, no. 3 (July 2010): 561–77.

11. L. Marx, 564. See also Merritt Roe Smith and Leo Marx, eds., *Does Technology Drive History? The Dilemma of Technological Determinism* (Cambridge, Mass.: MIT Press, 1994).

12. Eric Schatzberg, *Technology: Critical History of a Concept* (Chicago: University of Chicago Press, 2018).

13. Eric Schatzberg, "*Technik* Comes to America: Changing Meanings of Technology before 1930," *Technology and Culture* 47, no. 3 (July 2006): 486–512. Schatzberg calls *Technik* a German import and attributes the role of the importer, above all, to Thornstein Veblen. Schatzberg, 487.

14. Schatzberg, 496–507. For a discussion of how the term *technology* elevated the useful arts from the realm of artisans and manufacture to that of big business and the university, see Leo Marx, "The Idea of 'Technology' and Postmodern Pessimism," in Smith and Marx, *Does Technology Drive History?*, 238–57. For an exploration of how technology was gendered male, see Ruth Oldenziel, *Making Technology Masculine: Men, Women, and Modern Machines in America, 1870–1945* (Amsterdam: Amsterdam University Press, 1999).

15. Lewis Mumford, *Art and Technics* (New York: Columbia University Press, 1952), 15.

16. On disciplinarity of architecture, see Mark Wigley, "Prosthetic Theory: The Disciplining of Architecture," *Assemblage*, no. 15 (August 1991): 6–29; Mark Jarzombek, "A Prolegomena to Critical Historiography," *Journal of Architectural Education* 52, no. 4 (May 1999): 197–206; Zeynep Çelik Alexander, "Neo-naturalism," in "New Ancients," ed. Dora Epstein Jones and Bryony Roberts, special issue, *Log*, no. 31 (Spring/Summer 2014): 23–30; and Zeynep Çelik Alexander, "The Core That Wasn't," *Harvard Design Magazine*, no. 35 (Fall/Winter 2012): 84–89.

17. The most comprehensive examination of the tectonic in architectural modernism remains Kenneth Frampton, *Studies in Tectonic Culture: The Poetics of Construction in Nineteenth- and Twentieth-Century Architecture,* ed. John Cava (Cambridge, Mass.: MIT Press, 1995). See also Harry Francis Mallgrave, *Modern Architectural Theory: A Historical Survey, 1673–1968* (Cambridge: Cambridge University Press, 2009), 91–139.

18. Karl Bötticher, *Die Tektonik der Hellenen,* vol. 1 (Potsdam: Ferdinand Riegel, 1852), 1. See also Mitchell Schwarzer, "Ontology and Representation in Karl Bötticher's Theory of Tectonics," *Journal of the Society of Architectural Historians* 52, no. 3 (September 1993): 267–80; and Hartmut Mayer, *Die Tektonik der Hellenen: Kontext und Wirkung der Architekturtheorie von Karl Bötticher* (Stuttgart: Axel Menges, 2004).

19. Gottfried Semper, *Die Vier Elemente der Baukunst* (Braunschweig: Vieweg und Sohn, 1851), translated by Wolfgang Herrmann and Harry Francis Mallgrave as *Four Elements of Architecture and Other Writings* (Cambridge: Cambridge University Press, 1989). See also Gottfried Semper, *Der Stil in den technischen und tektonischen Künsten,* vol. 1, *Textile Kunst* (Frankfurt: Verlag für Kunst und Wissenschaft, 1860), and vol. 2, *Keramik, Tektonik, Stereotomie, Metallotechnik* (Munich: Friedrich Bruchmann, 1863), translated by Harry Francis Mallgrave and Michael Robinson as *Style in the Technical and Tectonic Arts* (Los Angeles: Getty Research Institute, 2004). For more recent and sophisticated understandings of Semper, see Harry Francis Mallgrave, *Gottfried Semper: Architect of the Nineteenth Century* (New Haven, Conn.: Yale University Press, 1996); Winfried Nerdinger and Werner Oechslin, eds., *Gottfried Semper, 1803–1879: Architektur und Wissenschaft* (Munich: Prestel, 2003); and Mari Hvattum, *Gottfried Semper and the Problem of Historicism* (New York: Cambridge University Press, 2004).

20. Eugène-Emmanuel Viollet-le-Duc, *Entretiens Sur l'Architecture,* 2 vols. (Paris: A Morel, 1863–72). Barry Bergdoll and Martin Bressani have complicated this picture: Barry

Bergdoll, "Of Crystals, Cells, and Strata: Natural History and Debates on the Form of a New Architecture in the Nineteenth Century," *Architectural History* 50 (2007): 1–29; Martin Bressani, "Notes on Viollet-le-Duc's Philosophy of History: Dialectics and Technology," *Journal of the Society of Architectural Historians* 48, no. 4 (December 1989): 327–50; and Martin Bressani, *Architecture and the Historical Imagination: Eugène-Emmanuel Viollet-le-Duc, 1814–1879* (Farnham, Surrey: Ashgate, 2014).

21. For a sophisticated critique of this idea, see a lucidly written essay by Antoine Picon, "Notes on Modern Architecture," *Positions*, no. 0 (Fall 2008): 78–83. For a discussion of the "tectonic unconscious" in the split between engineers and architects, see Sigfried Giedion, *Bauen in Frankreich, Eisen, Eisenbeton* (Leipzig: Klinkhardt & Biermann, 1928), translated by J. Duncan Berry as *Building in France, Building in Iron, Building in Ferro-Concrete* (Santa Monica, Calif.: Getty Center for the History of Art and the Humanities, 1995); and Sigfried Giedion, *Space, Time and Architecture: The Growth of a New Tradition* (Cambridge, Mass.: Harvard University Press, 1941).

22. I am thinking here of Fritz Neumeyer, "A World in Itself: Architecture and Technology," in *The Presence of Mies*, ed. Detlef Mertins (Princeton, N.J.: Princeton Architectural Press, 1994), 50–58; and Joanna Merwood-Salisbury, *Chicago 1890: The Skyscraper and the Modern City* (Chicago: University of Chicago Press, 2009), esp. 38–54.

23. Once again, Semper has an important place in these historiographical revisions. See, for example, Spyros Papapetros, "World Ornament: The Legacy of Gottfried Semper's 1856 Lecture on Ornament," *RES: Anthropology and Aesthetics*, no. 57/58 (Spring/Autumn 2010): 309–29. See also Gülru Necipoglu and Alina Payne, eds., *Histories of Ornament: From Global to Local* (Princeton, N.J.: Princeton University Press, 2016); Antoine Picon, *Ornament: The Politics of Architecture and Subjectivity* (Chichester: Wiley, 2013); and Mark Wigley, *White Walls, Designer Dresses: The Fashioning of Modern Architecture* (Cambridge, Mass.: MIT Press, 1995).

24. Paradoxically, Semper also became the locus of an antitectonic preoccupation with surface and ornamentation in North America. See, for example, the introduction to the special issue "Unraveling the Textile in Modern Architecture," ed. Kate Holliday, *Studies in the Decorative Arts* 16, no. 2 (Spring/Summer 2009): 2–6; Robert Levit, "Contemporary 'Ornament': The Return of the Symbolic Repressed," *Harvard Design Magazine*, no. 28 (Spring/Summer 2008): 70–85; and Jeffrey Kipnis, "The Cunning of Cosmetics (A Personal Reflection on the Architecture of Herzog & De Meuron)," in *Herzog and De Meuron 1981–2000* (Madrid: El Croquis, 2000), 404–11.

25. Siegfried Giedion, *Mechanization Takes Command: A Contribution to Anonymous History* (New York: Oxford University Press, 1948), here 2.

26. Giedion, 3.

27. Reyner Banham, *Architecture of the Well-Tempered Environment* (London: Architectural Press, 1969). See also Michael Osman, "Banham's Historical Ecology," in *Neo-Avant-Garde and Postmodern: Postwar Architecture in Britain and Beyond*, ed. Mark Crinson and Claire Zimmerman (New Haven, Conn.: Yale University Press), 231–51.

28. Banham, *Architecture of the Well-Tempered Environment*, 14.

29. Banham wrote that he thereby corrected his "guesswork" in *The Architecture of the Well-Tempered Environment*. Reyner Banham, "The Services of the Larkin 'A' Building," *Journal of the Society of Architectural Historians* 37, no. 3 (October 1978): 195–97.

30. On this, see Michael Osman, *Modernism's Visible Hand: Architecture and Regulation in America* (Minneapolis: University of Minnesota Press, 2018); and Zeynep Çelik Alexander, "The Larkin's Architectural Technologies of Trust," *Journal of the Society of Architectural Historians* 77, no. 3 (September 2018): 300–318. For the same point about Lewis Mumford's blindness to technics of control, see David Mindell, *Between Human and Machine: Feedback, Control, and Computing before Cybernetics* (Baltimore: Johns Hopkins University Press, 2002).

31. It is telling that around the same time, another historian was critiquing the machine aesthetic from another perspective. See Charles S. Maier, "Between Taylorism and Technocracy: European Ideologies and the Vision of Industrial Productivity in the 1920s," *Journal of Contemporary History* 5, no. 2 (1970): 27–61.

32. On the problem of the digital and the analog, see Kyle Stine, "The Coupling of Cinematics and Kinematics," *Grey Room*, no. 56 (Summer 2014): 34–57.

33. On the question of the digital in architectural discourses, among the many available works, see especially Antoine Picon, *Digital Culture in Architecture: An Introduction for Design Professionals* (Basel: Birkhäuser, 2010); and Mario Carpo, *Alphabet and the Algorithm* (Cambridge, Mass.: MIT Press, 2011).

34. Branko Kolarevic, *Architecture in the Digital Age* (New York: Taylor and Francis, 2003), 1.

35. Kolarevic, 2.

36. Kolarevic, 3.

37. For these developments, see Lanier Anderson, "The Debate over the *Geisteswissenschaften* in German Philosophy," in *The Cambridge History of Philosophy, 1870–1945*, ed. Thomas Baldwin (New York: Cambridge University Press, 2003), 223–25; Uljana Feest, ed., *Historical Perspectives on Erklären and Verstehen* (New York: Springer, 2010); and Karl Popper, "The Logic of the Social Sciences," and T. W. Adorno, "On the Logic of the Social Sciences," in *The Positivist Dispute in German Sociology*, trans. Glyn Adey and David Frisby (London: Heinemann, 1976), respectively 87–104 and 105–22.

38. In addition to Foucault, *The Order of Things*, see Michel Foucault, *The Archaeology of Knowledge*, trans. Allan Sheridan (New York: Harper and Row, 1972).

39. G. M. Trevelyan, *British History in the Nineteenth Century (1782–1901)* (London: Longmans, 1922), 292.

40. I am referring here to Ulrich Beck, *Risk Society: Towards a New Modernity*, trans. Mark Ritter (London: SAGE, 1992). Here it is also important to acknowledge the contributions of the Posthumanities series from the University of Minnesota Press.

41. Heinrich Wölfflin, *Kunstgeschichtliche Grundbegriffe: Das Problem der Stilentwicklung in der Neueren Kunst* (Munich: Bruckmann, 1915), 46, translated by Jonathan Blower as *Principles of Art History: The Problem of the Development of Style in Early Modern Art* (Santa Monica, Calif.: Getty Research Institute, 2015), 72; Giedion, *Mechanization Takes Command*, v.

42. Giedion, *Mechanization Takes Command*, v.

43. Mumford, *Technics and Civilization*, 6. David Mindell has observed, however, that humans disappeared altogether from Mumford's neotechnic phase: "In this vision people disappear from even the shiniest vehicles: for Mumford automobiles and airplanes were about gasoline and speed, not driving or piloting. However clean and electrical, machinery for Mumford remained inert and mechanistic, not actively involved with human beings." David A. Mindell, *Between Human and Machine: Feedback, Control and Computing before Cybernetics* (Baltimore: Johns Hopkins University Press, 2002), 1–2.

44. Giedion discusses the split between the constructor and the architect (*Building in France, Building in Iron, Building in Ferro-Concrete*, 94–96) and the schism between architecture and technology (*Space, Time, and Architecture*, 211–18) as a modern cognitive incompatibility between feeling and thought. Mumford discusses a similar alienation: "Our age is passing from the primeval state of man, marked by his invention of tools and weapons for the purpose of achieving mastery over the forces of nature, to a radically different condition, in which he will not only have conquered nature but detached himself completely from the organic habitat." Lewis Mumford, "Technics and the Nature of Man," *Technology and Culture* 7, no. 3 (1966): 303.

45. Banham, *Architecture of the Well-Tempered Environment*.

46. Otto Neurath, "Anti-Spengler" (1921), in *Empiricism and Sociology*, by Otto Neurath, ed. Marie Neurath and Robert S. Cohen (Dordrecht: Reidel, 1973), 199. Neurath used the metaphor throughout his career. For a good summary, see Nancy Cartwright, Jordi Cat, Lola Fleck, and Thomas E. Uebel, "On Neurath's Boat," in *Otto Neurath: Philosophy between Science and Politics* (New York: Cambridge University Press, 1996), 89–166.

CHAPTER 1

RENDERING

On Experience and Experiments

LUCIA ALLAIS

> The shades and shadows of architectural objects are architectural things, not mathematical things.... The fact that a draftsman of great skill and long experience will often make a very admirable drawing with poor instruments or materials is no reason why the beginner can do so.
>
> —Henry McGoodwin, *Architectural Shades and Shadows* (1904)

> I can't imagine that anyone without an architectural training could produce a good picture.... Often in our office it is not the computers that calculate the reflections, rather we do it ourselves by hand.... If I want shadows, I integrate these into the picture; if I don't, I move the sun.
>
> —Eric de Broche des Combes (2015)

Two lessons in architectural rendering, published more than a century apart, emphasize that when architects learn how to render, they are not only vested with a drawing skill but also implicated in a vast epistemic scheme that projects mathematics and its certainties onto buildings and their shadows. Today, digital renderings are the kind of image that elicit principled convictions. Commercial renderings, especially, images used to sell buildings, are seen as engines of superficiality because they are aimed at nonarchitects and also often outsourced to unseen software workers. "Architectural renderings are meant to seduce," reads a recent critique; they are "produced by people with no design training" who work in "image factories" creating "fantasies" unrelated to any "working building."[1] To preempt these critiques, architectural visualization firms reassure their clients that rendering is handiwork. In the 2015 interview cited above, Eric de Broche des Combes explains that in his firm, Luxigon (Figure 1.1), they do calculations "by hand."[2] These may sound like the modest words of an artisan, but they are

Figure 1.1. Digital rendering of Rex's design for the Calgary Central Library, 2017. Image and copyright by Luxigon.

a way to claim technical control far beyond architecture. Thus des Combes cannot resist adding that he is able to "move the sun," as if the goal of architectural rendering was not only the predictable appearance of buildings but the mathematization of the world itself.

Today the agent of this calculative power is imagined to be a computer. But the promise that rendering is a technique for channeling the forces of a possibly pervasive mathematical enslavement long predates the digital revolution. When the American architect Henry McGoodwin, who had trained at the École des Beaux-Arts in Paris, published a rendering manual in 1904, he assured his readers that shades and shadows of buildings were "architectural things, not mathematical things" and that he could manipulate them at will. Euclidian geometry was only an instrument, "a means having no greater architectural importance than the scale or triangle." To demonstrate his mastery, McGoodwin painstakingly drew figure after figure projecting the shadows cast by the sun onto the intricate outlines of the classical orders (Figure 1.2). Although these shadows had "form, mass

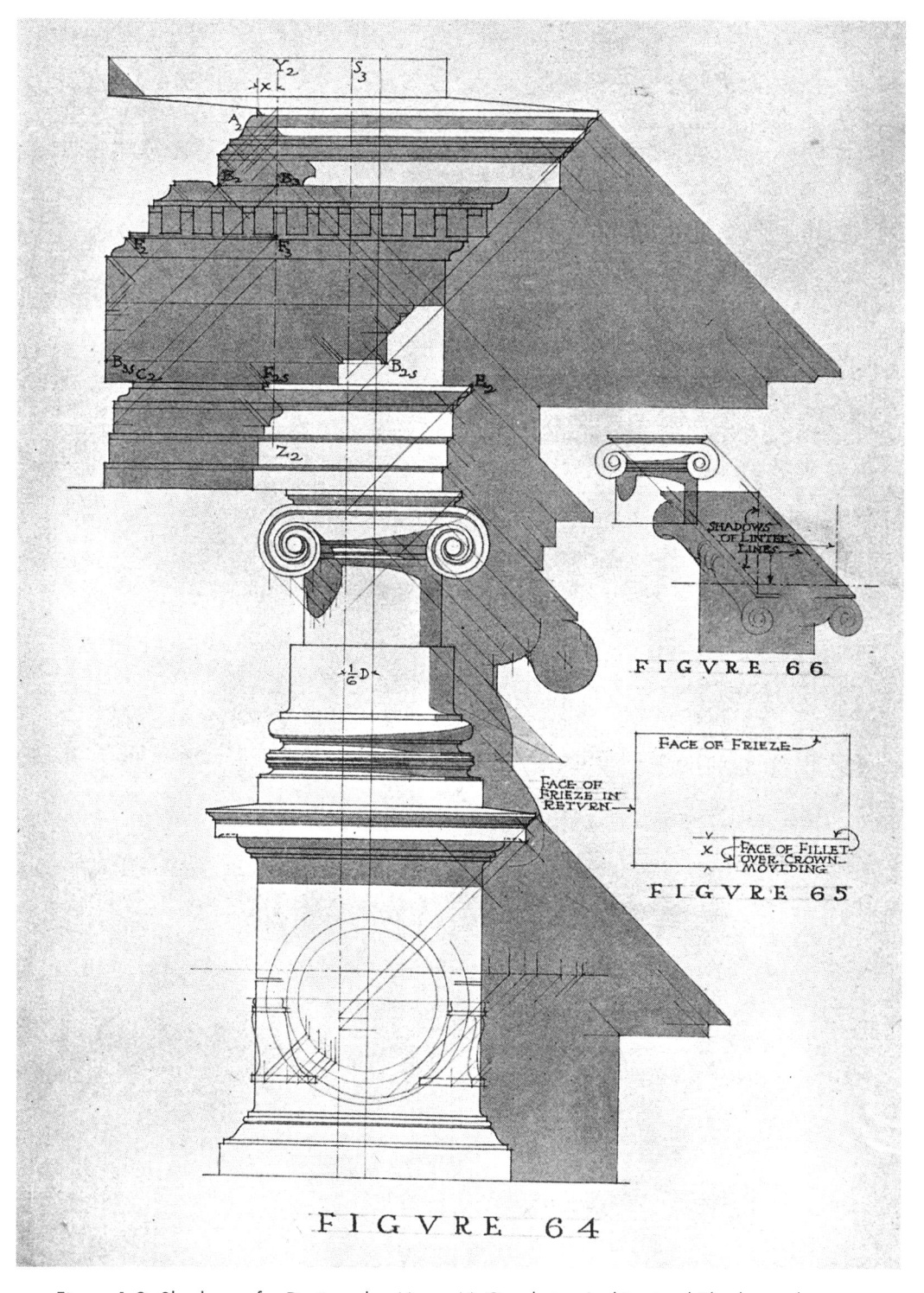

Figure 1.2. Shadows of a Doric order. Henry McGoodwin, *Architectural Shades and Shadows* (Boston: Bates & Guild, 1904).

and proportions" that could be immediately apprehended, McGoodwin cautioned against shaping them through intuition alone. For "inexperienced draftsmen," geometry was a tool that could substitute for the "great skill" of more experienced architects.[3]

Like his digital descendants, McGoodwin made a claim for rendering that was not so modest after all: a claim to have created, through architecture, a shortcut between two meanings of the term *experience*. When he spoke of shadows as having apprehensible form, he spoke of experience as given from external reality—as an *input* to the senses, we might say anachronistically. Whereas when he promised that "experienced draftsmen" would develop "an expressive 'touch' or technique," he described experience as something constructed through practice and repetition—as an *output* of the body.[4] To be less anachronistic, we could rephrase this distinction in terms of the philosophies of experience that proliferated in Germany and America around the time of McGoodwin's writing, from Wilhelm Dilthey to John Dewey and Edmund Husserl.[5] Architecture's shadows could be experienced by a passerby through *Erlebnis*, "a kind of passivity in activity," available in the lived moment.[6] But the painstaking experience of learning to draw delivered practical knowledge over time, what in German one would call *Erfahrung*. These two kinds of experience were increasingly split, philosophers warned. The promise of rendering, then, was to reconnect them, and it is a promise as alluring today as it was in 1904. Digital media enthusiasts claim that architects who use computer visualization can "empathize with the users of their projects," and especially those who "relate experientially and aesthetically to urban life as an interactive commodity."[7] Now that the public's senses have been habituated to digital media, the argument goes, every *Erlebnis* can become the input, and every *Ehrfahrung* the output, in an algorithm-fueled experience economy.[8]

Thus, our two rendering lessons lie on either side of a presumably irrevocable digital divide. But our computational vernacular, where terms like *input* and *output* evoke a world coursed-through with data and where "a rendering," or even "a render," has come to mean *any* computer-made image, is singularly helpful to flesh out retroactively how mathematics have inflected concepts of architectural experience and how design's labor has reflected notions of productivity. None of these oppositions map neatly onto one another—building / shadow, architectural thing / mathematical thing, architect / draftsman, *Erlebnis* / *Erfahrung*, input / output. An archaeology of rendering practices helps disambiguate the slippages between them. This essay offers one such archaeology: a history of rendering as a history of experience.

Existing histories of the architectural sciences have tended to distinguish between the shadow and the line—the former fuzzy and vague, the latter a tool of precision. Architectural historians have tied architecture's modernity to the development of linear graphic representation, specifically the "cult of the line" that was codified through the French tradition of *dessin* in the seventeenth century and achieved "hegemonic dominance" in nineteenth-century academicism, later migrating to the United States and beyond, through Beaux-Arts pedagogy and the artistic avant-gardes, after 1900.[9] In this account, lines contributed to architecture's scientific legitimacy, while shadows increasingly became a decorative flourish. The split between line and shadow is usually seen to originate with Leon Battista Alberti, who in 1452 defined "delineation" as the essence of architectural design. According to Alberto Pérez-Gómez, Alberti set the stage for a "loss of embodied experience" from architecture as "the sciences" increasingly encroached on design.[10] In his story, the line replaced a good kind of architectural mathematics (symbolic, poetic, metaphysical) with a bad geometricization of space (flat, secular, technological).

Yet computers have upset the old distinction between arithmetic and geometry upon which this line/shadow division was founded. As Friedrich Kittler and other media theorists have shown, the "code" that underlies digital culture is a written, nonvisual medium that can generate entire perspectival universes without using any lines at all—except a few lines of ones and zeros.[11] To account for this return of the digit, new histories have anchored Albertian *disegno* in a different historical arc that terminates in the digital present. Mario Carpo has argued that digital computation tools "unfroze" for architects the technological creativity and numerical "open-endedness" that had been latent in Alberti all along.[12] In his version of events, line and shadow are now equally obsolete because a deeper link between number and image, which the line could only ever approximate, has been recovered through the computer.

Such narratives of loss and recovery are of little use, however, for explaining the persistence of rendering and shadows in a history of architectural visualizations dominated by lines. As I want to show, it is the *operational* line that constitutes the architectural rendering's relevant legacy in digital culture today. In the training of architects, especially, rendering the shades and shadows of buildings has been an architectural technique for connecting professional experience to a sensorial world through threads of thinking and doing. By retracing this legacy, we will find not a gradual weakening of architecture's grasp on the real, nor its inevitable submission to mathematics. Rather, we will find a stubborn tendency of architectural visualization to be used and useful when the sciences have made claims on experience as a human faculty.

Architectural rendering, I will argue, has woven between experience as constructed and experience as received, and more specifically between the acquiring of disparate or discrete units of experience and the delivery of experience as sensible completeness. In this sense, an implicit phenomenology has driven the development of architectural rendering. I do not mean phenomenology as a design philosophy, for example, that of 1970s architects who wanted to accommodate the features of dwelling bodies, or that of recent proponents of embodied computation and its affordances.[13] I mean the formidable philosophy of experience that was invented by Edmund Husserl in the first half of the twentieth century, based on a study of mathematics. By his definition, phenomenology is a philosophical attitude to the real, which asks the mind to bracket off the question of whether things-in-themselves (say, buildings) exist, and instead directs the attention to phenomena as they appear, deriving philosophical principles about human cognition from the way these appearances are experienced. Historians of architectural drawing have referred to Husserl, but largely to borrow his idea that a "crisis" lies at the basis of the modern sciences. In Pérez-Gómez's aforementioned influential history, "a substitution . . . occurred as early as Galileo . . . of the mathematically substructed world of idealities for the only real world, the one that is actually given through perception, that is ever experienced and experienceable."[14] Instead, I propose to take the philosophical notions Husserl offered—wholeness, completion, and substitution—as technical and aesthetic tropes that have steadily characterized the making and recording of architectural shades and shadows across three supposed ruptures in architecture's history: the scientific, the industrial, and the digital. My goal is not to build a new grand narrative of architecture as a techno-science. It is to see architecture as a discipline through which scientific rationality has traveled historically, and where mathematics has resided as a kind of tradition. Husserl himself set the stage for this historical interpretation in "The Origins of Geometry," where he described geometry as a historical tradition, whose self-evidence relied on the "sedimentation of truth-meanings"—or, as Jacques Derrida put it, a "tradition of truth."[15]

After all, architectural drawing is a minor branch of modern image-making, yet it looms surprisingly large in visual culture. The truth it conveys is socially mediated, a thruway for the development of what Theodore M. Porter has called "trust in numbers."[16] According to Porter, quantification triumphed in the modern sciences to compensate for a perceived loss of any trustworthy community. Architectural rendering, as we will see, contributed to the rise of this compensatory social trust, as a tool both to produce new buildings and to record existing ones.

TABLETOP SCIENCES, CA. 1780

Despite the emphasis that has been placed on the Renaissance origins of architectural delineation, "the line" as a combined graphic tool for architecture's design,

Figure 1.3. Shadows used as part of naturalist artifice in the elevation of the Arch of Titus at Rome. Antoine Desgodetz, *Les Edifices antiques de Rome: Dessinés et mesurés tres exactement* (Paris: Coignard, 1682).

execution, and presentation did not coalesce until the late eighteenth century. Until then, drawing shadows had been one way among others to denote precision in the plates of architectural treatises. For example, in the mid-sixteenth century Andrea Palladio invented one convention: draw the proportions of the classical orders as outlines if they are taken from written texts, or give them shadows if they are measured from buildings.[17] After Palladio, wherever there was a line, there was a measurement; if there was a shadow (and additional reality effects such as plants overgrowing a ruin), there was a building (Figure 1.3).[18]

Once geometry became "descriptive" in the eighteenth century, what had been a surveying tool became an instrument for design, and a systematic realignment of drawings and their objects took place. The line became the most authoritative descriptor of reality. "Geometric learning" was called upon to replace "what would otherwise be acquired by induction, through lengthy copying."[19] This does not mean that shadows disappeared; on the contrary, any line could now generate a shadow. Treatises on shadow casting proliferated, especially after descriptive geometry became a required field of training in France's new engineering schools.[20] According to one 1754 textbook (Figure 1.4), shadows demonstrated that the same geometric operation—drawing a line—could be used to cut stone, train the engineer, and represent volumes in space, "rendering objects as perfect(ly) as they could be to the understanding of others."[21] The word *render* expressed a kind of cognitive productivity.

Barely half a century after being introduced in engineering schools, descriptive geometry and its associated "science of shadows" were made a compulsory part of architectural training in France. Again, shadows survived, but in a radically different way from the naturalist artifice that had characterized the plates of

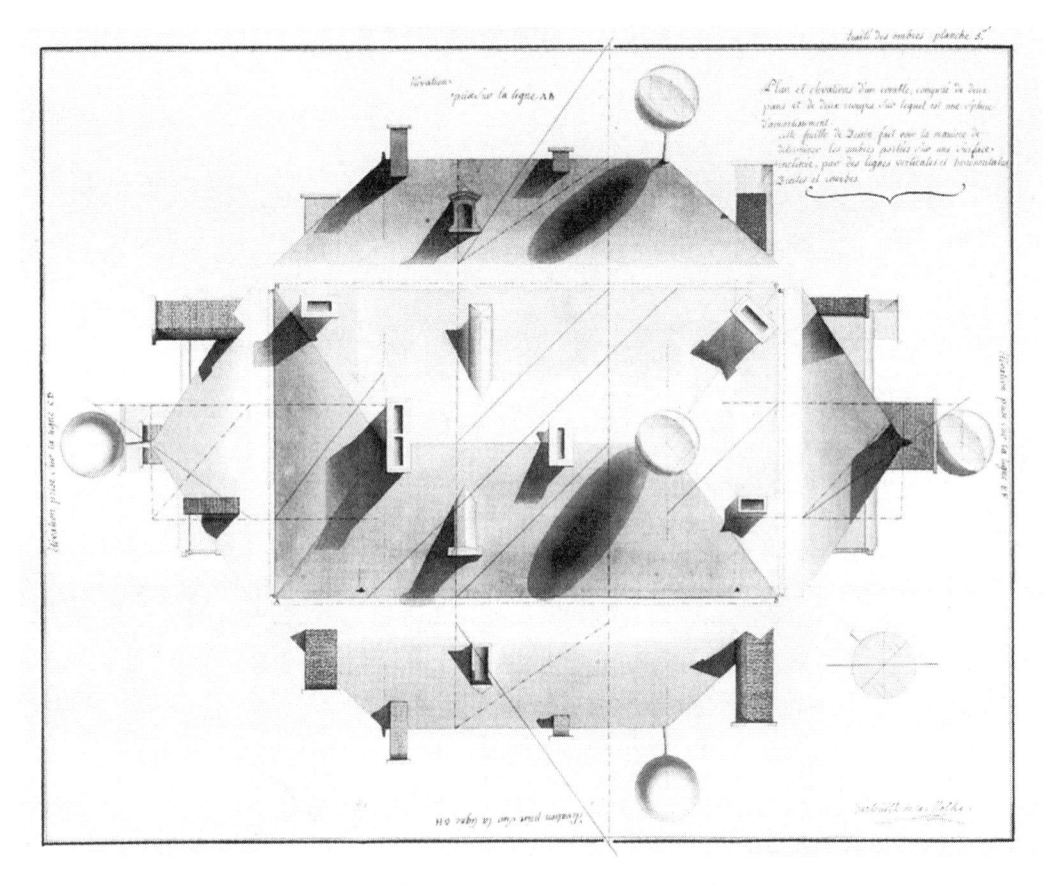

Figure 1.4. Roof plan showing off the new science of shadows. N.-F.-A. de Chastillon, *Traité des ombres dans le dessin géometral* (1754).

Vitruvian architectural treatises. Stanislas L'Éveillé, who wrote the first shadow-casting manual for architects in 1812, vaunted that he had literally "cast a new light" on the architectural canon, and depicted the paper on which his figures were drawn.[22] For architects, the burden was now to represent in three dimensions the space in which each line existed. The growing material reality that architects sought to encompass under a single graphic umbrella challenged what had seemed, to engineers, to be the metaproperties of the line. Stone and wood were soon joined by other media, including paper itself.

Such "cascading" of graphic media, as Bruno Latour has called it, is symptomatic of the rise of the experimental sciences in the late eighteenth century, with their distinct laboratory apparatuses, methods, and terminology.[23] As Raymond Williams has pointed out, this was also the period when *experience* and *experiment,* two words once meaning the same thing, underwent a split. *Experience* began to be seen as conservative, whereas *experiment* was forward-looking, linked to revolution. If experiments were events that took place in laboratories, experience became conceived as "against innovation," as "an appeal to the whole of consciousness, the whole being, as against reliance on a more specialized or more limited states or faculties."[24] Of course, artisanal experience continually crept into the world of experimental truth-making.[25] Painting, drawing, modeling—and handiwork from the makerly to the gestural—were pervasive in scientific laboratories, helping co-mingle experience and experiment into hybrid modes of knowing.[26] Rendering was one such practice. Certainly chemistry's experimentalists visualized their apparatus with shades and shadows rather than in outline. Robert Boyle's famous air pump was rendered as a three-dimensional volume when it was published—an additional cost that was expended so his groundbreaking "experiment" could be "experienced" by the reading public. Simon Schaeffer and Steven Shapin have called this phenomenon "virtual witnessing," and John Bender has even found *actual* witnesses in the plates of treatises in this period, drawn in three dimensions and out of scale, among rendered instruments and tabulated results.[27]

Rendered drawings also performed this virtual witnessing function in the architectural sciences, especially in the emerging field of structural engineering.[28] In 1787 the French engineer Jean-Baptiste Rondelet introduced his newest invention, a "machine for crushing stones," by publishing a rendered view of his workshop where an elaborate system of levers and pulleys, and solid blocks that lay waiting to be crushed, were dramatically lit from the side (Figure 1.5).[29] The machine itself was reinstalled at the École Polytechnique as an exhibition piece. As for the blocks, they were samples of the stone that Rondelet's mentor, the architect Jacques-Germain Soufflot, had used to build the church of Sainte-Geneviève.

Figure 1.5. Engraving of a "Machine for Crushing Stones." Jean-Baptiste Rondelet, *Traité théorique et pratique de l'art de bâtir* (Paris: n.p., 1787).

When the stones had been tested for structural failure, the results had been drawn in section, with no shadows at all, only cracks and fissures hatched in. Renderings, in other words, had been made for the public, while hatching had been kept for the specialists.

One of the most telling instances when architectural rendering helped *both* expand a science's experiential appeal with the public *and* perfect its experimental apparatus for the specialist came not from engineering but from city planning, or rather its precursor, urban topography. In 1792 Edme Verniquet published the first complete urban survey of Paris, a plan of such unprecedented accuracy that it served as the base map for a century's worth of visionary urban reforms, including Georges-Eugène Haussmann's.[30] Verniquet produced his plan by measuring the distances between Paris's architectural landmarks, triangulating these measures to get a basic layout of the city, and then filling in the rest with street-by-street measurements of the city's fabric.[31] The most famous spread of Verniquet's oversized book is a "demonstrations sheet" that combines all his triangulations into a blanked-out plan of the city walls, traversed by nothing but the outline of the Seine, as in a portolan nautical chart showing coastlines amid a network of rhumb lines. The sheet seems to represent the virtual conquest of urban space by pure linear geometry, and indeed it served as internal "proof" of the accuracy of Verniquet's calculations.[32] Verniquet was even asked to reenact his trigonometric operations in a session at the Jardin du Luxembourg, where two scientists from the French Academy of Sciences observed him redraw all his measurements on a new sheet and arrive at identical results (Figure 1.6).[33] Verniquet was no experimentalist, but he was a keen participant in the culture of "science and spectacle" that pervaded late eighteenth-century Paris.[34] His own workshop, a space rented out in the Convent des Cordeliers from 1783 to 1787, became a must-see stop for notables visiting the city.[35] Here is what these visitors saw: a massive horizontal surface—a table 16.5 feet long by 13 feet wide—where two hundred

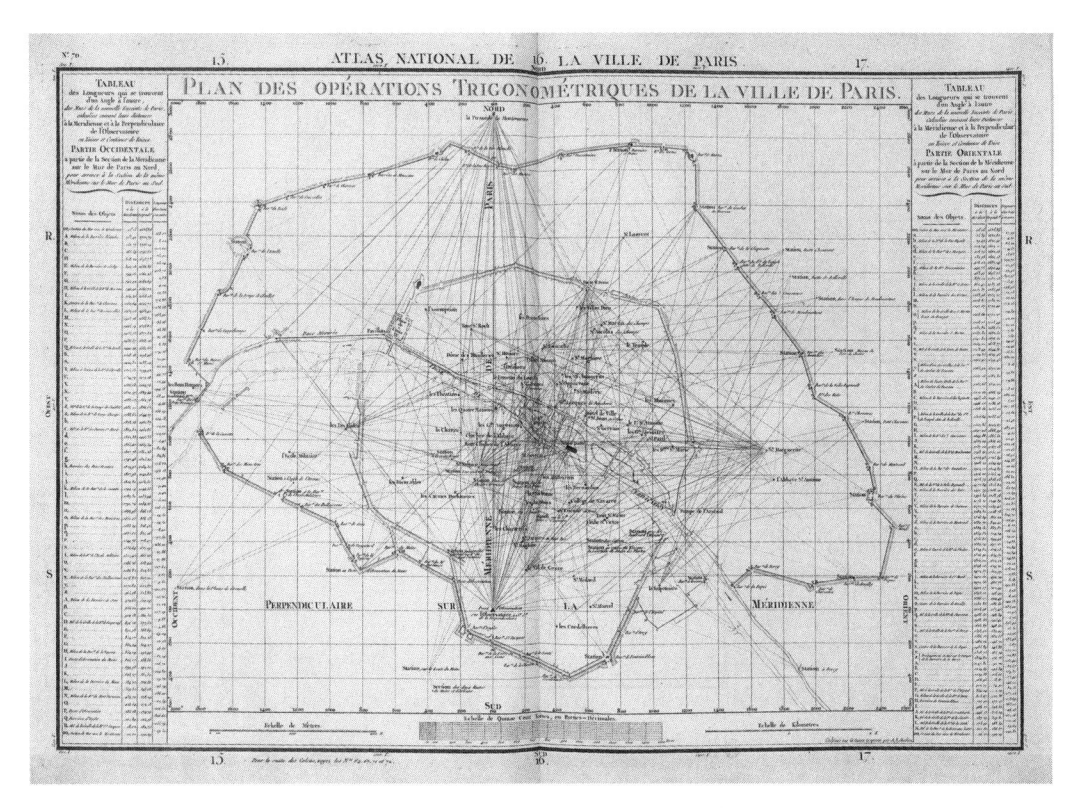

Figure 1.6. Plan of trigonometric operations. Edme Verniquet, *Plan de la Ville de Paris* (Paris: Verniquet, 1792). Courtesy of Bibliothèque nationale de France.

draftsmen assembled the information collected by more than sixty surveyors, returning from nightly excursions measuring streets by torchlight, or climbing to the tops of buildings by day. This tabletop was the representational space from which a new measurable Paris originated.

Once Verniquet published his map as an atlas, however, he complemented this geometric aesthetics with another type of drawing where shadows were added to convey truthfulness to an expanded readership. Here, Verniquet rendered each monument as a colossal and façade-less platonic volume, casting dramatic shadows on the page and also intersected by three lines—experiential monuments amid a mathematicized world. The baroque church of Saint-Sulpice, for instance, was represented by a plan of the cylindrical drum of its northern tower, extracted from the rest of the building, and casting a shadow leftward at forty-five degrees, according to the architectural convention set by Julien Le Roy in 1749 and still followed by contemporaneous visionary architects such as Etienne-Louis Boullée (Figure 1.7).[36] Alone or in groups of three, these volumes turned Parisian landmarks into "virtual witnesses" of Verniquet's procedure. [37]

So even without any descriptive geometry to teach, and without any Vitruvian theory to transmit, Verniquet's laborious effort to commit the buildings of Paris to paper amounted to a demonstration that architecture could supply a reliable source of data and comprehensive field of empirical reality to feed the new scientific mentality. His procedure was not called "rendering," but it corresponds to the old Roman word *redere,* to "give back," as in "render unto Caesar."[38] Mapping this much architecture necessarily implied a recipient with administrative authority and vast storage capacity. And although Verniquet began his measurements under the ancient regime, his project survived the French Revolution, his results and their public utility passing into the hands of the new nation-state.[39]

THE BEAUX-ARTS RENDERING AS WORKING DRAWING

The rendering only became a noun, *le rendu,* when architectural education was codified by the postrevolutionary French state throughout the nineteenth century. This transformation of rendering from process to thing closely followed the desire to quantify the mechanical productivity of the world. The term connoted quantification in several ways. In economics, the noun *rendement* meant the productive "yield" either of an agricultural enterprise or of a machine.[40] As an adjective, *rendu* was first associated with accounting, after finance minister Jacques Necker produced his Rendered Account (Compte Rendu) of the state's finances in 1781. At the École des Beaux-Arts, these two productive qualities combined with a third medium-specific one: *rendu* was something that happened to paper,

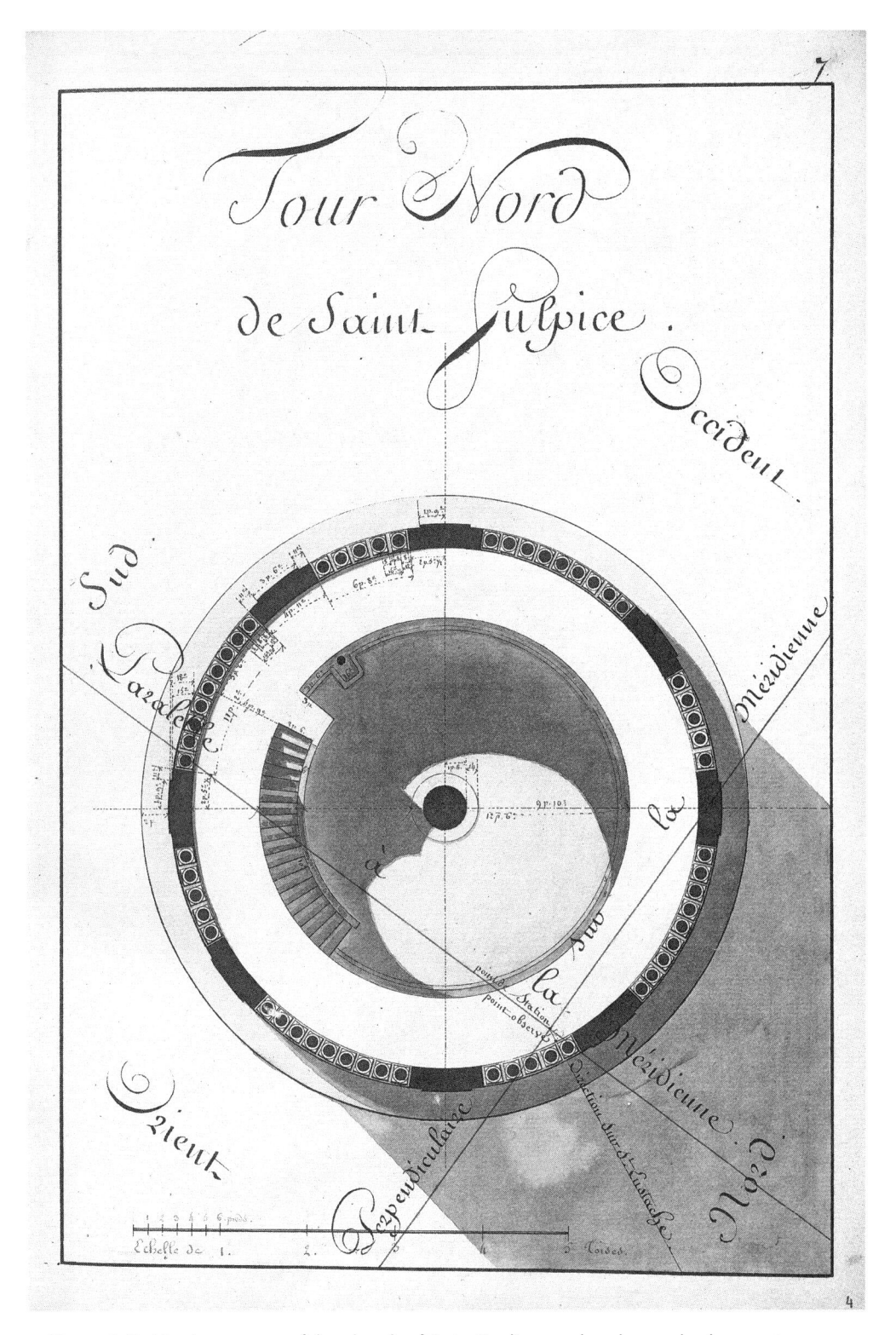

Figure 1.7. Northern tower of the church of Saint-Suplice rendered as a shadow-casting volume traversed by measuring lines. Edme Verniquet, *Plan de la Ville de Paris* (Paris: Verniquet, 1792).

specifically, "heavy stock such as Wattman paper," when it was worked over with "pencil and pen, and a bubble of China ink or sepia, and watercolor." [41] Within the arts, it was in architecture that *rendu* acquired its ultimate triple meaning as quality, thing, and procedure: "the coloring of a project; also, the finished project; also, the delivery of the project."[42]

When designing a project at the École des Beaux-Arts, to render meant to make complete. As the school's chief pedagogue, Antoine-Chrysostôme Quatremère de Quincy, put it in 1832, "rendered" was as a "synonym for *finished, done, completed*." Indeed, no drawing at the École was considered complete until it had been granted the "highest level of execution to even the smallest details and effects."[43] In the elevation drawings for any prize-winning competition entry, not a single line was left without volumetric or atmospheric enhancement—not a façade without a shadow, not a niche left empty of sculpture, not a sculpture left unshaded; every triptych and metope raised off the cornice and off the page, and every marble vein drawn in.

At the competing École Polytechnique, Jacques-Nicolas-Louis Durand complained that such "rendered drawings offer nothing geometrical to our eyes."[44] Charged with the architectural curriculum for the training of a quasi-military corps of engineers, Durand decided to adapt the Beaux-Arts system by removing the rendering phase of the project altogether. Anyone who obsessed over the surface of his drawings in this manner, he argued, could only get "confused" and produce an architecture of superficial façadism.[45] After all, it was at the Polytechnique that descriptive geometry flourished as pedagogical tool, providing a visual complement to the mathematics that were taught for mental rigor.[46] Durand thought architecture could contribute to training the engineering mind through graphic efficiency. "Reducing drawing to a simple trace," "gathering as many architectural objects as possible on one page" so that "shared lines coursed through them," and using watercolor washes *only* as a means of "distinguishing solid from void"—these economies of representation would yield visual, constructive, and professional clarity.[47] And this collapse of paper and wall was also stylistically fortuitous: drawing this way, it was possible to strip geometry bare (of patterns), much as a contemporary neo-Palladian taste demanded that walls be "denuded" of decoration.[48]

But visualization skills at the École des Beaux-Arts were also motivated by a professional economy. To begin with, the labor of rendering at the École was used to align a building and its representation not vertically through elevations but horizontally, in plan.[49] The plan was the privileged drawing at the École and, despite being taken from an impossible viewpoint (a horizontal cut taken a meter above the ground), it was extensively rendered. One vignette of an architectural student at work shows him hunched over his drafting desk, almost horizontal himself (Figure 1.8).[50] As David Van Zanten has described, rendered plans synchronized the movement of the hand of the architect with the bodies of the building's visitors, transforming the experience of composing a building into the experience of proceeding through it.

> Looking down into a fully rendered Beaux-Arts student plan, seeing the spaces assert themselves over the wall masses and push open a canyonized landscape of linked chambers, one's eye walks back and forth between the cliff-like walls, experiencing the composition the way [the architects] meant one to experience the composition of the buildings . . . itself.[51]

Rendering was a tool for thinking about architecture as made not of walls but of spaces. Second, then, composition of these spaces contained a certain collective ideal, driven as it was by the *marche* of a plan, a word that connoted both the fact that it "worked" (marcher) like a machine but also that it could be "marched through" as though by an army (Figure 1.9).[52] This operability embedded an entire system of bourgeois social values into academic architecture. Through drawing, hierarchy was engrained into architects and buildings alike, much more powerfully than rote repetition of the principles, such as propriety, decorum, and fit, that were supposed to regulate neoclassicism as a style.[53]

Rendering at the École des Beaux-Arts was also a way to systematize the production of architects, and to internalize the experiential basis of design in the person of the architect.[54] The ritualized culmination of any studio project was "the day of rendering" *(jour de rendu)*. Students gathered in the *salle Melponène* to stretch their drawings on canvases and register them with an attendant, who would then arrange to have them carried through Paris on a cart *(charrette)* so they could be "handed in" *(rendu)* to a jury of critics. At the end of the student's education, too, the architect was supposed to build up a cache of firsthand experiences (hopefully by winning the Grand Prix de Rome and traveling to Italy), process them, and deliver them via rendered drawings that were sent home once a year.[55] Henri Labrouste's 1828 reconstruction of the temple of Paestum was one such oversized envoi whose sheer material presence—overworked, difficult to store, cumbersome to display—was a testament to the immersive experience of the Rome Prize (Figure 1.10). Nineteenth-century Paris was flooded with architectural experiences, if we are to believe reports of the surplus of rendered paper in the city's market for drawings and complaints that such finished drawings appeared to proliferate in inverse proportion to the number of buildings actually built.[56]

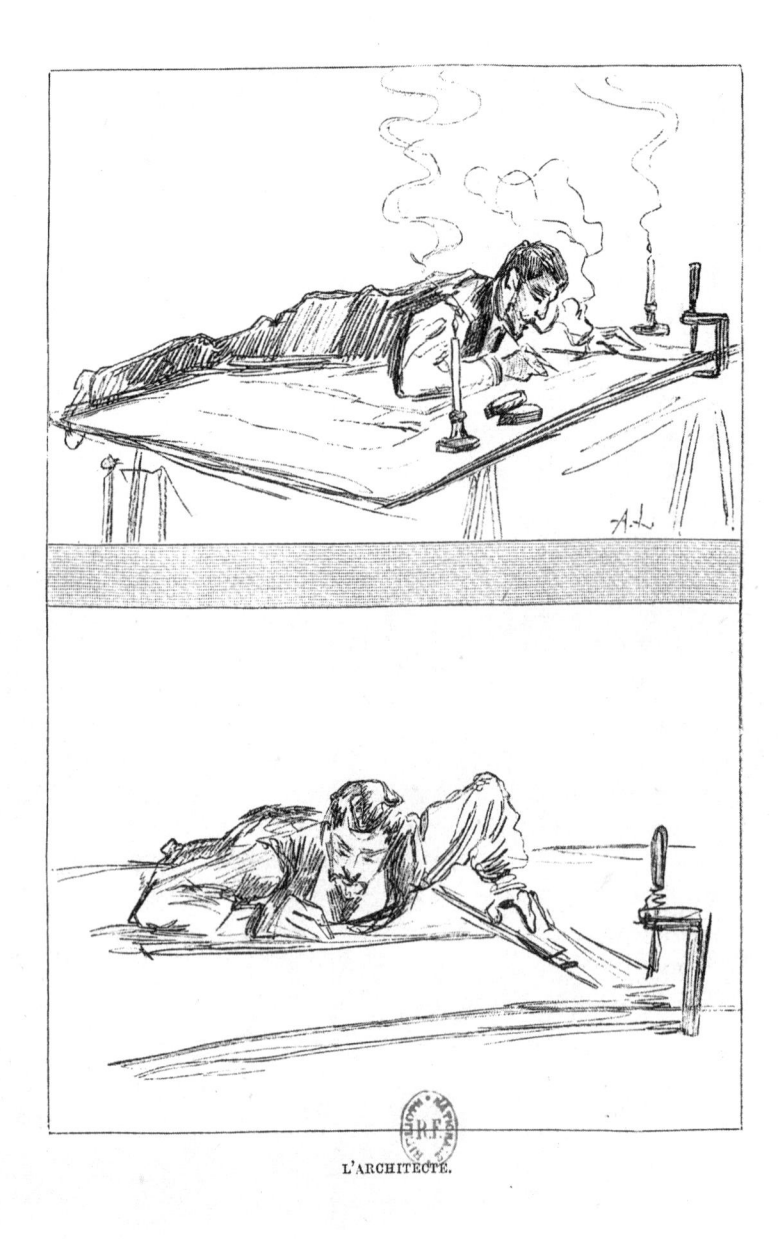

Figure 1.8. Vignette of the Beaux-Arts architect at work, almost horizontal himself. Alexis LeMaistre, *L'École des Beaux-arts, Dessinée et racontée par un élève* (Paris: Firmin-Didot, 1889).

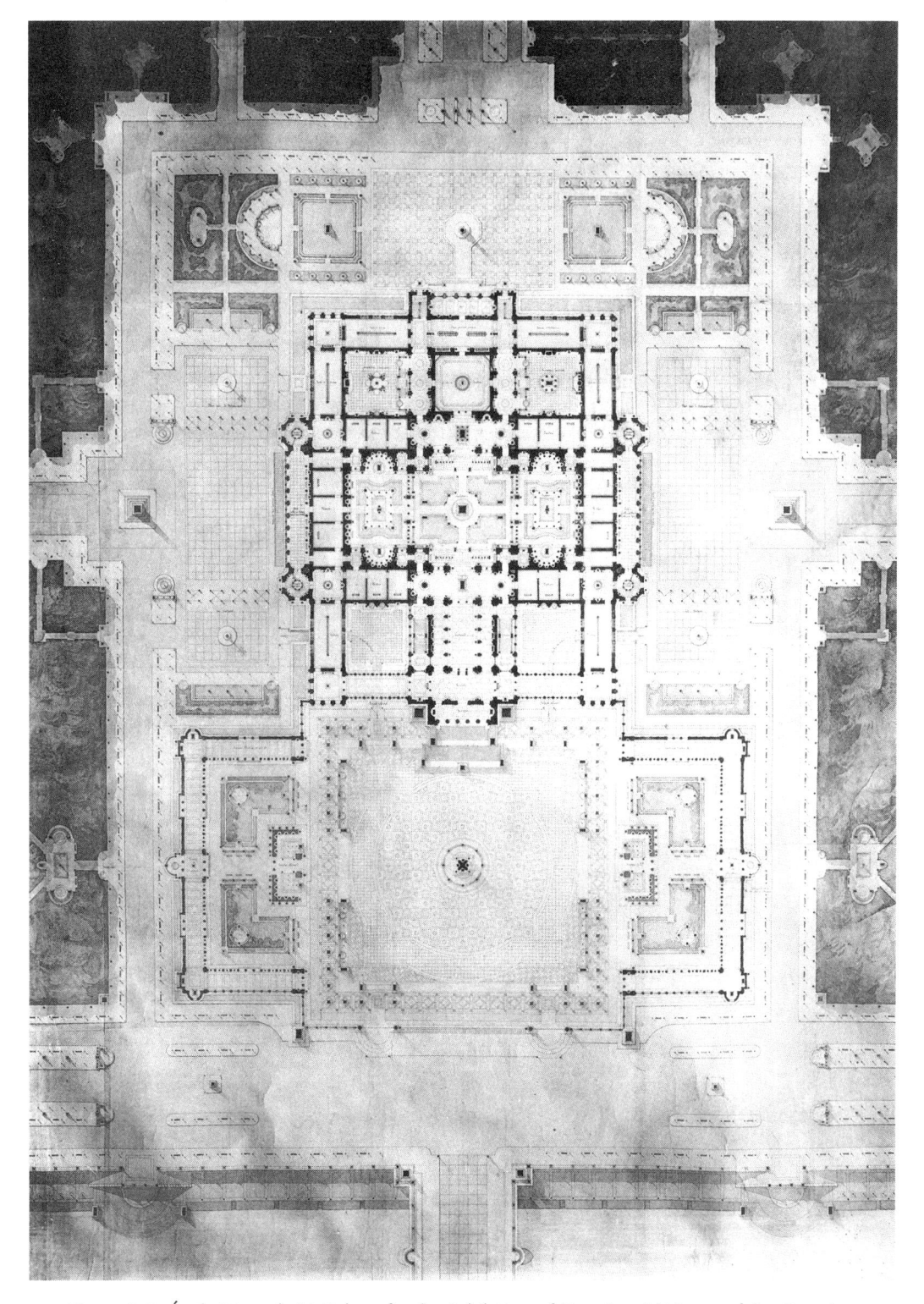

Figure 1.9. Émile Bénard, "A Palace for the Exhibition of Fine Arts," Winner of the Grand Prix de Rome, 1867. *Les grands prix de Rome d'architecture de 1850 á 1900: Avec les programmes des concours* (Paris: A. Guérinet, 1909), pl. 91.

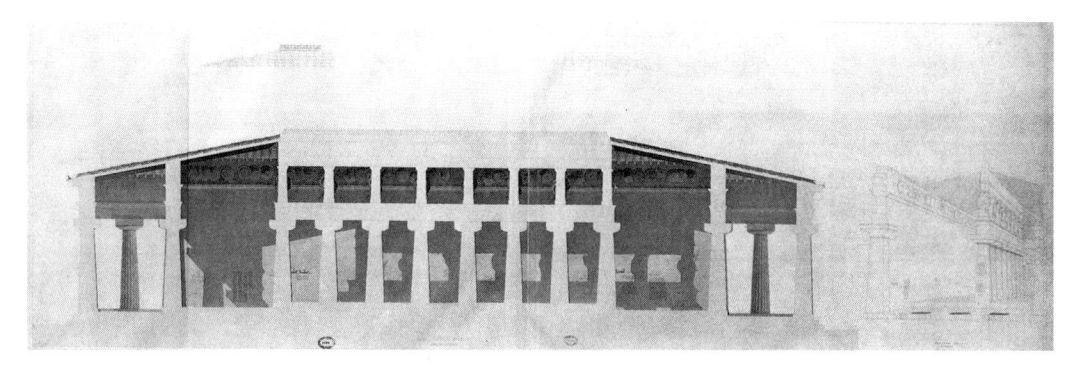

Figure 1.10. Henri Labrouste, longitudinal cross-section of the restoration of the Temple of Paestum, fourth-year submission from Rome, 1828–29. École nationale supérieure des beaux-arts, Paris.

But if the growth of the architectural drawing as a seductive commodity in the nineteenth century shows that architects increasingly took part in selling experiences, it also hints that what a rendering makes palpable is not always the building it depicts. Consider the flat pink profiles of columns in Labrouste's Paestum drawing, which give the section depth. In contrast to the shades of black ink Labrouste used to cast deep shadows into the cavernous interior, or the full spectrum of paints representing the ancient polychromy of the murals within, these pink profiles cut through stone and remain flatly on the surface of the page. Pink is essentially the color of rendered paper.[57] In that sense it is closer to the blue Labrouste used in his later drawings for the Bibliothèque Sainte-Geneviève, a medium-specific code indicating iron as construction material. These pink profiles materialized on paper the stereotomic-cum-analytical power that had been granted to the geometric line a century earlier. Given this new currency, the "cut" helped commodify the experience not only of Paestum but also of all the spaces where architects operated: the Parisian atelier, the salons of the city of Europe, the academies of Rome and Athens, and, increasingly, the industrial materials they specified.[58]

The apparent visual cohesion that emanated from the Beaux-Arts rendering, and the social distinction bestowed upon its author, actually relied on a strictly hierarchical division of graphic labor. Only a few students won the Rome Prize; most spent their time rendering in a piecemeal fashion and on behalf of someone else. The École's competition system was a pyramidal scheme where younger students who did not make it to the next round became helpers for those who did.[59] In the professional *ateliers,* every final drawing was rendered not by a single author but by an entire cohort of rendering hands, each working on separate portions of a single extensive surface (Figure 1.11). By the end of the nineteenth

Figure 1.11. Claude Hertenberger, "L'Atelier," 1937. *École Nationale Supérieure des Beaux-Arts* (Paris: La Grande Masse, 1937). Copyright by La Grande Masse des Beaux-Arts.

century, rendering had become a tedious and repetitive task delegated to a specialized subclass of image workers who called themselves "nègres." In a sure sign of the influence of industrial-era labor movements onto architectural culture, students started calling themselves the "great mass" in the early twentieth century, while the interns, still using the racist slur, tried to unionize.[60]

The Beaux-Arts system of distinction was only truly massified in the early twentieth century, however, when Beaux-Arts pedagogy was exported worldwide, and especially across architecture schools in the United States. American textbooks appeared to confirm the conflation of rendering with visual and professional finishing. John Harbeson published *The Study of Architectural Design* in 1927, for instance, to explain how the juried competition system worked, and to nationalize the standards for its associated medium, the rendered drawing.[61] The "time schedule" he published for a project broke down the system into incremental steps and even announced an automation of design.

```
Nov 31      Start inking final drawings
Dec  1
     2
     3
     4          Cast shadows
     5 Sat.    Render
     6          "
     7 Mon.   Problem due 10 A.M.[62]
```

Unlike all the other steps, "render" became a repeatable loop, through a single typographic mark, ". Harbeson also broke down the training of the eye visually. Devoting two chapters to rendering, he drew a full-page grid of "effects" that could be achieved with a single watercolor brush (Figure 1.12). The structure of this drawing (each cell in the grid cuts out a window through the page; each window is given its own depth effect) is strikingly similar to that of digital software tools; it looks like a hand-rendered version of the palette of options a Photoshop user can click on today.[63] But since there was no "clicking" possible, this menu offered no actions, only a sampler of architectural experiences and a serialized appeal to the senses.

As photography entered the design studio, the mechanization of vision also became useful to standardize rendered effects. Photographs pervade the manual I started with, Henry McGoodwin's *Architectural Shades and Shadows,* and his terminology too, as when he recommends using washes "to 'focus' the drawing at the principal plane."[64] Indeed McGoodwin directed his camera's lens at an already

Figure 196. Graded Washes of Water Color.

Figure 1.12. "Graded Washes of Water Color." John F. Harbeson, *The Study of Architectural Design* (New York: Pencil Points Library, 1927).

dissected reality, by taking photographs of plaster casts of capitols, carefully disposed atop column stubs, and artificially lit in front of a neutral backdrop. Bringing the rendering-real of the analytical "cut" full circle, McGoodwin dissected an architectural order in plaster, only in order to render it complete again via drawing. Gone were the polychromous backgrounds of Labrouste's Paestum reconstruction. Instead, the backdrop for rendering was that most modernist of three-dimensional décors, the naked white wall (Figure 1.13).

PHOTOGRAMMETRY AS MECHANICAL RENDERING

It is a point of historical consensus that the architects of the modern movement eschewed hand-rendering and preferred to visualize their projects with mechanical media that conveyed the disjointed and fragmented nature of modern experience.[65] According to Manfredo Tafuri, the architectural avant-gardes used mixed media and photo collage to mimic the assembly method of industrial production, eventually allowing the bourgeois public to "absorb and transmit" the "experience of shock suffered in the city."[66] Still, insofar as they combined drawn outlines with photographic shadows, especially through collage, many modernist architects can be said to have operated within a rendering paradigm. In his Klee collage for the 1939 Resor House, Mies van der Rohe used planes of color and texture to flatten the page, and naked lines for perspectival illusion.[67] When Le Corbusier collaged his *Plan Voisin* onto an aerial photograph of Paris, rendered plan and horizontal photography offered two parallel illusions of planimetric depth, side by side.

This interpretation of modernist collage is only one side of the story of mechanized visualization in architecture, however. A perceptual modernization of the built environment also took place in the late nineteenth and early twentieth centuries through surveying by way of photogrammetry—a technology that derives mathematical information from photographs to produce line drawings.[68] The optical principles of photogrammetry were already known to Renaissance surveyors, who traced city views onto large vertical glass plates. In the nineteenth century, these plates were replaced with photographs, which could be traced over offsite.[69] By the time the German engineer Albrecht Meydenbauer coined the word *photogrammetry* in the early twentieth century, it was largely a way to process the data contained in the vast photographic archives of historic monuments amassed by nation-states, creating measured drawings for them.[70] With the addition of stereoscopy—a technology that produces the impression of three-dimensional depth by taking two photographs of the same object spaced almost imperceptibly apart—photogrammetry became the dominant architectural surveying system

Figure 1.13. Photograph of a plaster cast used to practice drawing shadows. Henry McGoodwin, *Architectural Shades and Shadows* (Boston: Bates & Guild, 1904).

across Europe. Geometrically, the principle is the same as Verniquet's triangulation: from two views, one can derive a physical measure. But here one of the sides of the triangle is always composed by the very short distance between the viewer's two eyes.[71] The machine used to render the three-dimensional image—a "restitutor"—works by assigning each of these images to one eye of a human (Figure 1.14). This human is then asked to trace the position of a virtual "dot" that appears to "float" on the surface of a building as she sees it in three dimensions. Through a system of pulls and levers—right hand, left hand, and feet all operating a different prosthetic extension—her movements are transmitted mechanically to a drafting machine that produces a contour drawing. Every element of the classical rendering system is present but reenacted mechanically and by an upright body. English-language manuals use the term *rendering* to describe the product of these actions.[72] But photogrammetry more properly performs an act of unrendering: it presents a shadow to the eye and uses a machine to produce lines.

Stereophotography completely transformed the practice of surveying, turning what had been an architectural art requiring a point a view into a technical practice suitable for anyone with two eyes. Such was, at least, the caution sounded by many architects in the 1930s. Delegating depth perception to a prosthesis was too dangerous, they argued. Lengthy debates over whether to adopt these new and experimental stereographic technologies or whether to stick with the old method of single-point photography can be understood essentially as a debate between two kinds of experience.[73] At the 1934 International Congress of Photogrammetry, French architects in favor of traditional photogrammetry (where an

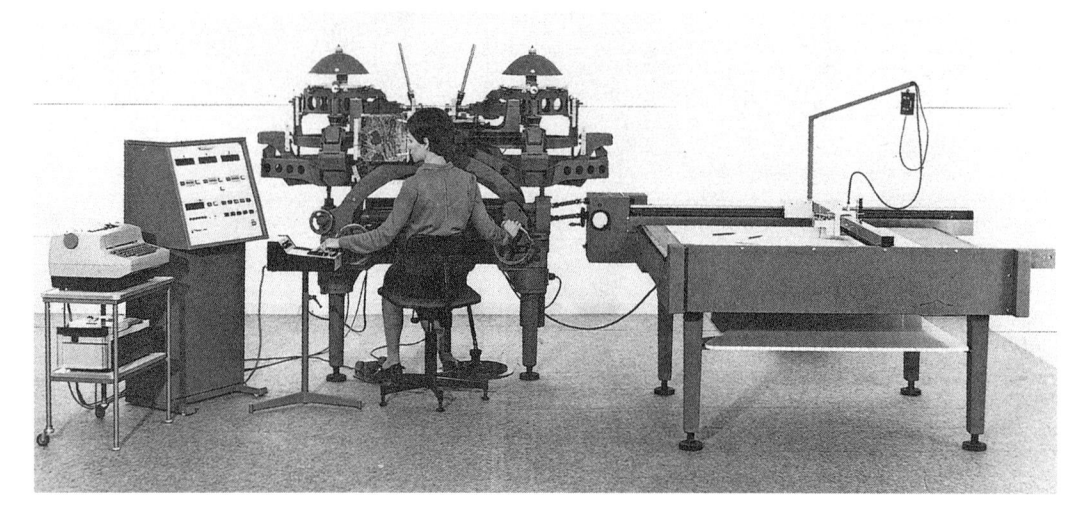

Figure 1.14. Wild A8 analog photogrammetry restitution machine, in use circa 1970. Jean-Paul Saint Aubin, *Le relevé et la représentation de l'architecture* (Paris: l'Inventaire, 1992).

architect traces over one photograph with ink) spoke of the convenience and mobility of their instruments and the continuing reliance on the traditional drawing skills of the architect. In contrast, the new stereoscopic "restitution machines" were large, expensive, and unwieldy. But the German delegation argued that they were more precise and reduced human error by requiring fewer measurements on site. The French side bet on the equation of human experience with mobility, predicting that stereo-photogrammetry would be adopted by architects only if smaller, more portable, and affordable photographic machines were made. But their German colleagues sought more accuracy by dividing up perception into minute, dispersed, and repeatable actions. They were proven right: oversized and expensive "restitutors" could be bought and maintained by state agencies and operated by a trained technician rather than an educated professional like the architect.[74] As control over the technologies was concentrated into state hands, so too was the architectural canon of buildings worthy of recognition and thus documentation. Photogrammetry brought a triple de-skilling of the architect: as a graphic artist, photographer, and cartographer.

Despite this de-skilling, claims that photogrammetric machines offered an experiential continuity were integral to their acceptance as truthful "restitutors" of reality. Although this system dramatically reduced the time that surveyors spent on building sites, it became known as a "tactile" technology, which could "cover the surface of the building in its actual state and with total continuity."[75] Maurice Carbonnel, one of the most famous architectural photogrammetrists of the twentieth century, vaunted he could "touch the image" and thus produce "threads of stone."[76] This cognitive metonymy is explained by the fact that de-skilling and re-skilling occurred at the scale of perception itself. Unlike collage, photogrammetry does not produce an image of disjunction. On the contrary, it offers the viewer an image of depth and wholeness but forbids him or her from experiencing it—from *receiving* it in the Husserlian sense. Instead, human operators follow a single "thread" between different media and their experience is discretized into separate channels. The fiction of wholeness persists only because of a continuous "line" in the instrumentation.

DIGITAL RENDERING: EXPERIENCE INTO EXPERIMENT

In our archaeology so far, we have already encountered several tools used by a digital renderer today: an iterative loop, a palette of shades, a menu of photorealistic effects, a nearly subocular visual increment (Figure 1.15). These segments of imaging processes have survived as digital operations, but only by being extracted from their technoscientific birthplaces. Photogrammetry offers an apt

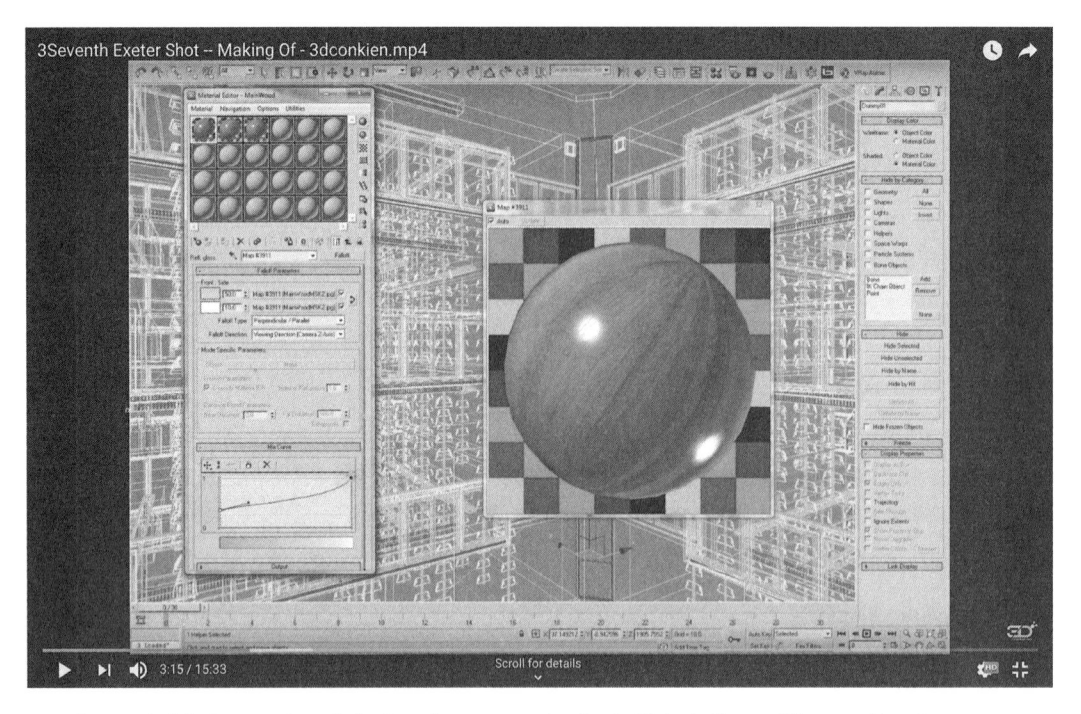

Figure 1.15. Screenshot of the interface to render Louis Kahn's Exeter Library. Alex Roman, "The Third & the Seventh," https://vimeo.com/7809605.

example. Its machine setup remained the same well into the 1980s—with a technician sitting at a viewing station, perceiving an illusion of depth, and producing architectural drawings using prosthetic drafting attachments. But after "restitution software" was introduced to replace the photo-mechanical viewing and plotting, it became unnecessary to measure the distance between the technician's eyes. All human input was reduced to viewing a single computer screen, sequentially clicking onto at least six points (three in one of two windows), then waiting for a progress bar to fill up to 100 percent.[77] That last step—the waiting—shows how the experiential basis of rendering's claim for a cognitive continuity has changed. Digital computing has all but removed the association of rendering with linear time, because software deals with time as a mathematical variable, to be computed and optimized.[78]

Architects today borrow their rendering tools from the computer graphics industry, where the tradeoffs about what deserves rendering time have already been made, often with the goal of maximizing spectacle.[79] The fly-through—borrowed from Hollywood film—has replaced the Beaux-Arts *marche* as the preferred way to walk through a building. For example, the most complete digital reconstruction of the site of Pompeii has been produced not by archaeologists but by the

CGI artists who made a three-minute sequence of the blockbuster film *Pompeii*, in which a camera flies over the city's streetscape as it is destroyed, first by massive balls of lava and then by an invading tsunami wave.[80] But to say architecture is submitted to spectacle is not saying much, given that the entire computer graphics industry has itself always been seen as a semiautonomous supplement to fundamental computing research. (This is the reason that graphics cards are bought separately, given a special "slot" in any computer today.) Computer graphics, the branch of computer science where rendering research takes place, is propelled by a desire to keep visualization fast, so it can be integrated into other coding endeavors.

There is no natural light in computing space, and also no difference between a shadow and a line: both need to be computed and rendered with equations. So, rather than relying on machines that see, rendering software models the behavior of light mathematically and optimizes the time to completion. There are two methods for doing this, each reliant on one of the basic operations of calculus, integration and differentiation. "Ray-tracing" imitates optical geometry by generating rays of light that bounce from the screen and toward an object, following them as they are reflected or refracted and rendering every point they encounter—a method best suited for visualizing shiny, isolated objects. "Radiosity" is borrowed from thermal engineering and works by computing the ability of surfaces to absorb and refract light against one another; it is best for rendering surface-bound environments.[81] Most rendering software uses a combination of both approaches, and because both are potentially indefinite operations, a certain processing time is set, after which the rendering process is cut off. The economy that drives the development of software has embedded criteria of visual "completion" into the rendering engines themselves.[82] But the machine "learns" what looks "finished" to the public at any given moment in time, not by comparing with an external referent.[83] Thus trust in computation differs from trust in numbers because every experiment contributes to perfecting this presumably growing machine intelligence.

Computer rendering was detached from sensory experience early on and explicitly distinguished from drawing or painting. Sketchpad, the earliest graphical computer interface, was presented in 1963 as based on "the medium of line drawing" in part to "make computers accessible to new classes of users (artists and draughtsmen among others)." But Ivan Edward Sutherland, Sketchpad's inventor, also argued the software would liberate them from "a lifetime of drawing on paper."[84] In other words, he hoped to enlist artists to help perfect his tool, but the tool would also transform their craft, retraining them to operate in computing space.

"Render" started to be used to mean an action performed by a computer a few years later, when computer scientists began to elaborate an inward-looking definition of sight called "machine rendering." Phrases such as "quantitative invisibility" and "conceptual opacity" (which paired mathematics and sensation) made the analogy possible.[85] As this new vocabulary developed, all the debates about epistemic substitution that had pertained to lines and shadows since the Enlightenment were transferred. For example, in order to make a surface, the computer had to be taught either to *not draw* the edges of certain objects or to *hide* certain lines. When the term *rendered* became applicable to actual surfaces, the two most important shading algorithms were invented by computer scientists, Henri Gouraud and Bui Tuong Phong, who had begun their careers in engineering schools in Paris and moved on to the pioneering computer graphics department at the University of Utah.[86]

At Utah and elsewhere, computer scientists working on this inward definition of machine vision routinely invoked architecture as an example of a renderable object. Architects had been early adopters of drafting software, and therefore computer scientists imagined that buildings could be made available in already digitized form rather than needing to be drawn from life. For example, in 1972 Martin Newell explained he wanted to avoid at all costs the impression that computer graphics were only a "sophisticated paintbrush," and therefore hoped to use "the output of design programs" as input.[87] (That is, rendering algorithms needed to be fed data not from empirical reality but from the output of other algorithms.) One of the primary uses of his research, he claimed, was "the assessment of the aesthetics of a new piece of architecture."[88] Already in 1968 a new ray-casting algorithm had been tested at IBM's Watson Laboratory on a number of digital objects, among them "an assembly of planes which make up a cardboard model of a building."[89] The model was of a courtyard building with low-slung canopies, clearly designed to produce a variety of shadow-casting conditions (Figure 1.16).

But the computer programming community eventually came to rely on a restricted repertoire of "standard objects," such as Newell's Utah teapot, to feed and perfect its ray-tracing algorithms, and not a single one of these objects was a building.[90] Architecture did periodically appear in the Utah experiments. Crude neoclassical forms, combining pedimented temples and circular domes, gave away that the problem being worked on was how to make a rounded surface look smooth. One striking example shows a perfectly smooth airplane dislodging the faceted dome of the U.S. Capitol building (Figure 1.17). By the time the Utah teapot was presented as standard, the renderer's ability to depict classical orders had markedly improved, but architecture's own standing had not. The famous "six platonic solids" displayed at SIGGRAPH '87 rested on top of fluted classical

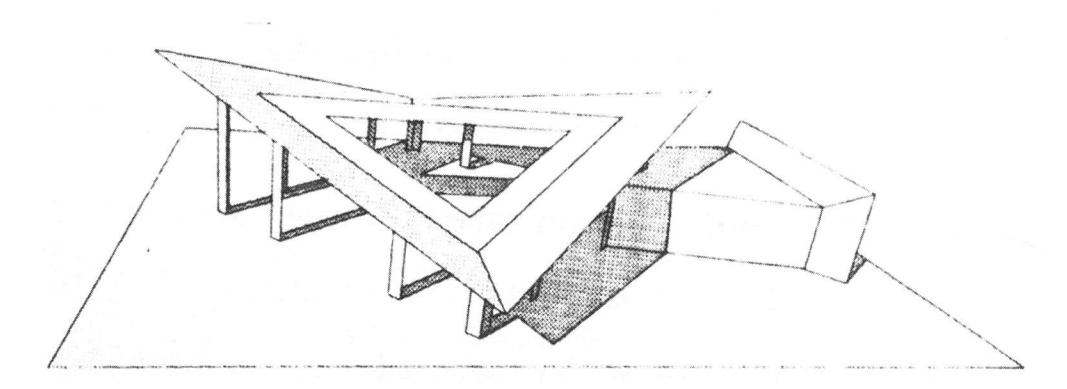

Figure 1.16. Cardboard model of a building. Arthur Appel, "Some Techniques for Shading Machine Renderings," in *Sprint Joint Computer Conference* (New York: ACM, 1968).

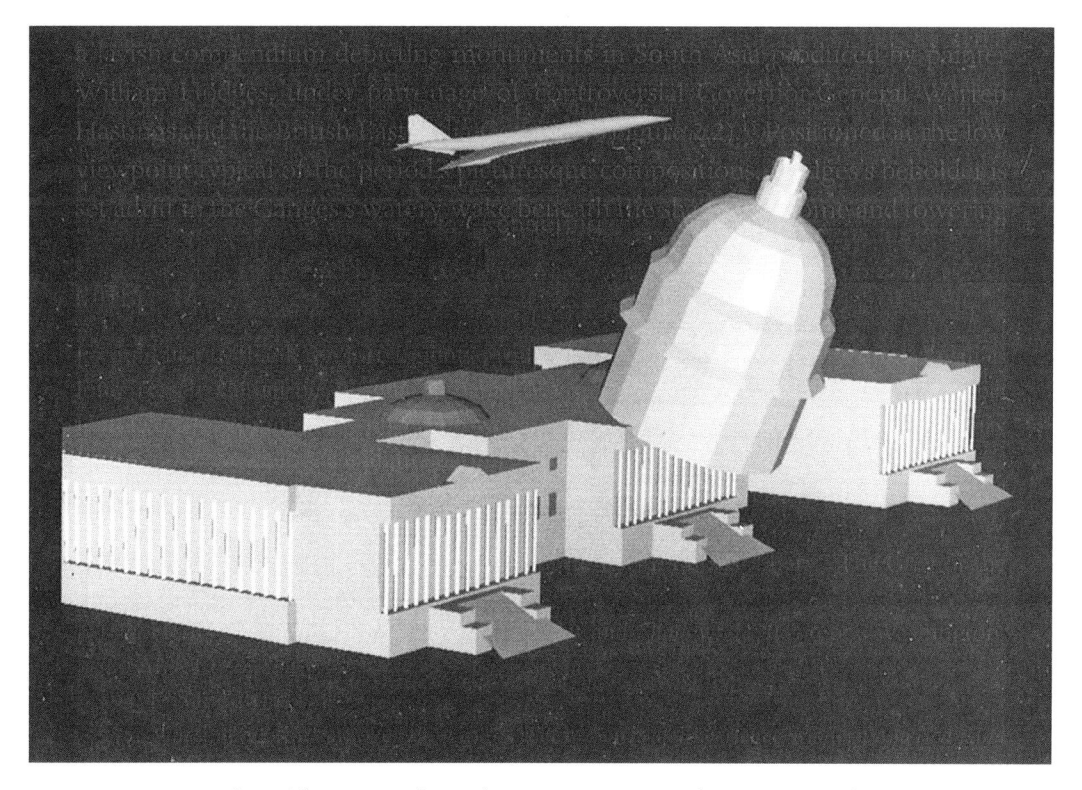

Figure 1.17. Polaroid from an early rendering experiment at the University of Utah. David C. Evans Photographic Collection, Special Collections, J. Willard Marriott Library, University of Utah.

pedestals, which look like highly stylized descendants of McGoodwin's academic plaster casts and column stubs (Figures 1.18, 1.13).[91]

This early history of computer graphics suggests that conventional architecture was consistently used to prop up engineering creativity. Even when the focus in rendering research turned from ray-tracing to radiosity in the 1980s (and digital objects were no longer rendered in isolation but were able to "bleed" their color onto wall surfaces in a scene), very little architectural specificity made it in.[92] Architectural planes in radiosity-rendered scenes were explicitly described as

Figure 1.18. James Arvo and David Kirk, "Six Platonic Solids," including the Utah teapot, 1987. Copyright by Apollo Computer Inc., reproduced on the cover of SIGGRAPH '87, Anaheim, Calif., July 27–31, 1987.

technically "passive." This meant, among other things, that these surfaces could become supports for mapping raster images. Architecture also became useful in experiments for computer-aided spatial navigation precisely by being unremarkably vernacular. The Aspen Movie Map, precursor to Google Earth, relied on two different definitions of mapping—one based on input, the other designed for output—that is strikingly reminiscent of Verniquet's dual use of trigonometry and shadows. On the one hand, Aspen's street geometry was extensively "mapped" (horizontally, by a drive-through) by surveying the city with a gyroscopic stabilizer; on the other, the resulting wireframe model was made virtually navigable through laboriously "mapping" (a kind of digital gluing) photographs of Aspen's banal streetscape onto blank volumes.[93]

This expectation that architecture be used to make digital experiences "familiar" has only intensified in the so-called second digital age, defined by the internet rather than laboratory computing. To be sure, a blackbox mentality continues to drive the development of rendering tools through trial and error, feeding algorithms into algorithms and hoping for optimization. But a dispersed viewing public is also increasingly called upon to establish visual criteria of realism and protocols for virtual witnessing—and to help rendering algorithms learn.[94] The rendering studio has been transposed to the online forums frequented by software engineers. Here, rendering knowledge is advanced by a hacker's culture, where informal experiments are first circulated as nonstandard "tricks" or "hacks" and eventually adopted as industry standards.[95] Most rendering demonstrations are staged within a rendered environment and performed as if they were a first-person video game. One 2010 example, demonstrating how to render a brick wall, leads us into a postindustrial interior, lit by neon, where we circumvent a brick cube, watching it morph as mortar joints are given more or less depth. To modify Shapin and Schaeffer's terms only a little: the object of the game is to experience a first-person virtual witnessing of a rendering experiment.

THE AESTHETICS OF INCOMPLETION

To conclude, I would like to suggest that many in architecture have responded to this collapse of experience into experiment by bringing to their renderings a provisional theory of experience—a phenomenology, almost—that has manifested itself through an aesthetics of incompletion.

Consider the Experiential Technologies Laboratory, one of the first to produce digital reconstructions of monumental environments—for example, a fly-through of a computer model of the Egyptian site of Karnak—as sources of firsthand historical knowledge.[96] The laboratory promotes this new, "immersive" mode of architectural history in spite of the obvious deficiencies of its fly-throughs—the incompleteness of the buildings, their crude detailing, pastel coloring, absence of landscape features, flatness of the terrain, and the artificiality of the camera movements. These architectural historians are fully aware of the philosophical charge of the word *experience*. But they nevertheless claim the term because they compare their products not to experience as it is "given in reality," as Husserl would say, but rather to other typically choppy digital experiences—such as navigating Google Earth.[97] They bracket off photo-realism to achieve completion where it matters more—in an architectural sequence.

This bracketing strategy has been adopted by a remarkably diverse array of architectural producers. Consider the rendering software that the self-styled digital architectural avant-garde has experimented with since the 1990s to "shape" building forms. Greg Lynn has explained that he chose software originally designed for the entertainment industry, Maya, because it "produced the kind of smoothly rendered surfaces that he admires in the automotive and aeronautic industries."[98] Lynn uses an Arts and Crafts–inspired definition of rendering that applies to a building, whereby a "render" is a thin layer of cement applied by hand to waterproof external walls. But Lynn too is fully aware of Husserl's theory of reduction, and keeps these highly rendered objects scaleless and surreally elemental.[99] If the historians of the ETL perform a Husserlian bracketing to access Karnak as pure "phenomenon," in contrast, Lynn brackets off context to achieve completion in representing "elements" such as fire, water, and air in a way that recalls Gaston Bachelard.[100]

Other branches of architectural rendering could productively be related to other schools of phenomenological thought. A Merleau-Pontian branch, especially visual, could be identified in the work of millennial architects who embrace what Hito Steyerl has called "the poor image" and hope to derive innovative building forms from its lossy aesthetic.[101] Even corporate images that "drip a glossy resolution" can be classified as flirting with digital dissolution.[102] Luxigon describes its rendering of REX's proposal for the Calgary Central Library as showing "the drama of the experience" by "radiating a warm and welcoming civic face."[103] But the refracted light in the falling snow that sprinkles across the foreground also seems to puncture through the image to the artifice that lies beneath (Figure 1.1). Such acts are twenty-first-century updates to the technique of rendering the "cut," which revealed and aestheticized an analytical operation all at once. Most common perhaps are architectural renderings that promise experiential insight through the destruction, or taking apart, of immersive environments, and which we could call Heideggerian.[104] Scientific communities have perfected this art of the digital disassembly. For example, a team of structural engineers and computer scientists at Purdue University rendered a sequence that shows two planes hitting the World Trade Center towers on September 11, 2001. Each act of this animated video repeats the destruction, each time "hiding" a different layer of the plane-building complex: the steel, the fuel, the glass, and so on. Although the goal is presumably scientific comprehensiveness, the effect is of a destruction whose causes are hauntingly remote—a building destroyed by a ghost (Figure 1.19).

To call architectural renderers phenomenologists is neither to elevate them into philosophers nor to vulgarize phenomenology. It is one way to illustrate how architectural renderings participate in working out standards for experiential completion and incompletion, now that "trust in numbers" is placed on thinking machines that need somehow to have a working theory of experience. Architectural visualization is ever-more relevant because of its long history of debates about epistemic substitutions: practice substituting for skill, geometry substituting for consensus, machines substituting for organs. After all, as Peter Gordon argued, phenomenology's philosophical authority has fundamentally shifted now that science no longer "enjoys a special access to a deworlded reality" but is "merely one world among others."[105] Architecture is one such world. Recent genealogies have emphasized its role in the emergence of an "interactivity" paradigm since the 1960s, but our longer archaeology of rendering cautions us not to believe that an age of unmediated spatio-temporal agency is upon us.

For most of the modern period, to render meant to recover experiences from an apparent loss or lack. In the eighteenth and nineteenth centuries, this loss was framed historically: renderings were a medium of the historical imagination, related to other acts of material recovery such as restitution, restoration, and reconstruction.[106] As rendering encountered mechanization, its tempo quickened (render, repeat). In the twentieth century, rendering became an operator in its own right, delegating productivity across the social order. In the twenty-first century, computer rendering instruments operate through a scattering of perceiving units across the globe, continuing this act of social ordering and delegation. On the one hand, architecture as a service industry allows instruments invented for knowledge production to be adapted to public use. On the other hand, the ubiquity of buildings makes their survey, through attention to the shadows they cast and colors they emit, especially useful for fine-tuning nonarchitectural technologies that rely on specialized access to the human senses. What this archaeology of rendering teaches us is to be attuned not to interactivity but rather *interpassivity*: our willingness to let others do the experiencing for us.[107]

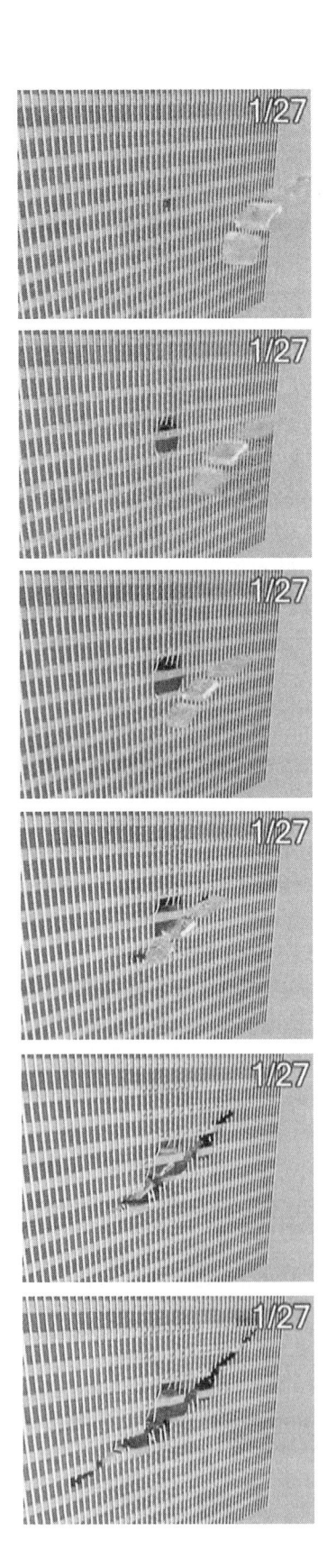

Figure 1.19. Paul Rosen, Voicu Popescu, Christopher Hoffmann, and Ayhan Irfanoglu, stills from "A High-Quality Physically-Accurate Visualization of the September 11 Attack on the World Trade Center," 2007. Courtesy of Paul Rosen.

NOTES

I would like to thank the instruments group for many productive discussions, as well as John Tresch, Catherine Ingraham, Daniel Maslan, and the Media Seminar at Columbia University, for commenting on various versions of this essay. Thank you to Jacob Gaboury for a productive dialogue and for sharing archival material.

1. Adam Nathaniel Mayer, "Urban Fantasies in China: Architectural Visualization," *Clog: Rendering,* August 2012, 31–33.

2. Eric de Broche des Combes, in an interview with Lutz Robbers, "The Grey of the Sky," *Candide,* no. 9 (June 2015): 116.

3. Henry McGoodwin, *Architectural Shades and Shadows* (1904; repr., Washington, D.C.: AIA, 1989), 1, 2.

4. McGoodwin, 1.

5. Martin Jay offers an overview in his recent *Songs of Experience: Modern American and European Variations on a Universal Theme* (Berkeley: University of California Press, 2005). See also Mark Jarzombek, *The Psychologizing of Modernity* (New York: Cambridge University Press, 2000).

6. For an overview of the *Erfahrung/Erlebnis* distinction, see C. Jason Throop, "Articulating Experience," *Anthropological Theory* 3, no. 2 (2003): 231. Wilhelm Dilthey is usually credited for originally popularizing this distinction. See Wilhelm Dilthey, *Das Erlebnis und die Dichtung* (Leipzig: Teubner, 1905). On Dilthey, see Jay, *Songs of Experience,* 222–41.

7. Amelia Taylor-Hochberg, "AfterShock #1: Architectural Consumers in the Experience Economy," *Archinect,* September 11, 2013, https://archinect.com.

8. B. Joseph Pine II and James H. Gilmore, *The Experience Economy* (Boston: Harvard Business School Press, 1999).

9. For a history of "respect for the line and cult of dessin," see Richard A. Moore, "Academic 'Dessin' Theory in France after the Reorganization of 1863," *JSAH* 36, no. 3 (October 1977): 145–17. See also Marco Frascari, "Lines as Architectural Thinking," *Architectural Theory Review* 14, no. 3 (2009): 200–212.

10. "First we observed that the building is a form of body, which like any other consists of lineaments and matter, the one the product of thought, the other of Nature." Leon Battista Alberti, *De re aedificatoria* (ca. 1450), translated by Joseph Rykwert, Neil Leach, and Robert Tavernor as *On the Art of Building in Ten Books* (Cambridge, Mass.: MIT Press, 1988). Alberto Pérez-Gómez posits Euclidian geometry as "intuitively sensible," whereas non-Euclidian forms provoked a "recentering of the world." He sees the shadow being gradually subjected to the same kind of "abstraction" as architecture itself—for example, as buildings went from acting as physical shadow tracers to featuring elaborate false perspectives. Alberto Pérez-Gómez, "Architecture as Drawing," *Journal of Architectural Education* 36, no. 2 (Winter 1982): 2–7; Alberto Pérez-Gómez and Louise Pelletier, *Architectural Representation and the Perspective Hinge* (Cambridge, Mass.: MIT Press, 2000), 112–25. See also Alberto Pérez-Gómez, *Architecture and the Crisis of the Modern Sciences* (Cambridge, Mass.: MIT Press, 1984).

11. Friedrich Kittler, "Computer Graphics: A Semi-Technical Introduction," *Grey Room,* no. 2 (Winter 2001): 44. See also Friedrich Kittler, "Real Time Analysis: Time Axis

Manipulation," in *Draculas Vermächtnis: Technische Schriften* (Leipzig: Reclam, 1993), 182–207; and Friedrich Kittler, "Perspective and the Book," *Grey Room*, no. 5 (Fall 2001): 38–53.

12. Mario Carpo, *The Alphabet and the Algorithm* (Cambridge, Mass.: MIT Press, 2010), 45. Carpo argues that Alberti's invention was not a geometric nomenclature but a humanist ideal of reproduction (what he calls "identicality"). This ideal was already revived in the early twentieth century when modern architects hoped to standardize architecture's design and its production. But according to Carpo, it was not until the late twentieth century that identicality and difference were remarried to their full extent.

13. For a description of the 1970s movement, see Jorge Otero-Pailos, *Architecture's Historical Turn: Phenomenology and the Rise of the Postmodern* (Minneapolis: University of Minnesota Press, 2010); see esp. "Polygraph of Architectural Phenomenology," 14–17.

14. Edmund Husserl, *The Crisis of the European Sciences and Transcendental Phenomenology*, trans. David Carr (Evanston: Northwestern University Press, 1970), 48. Lines and shadows played a role in the history of science according to Husserl. For example, Galileo owed his scientific fame in no small part to his careful and repeated hand-rendering of the shadows cast by the Earth onto the surface of the moon. See Samuel Y. Edgerton, "Galileo, Florentine 'Disegno' and the 'Strange Spottednesse' of the Moon," *Art Journal* 44, no. 3 (Autumn 1984): 225–32. And Husserl cited "the practical art of surveying, which knew nothing of idealities," as a precursor to the Galilean mathematization of the world. Husserl, *Crisis*, 48–49.

15. Edmund Husserl, "The Origins of Geometry," in Jacques Derrida, *Introduction to the Origin of Geometry* (1962), trans. John P. Leavey Jr. (Lincoln: University of Nebraska Press, 1989), 172–73. Derrida and others have provocatively argued that because Husserl set aside, or "bracketed," the question of what constituted the real, he developed an understanding of science not as an empirical pursuit but rather as historical practice, a passing down of transcendental truths. Derrida, 59. Also useful is Georges Canguilhem: "The history of science is the explicit, theoretical recognition of the fact that the sciences are a critical, progressive discourse for determining what aspects of experience must be taken as real." Georges Canguilhem, *A Vital Rationalist*, trans. Arthur Goldhammer (New York: Zone Books, 2000), 28. For a history where "emotion and aesthetic experience were valued on a par with technical and rational mastery," see John Tresch, *The Romantic Machine* (Chicago: University of Chicago Press, 2012), 1.

16. Theodore M. Porter, *Trust in Numbers: The Pursuit of Objectivity in Science and in Life* (Princeton, N.J.: Princeton University Press, 1995). For a sociotechnical history of "projecting" in the French architectural profession, see Jacques Guillerme, *L'Art du projet: Histoire, technique, architecture* (Paris: Mardaga, 2008).

17. Nicholas Savage, "Shadow, Shading and Outline in Architectural Engraving from Fréart to Letarouilly," in *Dealing with the Visual: Art History, Aesthetics and Visual Culture*, ed. Caroline van Eck and Edward Winters (London: Ashgate, 2005), 242–83.

18. When Antoine Desgodetz was commissioned to measure all the monuments in Rome in 1674, he returned to Paris with drawings whose outlines were drawn "very precisely" but also augmented with shadows that situated the ruins in three dimensions. Antoine Desgodetz, *Les Edifices antiques de Rome: Dessinés et mesurés tres exactement* (Paris:

Coignard, 1682). See also Wolfgang Herrmann, "Antoine Desgodetz and the Academie Royale d'Architecture," *Art Bulletin* 40 (1958): 23–53; and Henry Lemonnier, "Les dessins originaux de Desgodetz pour 'Les Édifices antiques de Rome' (1676–1677)," *Revue Archéologique* 6 (July–December 1917): 213–30.

19. Dupain l'Aîné, *La Science des ombres par rapport au dessein* (Paris, 1750), cited in Guillerme, *L'Art du projet,* 169.

20. On Gaspard Monge's transformation of geometry from a surveyor's tool into an architectural one, see Joel Sakorovitch, *Épures d'architecture* (Basel: Birkhäuser Verlag, 1998), 91.

21. N.-F.-A. de Chastillon, *Traité des ombres dans le dessin géométral* (1754), reprinted in Théodore Olivier, *Applications de la géométrie descriptive aux ombres à la perspective, à la gnomonique et aux engrenages* (Paris: Carilian-Goeury et V. Dalmont, 1847), 6. See also Joël Sakarovitch, "The Teaching of Stereotomy in Engineering Schools in France in the XVIIIth and XIXth Centuries," in *Entre méchanique et architecture,* ed. Patricia Radelet-de-Grave and Edoardo Benvenuto (Basel: Birkhäuser, 1995).

22. Stanislas L'Éveillé, *Etudes d'ombres, à l'usage des écoles d'architecture* (Paris: Truttel Wurtz, 1812), iii.

23. "The cascade of ever simplified inscriptions . . . allow harder facts to be produced at greater cost." Bruno Latour, "Visualisation and Cognition: Drawing Things Together," *Knowledge and Society: Studies in the Sociology of Culture Past and Present* 6 (1986): 16.

24. Raymond Williams, "Experience," in *Keywords: A Vocabulary of Culture and Society* (New York: Oxford University Press, 1985), 126–29. See also Peter Dear, *Discipline and Experience* (Chicago: University of Chicago Press, 1995).

25. Art historian Michael Baxandall has theorized the art of the Enlightenment along the lines of this bifurcation, detecting a "shadow epistemology" in drawings of Enlightenment artists. "Two modes of perceptive attentiveness" arose, he argues, with the line corresponding to the "local focus" required by scientific pursuit and the shadow providing "global awareness" of the kind "required by experience." Michael Baxandall, *Shadows and Enlightenment* (New Haven, Conn.: Yale University Press, 2007), 35, 48. See also Victor I. Stoichita, *A Short History of the Shadow* (London: Reaktion Books, 1997).

26. Pamela Smith, *The Body of the Artisan: Art and Experience in the Scientific Revolution* (Chicago: University of Chicago Press, 2004); Matthew C. Hunter, *Wicked Intelligence: Visual Art and the Science of Experiment in Restoration London* (Chicago: University of Chicago Press, 2013); Zeynep Çelik Alexander, *Kinaesthetic Knowing* (Chicago: University of Chicago Press, 2017).

27. Steven Shapin and Simon Schaffer, *Leviathan and the Air-Pump: Hobbes, Boyle and the Experimental Life* (Princeton, N.J.: Princeton University Press, 1985), 22–79; John Bender, "Matters of Fact: Virtual Witnessing and the Public in Hogarth's Narratives," in *Ends of Enlightenment* (Stanford: Stanford University Press, 2012), 57–78; John Bender and Michael Marrinan, *The Culture of the Diagram* (Stanford: Stanford University Press, 2010).

28. Antoine Picon argues that engineers operated "between sensation and calculation." Antoine Picon, *French Architects and Engineers in the Age of Enlightenment,* trans. Martin Thom (New York: Cambridge University Press, 1992), 148.

29. Jean-Baptiste Rondelet, *Traité théorique et pratique de l'art de bâtir* (Paris: n.p., 1802–17).

30. Verniquet's plan was the basis for the 1794 *Plan des artistes*; Antoine Picon calls it "the climax of the quest of accuracy" in the history of Parisian cartography. Antoine Picon, "Nineteenth-Century Cartography and the Urban Ideal," *Osiris* 18, 2nd ser. (2003): 135–49. See also Jean-Paul Robert and Antoine Picon, *Le dessus des cartes: Un atlas parisien* (Paris: Picard, 1999).

31. For an overview, see Jean-Marc Leri, "Edme Verniquet (1727–1804) cartographe du grand plan de Paris," in *Les architectes des lumières,* ed. Annie Jaxques and Jean-Pierre Mouilleseaux (Paris: ENSBA, 1989), 202–9. See also Jeanne Pronteau, *Edme Verniquet* (Paris: Commission des travaux historiques de la ville de Paris, 1986), 340; and Placide Mauclaire, *La vie et l'oeuvre de Verniquet, architecte, auteur du grand plan de Paris* (Paris: Picard, 1940).

32. See H. Monin, "Travaux d'Edme Verniquet, et en particulier sur le plan dit 'des artistes,'" *Bulletin de la bibliothèque et des travaux historiques* 1–4 (1898): xxiii.

33. Edme Verniquet, *Plan de la Ville de Paris* (Paris: Verniquet, 1792), 70–71. In Latour's words, the plan was an "immutable mobile." Latour, "Visualisation and Cognition," 21.

34. Liliane Pérez describes how "alongside monuments, museums and cabinets, engines and workshops were integrated into the range of economic curiosities." Liliane Pérez, "Technology, Curiosity and Utility in France and in England in the Eighteenth Century," in *Science and Spectacle in the European Enlightenment,* ed. Bernadette Bensaude-Vincent and Christine Blondel (London: Ashgate, 2008), 36.

35. Verniquet himself vaunted the "splendid testimony that all of the French and foreign scientists and artists who have visited the work have given as to its perfection." "Lettre de Verniquet, addressee a l'Assemblée Nationale en 1791," reprinted in Monin, "Travaux d'Edme Verniquet," xv.

36. See Basile Baudez, "L'Europe architecturale du second XVIIIe siècle: Analyse des dessins," *Livraisons de l'histoire de l'architecture* 30 (2015): 43–58.

37. The relational epistemology that arises from Verniquet's page can in no uncertain terms be related to the space of Verniquet's workshop, and to his own biography as a transitional figure in the French architectural profession of the late Enlightenment. As one historian has summarized, Verniquet was hired by the regime to make a complete survey of streets not because of his training but because he had become "the indispensable man [*l'homme indispensable*]," through his "experience and his works." Monin, "Travaux d'Edme Verniquet," xv.

38. *Oxford English Dictionary,* s.v. "render, v." III. "To return (something)," accessed October 30, 2014, https://www.oed.com. And specifically, 16a. "to restore, return, give back." See also "3b. To represent or reproduce, esp. artistically; to depict, portray."

39. His heirs spent a century attempting to secure retroactive payment for his work, as well as the "return" of the original plans, which, by the new republican standards, rightly belonged to him. The workshop's locus was a crucial datum in the debate. The inheritors argued that the plan that Verniquet had nailed to the table for his famous demonstration was one of three original drawings, now lost; the French National Assembly argued that it was an engraved reproduction of his atlas. Monin, "Travaux d'Edme Verniquet," xxi.

40. "Rendement," in *Dictionnaire de la langue française*, vol. 4, ed. M. P. Émile Littré (n.p.: n.p., 1873). On the use of "rendement" to refer to the efficiency of machines after accounting for friction and loss of energy, and eventually of bodies *(rendement de la machine humaine)*, see Anson Rabinbach, *The Human Motor* (Berkeley: University of California Press, 1992), 185.

41. Ernest Bosc, "Rendre," in *Dictionnaire raisonné d'architecture*, vol. 4 (Paris: Firmi-Didot, 1883).

42. John F. Harbeson, "Rendu," in "A Vocabulary of French Words Used in the Atelier," appendix to *The Study of Architectural Design* (New York: Pencil Points, 1927).

43. Antoine-Chrysostôme Quatremère de Quincy, "Rendre" and "Rendu," in *Dictionnaire historique d'architecture*, vol. 2 (Paris: Le Clere, 1832), 370. On Quatremère de Quincy and drawing, see Sylvia Lavin, *Quatremère de Quincy and the Invention of a Modern Language of Architecture* (Cambridge, Mass.: MIT Press, 1992), 158–64.

44. "Consequently the rendering of geometrical drawings, far from adding to the effect or the intelligence of these drawings, can only make them cloudy and equivocal." Jacques-Nicolas-Louis Durand, *Précis of the Lectures on Architecture* (1802–5), trans. David Britt (Santa Monica, Calif.: Getty Research Institute, 2000), 34. See also Anthony Vidler, "Diagrams of Diagrams: Architectural Abstraction and Modern Representation," *Representations* 72 (Autumn 2000): 1–20.

45. Durand, "Les principes et le mécanisme de la composition," in *Précis of the Lectures on Architecture*, 20. See also Picon's introduction, "From 'Poetry of Art' to Method: The Theory of Jean-Nicolas-Louis Durand," in Durand, *Précis of the Lectures in Architecture*, 1–72.

46. Guy Lambert and Estelle Thibault, "L'importance du savoir graphique," in *L'atelier et l'amphithéâtre* (Paris: Mardaga, 2011), 136–40.

47. Durand, "Préface," in *Précis des leçons d'architecture données à L'École Polytechnique* (Paris: Bernard, 1805), vi. See also Antoine Picon's note that at the École des Ponts et Chaussées, around 1800 a "dryer, more abstract cartography, often executed in black and white, began to replace the heightened realism of the previous period." Picon, *French Architects and Engineers*, 247.

48. On Durand and neo-palladian taste for *"nu du mur,"* see Jean-Philippe Garric, "Durand ou Percier? Deux approches du projet d'architecture au début du XIXe siècle," in *Bibliothèques d'atelier: Édition et enseignement de l'architecture, Paris, 1785–1871* (Paris: INHA, 2014).

49. On the plan, see Jacques Lucan, *Composition, Non-composition* (Lausanne: Presses polytechniques et universitaires romandes, 2010), esp. 122–23, 187–89; and the critique of Paul Cret of the "plan as 'a pleasing image'" (227).

50. Alexis LeMaistre, *L'École des Beaux-arts, Dessinée et racontée par un élève* (Paris: Firmin-Didot, 1889).

51. David Van Zanten, "The Beaux-Arts System," in *AD Profile: The Beaux-Arts*, ed. Robin Middleton (London: AD Editions, 1977), 66–78.

52. Durand uses *marche* in *Précis of the Lectures on Architecture*, 20. The word *marche* evolved from a synonym for a territorial border, to a noun for the movement of marching

troops, to a step in a stair or ladder, also acquiring ceremonial connotations, musical ones, even the one of chess-playing strategy, only to finally acquire both its scientific meaning (the movement of celestial bodies) and its mechanical one (the clock-works) by 1837. *Dictionnaires d'autrefois,* s.v. "Marche," accessed April 8, 2015, https://artfl-project.uchicago.edu/content/dictionnaires-dautrefois.

53. Alan Colquhoun, "The Beaux-Arts Plan," in Middleton, *AD Profile,* 61–66.

54. Annie Jacques, *La carrière de l'architecte aux 19.e siècle* (Paris: Musée d'Orsay, 1986). See also Annie Jacques and Richi Mikayé, *Les dessins d'architecture de l'École des Beaux-Arts* (Paris: Arthaud, 1988); and Jean-Michel Léniaud, *Les bâtisseurs d'avenir* (Paris: Fayard, 1998), 72.

55. Pierre Pinon and Francois-Xavier Amprimoz, "La fortune des Envois," in *Les Envois de Rome: Architecture et archéologie* (Paris: Diff. de Boccard, 1988); *Les grands prix de Rome d'architecture de 1850 á 1900: Avec les programmes des concours* (Paris: A. Guérinet, 1909).

56. As one commentator noted, "If every building of Rome had occupied the same space that its drawings sent from Rome occupy every year, Rome and its monuments would have invaded all of Italy." Charles Blanc, *Les artistes de mon temps* (n.p.: Nabu, 2010), cited in Lucan, *Composition, Non-composition,* 123. See also Quatremère de Quincy, "Dessiner," in *Dictionaire historique d'architecture,* 520.

57. In 1826 a textbook advised that the tints could be blue, pink, or black, and that black of a cut could be "substituted for pink." Pink had been used as replacement for black *poché* in the sixteenth century to represent the massive brick ballasts of military architecture and were popularized by the sensationalist architects of the late eighteenth century to create an architecture of sublimity. Basile Baudez, "Inessential Colors: A History of Color in Architectural Drawings, 16th–19th Centuries" (Françoise and Georges Selz Lectures on Eighteenth- and Nineteenth-Century French Decorative Arts and Culture, October 3, 2017); Basile Baudez, "L'Europe architecturale du second XVIIIe siècle: Analyse des dessins," *Livraisons d'histoire de l'architecture* 30 (2015): 43–58. But, as Sylvia Lavin has noted, this seductive pink survived decades after the sublime mission was dropped. Sylvia Lavin, "What Color Is It Now?," *Perspecta* 35 (2004): 98–111.

58. Jacques and Mikayé, *Les dessins d'architecture de l'École des Beaux-Arts,* 138.

59. One English-language source on this labor hierarchy is William H. White, "A Brief Review of the Education and Position of Architects in France since the Year 1671," *The Transactions,* September 1884, 93–120, esp. 112–15 (remarks by R. Phené Spiers).

60. See André Dubreuil and Roger Hummel, "Rassemblement: Devoirs du nègre et devoirs du patron," *Grande Masse,* no. 7 (April 1929): 23–25.

61. On the Beaux-Arts in America, see Paul Cret, "The École des Beaux-Arts and Architectural Education," *JSAH* (April 1941): 3–15.

62. Harbeson, "Time Schedule for Analytique for which Five Weeks Are Allowed," in *The Study of Architectural Design,* 14.

63. Harbeson, 142.

64. McGoodwin, *Architectural Shades and Shadows,* 96. On photography of the Beaux-Arts, see Anne-Marie Garcia, *La photographie avec les Arts* (Paris: ENSBA, 2015).

65. As Anthony Vidler has put it, the "white crusade" of architectural modernism was directed against the "brown world" of the Beaux-Arts, where brown was the color both

of rendered paper and of "19th-century bourgeois kitsch." Anthony Vidler, "The Modernist Vision," in *Open Plan: Architecture in American Culture* (New York: Institute for Architecture and Urban Studies, 1977). Vidler adapted this opposition from none other than Theo van Doesburg, who had advocated a new "white world" in contradistinction to a "brown world" implied in the cardboard hues of cubism.

66. Manfredo Tafuri, *Architecture and Utopia: Design and Capitalist Development* (Cambridge, Mass.: MIT Press, 1977), 86. See also Benjamin's "Experience and Poverty" (1933), in *Selected Writings,* vol. 2, *1927–1934,* trans. Rodney Livingstone (Cambridge, Mass.: Belknap Press of Harvard University Press, 1992), 731–36.

67. On collage, see also Martino Stierli, "Photomontage in/as Spatial Representation," *Photoresearchers* 18 (2012): 32–43.

68. On photogrammetry, see Albrecht Grimm, "The Origin of the Term Photogrammetry" (ISPRS Congress, Hamburg, 1980); Joerg Albertz, "A Look Back: 140 Years of Photogrammetry," *Photogrammetric Engineering and Remote Sensing* 73, no. 5 (May 1987): 503–6; Maurice Carbonnell, "L'Histoire et situation presente des applications de la photogrammetrie à l'architecture" (International Council of Monuments and Sites, Paris, 1968); and R. Burkhardt, *Historical Development of Photogrammetric Methods and Instruments* (Falls Church, Va.: American Society of Photogrammetry and Remote Sensing, 1989).

69. The surveyor took photographs from two specifically marked positions, then traced perspective lines on top of them, "searching for the focal point." On Eugène-Emmanuel Viollet-le-Duc's use of this technique, see Aaron Vinegar, "Panoramic Photography as Imagination Technology: Viollet-le-Duc and the Restoration of the Château of Pierrefonds," in *Essays on Viollet-le-Duc,* ed. Werner Oechslin (Zürich: ETH / Geschichte und Theorie der Architektur Verlag, 2010), 92–109. See also Peter Collier, "The Impact on Topographic Mapping of Developments in Land and Air Survey: 1900–1939," *Cartography and Geographic Information Science* 29, no. 3 (2002): 155–74.

70. Albrecht Meydenbauer, *Handbuch der Meßbildkunst in Anwendung auf Baudenkmäler und Reiseaufnahmen* (Halle: Knapp Verlag, 1912). See Albrecht Grimm, "Zwei Meydenbauer'sche Instrumente für die Architektur-Photogrammetrie wiedergefunden," *Bildmessung und Luftbildwesen* 46, no. 2 (1978): 33–34; and R. Meyer, *Albrecht Meydenbauer—Baukunst in historischen Fotografien* (Leipzig: Fotokinoverlag, 1985). The loop from surveying to building was closed half a century later, as these archives were used to rebuild Europe's destroyed monuments after World War II.

71. A straightforward description of the apparatus is found in Jean-Paul Saint Aubin, *Le relevé et la représentation de l'architecture* (Paris: Éditions de l'Inventaire, 1992), 24–25.

72. See, for example, Otto von Gruber, "The Rendering of Details in Photographs," in *Photogrammetry: Collected Lectures and Essays,* ed. Otto von Gruber, trans. G. T. McGraw and F. A. Cazalet (Boston: American Photographic, 1932), 51–56.

73. M. Walther, "L'application de la photogrammétrie à l'architecture en allemagne," in *Quatrième Congrès International de Photogrammétrie: Procès Verbaux des Séances des Commissions* (Paris: Société Géographique de l'Armée Française, 1936), 305–22.

74. National bureaucracies used these machines first vertically, to record monuments, and then to map their territories horizontally, through aerial photography. On

photogrammetry as a precursor to "remote sensing," see John J. May, "Sensing: Preliminary Notes on the Emergence of Statistical-Mechanical Geographic Vision," *Perspecta* 40 (2008): 42–53.

75. Maurice Carbonnel, *Le fil des pierres: Photogrammétrie et conservation des monuments* (Paris: Institut Géographique National, 1978), 8.

76. "The operator perceives a mark, in the same visual space as the image in relief and, with the appropriate command tool, he can apparently 'touch' the image with this mark, and make it follow whatever lines one wishes to record." Carbonnel, 12.

77. ADAM Technology, "How Does Photogrammertry Work?," September 3, 2010, http://www.adamtech.com.au.

78. On temporality in cybernetics, see Orit Halpern, "Dreams of Our Perceptual Present," *Configurations* 13, no. 2 (Spring 2005): 283–319.

79. As Matthew Allen summarizes it, recent histories have tried to dispel the notion "that experimentation was driven by young practitioners playing around with fancy software and stumbling upon flashy effects." Matthew Allen, review of "Archaeology of the Digital," *Domus,* May 15, 2013, https://www.domusweb.it. See also Greg Lynn, ed., *The Archaeology of the Digital* (Montreal: Canadian Centre for Architecture; Berlin: Sternberg, 2013).

80. One recent reconstruction of the Forum in Pompeii is Gabriele Guidi, Fabio Remondino, Michele Russo, Fabio Menna, and Alessandro Rizzi, "3D Modeling of Large and Complex Site Using Multi-sensor Integration and Multi-resolution Data," in *VAST 2008: Proceedings of the 9th International Symposium on Virtual Reality, Archaeology and Cultural Heritage,* ed. M. Ashley, S. Hermon, A. Proenca, and K. Rodriguez-Echavarria (Aire-la-Ville: Eurographics Association, 2008). On the integration of digital models, including GIS, into the new plans for a "sustainable Pompeii," see Giovanni Longobardi, ed., *Pompei Sostenibile* (Rome: L'Erma di Bretschneider, 2002), 121–23. For the Hollywood film, see Ian Failes, "Stories from *Pompeii,*" March 3, 2014, http://www.fxguide.com.

81. In "Computer Graphics," Kittler summarizes that ray-tracing renders the world as a still life and radiosity reproduces the atmosphere of a genre painting. For an art historical perspective on the same distinction, see James Elkins, "Art History and the Criticism of Computer-Generated Images," *Leonardo* 27, no. 4 (1994): 335–42.

82. Kittler, "Computer Graphics," 44.

83. A computer, in information theory, is defined as an electronic machine in which the line between input and output includes feedback. Succinct and helpful descriptions of this feedback system are in Peter Galison, "Ontology of the Enemy," *Critical Inquiry* 21, no. 1 (Autumn 1994): 228–66; and John Harwood, *The Interface* (Minneapolis: University of Minnesota Press, 2010).

84. Ivan Edward Sutherland, "Sketchpad: A Man-Machine Graphical Communication System" (PhD diss., MIT, 1963), 17.

85. Arthur Appel, "The Notion of Quantitative Invisibility and the Machine Rendering of Solids," *Proceedings of ACM National Meeting* (1967): 387–93. On "conceptual opacity," see Sutherland, "Sketchpad," 1.

86. Henri Gouraud, "Computer Display of Curved Surfaces" (PhD diss., University of Utah, 1971); Bui Tuong Phong, "Illumination of Computer-Generated Images" (technical report, Department of Computer Science, University of Utah, UTEC-CSs-73-129, July 1973). For an example of the literature that builds on their work, see A. Glasner, "Situation Normal," *IEEE Computer Graphics and Applications* 17, no. 2 (March/April 1997): 87–92; Isabelle Bellin, "Images de Synthèse: Palme de la longévité pour l'ombrage de Gouraud," *Interstices,* September 15, 2008, https://interstices.info.

87. The "production of shaded pictures" had evolved "using the results of design programs as input." M. E. Newell, R. G. Newell, and T. L. Sancha, "A Solution to the Hidden Surface Problem," *Proceedings of the ACM National Meeting* (1972): 448.

88. Newell, Newell, and Sancha, 448.

89. Arthur Appel, "The Visibility Problem and Machine Rendering of Solids" (IBM Research Report RC 1611, May 20, 1966). See also Arthur Appel, "Some Techniques for Shading Machine Renderings of Solids," in *Sprint Joint Computer Conference* (New York: Association for Computing Machinery Press, 1968), 37–45.

90. Jacob Gaboury, "Image Objects: An Archaeology of 3D Computer Graphics, 1965–1979" (PhD diss., New York University, 2014), 133–75.

91. "Platonic Solids," published by James Arvo and David Kirk in "Fast Ray Tracing by Ray Classification," *Computer Graphics* 21, no. 4 (July 1987): 55–64.

92. See Alan Watt and Mark Watt, *Advanced Animation and Rendering Techniques* (New York: Association for Computing Machinery Press, 1991) 294.

93. For a description of how the Aspen movie map was made, see Molly Wright Steenson, *Architectural Intelligence* (Cambridge, Mass.: MIT Press, 2017), 202–8; for the way it produced a cognitive "familiarity" with the town of Aspen, see Felicity Scott, *Outlaw Territories* (New York: Zone Books, 2018), 413.

94. See Wendy Hui Kyong Chun, *Control and Freedom* (Cambridge, Mass.: MIT Press, 2005); and Wendy Hui Kyong Chun, "On Software, or the Persistence of Visual Knowledge," *Grey Room,* no. 18 (Winter 2005): 26–51.

95. Isaac Kerlow, "Selected Rendering Hacks," in *The Art of 3d Computer Animation and Effects,* 4th ed. (New York: Wiley & Sons, 2008), 285. This is how the global illumination (GI) problem was solved. One textbook recounts that "the mathematical foundations of GI were essentially complete by the middle of the 1980s but the cost of computing indirect lighting to a visually acceptable accuracy was a major obstacle to its practical use." Nokiro Kurachi, *The Magic of Computer Graphics,* ed. Michael Stark (New York: Taylor and Francis, 2011), 23. This problem of cost and practicality led developers to design various hacks, one of which, called "ambient occlusion," relies on the creation of a "virtual sky" in order to "recreate the effect of a luminous but overcast day." Kerlow, 253.

96. Diane Favro, "*Se non e vero, e ben trovato*: Digital Immersive Reconstructions of Historical Environments," *JSAH* 71, no. 3 (September 2012): 273–77. Favro explicitly describes these experiments as "phenomenological." Diane Favro and Christopher Johanson, "Death in Motion: Funeral Processions in the Roman Forum," *JSAH* 69, no. 1 (March 2010): 12–37.

97. For a review of Google Earth as "the experience of a map in motion," see Laura Kurgan, "Google Earth 5.0," *JSAH* 68, no. 4 (December 2009): 588–90.

98. Lawrence Bird and Guillaume LaBelle, "Re-Animating Greg Lynn's Embryological House: A Case Study in Digital Design Preservation," *Leonardo* 43, no. 3 (2010): 242–49; Howard Shubert, "Embryological House," Canadian Centre for Architecture, April 6, 2009, http://www.cca.qc.ca. See also Randall Newton, "Using Rendering Technology to Revolutionize Yacht Design," *GraphicSpeak,* October 11, 2013. This reference is to the use of modeling software for ballistics and aeronautic design, a well-covered aspect of computer engineering history. For an architectural history of computation that incorporates this history, albeit briefly, see Mario Carpo, *Design in the Second Digital Age* (Cambridge, Mass.: MIT Press, 2017).

99. For Lynn's reading of Husserlian "reduction," see Greg Lynn, "New Variations on the Rowe Complex," in *Folds, Bodies & Blobs: Collected Essays* (Paris: La Lettre Volée, 1998), 209. For the claim that computers allow designers to "draw and sketch using calculus," see Greg Lynn, *Animate Form* (New York: Princeton Architectural Press, 1999), 17.

100. Two helpful excerpts that highlight the difference in two philosophies are as follows: "The transcendental Ego emerged out of my parenthesizing of the entire Objective World and all other (including all ideal) Objectivities." Edmund Husserl, "Fifth Meditation," in *Cartesian Meditations: An Introduction to Phenomenology,* trans. Dorian Cairns (Amsterdam: Kluwer, 1960), 99. "Everyone must learn to escape from the rigidity of the mental habits formed by contact with familiar experiences. . . . To the imagination, fire is not a separable datum of experience: it is already linked by analogy and identity to a dozen other aspects of experience." Gaston Bachelard, *The Psychoanalysis of Fire,* trans. Alan Ross (London: Routledge, 1963), 1, vi

101. Hito Steyerl, "In Defense of the Poor Image," *e-flux,* no. 10 (November 2009). Sam Jacob makes a related argument about a new generation rejecting the high resolution in "Rendering: The Cave of the Digital," *e-flux,* February 2, 2018, https://www.e-flux.com.

102. Francesca Hughes, *The Architecture of Error* (Cambridge, Mass.: MIT Press, 2015), 218.

103. REX, "Calgary New Central Library," caption for image 20 of 24, accessed June 1, 2019, https://rex-ny.com.

104. Martin Heidegger, "Time and Being" (1962), in *On Time and Being,* trans. Joan Stambaugh (Chicago: University of Chicago Press, 2002). On *Abbau* and *Destruktion* as a phenomenological method, which Heidegger substituted for Husserl's *Reduktion,* see Brian Elliot, *Phenomenology and Imagination in Husserl and Heidegger* (New York: Routledge, 2005), 70.

105. Peter Eli Gordon, "Realism, Science, and the Deworlding of the World," in *A Companion to Phenomenology and Existentialism,* ed. Hubert L. Dreyfus and Mark A. Wrathall (London: Wiley-Blackwell, 2009), 425–44.

106. For a "media archaeology of the historical imagination," see Wolfgang Ernst, "Let There Be Irony: Cultural History and Media Archaeology in Parallel Lines," *Art History* 28, no. 5 (November 2005): 582–603.

107. Slavoj Žižek, "The Interpassive Subject: Lacan Turns a Prayer Wheel," in *How to Read Lacan* (New York: W. W. Norton, 2006), 23–39.

CHAPTER 2

MODELING

A Secret History of Following

MATTHEW C. HUNTER

In the late 1990s, scientists at Princeton University seeking to understand circadian rhythms constructed an oscillatory network. Working within a tradition dating to the 1960s of studying biological clock phenomena via feedback systems drawn from engineering and statistical mechanics, researchers Michael B. Elowitz and Stanislas Leibler ran computer simulations of their oscillator's behavior. But they also went further. Elowitz and Leibler grew a living clock network from *Escherichia coli* protein (Figure 2.1).[1] The scientists called their creation "the repressilator," a name meant to signify how the network's genetic components (LacI, TetR, and λ cI) would strategically cancel out each other's activity. The repressilator served as an investigative tool. Not only was it designed to oscillate at much slower rates than actual cellular networks, but it would disclose periods of activity with bioluminescent display—by fluorescing green. Could those intermittent, green pulsations resolve into a stable rhythm? Or would temporal oscillations made bioluminescent devolve into stochastic noise? "Because individual cells have no apparent means of maintaining synchronization," Elowitz and Leibler explained, "we studied the repressilator by isolating single cells under the microscope and monitoring their fluorescence intensity as they grew into small two-dimensional microcolonies consisting of hundreds of progeny cells."[2] From a mathematical model based on an engineering formalism, the synthetic repressilator was then subject to experiments with living cellular networks.

While its hybrid fusion of mathematical modeling and experimentation on living model organisms could surely say much about the brave new worlds of synthetic biology, the repressilator has also spoken to investigators heeding a clarion call.[3] "Natural science since the seventeenth century has been the adventure of the interlocking of representing and intervening," as philosopher Ian Hacking

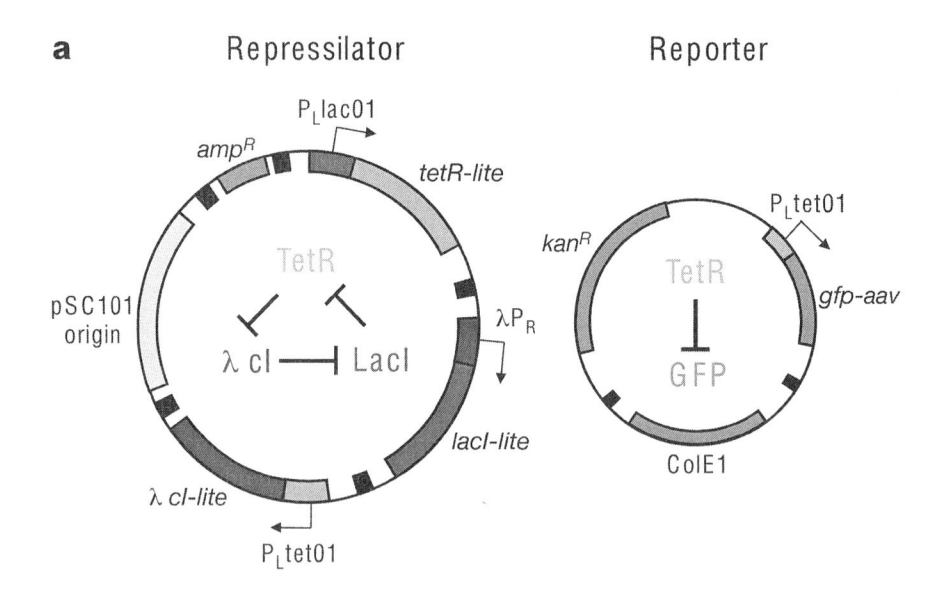

Figure 2.1. Synthetic "repressilator" network and reporter plasmid. Michael B. Elowitz and Stanislas Leibler, "A Synthetic Oscillatory Network of Transcriptional Regulators," *Nature* 403, no. 6767 (2000): 336.

declared in a classic study from 1983: "It is time that philosophy caught up to three centuries of its own past."[4] The impulse to locate modeling in those spaces between theoretical representation and more direct intervention into the material stuff of the world has since found numerous votaries among historians and philosophers of science. Such an impulse might also be detected in contemporaneous architectural conversation. Voiced in Peter Eisenman's speculation of 1981 that "models, like architectural drawings, could well have an artistic or conceptual existence . . . relatively independent of the project that they represented," modeling has been viewed as a site of mediating action.[5] Moving from analogy to ontology, the architect's models "cause to be made manifest—and hence allow for the revealing, touching, tweaking, or accessing—*the actual forces*" underpinning construction, as recent commentators put it.[6] And beyond positing some loose resemblance between the repressilator's scalar relations and the proportions of working models used by architects to design and manage buildings, the synthetic network might be said to share a quasi-autonomous existence with the models of architectural discourse. Each possesses "a life of its own."[7]

How, though, are insights extracted from modeling?[8] What modes of comportment have been proper to models in the intersecting histories of the arts and sciences? And what kind of an enterprise is modeling now? A story recently told by architectural historian Mario Carpo suggests that, until a recent digital rift, such matters had been all but sewn up by the late fifteenth century. In the hands of Leon Battista Alberti, modeling was arrogated unto the architect's design process. Notation of finished plans was exported to the building site for fabrication with all the exactitude demanded of what Carpo casts as the printing press's "mass-produced, exactly repeatable mechanical imprints."[9] This essay argues that models' vexing questions were very much alive and kicking well beyond that seventeenth-century scientific moment invoked by Hacking. Canvassing three likely stories then told about models, I focus attention on a formula into which Immanuel Kant would resolve modeling's vagaries. Modeling meant following. I explore this coupling not out of some antiquarian interest but as a means of highlighting key features in an ongoing conversation about models advanced by philosophers of science who have followed the call of Hacking and contemporaries such as Nancy Cartwright.[10] Providing a point of entry to a lively debate about models' mediation, fictionality, and related problems that have only recently begun to move beyond the confines of analytic philosophy, this essay means to open the possibilities and stakes of thinking the modeling/following couplet in the history and theory of architecture as well.[11] Philosopher Mary S. Morgan has identified a shift in the history of modern economics from "reasoning with words to reasoning with models."[12] Here, I aim to ask: What are the implications of working with—relying on—cognitive instruments that require not reading but following?[13]

MYTHOLOGIES: MECHANICAL, INSTRUMENTAL, WAYWARD

In his *Discourse XIII* of 1786, Sir Joshua Reynolds waged an assault on an art-theoretical standard: the imitation of nature. Admiringly noting how poets exaggerate meter and rhyme scheme to sway listeners, Reynolds (painter and first president of Britain's Royal Academy of Arts) directed the aspiring visual artist away from mimicking "the narrow idea of nature, and the narrow theories derived from that mistaken principle." Instead of the "natural representation of a given object," the painter should pursue "what it is natural for the imagination to be delighted with."[14] In Reynolds's argument, that shift from nature's means to the subject's ends should also extend to architects. As a prompt for expanding architecture's imaginative address, the painter recommends *Select Views in India* (1775), a lavish compendium depicting monuments in South Asia produced by painter William Hodges, under patronage of controversial Governor-General Warren Hastings and the British East India Company (Figure 2.2).[15] Positioned at the low viewpoint typical of the period's picturesque compositions, Hodges's beholder is set adrift in the Ganges's watery wake beneath the shadowed dome and towering

Figure 2.2. William Hodges, "View of Part of the City of Benares, upon the Ganges," February 24, 1787. William Hodges, *Select Views in India, Drawn on the Spot . . .* (London: Printed [by Joseph Cooper] for the author, 1785).

minarets of the Gyan Vapi mosque. Up the distant, illuminated steps, aquatint washes direct the beholder's attention to an architectural site of sectarian conflict: a mosque constructed for Mughal emperor Aurangzeb (1618–1707) on a destroyed Hindu temple.[16] For Reynolds, Hodges's work gives not political history but formal suggestion. "The Barbarick splendor of those Asiatick Buildings," as he puts it, "may possibly . . . furnish an Architect, not with models to copy, but with hints of composition and general effect, which would not otherwise have occurred."[17]

Numerous though its blind spots are, Reynolds's passage is instructive in its coupling of the model with copying (the latter a "delusive kind of industry" in his consistently pejorative usage).[18] It gestures to three oft-told tales about models and modeling in the early modern period—stories that feature the model's troubling mechanicity, its instrumentalizing function, and ultimately its wayward drift. I begin with mechanicity. Like the early modern French "modelle" in its derivation from the Renaissance Italian "modello" or exemplar used in metal casting, the English term *model* denotes a heterogeneous, often diminutive, preliminary object embedded into a sequence of making.[19] Modeled (meaning copied exactly) from Antoine Furètiere's standard craft dictionary, English encyclopedist Ephraim Chambers defined *model* in the early eighteenth century as "an artificial pattern made of wood, stone, plaister, or other matter, with all its parts and proportions; in order for better conducting and executing some great work, and to give an idea of the effect it will have in large."[20] Used extensively in the design, funding, and fabrication of spaces and artifacts, models figured in the technics of repetition vital to early modern art and architecture, if often straying to the wrong side of the ledger.[21] In the wake of Caravaggio's so-called naturalism, painters' dependence on human studio models became a cipher for failure of the elevated capacity to create ideas in the mind, a power newly asserted by artists.[22] One such Caravaggisto was ridiculed by contemporaries when his elaborate apparatus for modeling a commission of St. Jerome went awry and "an old man, hung upside down from a ceiling to pose as God . . . crashed to the floor."[23]

Reynolds was no stranger to such usage. In a discourse from 1788, he described as "contemptible and mischievous trifling" the practice of fellow portrait painter Thomas Gainsborough, who "framed a kind of model of landskips, on his table; composed of broken stones, dried herbs, and pieces of looking glass."[24] Narrow and narrowing, modeling as deadening *imitatio* opposed to liberal, tradition-enriching *emulatio* appears in full force with Antoine-Chrysostôme Quatremère de Quincy's subsequent distinction: "The model is an object that must be replicated exactly as it is. The *type,* on the other hand, is an object from which works can be made with little resemblance between them. All is precise and given in the model; all is more or less vague with the *type.*"[25] Model, in this sense, is a mechanism in the period's pejorative sense. It ties artist and architect unduly to the work of the hand rather than releasing them into the "liberal" realm of the mind.[26]

Commensurate with this mechanicity, a second likely story turns on modeling's instrumentality. Given its etymological relation to classical Latin "modulus," or the unit of length by which architectural proportions are determined, the model often plays into plots of instrumentalizing control. Henry A. Millon has traced a shift in Renaissance architecture from strategic abstraction to lavish projection, from the parsimonious working models used by Alberti and by Filippo Brunelleschi in the fifteenth century to the minutely detailed artifacts capable of simulating buildings' realized form as demanded by sixteenth-century clients.[27] The model's force as a tool of constraint was certainly felt by Christopher Wren, who commissioned from William and Richard Clere a massive object known as the "Great Model" when rebuilding St. Paul's Cathedral in 1670s London (Figure 2.3).[28] Scaled at one inch to two feet, the thirteen-foot-high model was "walkt through" by Robert Hooke and presented to King Charles II's rebuilding commission in 1674.[29] After a torrent of criticism was heaped on his "Model Design," Wren foreswore

Figure 2.3. "Great Model" of St. Paul's Cathedral, fabricated ca. 1673–74 by William and Richard Clere, in collaboration with Christopher Wren, Edward Woodroffe, and others. Copyright by the Chapter of St. Paul's Cathedral.

modeling as such. He vowed "to make no more Models, or publickly expose his Drawings, which, (as he had found by Experience,) did but lose Time, and subjected his Business many Times, to incompetent Judges."[30] By Adrian Forty's interpretation, Josiah Wedgwood and other eighteenth-century industrialists stripped models from any lingering vestige of makers' license as a central article of business. To achieve rigorous consistency in the Staffordshire pottery works, Wedgwood systematically undercut the traditional, individualizing privileges of high-status modelers as he sought to make "'Machines of the Men.'"[31] In this light, the promises of "unprecedented control over the quality and coordination" of architectural information captured digitally through contemporary techniques of building information modeling (BIM) might well be seen as a totalizing apotheosis of the early modern model's disciplining drives.[32]

Third, if tyrannically mechanical to idea-privileging liberal artists, models would simultaneously be damned from the opposite direction by practitioners in the natural sciences. Replete with concepts, modeling appeared to some experimental philosophers as mere illustrations dangerously void of the reference to nature critiqued by Reynolds. "The globes, the orrery, and other . . . means which ingenious men have hit upon, to explain their own conceptions of things," as charged by Wedgwood's sometime collaborator Joseph Priestley, were distinct from philosophical devices proper.[33] Priestley juxtaposed such pedagogical constructs to the air pump, the condensing engine, and other experimental tools that could put Lady Nature to the rack of what Francis Bacon had called "the vexations of art." Where models might help explain human ideas, only true philosophical instruments could actually body forth new natural facts (Figure 2.4). In the air pump that Hooke fabricated for his patron, Robert Boyle, Priestley found a crucial operation: "The laws of her [i.e., Nature's] action are observed, and the most important discoveries may be made; such as those who first contrived the instrument could have no idea of."[34] Models, by implication, are ideological; they give back what the maker believes. But experimental instruments challenge belief and politics alike—intervening into rather than representing nature, to return to Hacking's terms. Or, as Priestley had then proclaimed of Boyle's philosophical device: "The English hierarchy (if there be anything unsound in its constitution) has equal reason to tremble . . . at an air-pump or an electrical machine."[35]

Priestley did not target the term *model* for abuse per se; but French physicist and theorist Pierre Duhem felt no such restraint. Looking back on nineteenth-century science from his vantage point in the early twentieth century, Duhem laid blame for what he saw as the baffling character of English natural science at the feet of "that element, which nearly invariably accompanies the exposition of a theory, . . . the model [le *modèle*]."[36] If "les esprits abstraits" of French and German science yearned for rigorous, mathematical clarity, so Duhem argued as he took up a classification of intelligence made by Pascal, the ample, weak English mind ("l'esprit ample et faible") could arrive at scientific generalizations only by mimicking the wayward paths of models in all their quirks and material particularities.[37] "Recalling by certain more or less rough analogies the particular features of the theory being expounded," Duhem lamented, the mechanical model

> is a regular feature of the English treatises on physics. Here is a book intended to expound the modern theories of electricity and to expound a new theory. In it there are nothing but strings which move around pulleys, which roll around drums, which go through pearl beads, which carry weights; and tubes which pump water while others swell and contract; toothed wheels which are geared to one another and engage hooks. We thought we were entering the tranquil and neatly ordered abode of deductive reason, but we find ourselves in a factory.[38]

Domesticated by Wedgwood and other magnates of Britain's Industrial Revolution but rebuffed by its fine artists, models and their imaginative address were

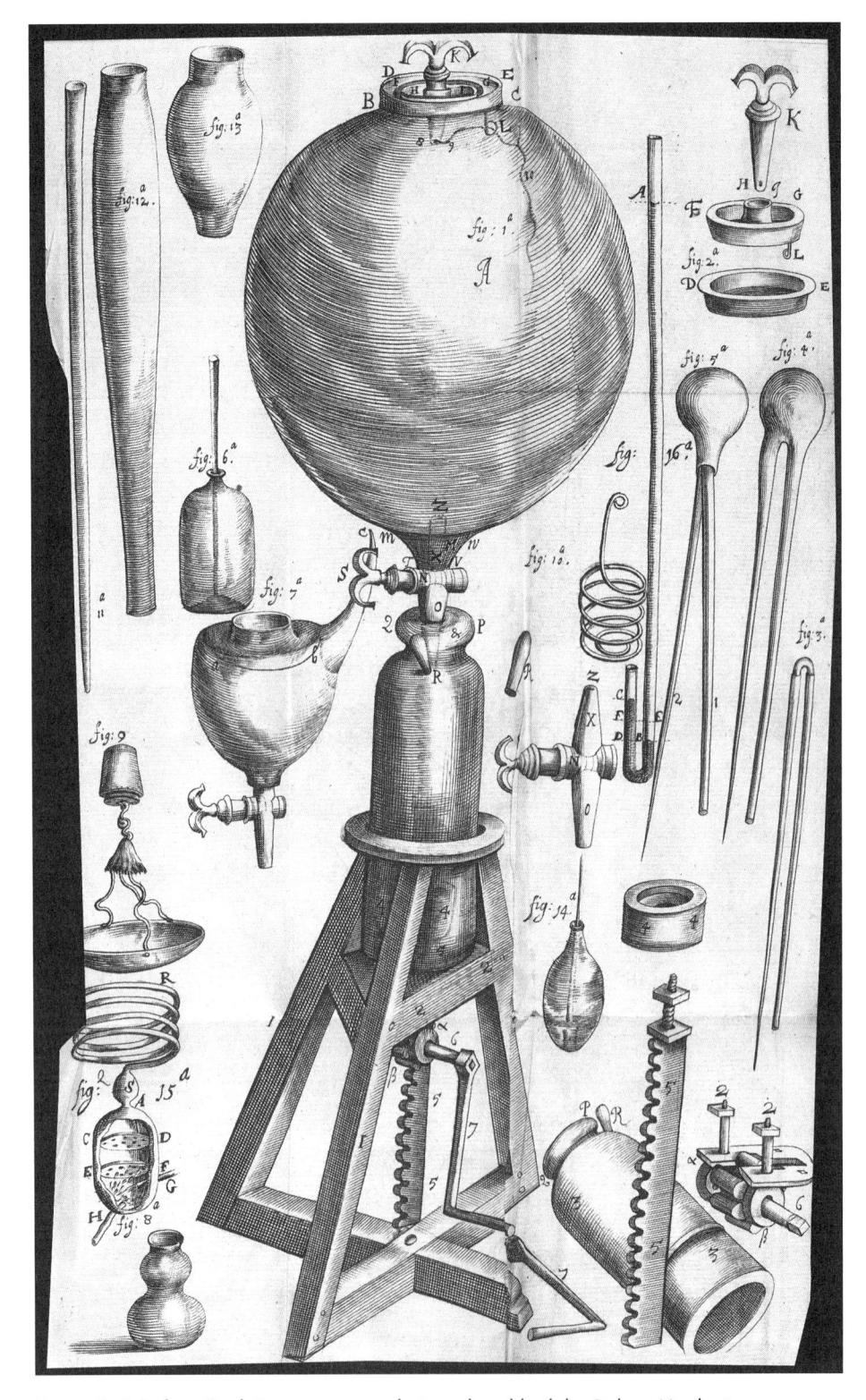

Figure 2.4. Robert Boyle's air pump as designed and built by Robert Hooke in collaboration with Ralph Greatorex. Robert Boyle, *New Experiments Physico-mechanicall, Touching the Spring of the Air, and Its Effects* (1660).

utterly anathema to Duhem's science. Sites of delusive industry for Reynolds, the models of English physicists were for Duhem "paintings [tableaux], and the artist, in composing each of them, has selected with complete freedom the objects he would represent and the order in which he would group them."[39] More child's play than the stuff of serious science, Duhem's conclusion for models' epistemic status was dire: "The logician would be out of place in being shocked by this; a gallery of paintings is not a chain of syllogisms."[40]

What, then, were models and the modeling done with them? For thinkers and practitioners of the long eighteenth century, central questions remained. Was modeling a bastard child of the Enlightenment's parting "two cultures," reconcilable with neither? Perhaps a vestige of imaginative analogy among modernizing regimes of art and science themselves commensurate in privileging abstraction? Did the model's thrum with industry disclose some narcissism of insignificant differences between those scientists who would rebuff it as interlarded with ideas but void of nature and those artists deeming models excessively natural yet insufficiently ideational? In the section that follows, I foreground an ingenious formulation by which philosopher Immanuel Kant then split those differences, outlining a view of models and their relations to art and nature alike. Modeling, we will see Kant arguing, possesses a peculiar relation to following. Rerouting Kant's formulation through a lively conversation about the model in contemporary analytic philosophy of science, I mean to suggest how this modeling/following couplet commands timely critical purchase.

NACHAHMUNG/NACHFOLGE

In *Kritik Der Urteilskraft* (*Critique of Judgment*, 1790), Kant claims that since the fine arts can neither be reduced to concepts nor their making explained by rules, they must require the intervention of a natural gift: "genius."[41] As art without intention would be mere product of chance *(ein bloßes produkt des Zufalls)* and "a product can never be called art unless it is preceded by a rule" *(ohne vorhergehende Regel ein Produkt niemals Kunst heißen kann),* rules operative in the original works of genius must be given by nature as it acts through the gifted artist.[42] Kant quickly qualifies that claim. Nonsense too can appear novel. In addition to displaying originality, then, Kant proposes: "The products of genius must also be models [*Muster*], i.e., they must be *exemplary* [*exemplarisch*]; hence, though they do not themselves arise through imitation [*Nachahmung*], still they must serve others for this, i.e., as a standard or rule by which to judge."[43] Unlike Joseph Priestley's mentalist contrivances of science that would want for nature's action, Kant's works of artistic genius show nature operating proleptically (through genius) in artifacts distinguished over time insofar as they become models for others.

By that account, modeling is the sign of—it is an action proper to—true specimens of fine art. Kant elaborates this point by contrasting the teachable, concept-based scientific achievements of Isaac Newton with the rules underpinning Homer's poetry. Where scientific principles could be studied and acquired systematically, natural rules imparted by genius in the fine arts "cannot be couched in a formula and serve as a precept. . . . Rather, the rule must be abstracted from what the artist has done, i.e., from the product, which others may use to test their own talent, letting it serve them as their model [*Muster*], not to be *copied* [*Nachmachung*], but to be *imitated* [*Nachahmung*]. How this is possible is difficult to explain."[44] Contemporaneously, Reynolds was looking to William Hodges's South Asian plates. He was recommending that the architect find in them implicit guidelines or "hints," a modern variant of *hent*, from the Old English *hentan*, "to handle, take hold of," likely from the Gothic *hinþan*, meaning "to seize." Recent historians have done much to illuminate how the early modern period's venatic epistemology literally made a science of such grasping and groping.[45] But Kant had apposite ideas of his own. A work of genius, he claims, "is an example that is meant not to be imitated [*der Nachahmung*], but to be followed [*der Nachfolge*] by another genius."[46]

This distinction between imitating and following is elaborated further in the third critique as Kant considers the exemplarity of a genius's production: "*Following* by reference to a precedent, rather than imitating [*Nachfolge, die sich auf einen Vorgang bezieht, nicht Nachahmung*], is the right term for any influence that products of an exemplary author may have on others; and this means no more than drawing on the same sources from which the predecessor himself drew, and learning from him only how to go about doing so."[47] Unlike the concepts and rule-boundedness of the sciences or mechanical arts, then, the fine arts require judgments of taste. And as taste is best formed by examples, so the truest guides are to be found in those works that have been (and will subsequently become) models for other geniuses.[48] Examples of natural, rule-establishing gift operating through human artifice, veritable works of genius become models not for copying in every particular but for following with some more capacious tolerance.[49] Whereas the *Encyclopédie* of Denis Diderot and Jean Le Rond d'Alembert contemporaneously defined a model as a specifically human exemplar, models for Kant were paradigmatic works that would disclose rules in time by subsequent acts of licensed following by followers.[50] Just as modeling reveals true works of artistic genius to those able to follow them, models were to be followed to see where they might lead.

If hardly central to the conversation, Kant's linkage of modeling and following is not altogether inimical to recent ways of talking about models and other epistemic representations. An image that goes before the maker, the model is certainly more than a blueprint or recipe-like plan of a work built from it. In a postmodern mood, we might cast such projective artifacts as totems, that distinctly modern entry to the pantheon of what W. J. T. Mitchell has called animated icons.[51] Mythically introduced into the English language in the 1790s by a British beaver trader tattooed with an image of his venatic target, the totem is a "brother of mine" in the language of the Ojibwa that founds and identifies a collective.[52] "Totems," Mitchell proposes, "are made things, artificial images. But they take on an independent life. They seem to create themselves, and to create the social formations that they signify."[53] Coined contemporaneously to Kant's third critique at a moment of intense concern for the powers of images to build social genealogies anew, the totem might well be imagined as denoting a domain of object relations of which the following practiced by the followers of the work of artistic genius qua model would be a subset.[54]

Some recent researchers have implicitly come back to Kant's modeling/following dyad in a different way by attending to the sprawling arrays of visualization technics used in contemporary architecture. As it poaches from other fields to satisfy what one theorist calls architects' "desire for emergence, complexity and control," architectural modeling figures as a promiscuous business.[55] To interrogate this veritable cascade of "virtual three-dimensional renderings, computer modeling, and walk-throughs and fly-bys," the methods of anthropological "following" pioneered by Bruno Latour in works like *Laboratory Life* ([1979] 1986) and *Science in Action: How to Follow Scientists and Engineers through Society* (1987) have proven attractive. "By following particular scaling moves as they run up and down," as one architectural historian recently argues along these lines, "I will expose the materialization of successive operations . . . through which architectural practices play out on a battlefield full of unknown internal streams, orders and disorders, flows and synchronization moves, polemics among architects, visual puzzles, and attempts to resolve disputed states of affairs through visual instruments and convincing images."[56] Its terms framed by the sociology of scientific knowledge, architectural modeling appears in this approach as one piece among ever-mobilizing techniques and an increasingly immutable dominion that must be followed by the investigator in quasi-ethnographic fashion. If modeling is a technique of power, then following would be its method of externalist apprehension.

Important as such approaches have been—as pleasurable as their particular hermeneutics of suspicion may be to repeat—it is time to stake out a new conception of the modeling/following relationship.[57] I move toward that configuration in the remainder of this essay by examining the aforementioned philosophical literature on modeling. If little known in art and architecture, the stakes of this conversation are high. For, after the collapse of logical positivism, many philosophers of science came to see scientific theories not as linguistic entities but as families of models.[58] Shifting away from talk about mimetic "morphisms" in set-theoretical terms privileged by the "semantic view" of scientific theories, this recent conversation has highlighted a far less elegant world—of models that leak, that mediate awkwardly, that would otherwise have outraged Duhem.[59] In the summa that follows, I stress three features of this literature, highlighting the partiality, procedural character, and fictionality of models. But, in drawing out some lessons from the analytic tradition applicable to architectural and humanistic interpretation, I also mean to tarry over the surprising relevance of Kant's strategy of *Nachfolge* to this conversation's implicit critique of science as such.

LEARNING FROM THE REPRESSILATOR

When researchers Elowitz and Leibler fashioned their repressilator, they created a new, intermittently fluorescing entity to better study "aspects of biological organization *in isolation*."[60] In this way, the repressilator can serve as representative of modeling activities increasingly important across the sciences—strategies highlighted in an expanding analytic literature. If often used to do representational work, this literature stresses, scientific models are frequently pragmatically selective and, consequently, plentiful.[61] Since the buzzing, blooming worlds explored by scientists are variously too big, distant, or complicated to study directly, researchers construct models that idealize, abstract, or otherwise stylize features of interest while omitting other key aspects of targeted phenomenon entirely. "The liquid drop model is useful for the production of nuclear fission," Mary S. Morgan and Margaret Morrison note of nuclear physics, "while the optical model serves as the basis for high energy scattering experiments."[62] Distinct and incompatible, these nucleus models each "fail to incorporate significant features of the nucleus.... They nevertheless are able to map onto technologies in a way that makes them successful, independent sources of knowledge."[63] Rather than providing conclusive evidence of models' cognitive waywardness as they had for Duhem, these distances from theory and observational data alike are seen as offering epistemic advantage via provisional flexibility. Philosopher Peter Godfrey-Smith captures this pragmatism: "A variety of people can use the same model while interpreting it differently. One person might use the model as a predictive device, something that gives an output, without caring how the inner workings of the model relate to the real world. . . . Another person might treat the model as representing *some* features, but only a few, of what is going on in the real system."[64] Just as a single problem or phenomenon can be modeled many different ways, so the same model may be variously construed according to researchers' discrete concerns or circumstances.

A second insight follows quickly from this usage. Reducible neither to theory nor observation while used to study some "target" in the world or no target at all, the scientific models described in this philosophical literature often figure as highly stylized representational enterprises. This point has been emphasized by recent studies that have built upon Nelson Goodman's devastating critique of imitation theories of representation.[65] The key claim, then, exceeds the Goodmanian insight that "virtually anything can be stipulated to be a representational vehicle for the representation of virtually anything," as Craig Callender and Jonathan Cohen have put it in a deflationary mood.[66] Instead, these studies stress how the kinds of representation practiced by modelers are complex, often multistage processes. Where older work by Ronald Giere detailed just how much distance stands between the pendulum in a grandfather clock and the axiomatic laws of motion in a physics textbook, Michael Weisberg has emphasized how scientists frequently construct a textual or mathematical "model description" to initiate the modeling inquiry.[67] "Take a very clear long cylindrical glass," Robert Hooke instructed his readers along these lines in the late 1670s: "Fill it three quarters full with water, and put into it a quarter of a pound of Oyl of Vitriol [sulfuric acid], and in the midst of this suspend by a small silver wire, a small wax-ball, rolled in filings of iron or steel."[68] This chemical recipe becomes a model description as Hooke specifies a set of allowances by which it can yield what he calls "a perfect representation of the Head, Halo, and Beard of . . . [a] Comet" (Figure 2.5).[69] At the very least, the iron-covered ball is to act as stylized approximation of the comet's core (stylized because, contrary to the superficial reaction of the recipe's wax ball, Hooke theorized comets to be rent by massive internal instabilities).[70] The bath of diluted acid stands in for the fluid "aether" through which a comet moves; principles of fluid dynamics governing the movement of bodies in liquids stand in for laws of celestial motion; and the force of terrestrial gravity acting upon the laboratory glass produced from the model description approximates the force of solar gravitation operating upon a comet visible from Earth. The fit between experimental situation and heavenly blaze is provisional (the recipe does not produce light as Hooke took comets to do, for example), and it must be kept flexible. "In some things analogous to the one, and somewhat to the other, though not exactly the same with either": so would Hooke aptly summarize his comet-modeling procedures.[71]

Figure 2.5. Robert Hooke's experiment reproduced by Matthew C. Hunter and Janek Syzchowski. Photograph by Matthew C. Hunter.

Hooke's model description would guide but not explain all the permutations to follow from the material model fashioned from it. So too would that chemical model betray fundamental differences from both the elegant comet theory it nominally illustrates and the celestial observations on which it was based.[72] Such shifty traffic between text, model, theory, and celestial target thus opens a broader view. Because model descriptions ask the reader-cum-experimentalist to stylize and then explore a trial scenario to generate insights that may or may not ultimately correspond to real-world phenomena, several philosophers have begun to investigate relations between modeling and literary fiction.[73] "When modeling the solar system as consisting of ten perfectly spherical spinning tops," Roman Frigg observes, "physicists describe (and *take themselves* to be describing) an imaginary physical system. . . . These are scenarios we can talk about and make claims about, yet they don't exist."[74] Consequently, Frigg has argued for an approach that foregrounds the imaginative interventions required for scientists to make and move among models: "The view of model systems that I advocate regards them as imagined physical systems, i.e. as hypothetical entities that, as a matter of fact, do not exist spatio-temporally but are nevertheless not purely mathematical or structural in that they would be physical things if they were real."[75] As visualized in his diagram (Figure 2.6), each facet of this modeling process—from the model description to its material incarnations and the mathematical formalisms possibly applied to it, along with various combinations of these parts—can be referred to as "the model."[76] Unlike older views that posited modeling as fundamentally mimetic or governed by criteria of resemblance, this recent literature stresses the cognitive utility and practical necessity of models that represent indirectly, through highly conventionalized techniques, and with substantial suspension of disbelief.[77]

Fabricated, sometimes physically; invested with imagined properties; and combined into internally inconsistent hybrids: models are a messy business. "The successes of models," Margaret Morrison notes, "are directly connected with highly questionable, sometimes explicitly false, assumptions.... We are left with little reason to give credence to any particular model or group of models."[78] So

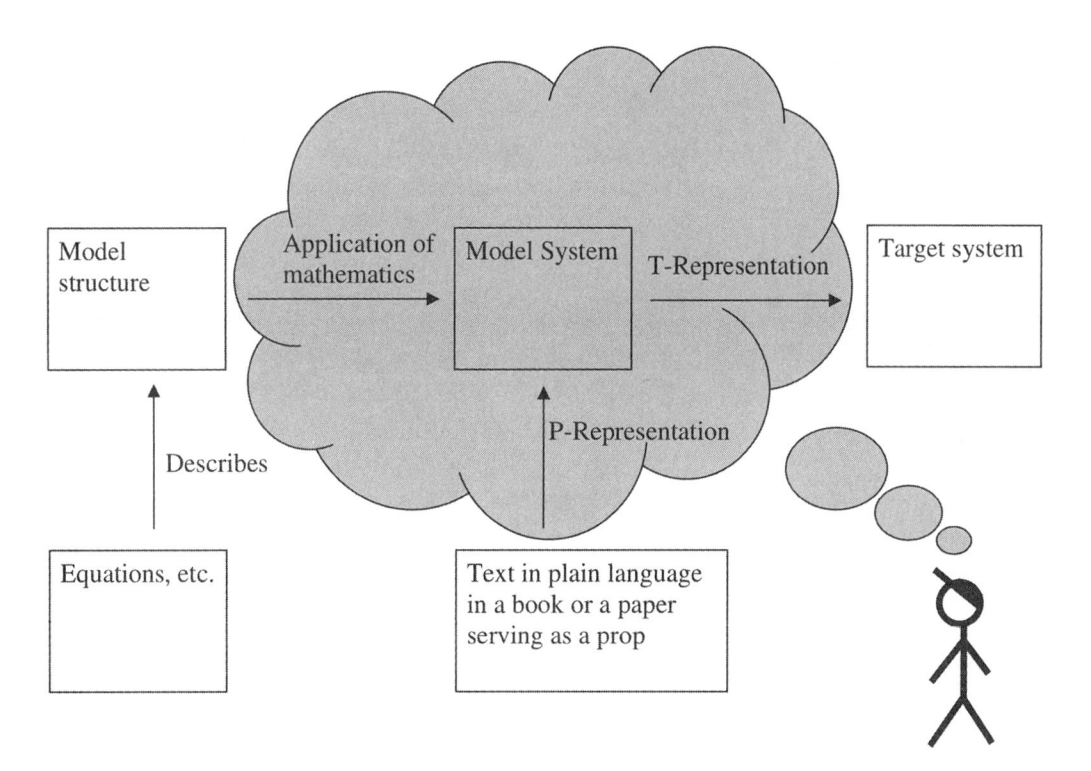

Figure 2.6. "The Elements of Scientific Modeling." Roman Frigg, "Models and Fiction," *Synthese* 172, no. 2 (2010): 266. Courtesy of Roman Frigg; reprinted with permission from Springer Nature.

how and why are models to be believed? A pathway out from this baffling thicket has been found by some recent philosophers in the "pretense theory" of representation advanced by philosopher Kendall Walton. Hailed at its publication as an important alternative to linguistic accounts of representation, Walton's *Mimesis as Make-Believe* (1990) proposes a view of art rooted in children's imaginative games.[79] For Walton, a work of art (be it plastic, textual, or otherwise) is a subset category among "props" to games of make-believe. Art works by issuing what Walton calls "a prescription or mandate in some context to imagine something. Fictional propositions are propositions that are *to be* imagined—whether or not they are in fact imagined."[80] Through abiding props' founding stipulations, players thus inhabit a social environment of make-believe in which knowledge can be gained within the space of play. Invoking a game where two players pretend that tree stumps found in the woods are bears, Walton describes the epistemic agency of props this way:

> [Props] give fictional worlds and their contents . . . an independence from cognizers and their experiences which contributes much to the excitement of our adventures with them. . . . The stump game shows that what is fictional, when props are involved, is detached not only from our imaginings but also from what they [i.e., game players] think and what they take to be fictional. We can be unaware of fictional truths or mistaken about them as easily as we can about those aspects of the real world on which they depend. [Prop users] Eric and Gregory are genuinely surprised to discover that a bear is lurking in the thicket. It is not thinking that makes it so; the prop does.[81]

Eschewing talk about modeling qua resemblance or imitation, Waltonian pretense theory casts works of art as directives to mental activity introduced among players as means to enhance the game and to generate truths within it.[82]

Walton's account of artistic props and their principles of generation have inspired at least two distinct, analytic camps to venture accounts of scientific modeling as make-believe.[83] When modeling with "frictionless planes, spherical planets, infinitely extended condenser plates, infinitely high potential walls, massless strings, populations living in isolation from their environment, animals reproducing at constant rate, perfectly rational agents, markets without transaction costs," and other idealizations, as Frigg has put it, scientists invite participants to imagine fictional worlds.[84] Yet rather than devolving into subjectivist indulgence as its appeal to make-believe and imagination might imply, the vision of scientific modeling crafted through Waltonian principles is extensively rule-bound. At its core, as Adam Toon observes, fiction in Walton's sense requires abiding direction: "To say that a proposition is fictional, on Walton's theory, is to say that there is a prescription to imagine it."[85] As with the children's games that become science's model, so claims philosopher of biology Arnon Levy in Waltonian mode, "there is a set of rules—often implicit—that determines what is to count as true in the game.... [These] principles of generation instruct participants what it is that they are to pretend when playing the game."[86]

Here, the appeal of Walton to philosophers seeking ways to make sense of scientists' models offers a return to Kant. A model is a prop to a game of make-believe; it attains epistemic force and generates new insights only as its constraining directives are discovered and pursued. Viewed through the prism of Waltonian make-believe, science bodies forth from models' initial, simplified props. Building in available theories and expanding through shared assumptions, it proceeds to hash out results by attending to models' implications.[87] "By being involved in such games," as Frigg and James Nguyen have recently put it, "physicists learn about the geometrical properties of orbits and population biologists about growth of populations, neither of which was explicitly mentioned in the model description."[88] The game of science only works, that is, when investigators agree to play along with its fictional objects and the imaginings they specify. What is more, as Frigg and Nguyen claim, Waltonian pretense theory and its rules offer a general "epistemology for model systems: exploring a model amounts to figuring out what follows from the basic assumptions and the principles of generation."[89] Just as the antirealism of representation in pretense theory stands apart from the mimetic commitments of Kant's *Nachahmung* or Reynolds's copying, so the science imagined after Walton's account emerges as its models are followed, made subject of what Kant calls *Nachfolge*. Following, in this sense, is the attitude proper to the model. Or, to say it the other way around, modeling requires following.

More than half a century ago, Thomas Kuhn's *The Structure of Scientific Revolutions* (1962) scandalized readers.[90] Kuhn positioned science's standard operating procedures not as some vigilant, "global" criticality but as a deeply conservative business. Science also worked in the manner of children's games: of puzzle-solving. With all the efficiency of the Elowitz/Leibler repressilator, Kuhn's scientists would winnow out details of problems with known solutions and suppress exceptions to an operative paradigm until a mass of anomalies proved positively overwhelming to their efforts. Now, as apologists for Ludwig Wittgenstein have argued, following cannot necessarily be reduced to some intellectual fascism of unquestioning obedience to rules. Building on Wittgenstein's likeness between rules and signposts, one commentator claims: "A signpost may serve to guide a walker along a footpath, but not by dragging him along an invisible set of rails.... Following a signpost is a paradigm of guidance without mechanism."[91] At what point, though, do the games of make-believe prompted by these invidiously machine-like models (at least per the long-eighteenth-century tradition canvassed here) become coercive tools for *making believe,* for instrumentalizing thought and its thinkers? Does the following generated by props answer to a desire to be governed best understood under a general history of governmentality?[92] One way of reading philosophers' recent approach to science via Waltonian make-believe could see it as a searching update of Kuhnian critique wherein rooting out anomalies in defense of paradigms (themselves subject to revolution) has morphed into immersion in the dappled worlds of models and the species of rule-following they mandate.

Given the significant theoretical potential of this modeling conversation against standing alternatives and the points of overlap it promises with thinking about architectural modeling gestured to above, the proposition of this essay is that sharpening such critiques and their targets should be keenly felt by historians, theorists, and practitioners alike. Many approaches to how modeling makes belief are available, including recourse to the varieties of ethnographic following noted above.[93] By taking up Kant's paired gerunds, though, I mean to move what has been an operation of methodological procedure to a more general level. I mean to highlight how, in this philosophical conversation, following has attained key epistemological function with ontological entailment. Modeling requires—in a sense, it is—following. Eschewing familiar assumptions about models as objects or images, modeling in this conception appears as a particular kind of sequential process. Forgoing talk of scale, similitude, or verism, models are mediators whose epistemic yield is taken to issue from principles of their own generation. Rather than preceding building or taking its brief from a mode of criticality based on reading linguistic texts, modeling follows.[94] The nature—better, the politics—of knowledge made by following and believing models needs to be a matter of expanded discussion among historians, theorists, makers, and critics across the arts and sciences.

NOTES

1. Michael B. Elowitz and Stanislas Leibler, "A Synthetic Oscillatory Network of Transcriptional Regulators," *Nature* 403, no. 6767 (2000): 335–38.

2. Elowitz and Leibler, 335.

3. See, for example, Tarja Knuuttila and Andrea Loettgers, "Causal Isolation Robustness Analysis: The Combinatorial Strategy of Circadian Clock Research," *Biological Philosophy* 26, no. 5 (2011): 773–91; and Tarja Knuuttila and Andrea Loettgers, "Synthetic Biology as an Engineering Science? Analogical Reasoning, Synthetic Modeling, and Integration," in *New Challenges to the Philosophy of Science,* ed. Hanne Andersen et al. (New York: Springer, 2013), 163–77.

4. Ian Hacking, *Representing and Intervening: Introductory Topics in the Philosophy of Natural Science* (New York: Cambridge University Press, 1983), 146.

5. Peter Eisenman, *Idea as Model,* ed. Kenneth Frampton and Silvia Kolbowski (New York: Institute for Architecture and Urban Studies, 1981), 1.

6. D. Graham Burnett and Jonathan D. Solomon, "Masters of the Universe," in *Models,* ed. Emily Abruzzo et al. (New York: Princeton Architectural Press, 2007), 44.

7. For a statement of this familiar adage, see Patrick Healy, *The Model and Its Architecture* (Rotterdam: 010 Publishers, 2008), 51. For scaling as criteria of architectural models, see Mark Morris, *Models: Architecture and the Miniature* (Chichester: Wiley-Academy, 2006), 9. For their concern with temporal scale, cf. Elowitz and Leibler, "A Synthetic Oscillatory Network," 336.

8. I use the terms *model* and *modeling* indifferently in this essay. I thank Axel Kilian for discussing his disagreements on this usage with me.

9. Mario Carpo, *The Alphabet and the Algorithm* (Cambridge, Mass.: MIT Press, 2011), 20–23, 4. For critiques of the venerable claims of Elizabeth Eisenstein, William Ivins, and preindustrial mass production—all of which subtend Carpo's argument—see, respectively, Adrian Johns, *The Nature of the Book: Print and Knowledge in the Making* (Chicago: University of Chicago Press, 1998), esp. 10–20; Peter Parshall, "The Education of a Curator: William Mills Ivins Jr. at the Met," in *The Power of Prints: The Legacy of William M. Ivins and A. Hyatt Mayor,* ed. Freyda Spira and Peter W. Parshall (New York: Metropolitan Museum of Art, 2016), 12–25; and John Styles, "Manufacturing, Consumption and Design in Eighteenth-Century London," in *Consumption and the World of Goods,* ed. John Brewer and Roy Porter (New York: Routledge, 1993), 527–54.

10. For a contemporaneous account with which Hacking engages extensively and that has done much to underwrite the recent modeling conversation, see Nancy Cartwright, *How the Laws of Physics Lie* (Oxford: Clarendon, 1983).

11. For recent interest in this philosophical conversation about modeling outside the analytic tradition, cf. Roman Frigg and Matthew Hunter, eds., *Beyond Mimesis and Convention: Representation in Art and Science* (New York: Springer, 2010); and Andrew Piper, "Novel Devotions: Conversional Reading, Computational Modeling, and the Modern Novel," *New Literary History* 46, no. 1 (2015): 63–98.

12. Mary S. Morgan, *The World in the Model: How Economists Work and Think* (New York: Cambridge University Press, 2012), 5–6.

13. For various perspectives on the redefinition of reading in the era of artificial intelligence, see Franco Moretti, *Graphs, Maps, Trees: Abstract Models for Literary History* (London: Verso, 2007); Jonathan Goodwin and John Holbo, eds., *Reading Graphs, Maps, Trees: Responses to Franco Moretti* (Anderson, S.C.: Parlor Press, 2011); Heather Love, "Close but Not Deep: Literary Ethics and the Descriptive Turn," *New Literary History* 41, no. 2 (Spring 2010): 371–91; and Nan Z. Da, "The Computational Case against Computational Literary Studies," *Critical Inquiry* 45, no. 3 (Spring 2019): 601–39. On the history of nonreading *(Nichtlesen),* see Zeynep Çelik Alexander, *Kinaesthetic Knowing: Aesthetics, Epistemology, Modern Design* (Chicago: University of Chicago Press, 2017).

14. Joshua Reynolds, *Discourses on Art,* 3rd ed., ed. R. W. Wark (New Haven, Conn.: Yale University Press, 1997), 234.

15. For more on Hodges's architectural views and position in larger histories of British imperial projects in South Asia, cf. Geoff Quilley and John Bonehill, *William Hodges 1744–1797: The Art of Exploration* (New Haven, Conn.: Yale University Press for the National Maritime Museum, Greenwich, 2004); and Natasha Eaton, "'Enchanted Traps?' The Historiography of Art and Colonialism in Eighteenth-Century India," *Literature Compass* 9, no. 1 (2012): 15–33.

16. For note of this history, see William Hodges, "View of Part of the City of Benares, upon the Ganges," in *Select Views in India, Drawn on the Spot* ... (London: Printed [by Joseph Cooper] for the author, 1785), n.p. More broadly, see Madhuri Desai, *Banaras Reconstructed: Architecture and Sacred Space in a Hindu Holy City* (Seattle: University of Washington Press, 2017).

17. Reynolds, *Discourses,* 242.

18. Reynolds, 29.

19. Compare Malcolm Baker, "Representing Invention, Viewing Models," in *Models: The Third Dimension of Science,* ed. Soraya de Chadarevian and Nick Hopwood (Stanford: Stanford University Press, 2004), 19–42; and Celina Fox, *The Arts of Industry in the Age of Enlightenment* (New Haven, Conn.: Yale University Press for the Paul Mellon Centre for Studies in British Art, 2009), 135–78.

20. Ephraim Chambers, "Model," in *Cyclopædia: Or, An Universal Dictionary of Arts and Sciences*..., vol. 3 (London: Printed for W. Strahan et al., 1778–88), n.p. Cf. Antoine Furetière, *Dictionnaire universel contenant généralement tous les mots françois tant vieux que modernes, & les termes de toutes les sciences et des arts,* vol. 2 (The Hague: Arnout et Reinier Leers, 1690), 645.

21. On this tradition, see Richard T. Neer, "Poussin, Titian, and Tradition: *The Birth of Bacchus* and the Genealogy of Images," *Word & Image* 18, no. 3 (2002): 267–81; Maria H. Loh, "New and Improved: Repetition as Originality in Italian Baroque Practice and Theory," *Art Bulletin* 86, no. 3 (September 2004): 477–504; and Paul Duro, "'The Surest Measure of Perfection': Approaches to Imitation in Seventeenth-Century French Art and Theory," *Word & Image* 25, no. 4 (October–December 2009): 363–83.

22. For these assertions, particularly north of the Alps, see Erwin Panofsky, "Artist, Scientist, Genius: Notes on the 'Renaissance-Dämmerung,'" in *The Renaissance: Six Essays,* ed. W. Ferguson (New York: Harper & Row, 1962), 121–82; and Joseph Leo Koerner, *The Moment of Self-Portraiture in German Renaissance Art* (Chicago: University of Chicago Press, 1993).

23. Patrizia Cavazzini, *Painting as Business in Early Seventeenth-Century Rome* (University Park: Pennsylvania State University Press, 2008), 74.

24. Reynolds, *Discourses,* 250.

25. "Le modèle, entendu dans l'exécution pratique de l'art, est un objet qu'on doit répéter tel qu'il est. Le *type* est, au contraire, un objet d'après lequel chacun peut concevoir des ouvrages qui ne se ressembleroient pas entr'eux. Tout est précis et donné dans le modèle, tout est plus ou moins vague dans le *type*." Antoine-Chrysostôme Quatremère de

Quincy, *Architecture,* vol. 3 (Paris: Panckoucke, 1825), 544. For more on this contrast, see Adrian Forty, *Words and Buildings: A Vocabulary of Modern Architecture* (New York: Thames & Hudson, 2000), 304–30.

26. On this point, see Joel Snyder, "Res Ipsa Loquitur," in *Things That Talk: Object Lessons from Art and Science,* ed. Lorraine Daston (New York: Zone Books, 2004), esp. 200–202. For the etymology of mechanism and its connections to the hand, see Philip Sohm, "*Maniera* and the Absent Hand: Avoiding the Etymology of Style," *RES* 36 (Autumn 1999): 100–124.

27. Millon clams: "There is less left undecided, less that the architect needs to or can alter during construction.... Fully detailed models also provide greater control for the client who is better able to assess and understand the whole and the detail." Henry A. Millon, "Models in Renaissance Architecture," in *The Renaissance from Brunelleschi to Michelangelo: The Representation of Architecture,* ed. H. A. Millon and V. M. Lampugnani (London: Thames & Hudson, 1994), 70.

28. See John Wilton-Ely, "Wren, Hawksmoor and the Architectural Model," in *English Architecture Public and Private: Essays for Kerry Downes,* ed. J. Bold and E. Chaney (London: Hambledon, 1993), 147–58.

29. See Robert Hooke, February 21, 1674, in *The Diary of Robert Hooke, 1672–1680,* ed. H. W. Robinson and W. Adams (London: Taylor & Francis, 1935), 87.

30. Christopher Wren Jr., *Parentalia; Or, Memoirs of the Family of the Wrens* (London: T. Osborn, 1750), 283.

31. See Adrian Forty, *Objects of Desire: Design and Society 1750–1980* (New York: Pantheon Books, 1986), esp. 30–38.

32. Tatjana Dzambazova, Eddy Krygiel, and Greg Demchak, *Introducing Revit Architecture 2010: BIM for Beginners* (Indianapolis, Ind.: Wiley, 2009), 5. For an opposing view that casts the model as index of the uncontrolled power of modern technology, see Albert C. Smith, *Architectural Model as Machine: A New View of Models from Antiquity to the Present Day* (Boston: Architectural Press, 2004), esp. 85.

33. Joseph Priestley, *The History and Present State of Electricity, with Original Experiments,* 3rd ed., vol. 1 (London: Printed for C. Bathurst et al., 1775), xii.

34. Priestley, xiii.

35. Joseph Priestley, *Experiments and Observations on Different Kinds of Air* (London: J. Johnson, 1774), xiv.

36. Pierre Duhem, *The Aim and Structure of Physical Theory,* trans. P. P. Wiener (Princeton, N.J.: Princeton University Press, 1954), 69. For the French, see Pierre Duhem, *La théorie physique: Son objet, sa structure* (1906; reprint, Lyon: ENS Éditions, 2016, http://books.openedition.org/enseditions/6077), chapter IV, para. 58 (subsequent citations to the French edition provide chapter and paragraph number of the electronic edition). The persistent force of this pejorative view of modeling is interestingly echoed in important studies that still feel compelled to justify work with models as a legitimate concern for philosophy of science. See, for example, Peter Godfrey-Smith, "The Strategy of Model-Based Science," *Biology and Philosophy* 21, no. 5 (November 2006): 725–40 (esp. 726–30). For a very different view of models contemporaneous to Duhem, see Ludwig Boltzmann,

"Model" (1902), in *Theoretical Physics and Philosophical Problems: Selected Writings,* ed. Brian McGuinness, trans. Paul Foulkes (Dordrecht: Reidel, 1974), 213–20.

37. Duhem, *La théorie physique,* IV: 8–13, 97; IV: 13.

38. Duhem, *The Aim and Structure,* 70–71 (translation modified). "L'emploi de semblables modèles mécaniques, rappelant, par certaines analogies plus ou moins grossières, les particularités de la théorie qu'il s'agit d'exposer, est constant dans les traités de Physique anglais. . . . Voici un livre destiné à exposer les théories modernes de l'électricité, à exposer une théorie nouvelle; il n'y est question que de cordes qui se meuvent sur des poulies, qui s'enroulent autour de tambours, qui traversent des perles, qui portent des poids; de tubes qui pompent de l'eau, d'autres qui s'enflent et se contractent; de roues dentées qui engrènent les unes dans les autres, qui entraînent des crémaillères; nous pensions entrer dans la demeure paisible et soigneusement ordonnée de la raison déductive; nous nous trouvons dans une usine." Duhem, *La théorie physique,* IV: 63.

39. Duhem, *The Aim and Structure,* 86. "Ce sont des tableaux, et l'artiste, en composant chacun d'eux, a choisi avec une entière liberté les objets qu'il représenterait et l'ordre dans lequel il les grouperait." Duhem, *La théorie physique,* IV: 118.

40. Duhem, *The Aim and Structure,* 86. "Le logicien serait mal venu de s'en choquer; une galerie de tableaux n'est pas un enchaînement de syllogismes." Duhem, *La théorie physique,* IV: 118.

41. This section expands on an earlier argument presented in Matthew C. Hunter, *Painting with Fire: Sir Joshua Reynolds, Photography, and the Temporally Evolving Chemical Object* (Chicago: University of Chicago Press, 2019), 86–87.

42. Immanuel Kant, *Critique of Judgment* (1790), trans. W. Pluhar (Indianapolis, Ind.: Hackett, 1987), § 46, 175. For the German, see Immanuel Kant, *Kritik Der Urteilskraft,* 5th ed. (Leipzig: Felix Meiner, 1920), 160. For an engagement of this famous passage with address to contemporary architecture and computational modeling, see Sean Keller, "Beauty, Genius, and Epigenesis: The Kantian Aesthetics of Computational Architecture," *Journal of Architectural Education* 65, no. 2 (April 2012): 42–51.

43. Kant, *Critique,* § 46, 175; Kant, *Kritik Der Urteilskraft,* 161. *Muster* can signify, among other things, model or pattern. Quoting Goethe, Lorraine Daston and Peter Galison render the term this way: "'The particular can never serve as a pattern [*Muster*] for the whole.'" Citing the same passage from Kant as I have quoted above, Paul Erickson and fellow coauthors (including Daston) translate this way: "Models [*Muster*] . . . must be exemplary." I follow that rendering. Cf. Lorraine Daston and Peter Galison, *Objectivity* (New York: Zone Books, 2007), 69–70; and Paul Erickson, Judy L. Klein, Lorraine Daston, Rebecca Lemov, Thomas Sturm, and Michael D. Gordin, *How Reason Almost Lost Its Mind: The Strange Career of Cold War Rationality* (Chicago: University of Chicago Press, 2013), 40. For an illuminating reading of *Muster* qua exemplarity in Kant, see David Lloyd, "Kant's Examples," *Representations,* no. 28 (Autumn 1989): 34–54.

44. Kant, *Critique,* § 47, 177; Kant, *Kritik Der Urteilskraft,* 163. As translator Werner S. Pluhar reports, Kant's repetition of "Nachahmung" in this passage has been noted by previous editors as a possible typographical error; more plausibly, it might be replaced by "Nachfolge," meaning that a work of artistic genius must act as a model to be followed.

45. Of the model of the sagacious philosopher who treats the inquiry into nature as a *venatio* or a hunt, William Eamon proposes: "Instead of 'groping in the dark,' he patiently reads the minute signs and clues that will lead him to his prey hiding in the dense thicket of experience." William Eamon, *Science and the Secrets of Nature: Books of Secrets in Medieval and Early Modern Culture* (Princeton, N.J.: Princeton University Press, 1994), 284. Cf. Carlo Ginzburg, "Clues: Roots of a Scientific Paradigm," *Theory and Society* 7, no. 3 (1979): 273–88; and Paolo Rossi, *Philosophy, Technology, and the Arts in the Early Modern Era* (New York: Harper & Row, 1970).

46. Kant, *Critique*, § 49, 186–87; Kant, *Kritik Der Urteilskraft*, 173.

47. Kant, *Critique*, § 32, 146–47; Kant, *Kritik Der Urteilskraft*, 133. For a suggestive meditation on the figure of the source, see Christopher S. Wood, "Source and Trace," in "Wet/Dry," special issue, ed. Christopher S. Wood, *RES: Anthropology and Aesthetics*, no. 63/64 (Spring/Autumn 2013): 5–19.

48. On taste guided by examples, see Kant, *Critique*, § 32, 147.

49. On this point about "tolerance" and followers, see Kant, *Critique*, 187.

50. See [Chevalier Louis de Jaucourt], "REGLE, MODELE (Synon.)," in *Encyclopédie, ou Dictionnaire raisonné des sciences, des arts et de métiers*, vol. 28, ed. Denis Diderot and Jean Le Rond d'Alembert (Lausanne: Les sociétés typographiques, 1780), 116–17; Erickson et al., *How Reason Almost Lost Its Mind*, 39–40.

51. See Karen Moon, *Modeling Messages: The Architect and the Model* (New York: Monacelli, 2005), 18.

52. See W. J. T. Mitchell, *What Do Pictures Want? The Lives and Loves of Images* (Chicago: University of Chicago Press, 2005), 174–76.

53. Mitchell, 105.

54. On these anxieties, particularly in the ambit of Jacques-Louis David, see Thomas E. Crow, *Emulation: Making Artists for Revolutionary France* (New Haven, Conn.: Yale University Press, 1995); and Satish Padiyar, *Chains: David, Canova, and the Fall of the Public Hero in Postrevolutionary France* (University Park: Pennsylvania State University Press, 2007).

55. Axel Kilian, "The Question of the Underlying Model and Its Impact on Design," in Abruzzo et al., *Models*, 208.

56. Albena Yaneva, "Scaling Up and Down: Extraction Trials in Architectural Design," *Social Studies of Science* 35, no. 6 (December 2005): 869. See Bruno Latour and Steve Woolgar, *Laboratory Life: The Social Construction of Scientific Facts* (Beverly Hills: SAGE, 1979); and Bruno Latour, *Science in Action: How to Follow Scientists and Engineers through Society* (Cambridge, Mass.: Harvard University Press, 1987).

57. Cf. Rita Felski, "Suspicious Minds," *Poetics Today* 32, no. 2 (2011): 215–34.

58. For an overview of these developments, see Roman Frigg and Matthew Hunter, "Introduction," in *Beyond Mimesis and Convention*, esp. xvi–xxi. An accessible overview of the larger analytic environment by a leading figure in the modeling conversation is Peter Godfrey-Smith, *Theory and Reality: An Introduction to the Philosophy of Science* (Chicago: University of Chicago Press, 2003). Cf. Paul Teller, "Twilight of the Perfect Model Model," *Erkenntis* 55, no. 3 (2001): 393–415.

59. For an important statement of the semantic view of models as nonlinguistic entities, see Patrick Suppes, "A Comparison of the Meaning and Uses of Models in Mathematics and the Empirical Sciences" (1960), in *Studies in the Methodology and Foundations of Science: Selected Papers from 1951 to 1969* (Dordrecht: Springer Netherlands, 1969), xx. On the emergence of the semantic view and its critique, see Frederick Suppe, *The Structure of Scientific Theories* (Urbana: University of Illinois Press, 1977). For exemplary case studies that have informed the larger, philosophical conversation, cf. Soraya de Chadarevian and Nick Hopwood, eds., *Models: The Third Dimension of Science* (Stanford: Stanford University Press, 2004); and Mary S. Morgan and Margaret Morrison, eds., *Models as Mediators: Perspectives on the Natural and Social Sciences* (New York: Cambridge University Press, 1999).

60. Knuuttila and Loettgers, "Synthetic Biology," 165.

61. The following four paragraphs build upon arguments presented in an earlier iteration in Matthew C. Hunter, "'Mr. Hooke's Reflecting Box': Modeling the Projected Image in the Early Royal Society," *Huntington Library Quarterly* 78, no. 2 (Summer 2015): 301–28, esp. 318–21.

62. Margaret Morrison and Mary S. Morgan, "Models as Mediating Instruments," in *Models as Mediators*, 23.

63. Morrison and Morgan, 23–24. For an expanded meditation on this problem of inconsistency, see Margaret Morrison, "One Phenomenon, Many Models: Inconsistency and Complementarity," *Studies in the History and Philosophy of Science* 42, no. 2 (June 2011): 342–51.

64. Godfrey-Smith, *Theory and Reality*, 188.

65. For the extensive place of Goodman in this conversation, cf. R. I. G. Hughes, "Models and Representation," *Philosophy of Science* 64, Supplement (December 1997): S325–S336; and Roman Frigg and James Nguyen, "The Fiction View of Models Reloaded," in "Scientific Fiction-Making," special issue, *The Monist* 99, no. 3 (2016): 225–42. For Goodman's arguments, see Nelson Goodman, *Languages of Art: An Approach to a Theory of Symbols* (New York: Bobbs Merrill, 1968), esp. 3–43.

66. Craig Callender and Jonathan Cohen, "There Is No Special Problem about Scientific Representation," *Theoria* 21, no. 55 (2006): 14.

67. Ronald Giere, *Explaining Science: A Cognitive Approach* (Chicago: University of Chicago Press, 1990), 62–90; Michael Weisberg, "Who Is a Modeler?," *British Journal for the Philosophy of Science* 58, no. 2 (2007): 217.

68. Robert Hooke, *Lectures and Collections* (London: J. Martyn, 1678), 31.

69. Hooke, 31.

70. Hooke, 11–12.

71. Hooke, 47.

72. For a provisional analysis of this model, see Matthew Hunter, "Experiment, Theory, Representation: Robert Hooke's Material Models," in Frigg and Hunter, *Beyond Mimesis and Convention*, 193–219.

73. Cf. Mauricio Suárez, ed., *Fictions in Science: Philosophical Essays on Modeling and Idealization* (New York: Routledge, 2009); Adam Toon, *Models as Make-Believe: Imagination, Fiction, and Scientific Representation* (New York: Palgrave Macmillan, 2013); Marion

Vorms, "Representing with Imaginary Models: Formats Matter," *Studies in History and Philosophy of Science* 42, no. 2 (2011): 287–95; and "Scientific Fiction-Making," special issue, *The Monist* 99, no. 3 (2016).

74. Roman Frigg, "Fiction and Scientific Representation," in Frigg and Hunter, *Beyond Mimesis and Convention,* 101.

75. Roman Frigg, "Models and Fiction," *Synthese* 172, no. 2 (2010): 253.

76. Frigg, "Fiction and Scientific Representation," 121–22. Each facet, that is, except the "target system."

77. For a classic account of modeling that stresses analogy, see Mary B. Hesse, *Models and Analogies in Science* (Notre Dame: University of Notre Dame Press, 1966).

78. Morrison, "One Phenomenon," 351.

79. For this reception, see Marguerite La Caze, *The Analytic Imaginary* (Ithaca, N.Y.: Cornell University Press, 2002), 147–48.

80. Kendall Walton, *Mimesis as Make-Believe: On the Foundations of the Representational Arts* (Cambridge, Mass.: Harvard University Press, 1990), 39.

81. Walton, 42.

82. For recent attempts to elaborate an "architecture of the cognitive mind" or "architecture of the imagination" enabling this kind of Waltonian pretending, cf. Shaun Nichols and Stephen Stich, "A Cognitive Theory of Pretense," *Cognition* 74, no. 2 (2000): 115–47; and Jonathan M. Weinberg and Aaron Meskin, "Puzzling Over the Imagination: Philosophical Problems, Architectural Solutions," in *The Architecture of the Imagination: New Essays on Pretence, Possibility, and Fiction,* ed. Shaun Nichols (Oxford: Clarendon Press, 2006), 175–202.

83. Among those who have recently taken up Walton's terms to study scientific models are Roman Frigg, Adam Toon, and Arnon Levy. For analyses of the important differences between the "direct" view of models advanced by Toon and Levy via Walton versus the "indirect" account proposed by Frigg and Nguyen, see Manuel García-Carpintero, "Fictional Entities, Theoretical Models and Figurative Truth," in Frigg and Hunter, *Beyond Mimesis and Convention,* esp. 159–63; and Tarja Knuuttila, "Imagination Extended and Embedded: Artifactual versus Fictional Accounts of Models," *Synthese* (2017): 1–21. For purposes here, I am more interested in what these accounts share than the differences between them.

84. Frigg, "Models and Fiction," 257.

85. Adam Toon, "Models as Make-Believe," in Frigg and Hunter, *Beyond Mimesis and Convention,* 80.

86. Arnon Levy, "Information in Biology: A Fictionalist Account," *Noûs* 45, no. 4 (2011): 648.

87. "Model systems are interesting," Frigg has written, "exactly because more is true of them than what the initial description specifies; no one would spend time studying models if all there was to know about them was the explicit content of the initial description." Frigg, "Models and Fiction," 258.

88. Frigg and Nguyen, "The Fiction View," 237–38.

89. Frigg and Nguyen, 239. For a critical assessment of Walton noting the importance of "dictatorial" rule-following to his account of representation, see La Caze, *The Analytic Imaginary*, esp. 160–61.

90. For a concise summary of this reception, see Godfrey-Smith, *Theory and Reality*, 77–86. For Kuhn's account, see Thomas S. Kuhn, *The Structure of Scientific Revolutions*, 3rd. ed. (1962; repr., Chicago: University of Chicago Press, 1996), esp. 23–91.

91. Gordon Baker, "Following Wittgenstein: Some Signposts for *Philosophical Investigations* §§143–242," in *Wittgenstein: To Follow a Rule*, ed. Steven H. Holtzman and Christopher M. Leich (London: Routledge & Kegan Paul, 198), 55. For Wittgenstein's teaching on rule-following claimed into an "antifoundationalist" account of artistic modernism, see Michael Fried, "How Modernism Works: A Response to T. J. Clark," *Critical Inquiry* 9, no. 1 (1982): 217–34 (esp. 227–28).

92. Cf. Michel Foucault, *The Birth of Biopolitics: Lectures at the Collège de France, 1978–1979*, ed. Michel Senellart, trans. Graham Burchell (New York: Palgrave Macmillan, 2008); Aggregate, *Governing by Design: Architecture, Economy, and Politics in the Twentieth Century* (Pittsburgh: University of Pittsburgh Press, 2012).

93. As but one example: Eva Kernbauer, "Establishing Belief: Harun Farocki and Andrei Ujica, *Videograms of a Revolution*," *Grey Room*, no. 41 (Fall 2010): 72–87.

94. Frigg and coauthor James Nguyen have recently underscored differences between learning from models and from texts in the following manner: "Studying the internal constitution of a model can provide information about the target. Not so with words. The properties of a word (consisting of so and so many letters and syllables, occupying this or that position in a dictionary, etc.) do not matter to its functioning as a word; and neither do the physical properties of the ink used to print words on a piece of paper. . . . [Unlike a model] the properties of a word as an object do not matter to its semantic function." Roman Frigg and James Nguyen, "Models and Representation," in *Springer Handbook of Model-Based Science*, ed. Lorenzo Magnani and Tomasso Bertolotti (New York: Springer, 2017), 51.

CHAPTER 3

SCANNING

A Technical History of Form

ZEYNEP ÇELIK ALEXANDER

Compare the following two "reading machines," precursors to today's scanners. Both were designed to read forms, checks, and other similar paperwork in large numbers at the bank, post office, and so forth, but did so using two distinct methods. The first one, patented in 1935 by the Austrian inventor Gustav Tauschek, was set up such that when the target character to be read was displayed on a screen, a disk right behind a lens would rotate until one of the disk's openings, each of which corresponded to a numeral between 0 and 9, coincided with the target exactly (Figure 3.1).[1] The machine recognized the numeral 1, for example, only when the target character matched one of the openings on the side of the disk so perfectly that little or no light passed through the overlap. The second reading machine, patented in 1953 by the American cryptologist David H. Shepard, consisted of a setup with similar elements, but in this case the light from the target character, after passing through an arrangement of lenses, was picked up by a rotating mechanism known as a Nipkow disk, which had on its surface a series of pinhole apertures that dissected the image into fragments as it rotated (Figure 3.2).[2] In the case of Shepard's machine, it did not matter whether the target character matched one in the machine's inventory of characters. Only when the machine consecutively registered the presence of dark areas in segments 2, 4, 1, 7, and 3 of the rotating disk, for example, did it recognize the scanned target as A.

However trivial these technical differences may appear, technologists in the 1960s and 1970s described the turn from readers like Tauschek's to Shepards's as pivotal.[3] Tauschek's reader sought forms that were intelligible to humans or, to use technical parlance, it recognized the "semantic value" of a character through an "instantaneous parallel comparison of the unknown character with a large

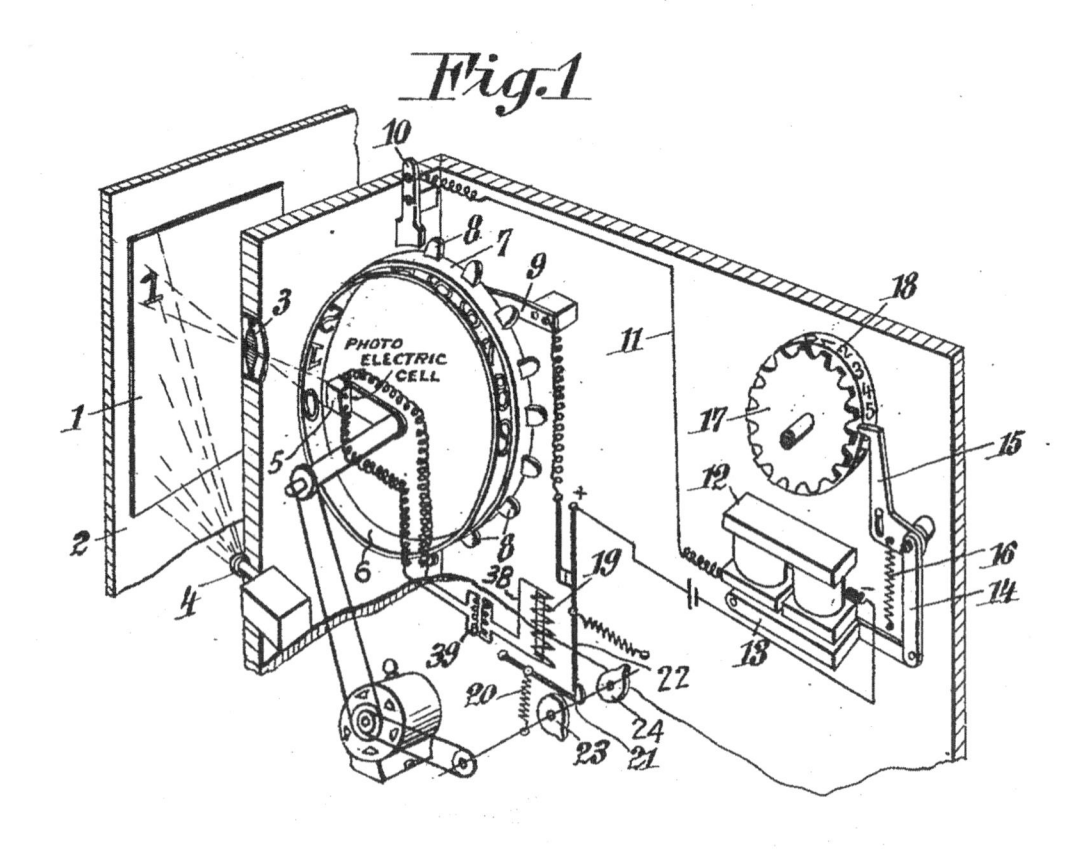

Figure 3.1. Reading machine, 1935. Gustav Tauschek, Reading Machine, U.S. Patent 2,026,329, filed May 27, 1929, and issued December 31, 1935.

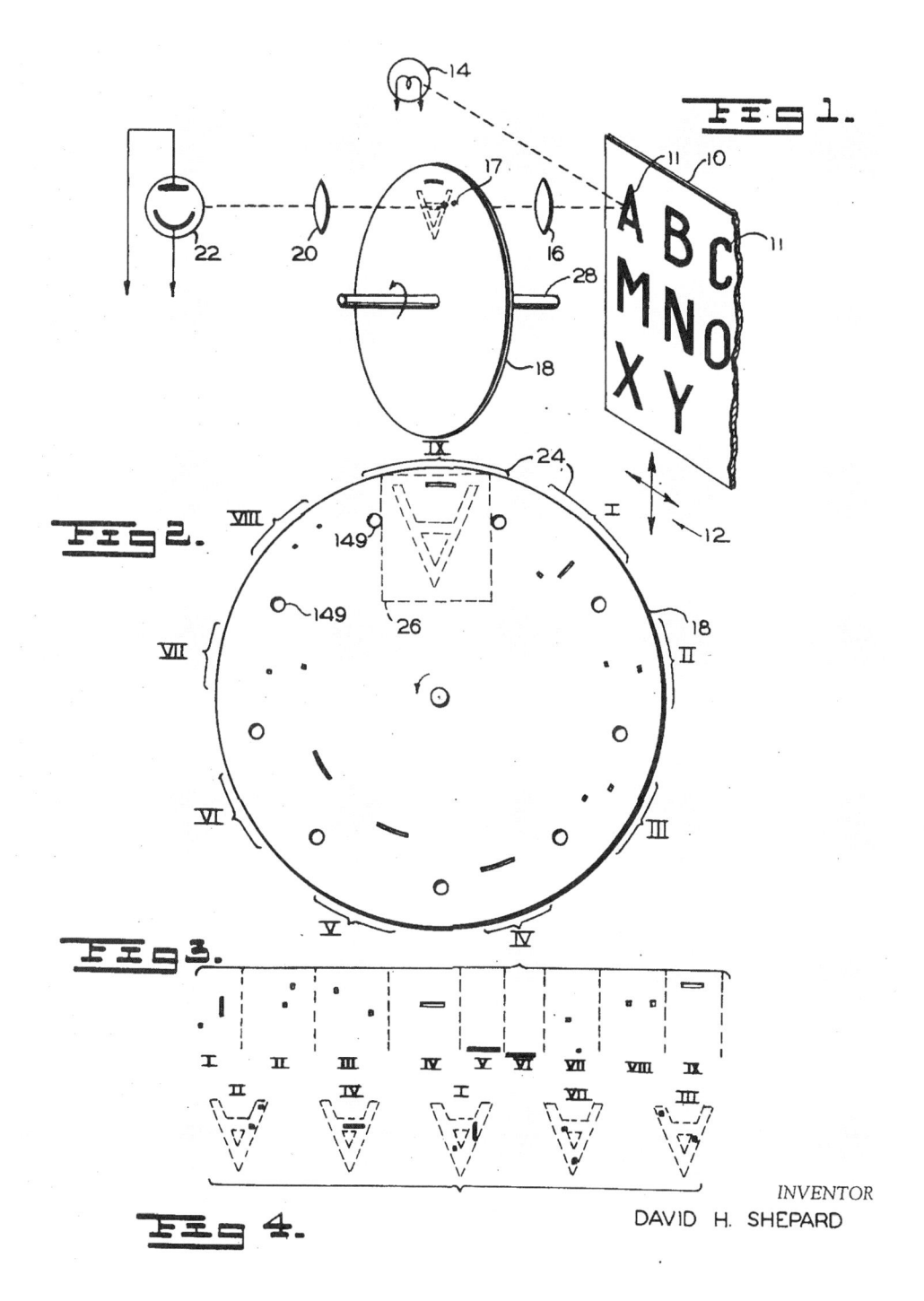

Figure 3.2. Reading machine, 1953. David H. Shepard, Apparatus for Reading, U.S. Patent 2,663,758, filed March 1, 1951, and issued December 22, 1953.

optical storage matrix."[4] This was called "parallel processing": "various features were inspected by little demons," as one technologist put it, which would "shout answers in concert to a decision-making demon."[5] Shepard's machine, by contrast, presumed no ghosts in the machine: it operated by discretizing images into fragments, breaking down the "semantic limits" of a pattern, and analyzing it statistically.[6] Legibility for Shepard's machine, in other words, was a matter of limits even when it dealt with the problem of recognizing coherent forms (Figure 3.3). As the technical literature on the topic would explain, such machines extracted "the characteristic or criterial features of exemplars of each character," calculated the "total probabilities" for each, and, finally, made a decision "by choosing the letter with the highest probability."[7] Shepard's method was more efficient as a result. Since it did not need to compare the target with each character in its inventory, it required less memory and thus a shorter computational time.[8] By the time Russell A. Kirsch constructed what is frequently credited as the first electronic scanner in 1957, machines like Tauschek's had been declared obsolete.[9] Scanning was now described as it is understood today: that is, as a process whereby "the light reflected from an opaque document" was converted "into a signal or series of signals which can be presented to the preprocessing and recognition units."[10]

At stake in these distinctions was more than the technicalities of scanning. In 1968, when the dust had seemingly settled on the question of which of the two scanning methods had triumphed, Jacob Rabinow, an optical character recognition expert, offered an explanation for the presumably wrong turn taken by the likes of Tauschek. These technologists had treated the problem of scanning as if the technician were "a minor god" charged with the task of designing a human being.[11] Contemporary scanners finally succeeded, according to Rabinow, when machine vision was conceptually separated from human vision—that is, when technicians finally abandoned the idea of building scanners that simulated the human cognitive apparatus. To use the formulation of the media theorist Wolfgang Ernst, Shepard's machine's ingenuity was to "desemanticize" vision so that seeing was replaced by "gazing/scanning" without any search of deep meaning.[12] (Optical recognition experts defined "meaning," it is worth mentioning, as merely a "set of connections."[13]) To the extent that these scanners could be said to possess "inwardness," it was as storage memory, employed not for in-depth exercises of hermeneutics but for far more mundane purposes such as directing mail to the appropriate bin in the post office.

Rabinow, then, had a point. Those like Tauschek who used parallel processing methods were unapologetic about the frequent use of anthropomorphic or biomorphic terminology.[14] Not only had Tauschek called an earlier version of his

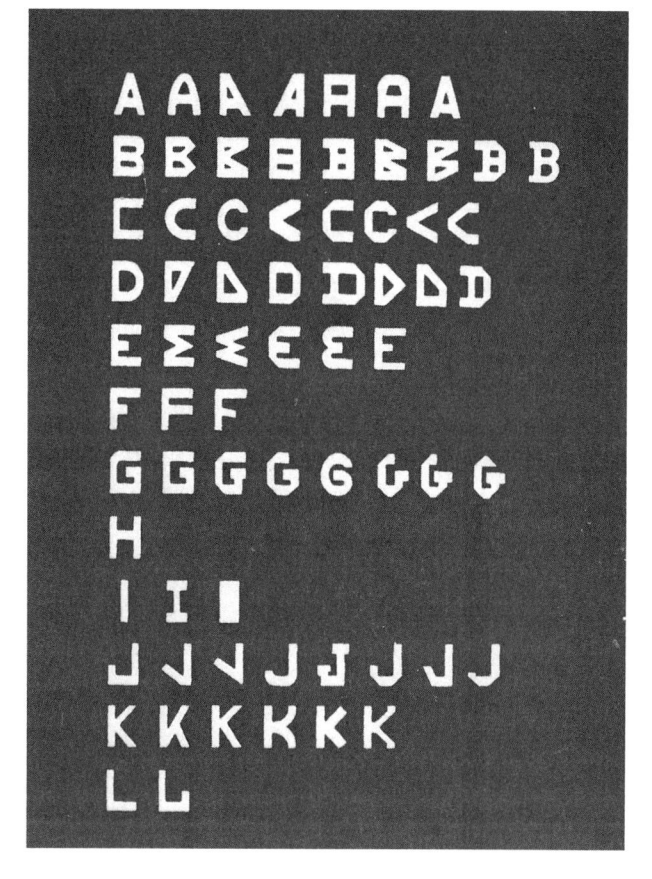

Figure 3.3. "Experimental designs" for improved raster-type data display. Leonard C. Moore and Paul M. Nida, *An Analysis of Lettering Styles for an Improved Raster-Type Data Display* (Indianapolis, Ind.: Technical Development Center, Federal Aviation Agency, 1958), Fig. 2A.

reader "Maschine mit Gesichtssinneffekt" (Machine with the effect of the sense of sight), but he had also claimed that it would "replace the human activity of reading," which he described for machine and human alike as "the perception of any image-impression and the memory-related comparison of the perceived with the results of simultaneous or earlier perceptions."[15] An autodidact who transformed himself into a prolific inventor while working for a metal manufacturing facility in Germany, Tauschek, in fact, resorted to such anthropocentric tropes throughout his career.[16] The so-called Tauschek system of punched cards, which he developed throughout the 1920s while working with machines provided by the International Business Machines Corporation, for example, distinguished itself from the more commonly used Hollerith system by being more readily perceived by the human eye—or at least so claimed their inventor.[17] Shepard's machine too simulated certain human cognitive processes but to the extent that it did not assume profound hermeneutic capacities, it was more akin to electronic scanners that would follow in its footsteps than Tauschek's psychologically ambitious machines.

My goal in juxtaposing Shepard's and Tauschek's readers here is not to construct a genealogy of scanning technologies in use today or attempt what is sometimes called "media archaeology," an excavation of histories that have been "left by the roadside out of negligence or ideological bias."[18] Instead, I hope to tease out of these outdated scanning devices a history of a concept that has been central to modernism generally and to the design disciplines specifically: the concept of form. For among the more significant differences between the two machines was their attitude toward formal structures. Shepard's reading machine, after all, differed from Tauschek's to the extent that it was oblivious to the overall *Gestalt* of a form; instead it sought patterns in discretized fragments. By contrast, Tauschek's reader was a formalist in its own right; its virtue was to be able to recognize *Gestalten* that would also be familiar to humans. If we take Tauschek's faith in formal coherence and Shepard's obliviousness to it seriously, could this technical history tell us anything new about the elusive concept of form?

Although such an approach may seem counterintuitive, I will argue in this essay that attempting a historical ontology of form from this unlikely perspective might provide unexpected rewards.[19] First, as I hope to show, such an account would provide much-needed specificity to histories that are usually presented as purely intellectual ones. Countless scholars have meticulously traced the emergence of the modern concept of form from Kantian aesthetics to twentieth-century modernism, but what if the concept's salience in modernist discourses also had to do with more mundane—what might perhaps be called "technical"—concerns?[20] Might such a technical history offer an account of a concept that numerous others written in the disciplines of philosophy, intellectual history, or art and architectural history have not already?

Second, such a "technical" history of form would upend some assumptions that persist in contemporary understandings of technology's relationship to humans. Conceiving technology as an extension of the human body has a long history from Karl Marx's theorization of machines to Ernst Kapp's organ projection (*Organprojektion*) and to Marshall McLuhan's formulation that media are extensions of the human sensorium.[21] In each case, the human comes first and technology follows. But what if, as the case of Tauschek might suggest, the precedence of the human is simply another anthropocentric assumption and that it is the prioritizing of the human that leaves ghosts—gods, demons, or otherwise—in the machine? That is to say, what if the stabilization of the category of the human has something to do with technics whose jurisdiction has historically been carefully demarcated from that of the human? What effect would this shifting of priorities have on our understandings of modernity and modernism? What would the concept of form's continuing hold on the design disciplines look like from this historical vantage point?

If such an account of form is to be historically specific, however, it cannot claim to be comprehensive. In what follows, therefore, I will attempt a history of the concept of form by focusing on a relatively short historical arc from the late nineteenth century onward within the relatively narrow confines of Germanic and, later, American discourses in which the term rose to prominence.

Midcentury technologists working on the problem of scanning took for granted that the storage of sensory stimuli in the human nervous system and information in a machine were analogous. As the psychologist Frank Rosenblatt, the theorist of the "perceptron," wrote in 1958, "the development of symbolic logic, digital computers, and switching theory" had "impressed many theorists with the functional similarity between a neuron and the simple on-off units of which computers are constructed."[22] The two kinds of scanning imagined by Tauschek and Shepard, then, implied a set of intertwined questions. Was information stored *topographically*—that is, "in the form of coded representations or images, with some sort of one-to-one mapping between the sensory stimulus and the stored pattern" much like a photographic negative?[23] Or did the similarities between a network of neurons and computers mean that "the central nervous system simply act[ed] as an intricate switching network"—that is, there was never any simple topographical mapping of the stimulus into memory but "the information [was] contained in connections or associations rather than topographic representations"?[24] The "coded memory theorists" in the first group concluded that "matching and systematic comparison"—an "a-ha moment," so to speak—was crucial for the organism to determine the appropriate response. Since vision for the "connectionist" group was a thoroughly desemanticized process—a process, in other words, oblivious to meaning—no such moment could be presumed. Instead, stimulus and response were linked not *topographically* but rather *statistically*.[25]

This presumption about the parallelism between the human and the machine, of course, had a much longer history, but discretization, which implied the absence of a topographical relationship between stimulus and response, became a question of epistemological import relatively late in Western intellectual life. Until the nineteenth century, thinkers in the West frequently conceptualized human perception as a process that entailed the projection of a static image of the world into the chamber of the human mind. It has been argued that this conception of the mind was informed by—and, in turn, informed—the camera obscura, which was not only a philosophical metaphor but also a viewing technology.[26] According to this view, the image of the world appeared on the retina as a whole—albeit upside down—just as it appeared on the back wall of a camera obscura.[27] Yet in the early nineteenth century, physiologists like Johannes Müller started to demonstrate experimentally that the relationship between stimulus and sensation was not what it had been assumed to be: not only was the relationship not topographically defined, their findings implied, but it was also possibly arbitrary. A uniform cause such as electricity, for example, could produce the sensation of light when applied to the eye and the sensation of touch when applied to the skin.[28] Müller's student Hermann von Helmholtz continued this line of thinking when he famously compared wires to nerves in 1868.

> The nerve-fibres have been often compared with telegraphic wires traversing a country, and the comparison is well fitted to illustrate this striking and important peculiarity of their mode of action. In the net-work of telegraphs we find everywhere the same copper or iron wires carrying the same kind of movement, a stream of electricity, but producing the most different results in the various stations according to the auxiliary apparatus with which they are connected. At one station the effect is the ringing of a bell, at another a signal is moved, and at a third a recording instrument is set to work. Chemical decompositions may be produced which will serve to spell out the messages, and even the human arm may be moved by electricity so as to convey telegraphic signals.... In short, every one of the hundred different actions which electricity is capable of producing may be called forth by a telegraphic wire laid to whatever spot we please, and it is always the same process in the wire itself which leads to these diverse consequences. Nerve-fibres and telegraphic wires are equally striking examples to illustrate the doctrine that the same causes may, under different conditions, produce different results.[29]

Wires, in fact, preceded nerves in Helmholtz's imagination. Historians have demonstrated how Helmholtz's conceptualization of a nervous system operating with discretized fragments rather than with wholes would have been impossible without the "materialities of communication" in such technologies as telegraphy.[30] Nor would the Nipkow disk have been possible: it turns out that one efficient means of transferring wholes across distances—whether between telegraphic operators or between the world and the human mind—was by breaking them down into discrete fragments, transferring them through a medium that was oblivious to the completeness of the original, and reassembling these fragments again at the destination.[31] It was while he was still working on his doctoral degree under the tutelage of Helmholtz in Berlin that Paul Gottlieb Nipkow invented the disk that would be named after him (although he never built a model of the invention and was surprised decades later to be hailed as the inventor of the mechanical television).[32] Nipkow's ingenuity was to realize that when great distances were involved, it helped to be looking at the target through a spinning disk. Punctuated in a spiral pattern with twenty-four square holes, Nipkow's "electrical telescope" rotated at six hundred revolutions per minute while light illuminated the target image. Selenium, an element whose photoconductive properties had only recently been discovered, captured the discretized fragments of the image and converted them into electrical pulses. A receiver with a synchronously spinning disk reversed the process by reconstituting the transmitted signals. The transmission was complete when what we would today call the "rasterized" image was projected onto a screen by means of the Faraday effect. Whereas film created the illusion of movement by projecting still, whole images at twenty-four frames per second, the Nipkow disk worked by breaking the whole image down to its components before reassembling it. No wonder that Nipkow spent the rest of his life as an engineer for a company that manufactured railway signaling equipment.[33]

Helmholtz's theory of nervous-electric transmission might have been shaped in the shadow of electrical telegraphy, but not all telegraphic technologies encrypted and decrypted messages in the binary code of dots and dashes. Alongside the better-known Morse code existed numerous nineteenth-century telegraphic languages that went to great lengths to simulate notational systems that were presumed to come more naturally to humans.[34] Compare, for example, Morse's telegraph to Reizen's (Figure 3.4). Messages conveyed through the latter system appeared on a pane of glass upon which were pasted strips of tinfoil cut out in the form of letters. When an electric spark was transmitted through the correct convoluted foil, the light at the interstices presented the form of the letter to the telegraph operator, who was already familiar with alphanumeric characters. The Morse code, by contrast, required that the operators both sending and receiving the message needed to be skilled at deciphering the code of dots and dashes in their heads. Other systems, such as Bakewell's image telegraph, relied on the continuity of electric currents rather than their discretization (Figure 3.5). Dubbed the "copying telegraphy," Bakewell's telegraph consisted of two cylinders—one at the point of origin and the other at the destination—that rotated simultaneously except when their movement was stopped by breaks, which were registered at the destination as the message that was meant to be conveyed.[35] Contemporaries noted how, unlike telegraphic technologies that used abstract machine languages, the image telegraph, by requiring neither special training nor any particular hermeneutic skill, proved immune to errors.[36] The ingenuity of the image telegraph was that it did not require any mechanical components—such as an elaborate escapement mechanism—to minimize hermeneutic mishaps. In a thoroughly

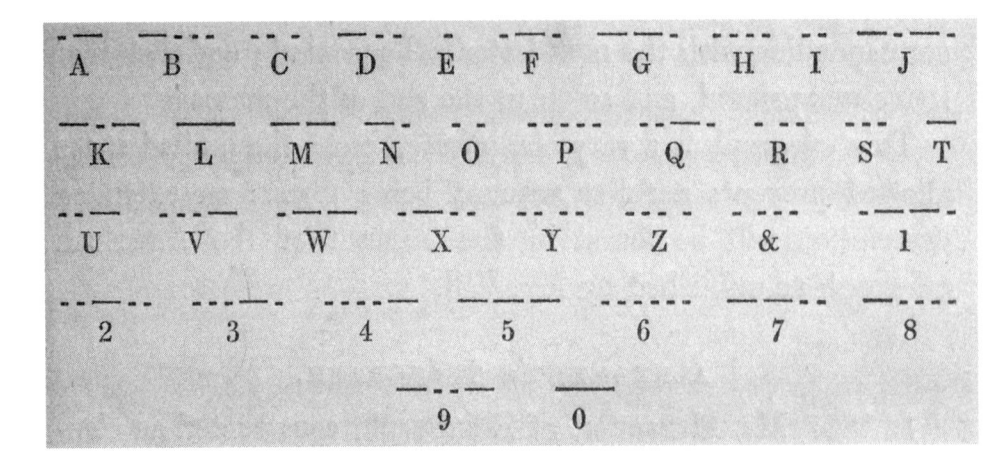

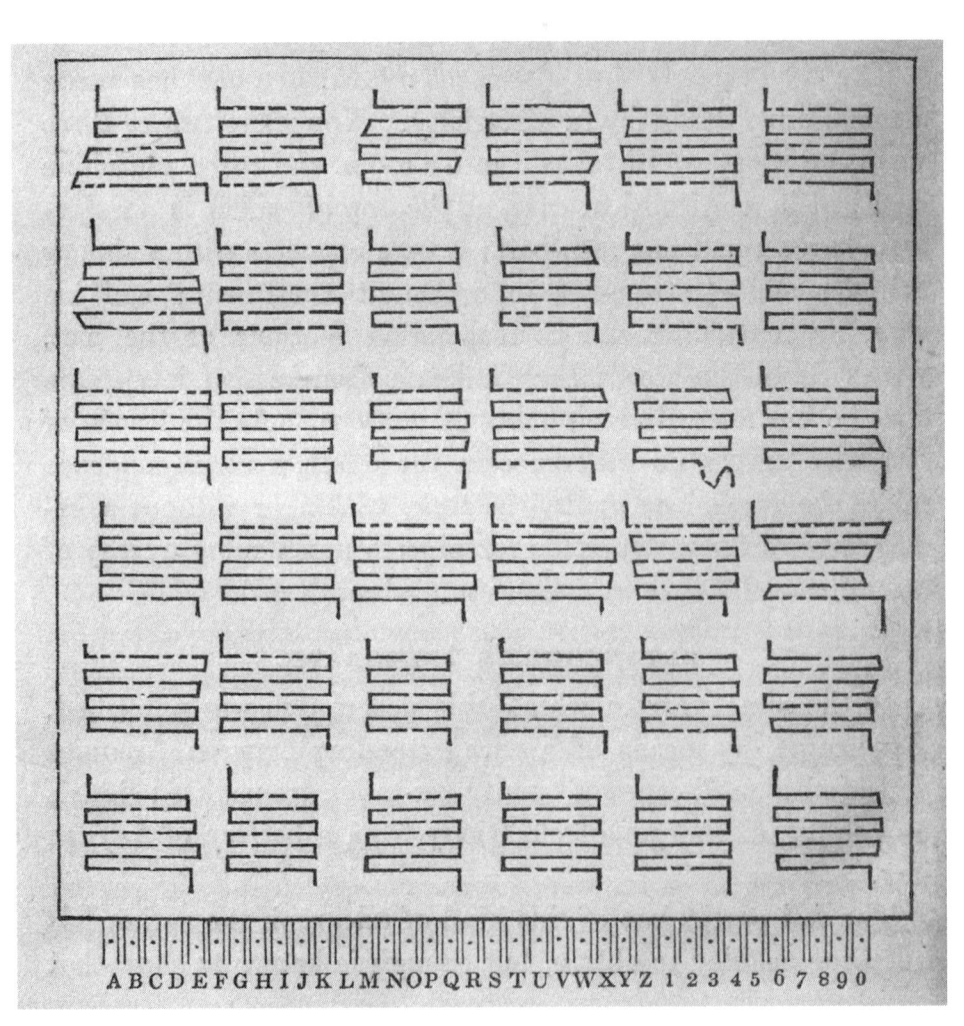

Figure 3.4. Telegraphic notations by Morse (above) and Reizen (below). Edward Highton, *Electric Telegraph: Its History and Progress* (London: John Weale, 1852), 42, 63.

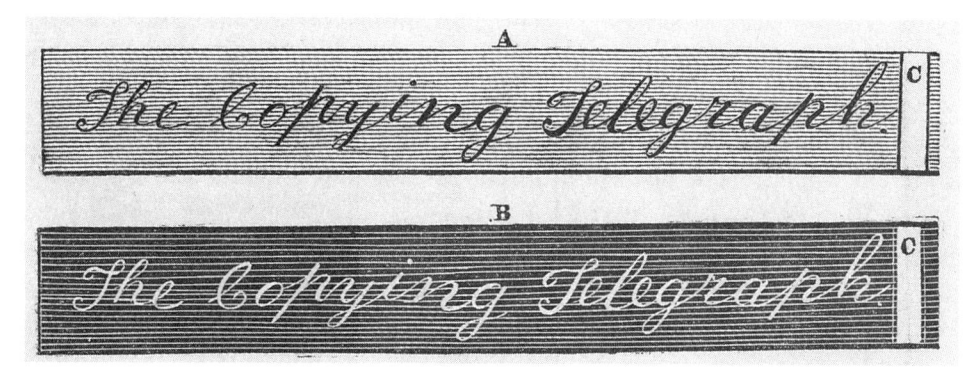

Figure 3.5. The copy electric telegraph. F. C. Bakewell, *Electric Science: Its History, Phenomena, and Applications* (London: Ingram, Cooke, 1853), 171.

mechanized system of sending and receiving signals, the ability to reproduce the idiosyncratic forms of the hand-drawn image turned out to be the most dependable safeguard against error or forgery.

Yet the Morse telegraph ultimately triumphed over other telegraphic technologies. Samuel Morse himself would claim that his invention was not a species but rather the genus to which all other telegraphic technologies belonged.[37] Morse did not attempt to convert discrete signals into continuous forms like Reizen, Bakewell, and countless others had attempted to do in the nineteenth century; the Morse code remained a pointedly discretized affair resistant to the temptations of form. This fundamental formlessness, according to the philosopher Georg Simmel, was the very essence of modernity.[38] Nothing demonstrated this condition better than money, which, Simmel pointed out, was inextricably connected with the metropolis and the modern subject who was subjected daily to an onslaught of fragmented sensations there. After all, decades before Simmel argued that money was not only "absolutely formless" but "the destroyer of form" tout court, Western Union had started enacting money's formlessness by allowing its customers to send and receive money via telegraphy.[39]

Simmel also observed that "the universal formlessness of money as money [was] certainly the root of the antagonism between an aesthetic tendency and money interests."[40] This meant that the modern malaise of formlessness could be cured through aesthetic means alone. Or so claimed the sculptor Adolf Hildebrand in his widely influential text *Das Problem der Form* in 1893.[41] According to Hildebrand, the human sensorium oscillated between two extremes. One extreme was the distant view. Because at a distance the sight lines of the observer remained parallel to each other and perfectly perpendicular to the object under examination, the distant view presented the object in its entirety as a total picture (*Gesamtbild* or

Flächenbild)—that is, as a form.[42] The other extreme was the near view. When the observer moved closer to the object, the sight lines formed increasingly narrower angles, which meant that the observer's eyes had to move incessantly across the surface of the object in order to connect the fragmented visual impressions into coherent wholes.[43] The near view produced formlessness. Hildebrand acknowledged that most perception was situated somewhere between these two extremes, but that did not prevent him from worrying that the pendulum of modernity had swung too far toward the near view, a condition that he described dramatically as the "sickness of the age."[44]

Others joined Hildebrand at the end of the nineteenth century in pathologizing the human eye that failed to convert the discreteness of the world's sensations into coherent wholes. With theoretical support from the emergent discipline of experimental psychology, which, in turn, borrowed its techniques from the nineteenth-century discipline of physiology, overactive eyes engaged in surface-scanning were denounced. The physician-cum-cultural theorist Max Nordau indicted eye movements that struggled to contend with the perception of a *Gesamtbild* as "degenerate" while the psychologist Richard von Krafft-Ebing classified the uncontrollable movements of the eye as "degeneration in the motor domain."[45] Arguing with more subtlety, the art historian Heinrich Wölfflin projected this modern pathology into the past: unlike the inherently linear Renaissance, he argued, the Baroque was "pathological" because it made it impossible for the eye to follow the contours of coherent forms.[46] No less detrimental were eyes that indulged in the pleasures of various nineteenth-century toys such as phenakistoscopes, stroboscopes, and zoetropes—to say nothing of photography and film, which, as its countless critics pointed out at the turn of the century, was an inherently disjointed and therefore inevitably hazardous medium.[47]

Form, by this logic, was not so much the problem as the solution to the problem of modernity. Hildebrand defined form as "the essential reality of things," "the sum total that we have extracted by comparing appearances."[48] Given the prevalent modern failure to cohere individual sensations into unified formal structures, Hildebrand reasoned, it was best to provide the incompetent viewer with the correct distant view of an artwork. It was for this reason that Hildebrand advocated relief sculpture as opposed to sculpture-in-the-round. The virtue of relief sculpture was that it impressed its form on the wax tablet of the modern mind, so to speak, without any room for misinterpretation (Figure 3.6). So strong was the pedagogical impulse in this late nineteenth-century brand of formalism that it was enthusiastically incorporated into general education in the newly unified Germany—that is, decades before it became the backbone of the new artistic education offered at institutions like the Bauhaus. The object lesson *(Anschauungsunterricht)* had a

Figure 3.6. Adolf von Hildebrand, Hymen relief. Villa Hildebrand, Brewster-Peploe Collection, the Conway Library, the Courtauld Institute of Art, London.

long history before the end of the nineteenth century; especially important in this history was the work of the Swiss educator Johann Heinrich Pestalozzi, who advocated for teaching *forms* before *words* and *letters*.[49] Starting in the 1870s, however, drawing and handicraft classes were introduced into primary and secondary schools and even at universities with unprecedented zeal on both sides of the Atlantic. Inherent in this new pedagogical program was the assumption that there existed a kind of knowledge—obtained through the body's experiential acquaintance with the world but nonetheless capable of competing in rigor with conceptual, propositional, discursive knowledge.[50] Formal training was offered at all levels of the education system for a subject imagined to be cognitively lesser than the will-centered, knowing subject that the tradition of *Bildung* had targeted since the beginning of the nineteenth century.[51] It was in this context that the meaning of *Gestaltung* as self-formation with *Gestaltung* as design and form merged into one (Figure 3.7).

Late nineteenth-century formalism frequently relied on the findings of experimental psychology, but that is not to say that the latter produced unequivocal evidence in support of the cognitive advantages of form. In the 1870s, for example, the French ophthalmologist Louis Émile Javal demonstrated in a series of experiments that reading, considered a high-order cognitive activity, was not what it was imagined to be at all. Against the prevalent method of reading instruction, which assumed that one learned to read whole words before distinguishing individual letters, Javal discovered that the eye did not move in a linear fashion across the page. Rather, it traversed the page saccadically—that is, in starts and stops, with fixations, interfixations, and regressions just like the Nipkow disk (Figure 3.8).[52] Others confirmed Javal's findings. Not only did "the path by which the eye passe[d] from one to another of these resting places ... not seem to depend very nicely upon the exact *form* of the line observed," the American psychologist G. M. Stratton wrote, but also there was a "grotesque unlikeness between the outline observed and the action of the eye in observing it."[53] According to these psychologists, then, the eye read by scanning—that is, it operated less like Tauschek's machine and more like Shepard's.

Such debates were not trivial. The question of whether human perception operated with wholes or fragments was among the most controversial in psychological circles at the end of the nineteenth century. According to the detractors of Wilhelm Wundt, the founder of arguably the first and certainly the most influential psychology laboratory in the world, the dividing line was between a psychology that *analyzed* or *dissected* (frequently described with the word *zergliedern* in German) the operations of the human mind and a psychology that more

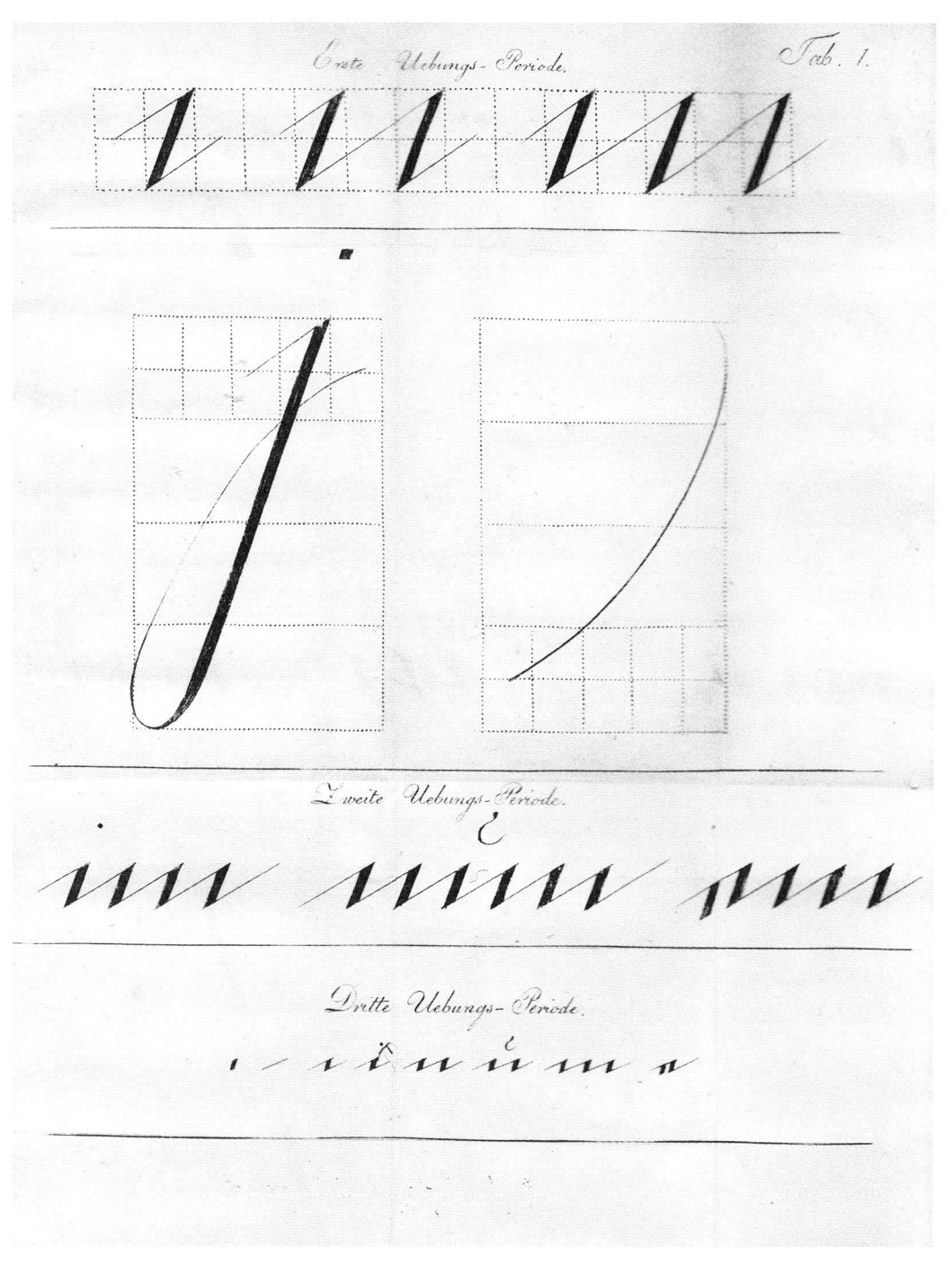

Figure 3.7. First three exercises according to the Pestalozzi curriculum. A. Soyaux, *Pestalozzi, seine Lehrart und seine Anstalt* (Leipzig: Gerhard Fleischer, 1803).

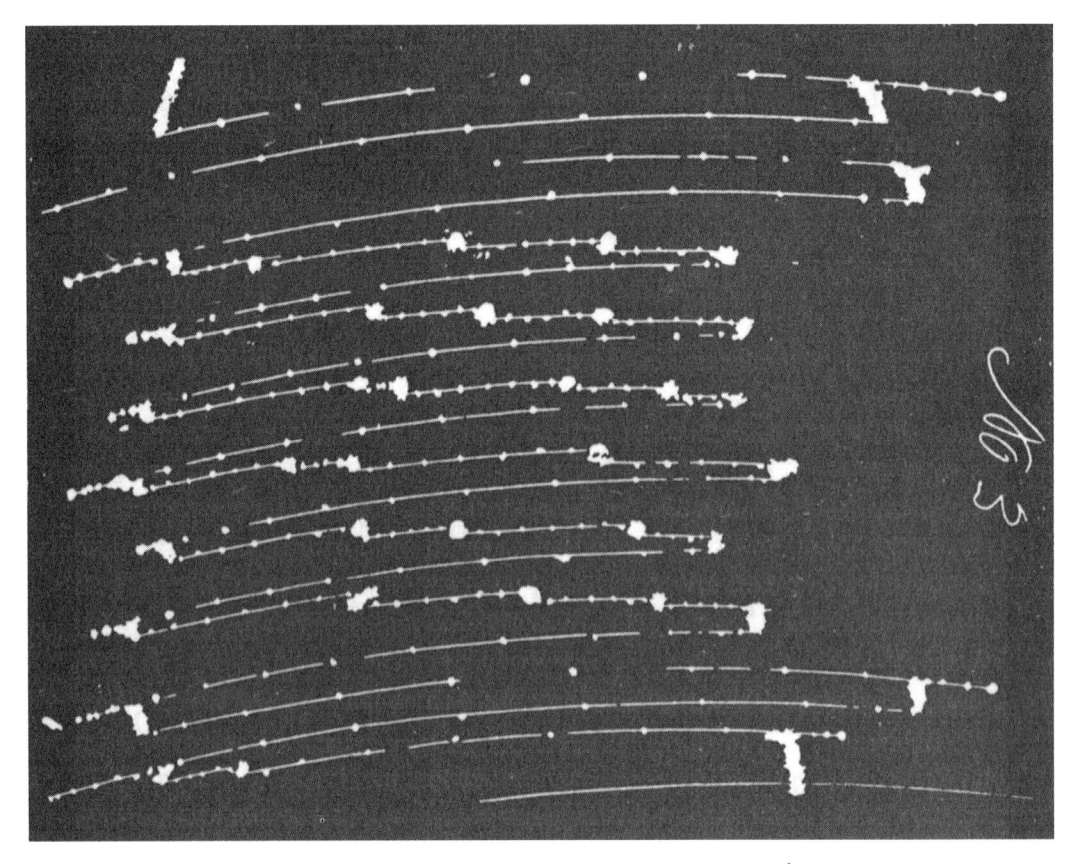

Figure 3.8. Saccadic movements of a reading eye according to Louis Émile Javal. Edmund Burke Huey, *The Psychology and Pedagogy of Reading with a Review of the History of Reading and Writing and of Methods, Texts, and Hygiene in Reading* (New York: Macmillan, 1908), 28.

modestly confined itself to *describing* them.[54] This debate too had a longer history: Helmholtz at midcentury had distinguished a descriptive science practiced by the likes of Goethe from the kind of analytic science in which he himself was engaged. The latter inquired into the question of deep causality, according to Helmholtz, while the former busied itself with a phenomenology of forms—whether of plants or the intermaxillary bone.[55] Continuing this line of thinking, critics of Wundt argued for a science anticipating phenomenology, a science dedicated to *understanding* the unity of experience as a whole rather than *analyzing* it through dissection.[56] While Wundtians might be busy in the laboratory measuring the pulse, heartbeat, and breathing that might accompany the perception of a particular color, these phenomenologically inclined psychologists would mock the experimenters' hubris.

> I stand at the window and see a house, trees, sky. Theoretically I might say there were 327 brightnesses and nuances of colour. Do I *have* "327"? No. I have sky, house, and trees. It is impossible to achieve "327" as such. And yet even though such droll calculation were possible—and implied, say, for the house 120, the trees 90, the sky 117—I should at least have *this* arrangement and division of the total, and, not, say, 127 and 100 and 100; or 150 and 177.[57]

It was out of late nineteenth-century critiques of Wundtian psychology, accused of dismembering the presumed unity of experience, that Gestalt psychology emerged in the twentieth century. As Edward Boring, an early historian of the discipline, explained, the primacy of formal structures in organizing consciousness was the fundamental principle of Gestalt psychology.[58] The psychologist Max Wertheimer summarized the fundamental "Gestalt formula" as follows: "There are wholes, the behavior of which is not determined by that of the individual elements, but where the part-processes are themselves determined by the intrinsic nature of the whole." If the Gestalt formula was to be followed, it was necessary to "not be satisfied with sham solutions suggested by a simple dichotomy of science and life." Science here was understood as any field of knowledge that took it upon itself to reduce "all wholes . . . to pieces and piecewise relations between pieces."[59] Against the psychological camps of "Introspectionists" and "Behaviorists," Gestaltists maintained that "instead of reacting to local stimuli by local and mutually independent events, the organism responds to the pattern of stimuli to which it is exposed; and that this answer is a unitary process, a functional *whole*" (Figure 3.9).[60] As the architectural critic Colin Rowe would put it later, Gestalt psychology assumed that the human sensorium was endowed with an inherent "organizing capacity."[61]

This was not to say that Gestalt psychology never took an interest in fragmentation. Gestalt psychologists preoccupied themselves with the saccadic movements of the eye too, but what some had considered degenerate only a generation ago was now theorized as a necessary component of pattern recognition. Take this experiment that the psychologist Kurt Gottschaldt wrote about in 1929: subjects, seated at a table, were asked to observe a projection screen and make drawings of figures that evolved from primary shapes into increasingly more complicated ones.[62] The task, however, was not as straightforward as it might sound. In front of the projection lens was placed an episcotister—a rapidly rotating disk with opaque and transparent sectors so that the subject's field of vision would be blocked as if by a Nipkow disk. After a "ready" signal, the subject was asked to call out every time he or she detected a different figure. The results were summarized in a table (Figure 3.10). Gottschaldt's conclusions were in support of

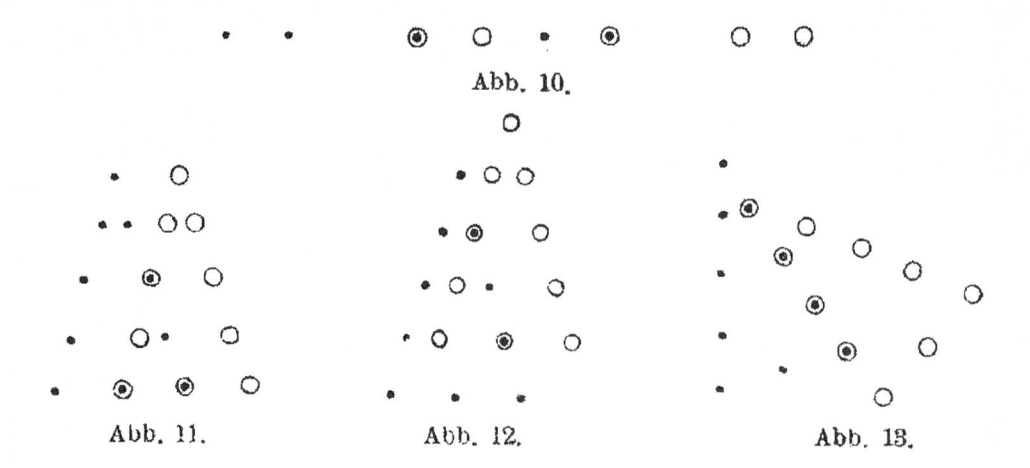

Figure 3.9. Perceptual organization of dots. Josef Ternus, "Experimentelle Untersuchungen über phänomenale Identität," *Psychologische Forschung* 7 (1926): 88.

the Gestaltist position: the "after-effect of [prior] experience was so small as to be virtually non-existent."[63] Regardless of how frequently and for how long the initial shapes had been shown, the final figures' internal unity proved to be the strongest factor in perception. Formal organization outdid every other factor.

Gottschaldt's experiment replaced the machine vision in Nipkow's apparatus with human eyes but only to reinforce the distinction between the human and the machine: creating and recognizing formal unities was a uniquely organic—if not exclusively human—capability. (Gestaltists made a point of stressing that variations of it were, in fact, found in birds, bees, and other animals.[64]) Scanning experts at mid-twentieth century would agree with Gottschaldt's conclusion. "The human visual system categorizes; it does not analyze," one optical character recognition expert argued, as if rehearsing late nineteenth-century psychological debates about morphology versus dissection, and "it forms hypotheses and makes decisions. . . . It does not typically decompose the world into its elements."[65] Even when listening to the Morse code, others wrote, the human operator "does not hear dots and dashes at all, but perceives the characters as wholes."[66] In other words, even before the emergence of today's CAPTCHA technology that determines if an online user is a human or a robot, form was that which authenticated—and, one might even say, stabilized—the category of the human at precisely the moment when the unity of that concept was being demonstrably discretized by an expanding range of technical practices.

In pursuing the integrity of wholes, Gestaltists, in fact, were also following the thinking of the philosopher Wilhelm Dilthey. Against the fragmented subject that

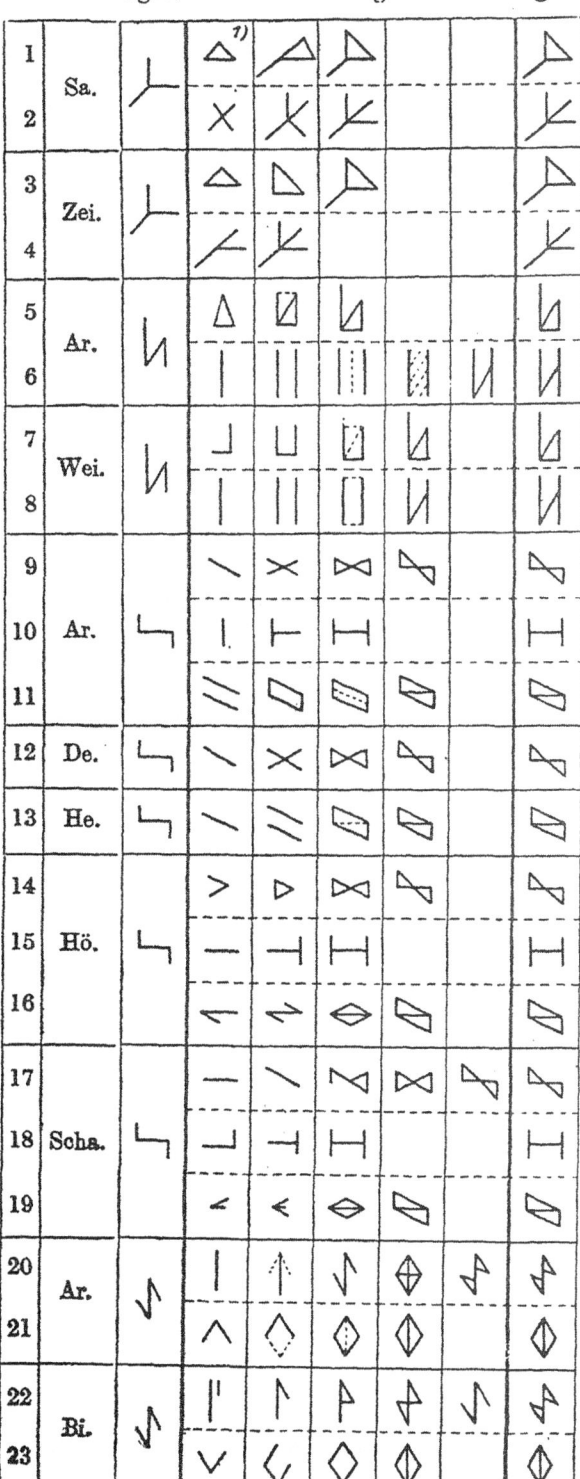

Figure 3.10. Results of experiments with forms. Kurt Gottschaldt, "Gestalt Factors and Repetition" (1929), in *A Source Book for Gestalt Psychology* (1938; repr., Norwich: Routledge, 1950), 127.

has been the protagonist of so many accounts of modernity, Dilthey repeatedly imagined a human subject held together by an elusive "lived nexus" *(der erlebte Zusammenhang)*. "In inner experience," he wrote, "not only are the processes of interaction given, but also the way particular functions relate to the whole of psychic life as its individual constituent parts."[67] More significantly, because it was, above all, this connectedness that held together the human, the human sciences (which in the German context signified what in North America is referred to as the humanities and the social sciences) were to be distinguished from the natural sciences on the basis of this principle: "The methods by means of which we study psychic life, history, and society," Dilthey wrote, are "very different from those that have led to the conceptual cognition of nature."[68] A descriptive psychology that privileged the continuum of life was poised to be the key science in such an endeavor. Even though Dilthey's vision for the arrangement of the discipline with phenomenology as the queen science lost to the neo-Kantian solution in the end, the separation of the human sciences from the natural sciences would not only follow the logic of the separation of the human from everything else but would also perpetuate it in the twentieth century.[69] A primary reason why the distinction between the human and the machine persisted, in other words, was because it was built into the structure of the disciplines at the university.

Calls for a "whole man" were as old as the ideal of *Bildung* itself. It was none other than Wilhelm von Humboldt, the architect of the Prussian educational system and the modern research university, who had imagined this "whole man" as a bulwark against the fragmented self that French revolutionaries had borrowed from sensationalist philosophy.[70] According to Humboldt, the goal of education was to "review our inward being in its whole extent and from all sides" so as to arrive at a "whole being."[71] As Fritz Ringer has demonstrated, the meaning of *Bildung* changed dramatically from the turn of the nineteenth century to the turn of the twentieth, but by 1929 László Moholy-Nagy, teaching at the Bauhaus, was still defending the *Bildung* ideal when he argued that the formal education attempted in the school's preliminary design course *Vorkurs* was a "ripening of sense, feeling, and thought" that was necessary for the formation of the "whole man."[72] Walter Gropius, the founder and the first director of the school, would agree, even from the other side of the ocean: "preliminary artistic training" was not only specialized training, Gropius wrote; the ability to see and make forms—especially of the "spatial kind"—was a necessary part of all education, which itself was to grow "concentrically, like the annular rings of a tree, embracing the whole from the beginning and, at the same time, gradually deepening and extending it."[73]

Following World War II, advocates for visual education in America, deeply indebted to the version of formalism taught at institutions like the Bauhaus and emboldened by postwar calls to revive the Germanic ideal of *Bildung* under the guise of liberal arts (so that a "broad sense of completeness as a human being" would be cultivated "rather than in the narrower sense of competence in a particular lot") once again turned to form as savior.[74] Primary among them was György Kepes, who, after teaching at Moholy-Nagy's New Bauhaus in Chicago, was hired as a professor of "freehand drawing" at MIT at a moment when the institution was busy transforming itself from an engineering school to a science-based research university with ambitions to offer an all-around general education. Like Bauhäusler from the Old World, Kepes cited the "tragic formlessness" of modernity and proposed form as the magical force that would "re-integrate" the disjointed human faculties, on the one hand, and the increasingly specializing sciences, on the other.[75]

> This new knowledge can only be in the living fibre of integration if man experiences it with the wholeness of his being. Human faculties, however, have been dulled and have disintegrated in a climate of frustration. Experience has tended to become only a stepping-stone to an exploitation of nature of man and of man. Experiences are isolated pigeon-holes; they display only single aspects of human beings. To function in his fullest scope man must restore the unity of his experiences so that he can register sensory, emotional, and intellectual dimensions of the present in an indivisible whole. The language of vision, optical communication, is one of the strongest potential means both to reunite man and his knowledge and to re-form man into an integrated being.[76]

These words might as well have been from the nineteenth century. Yet even while Kepes's call for wholenesss sounded like Dilthey's, in fact it signaled a new definition of disciplinary unification: not of the early Gestaltist kind that fantasized about the arrangement of the human disciplines around the nexus of lived experience but rather of the kind that favored "integration." This resulted in courses that continue to be called "visual communication."[77] Orit Halpern has argued compellingly that by asking his students to engage in "scanning" rather than "looking," Kepes reconfigured the categories of "cognition, perception, and sense" into those of "algorithm, pattern, and process."[78] In the postwar period the latter terms aligned more easily with such war-driven "intersciences" as cybernetics, computation, operations research, and game theory, which were beginning to constitute the lingua franca at institutions like MIT. Yet, Peter Galison has argued, this lingua franca was not a universal language: its idea of wholeness differed from its prewar and continental equivalents in that it was "a unification through localized sets of common concepts." In other words, an "interscience" was a science unified in pieces as if in a patchwork manner.[79] It no longer had the ambition of transdisciplinarity that the likes of Dilthey entertained a few decades ago. In practical terms this meant that one or more disciplines would come together in "centers of research" such as Kepes's CAVS at MIT.[80] Such centers undertook what Kepes called "the task to establish an organic interconnection of the new frontiers of knowledge." "Integration, planning, and form are the key words of all progressive efforts today," Kepes wrote, and "the goal is a new vital structure-order, a new form on a social plane, in which all present knowledge and technological possessions may function unhindered as a whole."[81] Remarkably, then, even after the disciplinary and institutional rearrangements undertaken during and after World War II and on another continent, form lost none of its presumed magical power to achieve wholeness.[82]

In this new context, *Gestalt* too acquired new valency. The question of optical illusions is a good case in point. If in the camera obscura model of perception, optical illusions were nothing more than illusionary sensations that were stumbling blocks on the path to true knowledge, for Helmholtzian epistemology, they were the exceptions that reassuringly proved the rule: if human judgment prevailed even when confronted with such tricks, Helmholtz argued, so would Enlightenment reason. Gestalt psychology, by contrast, recognized illusions as the intermediary step between unprocessed sensation and apperceived judgment. This meant that even after determining the length of the two lines in a Müller-Lyer diagram to be equal, one had to accept that it was impossible to eliminate the illusion that one line appeared longer than the other (Figure 3.11). In one of the several volumes edited by Kepes, however, the art theorist Anton Ehrenzweig tellingly attributed a new role to optical illusions. Echoing Hildebrand's distinction from the past century, Ehrenzweig distinguished between two kinds of vision: a clear, precise visualization that he called "conscious planning" versus an imprecise, intuitive visualization that he dubbed "unconscious scanning." But, unlike Hildebrand, Ehrenzweig privileged the latter.[83] Examining the optical illusion in an exercise from a basic design course (Figure 3.12), for example, he dismissed the Gestaltist argument that "one's attention jump[ed] between the two alternative modes of configuration," arguing instead that "the student must learn to wipe out all precise visualization and comprehend both mutually exclusive possibilities . . . in a single glance."[84] Just as was the case with Shepard's reader, which triumphed over Taushchek's because it did not need as comprehensive a storage, this was, above all, a matter of efficiency. "Conscious visualization can deal only with one alternative at a time," wrote Ehrenzweig, whereas "unconscious visualization has a wider focus and so is capable of scanning with a single glance all the many ramifications of the way ahead and assists in making the right choice."[85] Ehrenzweig predicted the triumph of unconscious scanning: scanning numerous

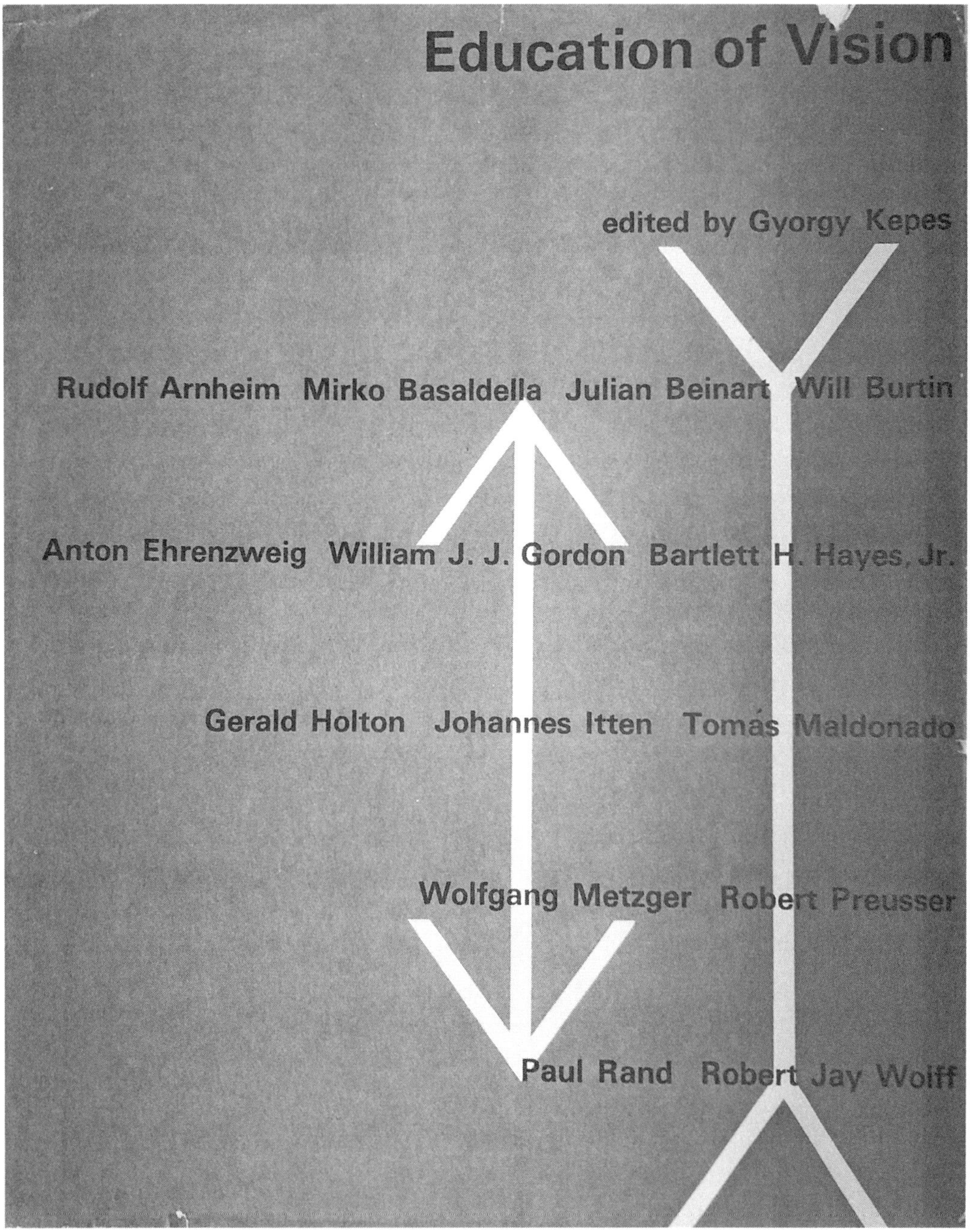

Figure 3.11. Müller-Lyer diagram. Cover image of Gyorgy Kepes, ed., *Education of Vision* (New York: George Braziller, 1965).

Figure 3.12. Exercise from the basic design course at the London Central School of Arts and Crafts. Anton Ehrenzweig, "Conscious Planning and Unconscious Scanning," in *Education of Vision*, ed. Gyorgy Kepes (New York: George Braziller, 1965), 35. Copyright 1965 by George Braziller, Inc. Reprinted with the permission of George Braziller, Inc. (New York), www.georgebraziller.com. All rights reserved.

low-resolution images was more effective than examining at length a few high-resolution ones. Scanning, in other words, was not only appropriate now but also welcome, even for human eyes.

Yet this did not amount to the blurring of the boundaries that had been established a century ago. At the moment that Ehrenzweig was lecturing on the virtues of what might today be called "distant reading," American humanists were doubling down on the hermeneutic tradition and insisting on the necessity to engage in "close reading."[86] New Criticism in the 1940s and 1950s dismissed all factors deemed "external" to a literary text—history, cultural context, or politics—focusing instead exclusively on its "internal" consistencies. A text was seen as an organic unity: "Through intentional acts of reading," wrote one critic, "the different strata of the literary work are simultaneously constituted into a unity within which they can interact, and, as it were, comment upon one another."[87] Even Clement Greenberg's formalism, despite his self-professed goal to expunge the literary from the visual in the name of achieving medium purity, was indebted to New Criticism's notion of close reading.[88]

Paradoxically, however, both Ehrenzweig's distant reading and New Criticism's close reading were engaged in analyzing formal qualities. In other words, instead of giving way to some fragmented, mechanistic modern subject, the mythical creature that is the protagonist of so many accounts of the twentieth century, the nineteenth-century post-Kantian subject—will-centered and indivisible—received a boost from technologies of discretization. The ability to recognize and make form remained crucial to the integrity of this subject. As the categories of the human and the machine were made and remade through their disciplinary frameworks, the elusive concept form was conjured time and again as the force that would make these inherently unstable categories stable. Viewed from this technical perspective, history of the humanities in modernity might well be the history of this persistent nineteenth-century subject and its formalist techniques.

NOTES

I thank Elliott Sturtevant for the invaluable research support that he provided.

1. Gustav Tauschek, Reading Machine, U.S. Patent 2,026,329, filed May 27, 1929, and issued December 31, 1935.

2. D. H. Shepard, Apparatus for Reading, U.S. Patent 2,663,758, filed March 1, 1951, and issued December 22, 1953.

3. G. J. Balm, "An Introduction to Optical Character Reader Considerations," *Pattern Recognition* 2, no. 3 (1970): 159. According to Balm, if abstraction was taken as the primary criterion, machines like Tauschek's and Shepard's represented the two extremes of

existing optical character recognition technologies. These two extremes were "entire character (gestalt) recognition" and "information transformation," respectively, and in between were the options of "essential feature extraction" and "threshold logic or decision functions."

4. W. J. Hannan, "The RCA Multi-Font Reading Machine," in *Optical Character Recognition,* ed. George L. Fischer Jr. et al. (Washington, D.C.: Spartan Books, 1962), 6.

5. Parallel processing, it was claimed, was not the natural language for machines, which operated better with sequential processing. Oliver G. Selfridge and Ulrich Neisser, "Pattern Recognition by Machine," *Scientific American* 203, no. 2 (August 1960): 66.

6. A pattern was defined as "an arrangement or interorientation with no necessary semantic value." D. A. Young, cited in Mary Elizabeth Stevens, *Automatic Character Recognition: A State-of-the-Art Report* (Washington, D.C.: United States Department of Commerce, 1961), 2.

7. Mary Elizabeth Stevens, "Introduction to the Special Issue on Optical Character Recognition (OCR)," *Pattern Recognition* 2, no. 3 (September 1970): 147; Selfridge and Neisser, "Pattern Recognition by Machine," 68. Even error was a matter of statistical analysis: "If three sides of a black element are white, the element should be white. If three sides of a white spot are black, the machine converts the white spot to black." Jacob Rabinow, "The Present State of the Art of Reading Machines," in *Pattern Recognition,* ed. L. M. Kanal (Washington, D.C.: Thompson, 1968), 14.

8. Jacob Rabinow, "Developments in Character Recognition Machines at Rabinow Engineering Company," in *Optical Character Recognition* (Washington, D.C.: Spartan Books, 1962), 38.

9. R. A. Kirsch, L. Cahn, C. Ray, and G. H. Urban, "Experiments in Processing Pictorial Information with a Digital Computer," in *Proceedings of the Eastern Joint Computer Conference* (New York: Institute of Radio Engineering and Association for Computing Machinery, 1957), 221–29.

10. Balm, "An Introduction to Optical Character Reader Considerations," 153.

11. Rabinow, "The Present State of the Art of Reading Machines," 16.

12. Wolfgang Ernst and Harun Farocki, "Towards an Archive for Visual Concepts," in *Harun Farocki: Working on the Sight-Lines,* ed. Thomas Elsaesser (Amsterdam: Amsterdam University Press, 2004), 272. Ernst and Farocki's goal is to imagine a "new image archaeology that has as its aim the rethinking of the notion of images from the vantage point of the process of archiving." They continue: "In sharp contrast to traditional hermeneutics, the media-archaeological investigation of image archives does not regard images as carriers of experiences and meanings. . . . Image processing by computers can no longer be re-enacted with the anthropological semantics of the human eye." Ernst and Farocki, "Towards an Archive for Visual Concepts," 262.

13. Leonard Uhr, "Pattern Recognition," in *Electronic Information Handling,* ed. A. Kent and O. E. Taulbee (Washington, D.C.: Spartan, 1965), 51.

14. See, for example, the account by O. G. Selfridge, "Pandemonium: A Paradigm for Learning," in *Proceedings of the Symposium on Mechanisation of Thought Processes* (London: Her Majesty's Stationery Office, 1959), 513.

15. Gustav Tauschek, Lesende Maschine (Maschine mit Gesichtssinneffekt), Austrian Patent 116,799, filed May 30, 1928, and issued March 10, 1930, 1. Translations are mine unless otherwise noted.

16. Tauschek began his career after World War I as an errand boy in the Austrian National Bank in Vienna, where he devised a machine that produced guilloche patterns to be used on paper bills so that they could not be forged. This invention allowed him to secure a position at a metal production facility in Sömerda, Germany. For more on Tauschek's fascinating career in Europe and America, see Martin Helfert, Petra Mazuran, and Christoph Wintersteiger, *Gustav Tauschek und seine Maschinen* (Vienna: Universitätsverlag Rudolf Trauner, 2006). The appeal to qualities attributed to humans was evident in Tauschek's other inventions as well; among them are the following: Gustav Tauschek, Feeling Device for Machines for Interpreting Perforated Cards, U.S. Patent 1,745,388, filed February 9, 1928, and issued February 4, 1930; Gustav Tauschek, Sensing Mechanism, U.S. Patent 2,320,836, filed June 24, 1936, and issued June 1, 1943; and Gustav Tauschek and International Business Machines Corporation, Machine for Simulating Handwriting, U.S. Patent 2,049,675, filed December 7, 1935, and issued August 4, 1936.

17. Tauschek also left the lower half of his cards empty to provide room for handwritten notes, which, he thought, were indispensable. Gustav Tauschek, *Die Lochkarten-Buchhaltungs-Maschinen meines Systems* (Vienna: Meinhartsdorfergasse, 1930), 10.

18. For a partial but useful genealogy, see Jacob Rabinow, "Whither OCR and Whence?," *Datamation*, July 1969, 38–42. For one definition of this meaning of "media archaeology," see Erkki Huhtamo and Jussi Parikka, eds., *Media Archaeology: Approaches, Applications, and Implications* (Berkeley: University of California Press, 2011).

19. I am borrowing the term *historical ontology* from Ian Hacking, who defines it as "coming into being of the very possibility of some objects." Hacking, in turn, borrowed the term from Michel Foucault, who referred to a "historical ontology of ourselves." Ian Hacking, *Historical Ontology* (Cambridge, Mass.: Harvard University Press, 2002); Michel Foucault, "What Is Enlightenment?," in *Foucault Reader*, ed. Paul Rabinow, trans. Catherine Porter (New York: Pantheon Books, 1984), 32–50.

20. For a good summary, see Lucian Krukowski, Norton Batkin, and Whitney Davis, "Formalism: Overview," "Formalism in Analytic Aesthetics," and "Formalism in Art History," in *Encyclopedia of Aesthetics*, 2nd ed., ed. Michael Kelly (New York: Oxford University Press, 2014), 70–84.

21. Karl Marx, *Capital: A Critique of Political Economy*, vol. 1, ed. Ernest Mandel (London: Penguin, 1981); Ernst Kapp, *Grundlinien einer Philosophie der Technik* (Braunschweig: George Westermann, 1877); Marshall McLuhan, *Understanding Media: Extensions of Man* (New York: McGraw-Hill, 1964).

22. Frank Rosenblatt, "The Perceptron: A Probabilistic Model for Information Storage and Organization in the Brain," *Psychological Review* 65, no. 6 (1958): 387. For another example of this parallelism at midcentury, see Paul A. Kolers, "Some Psychological Aspects of Pattern Recognition," in *Recognizing Patterns: Studies in Living and Automatic Systems*, ed. Paul A. Kolers (Cambridge, Mass.: MIT Press, 1968), 4–61. See also Orit Halpern's essay in this volume.

23. Rosenblatt, "The Perceptron," 386.

24. Rosenblatt, "The Perceptron," 386–87.

25. Rabinow, "Developments in Character Recognition Machines," 38.

26. See Jonathan Crary, *Techniques of the Observer: On Vision and Modernity in the Nineteenth Century* (Cambridge, Mass.: MIT Press, 1990); and Martin Jay, *The Downcast Eyes: Denigration of Vision in Twentieth-Century French Thought* (Berkeley: University of California Press, 1993).

27. Crary has convincingly demonstrated how the camera obscura metaphor was challenged in the nineteenth century by a model of seeing that he dubbed "subjective vision." Crary, *Techniques of the Observer,* 67–96. According to Crary, this was the moment "when the visible escape[d] from the timeless order of the camera obscura and [became] lodged in another apparatus, within the unstable physiology and temporality of the human body." Crary, 70.

28. Crary, 90. Crary here refers to Johannes Müller's 1833 treatise *Handbuch der Physiologie des Menschen.*

29. Hermann von Helmholtz, "Die neueren Fortschritte in der Theorie des Sehens," in *Populäre Wissenschaftliche Vorträge* (Braunschweig: Friedrich Viewig, 1871), translated as "The Recent Progress of the Theory of Vision," in *Science and Culture: Popular and Philosophical Essays,* ed. David Cahan (Chicago: University of Chicago Press, 1995), 150.

30. Timothy Lenoir, "Helmholtz and the Materialities of Communication," *Osiris* 9, no. 1 (1994): 185–207.

31. Paul Nipkow, Elektrisches Teleskop, German Patent 30105, filed January 6, 1884, and issued January 15, 1885.

32. "Paul Gottlieb Nipkow," in *Encyclopedia of World Scientists,* ed. Elizabeth H. Oakes (2002; repr., New York: Facts on File, 2007), 543. According to historians, the myth of Nipkow as the inventor of the television was perpetuated during the Nazi era. Monika Elsner, Thomas Müller, and Peter M. Spangenberg, "The Early History of German Television: The Slow Development of a Fast Medium," in *Materialities of Communication,* ed. Hans Ulrich Gumbrecht and K. Ludwig Pfeiffer, trans. William Whobrey (Stanford: Stanford University Press, 1994), 129–30.

33. "Paul Gottlieb Nipkow," 543.

34. Robert Sabine, "Telegraphic Apparatus and Processes," in *Reports on the Paris Universal Exhibition 1867,* vol. 4 (London: George E. Eyre and William Spottiswoode, 1868), 521–607.

35. Frederick Collier Bakewell, *Electric Science: Its History, Phenomena, and Applications* (London: Ingram, Cooke, 1853), 160.

36. Bakewell, 171.

37. Joshua D. Wolff, *Western Union and the Creation of the American Corporate Order, 1845–1893* (Cambridge: Cambridge University Press, 2013), 21.

38. On the turn-of-the-twentieth-century theme of "formlessness," see Alexander Eisenschmidt, "The Formless Grosstadt and Its Potent Negativity: Berlin, 1910 through the Eyes of Endell, Scheffler, and Hegemann" (PhD diss., University of Pennsylvania, 2008).

39. Georg Simmel, *Philosophie des Geldes* (Leipzig: Duncker & Humblot, 1900), translated by David Frisby as *The Philosophy of Money* (New York: Routledge, 2011), 294.

40. Simmel, *The Philosophy of Money*, 294.

41. Adolf Hildebrand, *Das Problem der Form in der bildenden Kunst* (Strassburg: Heitz & Mündel, 1893), translated as "The Problem of Form in the Fine Arts," in *Empathy, Form, and Space: Problems in German Aesthetics, 1873–1893*, trans. Harry Francis Mallgrave and Eleftherios Ikonomou (Santa Monica, Calif.: Getty Center for the History of Art and the Humanities, 1994), 227–79.

42. Hildebrand, "The Problem of Form," 229–30.

43. Hildebrand, "The Problem of Form," 229. The English translation uses the word *scanning*.

44. Hildebrand, "The Problem of Form," 270.

45. Max Nordau, *Entartung*, 2 vols. (Berlin: Duncker, 1892–93), translated by George L. Mosse as *Degeneration* (New York: H. Fertig, 1968), 27; Richard von Krafft-Ebing, *Text-Book of Insanity Based on Clinical Observations for Practitioners and Students of Medicine*, trans. Charles Gilbert Chaddock (Philadelphia: Davis, 1904), 361.

46. The theme of formlessness runs through the work of Wölfflin, known as the father of formalism in art history. See Heinrich Wölfflin, *Renaissance und Barock: Eine Untersuchung über Wesen und Entstehung des Barockstils in Italien* (Munich: T. Ackermann, 1888), 30, translated by Kathrin Simon as *Renaissance and Baroque* (Ithaca, N.Y.: Cornell University Press, 1966). The term *pathological* was not used in the English translation of the book but appears on page 30 of the German edition cited here. See also Zeynep Çelik Alexander, "Baroque out of Focus: The Question of Mediation in Wölfflin," *New German Critique* 45, no. 1 (February 2018): 79–109.

47. Barbara Maria Stafford and Francis Terpak, eds., *Devices of Wonder: From the World in a Box to Images on a Screen* (Los Angeles, Calif.: Getty Research Institute, 2001). For a contemporaneous account of the disjointedness of film, see Konrad Lange, *Das Kino in Gegenwart und Zukunft* (Stuttgart: Ferdinand Enke, 1920), 52. For secondary literature on the suspect entertainment culture in Germany at the turn of the century, see Kaspar Maase and Wolfgang Kaschuba, eds., *Schund und Schönheit: Populäre Kultur um 1900* (Cologne: Böhlau, 2001).

48. Hildebrand, "The Problem of Form," 227–28.

49. Johann Heinrich Pestalozzi, *Sämtliche Werke*, vol. 22, *Über die Idee der Elementarbildung und den Standpunkt ihrer Ausführung in der Pestalozzischen Anstalt zu Iferten* (delivered in Lenzburg on August 30, 1809) (Berlin: De Gruyter, 1979), and vol. 5, *Wie Gertrud ihre Kinder lehrt: Ein Versuch den Müttern Anleitung zu geben, ihre Kinder selbst zu unterrichten* (Stuttgart and Tübingen: Gottaschen, 1820), translated by Lucy E. Holland and Francis C. Turner as *How Gertrude Teaches Her Children* (Syracuse, N.Y.: C. W. Bardeen, 1900).

50. For a longer history of this phenomenon, see Zeynep Çelik Alexander, *Kinaesthetic Knowing: Aesthetics, Epistemology, Modern Design* (Chicago: University of Chicago Press, 2017).

51. *Bildung* in German is a term that can be simply translated as "education," but historically it has signified both institutional instruction and individual self-cultivation.

For a good introduction to this complex context, see the excellent study by Suzanne Marchand, *Down from Olympus: Archaeology and Philhellenism in Germany, 1750–1970* (Princeton, N.J.: Princeton University Press, 1996); and the summary by Fritz Ringer, "Bildung and Its Implications in the German Tradition, 1890–1930," in *Toward a Social History of Knowledge: Collected Essays* (New York: Berghahn, 2000), 193–212.

52. Edmund Burke Huey, *The Psychology and Pedagogy of Reading with a Review of the History of Reading and Writing and of Methods, Texts, and Hygiene in Reading* (New York: Macmillan, 1908), 16.

53. G. M. Stratton, "Eye Movements and the Aesthetics of Visual Form," *Philosophische Studien* 20 (1902): 343, emphasis added; and G. M. Stratton, "Symmetry, Linear Illusions, and the Movements of the Eye," *Psychological Review* 13, no. 2 (1906): 94.

54. Starting in 1890, the journal *Zeitschrift für Psychologie und Physiologie der Sinnesorganen*, edited by Hermann Ebbinghaus and Arthur König, regularly aired objections against Wundtian psychology, propagated primarily through the latter's *Philosophische Studien*, published in Leipzig. This debate is too long to be explained in detail here, but it should suffice to mention that it had implications not only for psychology but for modes of explanation in the sciences and also for the organization of the disciplines at large. For a good examination of the various aspects of the debate, see Uljana Feest, ed., *Historical Perspectives on Erklären and Verstehen* (New York: Springer, 2010).

55. Hermann von Helmholtz, "Über Goethe's naturwissenschaftliche Arbeiten, Vortrag gehalten in Frühling 1853 in der deutschen Gesellschaft zu Königsberg" (1853), in *Populäre wissenschaftliche Vorträge* (Braunschweig: Friedrich Viewig und Sohn, 1865), 31–53, translated as "On Goethe's Scientific Researches," in *Science and Culture: Popular and Philosophical Essays*, ed. David Cahan (Chicago: University of Chicago Press, 1995), 1–17.

56. See, for example, Wilhelm Dilthey, "Ideen über eine beschreibende und zergliedernde Psychologie," *Sitzungsbeitrag der Berliner Akademie der Wissenschaften vom 20. Dezember 1894* (1895): 1309–1407, translated by Rudolf A. Makkreel and Donald Moore as "Ideas for a Descriptive and Analytic Psychology," in *Selected Works*, vol. 2, *Understanding the Human World*, ed. Rudolf A. Makkreel and Frithjof Rodi (Princeton, N.J.: Princeton University Press, 2010), 115–210.

57. Max Wertheimer, "Laws of Organization in Perceptual Forms" (1923), in *A Source Book for Gestalt Psychology* (1938; repr., Oxon: Routledge, 2007), 71.

58. Edwin G. Boring, *A History of Experimental Psychology* (1929; repr., New York: Appleton-Century-Crofts, 1957), 587–619.

59. Max Wertheimer, "Gestalt Theory" (1924), in *A Source Book for Gestalt Psychology*, 2.

60. Wolfgang Köhler, *Gestalt Psychology: An Introduction to New Concepts in Modern Psychology* (New York: Mentor, 1947), 62, emphasis added.

61. Colin Rowe, *As I Was Saying: Recollection and Miscellaneous Essays*, vol. 1, ed. Alexander Caragonne (Cambridge, Mass.: MIT Press, 1996), 103.

62. Kurt Gottschaldt, "Gestalt Factors and Repetition" (1929), in *A Source Book for Gestalt Psychology*, 123–31.

63. Gottschaldt, 123.

64. An entire section of *A Source Book for Gestalt Psychology* is dedicated to how animals make and perceive forms.

65. Kolers, "Some Psychological Aspects of Pattern Recognition," 56.

66. Selfridge and Neisser, "Pattern Recognition by Machine," 60.

67. Dilthey, "Ideas for a Descriptive and Analytic Psychology," 119–20.

68. Dilthey, "Ideas for a Descriptive and Analytic Psychology," 119–20.

69. R. Lanier Anderson, "The Debate over the *Geisteswissenschaften* in German Philosophy," in *The Cambridge History of Philosophy, 1870–1945*, ed. Thomas Baldwin (New York: Cambridge University Press, 2003), 223–25.

70. For the import of German ideas to postrevolutionary France, see Jan Goldstein, *The Post-Revolutionary Self: Politics and Psyche in France, 1750–1850* (Cambridge, Mass.: Harvard University Press, 2005).

71. Wilhelm von Humboldt, "Letter XXXI," in *Letters of William von Humboldt to a Female Friend*, vol. 2, trans. Catherine M. A. Couper (London: John Chapman, 1849), 121.

72. Ringer, "*Bildung* and Its Implications in the German Tradition"; László Moholy-Nagy, *Von Material zu Architektur* (Munich: Albert Langen, 1929), 11.

73. Walter Gropius, "Education toward Creative Design," *American Architect and Architecture* 150 (May 1937): 30.

74. James Bryant Conant, ed., *General Education in a Free Society* (1945; repr., Cambridge, Mass.: Harvard University Press, 1950), 4.

75. Gyorgy Kepes, *Language of Vision* (1944; repr., Chicago: Paul Theobold, 1969), 12. For Kepes's career at MIT, see Anna Vallye, "The Middleman: Kepes's Instruments," in *A Second Modernism: MIT, Architecture, and the "Techno-Social" Moment*, ed. Arindam Dutta (Cambridge, Mass.: MIT Press, 2013), 144–85; and Reinhold Martin, "Organicism's Other," *Grey Room*, no. 4 (Summer 2001): 34–51.

76. Kepes, *Language of Vision*, 13.

77. At the time of writing, such a course was offered in the Daniels Faculty of Architecture, Landscape, and Design at the University of Toronto, where I taught.

78. Orit Halpern, *Beautiful Data: A History of Vision and Reason since 1945* (Durham, N.C.: Duke University Press, 2014), 80.

79. Peter Galison, "The Americanization of Unity," *Daedalus* 127, no. 1 (Winter 1998): 67.

80. Vallye, "The Middleman," 162.

81. Kepes, *Language of Vision*, 4.

82. This is not to say formalism "migrated" from Europe to North America. American pedagogues were busy developing their version of formalism with ambitions similar to their counterparts in German-speaking lands. For an instance of influence in the other direction, see, for example, Ákos Moravanszky, "Educated Evolution: Darwinism, Design Education, and American Influence in Central Europe, 1898–1918," in *The Education of the Architect: Historiography, Urbanism, and the Growth of Architectural Knowledge* (Cambridge, Mass.: MIT Press, 1997), 113–37.

83. Anton Ehrenzweig, "Conscious Planning and Unconscious Scanning," in *Education of Vision*, ed. Gyorgy Kepes (New York: George Braziller, 1965), 27–49.

84. Ehrenzweig, 34.

85. Ehrenzweig, 28.

86. I am borrowing the term from Franco Moretti, *Distant Reading* (London: Verso, 2013). Moretti used quantitative methods to "distant-read" seven thousand novels written between 1740 and 1950. This approach has inspired much work in the digital humanities recently.

87. Roman Ingarden, *The Literary Work of Art* (1965; repr., Evanston: Northwestern University Press, 1973), xxiv.

88. Clement Greenberg, "Towards a Newer Laocoon," in *Clement Greenberg: The Collected Essays and Criticism,* vol. 1, *Perceptions and Judgments, 1939–1944,* ed. John O'Brian (1940; repr., Chicago: University of Chicago Press, 1986), 23–37. For Greenberg's indebtedness to New Criticism, see Caroline A. Jones, *Eyesight Alone: Clement Greenberg's Modernism and the Bureaucratization of the Senses* (Chicago: University of Chicago Press, 2005).

CHAPTER 4

EQUIPPING

Domestic Sleights of Hand

EDWARD A. EIGEN

The cover of Jean-Eugène Robert-Houdin's far from transparently factual memoir, *Confidences et révélations: Comment on devient sorcier,* says it all, and more (Figure 4.1). Below the title appears a mysterious design, drawn by the author, identified as a "calligraphic hodgepodge."[1] When the cover is held horizontally at eye level and then tilted, six hidden words emerge from its dense tatting of lines: "ROBERT-HOUDIN PRESTIDIGITATEUR MÉCANICIEN PHYSICIEN ST. GERVAIS P^{res} BLOIS" (Robert-Houdin Prestidigitator Mechanic Physicist Near Blois). Upon the decipherment of this code, the reader's initiation into conjury has begun: the first lesson being that things are often not as they first seem to be. The book reveals how the hidden words were intertwined in Robert-Houdin's storied career in natural magic. Yet the calligraph's final term, "Near Blois," requires separate contextualization.

After seven years as impresario of the Théâtre des Soirées Fantastiques, its program composed of "entirely new experiments" invented by the master conjurer, Robert-Houdin quit Paris for the town of Saint-Gervais, near his native Blois.[2] There he purchased a property once belonging to the Church of Saint Solemne, from which it derived its name: the Priory. Christened "The Abbey of Tricks" (L'Abbaye de l'Attrape, i.e., Trap[p]-ist Abbey) by one of its *habitués,* the house was equipped with the sort of machines and clockworks that Robert-Houdin had perfected for the stage. In his rigged home, he was eager to demonstrate the applicability of these "mysterious organizations" to the science of domestic life. Yet to read his memoir is to get the impression that Robert-Houdin, for whom domesticity itself was a mysterious hodgepodge of comfort and control, could only have been at home in such a contraptious setting.

The design of the Priory underscores an evident tension in Robert-Houdin's memoir between the desire for machines and the expectations of domestic life.

ROBERT-HOUDIN

CONFIDENCES
ET
RÉVÉLATIONS

COMMENT ON DEVIENT SORCIER

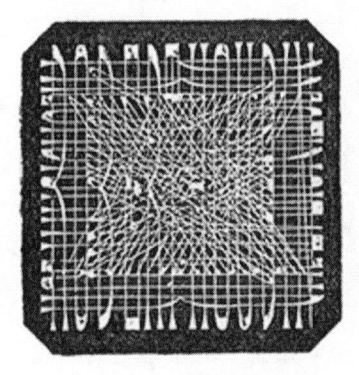

MACÉDOINE CALLIGRAPHIQUE
dans laquelle se trouvent six mots différents.

BLOIS
LECESNE, IMPRIMEUR-ÉDITEUR
RUE DES PAPEGAULTS

MDCCCLXVIII

Figure 4.1. Title page with the "calligraphic hodgepodge" in which are to be found six words spelling out elements of the author's identity: ROBERT-HOUDIN PRESTIDIGITATEUR MÉCANICIEN PHYSICIEN ST. GERVAIS P^res BLOIS. Jean-Eugène Robert-Houdin, *Confidences et révélations: Comment on devient sorcier* (Blois: Lecesne, 1868).

That the Priory was a place of "tricks" serves as but one indication that these desires were not finally reconciled. Wishing to disclose all its "little secrets," Robert-Houdin published *Le Prieuré: Organisations mystérieuses pour le confort et l'agrément d'une demeure* in 1867. In the pamphlet he summoned his powers as an "ex-sorcerer" to guide his readers on a visit while sparing them the fatigue of actual transit to Saint-Gervais. As it turns out, gaining entry to the property was no simple matter. The Priory's portal was equipped with an "electric concierge" in which the (all-knowing) person who customarily monitored the doorway was substituted by a system of electrically actuated latches, relays, and signals.[3] It was Robert-Houdin's genius to show how these mechanical devices could be used in the home. What he revealed in the process was the extent to which the home was already a machine for living (in), to borrow a defining trope of architectural modernity. The self-bestowed reward for his long "mechanical labors" in the service of illusion, the Priory offers a compelling study of how, by entering the home, artificious machines both articulated and disguised the ambiguous pleasure of yielding to the seductions of comfort. Hospitality at the Priory was a matter of being "taken in." The electromechanical doorbell was the first test.

COMFORT AND CONTROL

Before staging our interpretive visit to the Priory, the mixed pleasures of which are the modest but, it is hoped, appreciable reward of this essay, let us first investigate what may be meant by this juxtaposition of terms, *comfort* and *control*, beyond their alliterative effect. In her study of the invention of modern French living, circa 1670–1765, historian Joan DeJean examines the confident belief, itself an unevenly distributed luxury, that "we have a right to expect a high degree of comfort, above all, in the place where we can control it most easily, in our homes."[4] Apart from determining the locally appropriate measure of degree of comfort, it might also be asked what sort of comfort is derived from the expectation that such places as our homes are subject to control, even or perhaps especially by ourselves? The very question could be regarded as a breach of the decorum that governs, precisely by degree, the terms of hospitality and sociability that shape the home no less than its physical form and arrangement. And then there is the matter of "ease," a close but ultimately false friend of "comfort." For while dramatizing the passionate intelligence of Mesdames de Pompadour and de Montespan in defining the taste of the court of Louis XV, DeJean's attention to what took place *hors-scène* belies any sense that comfort is "easily" attained. She takes pains to describe a diverse corps of *ébénistes, tapissiers, menuisiers, doreurs, miroitiers*, etcetera—their tools, materials, and workplaces precisely and economically delineated in the pages of the *Encyclopédie* of Denis Diderot and Jean Le Rond d'Alembert, making visible the hitherto occult world of artisanry—by whose delicate labors a laboriously delicate "world of interior decoration" was brought into being.[5]

The object of this purposeful luxury was not merely to line the inner shell of an ungenerously scrupulous theater of social ostentation but also to provide the necessary increment of measure to a nascent inward opening into privacy. In his encomium to the "Ingenious Frenchmen" who had conceived these discrete and discreetly chambered interiors, the author, theorist of sensationalism, and architect Nicolas Le Camus de Mézières praised the "plans that you have devised."[6] These plans attain the status of intricate plots, newly embroidered brocades of ambition and desire, expressing the unspoken need to be left to (be) one's self. Like all such designs, they entail unperceived traps, the consequence if not also the source of their ingeniousness. Thus while Le Camus de Mézières wished to distill the minutely particular character of the diverse interior spaces that bear analogy with inwardly felt and often imperfectly expressed emotions, there remained the possibility for calculated misdirection. For comfort to emerge, an unperceived passage (*dégagement* was the term of art) needed to be contrived between formal exteriors and furnished interiors. In early eighteenth-century domestic planning, according to Robin Middleton, "magnificence and symmetry of the architecture as presented to the world was of far greater importance than ease of circulation or comfort. These might be sacrificed without qualm when rank and decorum dictated."[7] The tables were to be turned. Comfort was commensurate with the possibility of retreating from view, with draped and upholstered insulation from the requirements of how one needed to appear to, or in the estimation of, others. "You govern the motions of his heart," Le Camus de Mézières wrote of these ingenious Frenchmen, "and by a kind of magic you excite all manner of sensations at will."[8] These conjurers of interior worlds were, as such, only partially to be trusted. Where there is a will there must be a way *out*—a trapdoor, failing all else.

As a measure of control, then, let us take an admittedly quick glance at one of these magicians, or rather a duly appointed *mécanicien du roi* (mechanical engineer to the king), by the name of Antoine-Joseph Loriot. In presenting the most celebrated of his "very ingenious machines," the so-called *table volante* (flying table), the *Mercure de France* noted that Loriot first gained renown for his "secret" fixative for pastels.[9] This proprietary painterly substance solidified the delicate and powdery artistic medium without altering its distinctive *éclat*.[10] Loriot demonstrated the fixative, without elaborating on how it was produced, at the Salon of 1763, by applying it to one half of a portrait of himself done by the artist Jean

Valade. Reviewers of the Salon were unable to detect the treated portion, which was taken as an (in)visible sign of its effectiveness, and not incidentally Loriot's skill at self-presentation. Yet while the Salon was a transparent, Diderotian spectacle of opinion formation, following a script of unfixed critical dictates, the transformation achieved by the *table volante* was said to be "magical."[11]

When guests arrived in the dining room, so read the report's compact narrative, they did not detect the "least hint" of a table. All they saw was a seamless expanse of parquet flooring, the center of which was decorated with a rose. But with the "slightest signal" the rose opened, its leaves retracted under the floor, and a fully set table emerged, surround by four "servants" *(guéridons)* that also appeared from below. At the end of the meal, another barely discernible signal was given, and the table was made to descend, the floor restoring itself, leaving no "vestige" of the table having been there. The *Mercure de France* refrained from elaborating upon the presumably complicated mechanisms involved, suggesting that it would take "infinitely long" to do so.[12] This cunning reticence, the omission of required elaboration, extended into print the means by which the *mécanicien*'s own dexterity was demonstrated, that is to say, by the unmaking of expectation. But other actors, or rather other things, were also in on the performance.

The "servants" that appeared in the dining room were not, perhaps needless to say, flesh and bones table staff. The latter were sequestered below the rosaceous emblem in the parquet, the fragrant delicacies on the table, like attar, delivered as if by *the gift of screws* (with apologies to homebody Emily Dickinson). The term *servante* (sing. fem.) was used to designate a piece of furniture whose purpose was to replace an "absent domestic."[13] This absence was not a potentially socially stigmatizing mark of deficiency in matters of household management but rather an ingenious means of affording comfort and privacy. Sideboards and *guéridons* allowed diners to serve themselves without bothersome "recourse to domestics."[14] The need for these ancillaries, announced or otherwise, was a form of dependency, which is the near opposite of ease. In any case, they presented an undesirable audience for otherwise unguarded behavior and discourse. While they could be easily and indeed conspicuously overlooked, servants were nonetheless a source of inhibition, a controlling proscription of individual freedom. They were the potential source of self-consciousness and embarrassment, another form of want. To be truly comfortable was not the result of being served but of properly moderating the degree of self-control.

The *table volante* was merely the most elaborate of the servants by which all effort was made to disappear; it was the apparatus's mechanical self-removal—the *gift of screws*—that made it magical. We will return below to the matter of the signals that set this effect in motion, and whether the signal itself, conveyed by voice or gesture or even electromechanical conduits, was the embodiment of the ever-uneasy state between comfort and control. In any case, to be socially legible and meaningful as a facet of decorum, the signal must be considered alongside all those transformations of human behavior, like table manners, that reveal in their infinitesimal precision a world of refinement known to hosts and guests, ignorance of which is an innocent form of self-treachery (Figure 4.2).[15]

A final preliminary question is whether Robert-Houdin's theater at the Palais Royale provided a method of decoding the magical mechanisms set to work (and at play?) at the Priory, perhaps in the very manner editorially omitted by the *Mecure de France* due to a lack of space. Fittingly enough, the stage, as the self-designated *mécanicien* described it, "represented a sort of small Louis XV salon, in white and gold." But however stylish the set's appearance, each item had its place and purpose, with nothing sacrificed to luxury. Robert-Houdin insists it was

Figure 4.2. Louis XV–style salon that served as the stage set of the Théatre des Soirées Fantastiques. Jean-Eugène Robert-Houdin, *Magie et physique amusante* (Paris: Calmann Lévy, 1885).

"furnished solely with what was absolutely necessary for the purposes of my performance."[16] There was a center table, two consoles, two small *guéridons,* and a shelf running across the back of the stage, on which Robert-Houdin placed articles "intended for use." The conjurer's stage is designed not merely to "please the eye of the spectator," Robert-Houdin observed, but also to "facilitate the execution of many of his marvels." The tables, in particular, had an important function, "for by their assistance is generally effected the appearance or disappearance of articles too bulky to be concealed in the hands or the pockets of the performer."[17] These servants are undetected because unscrutinized. Attention is placed elsewhere, on the performer, whose own labors are spent in misdirection and producing a hiatus between perceived cause and effect. In any case, furniture, like the seats in the narrow theater, is meant for comfort, so why call it into question?

But the show was not confined to the stage. Like the undetectable portion of Loriot's portrait treated with a secret fixative to preserve its luminous effect, or the laborers beneath the rose-ornamented parquet, the ancillary or servant spaces that constituted Robert-Houdin's private domain were unseen by the audience. On each side of the stage was a pair of folding doors that opened to allow the passage of his "mechanical pieces," the objects of prestige (celebrated automata) upon which attention was focused, as opposed to the homely seeming pieces that furnished the stage.[18] The doors on the right of the stage led to a room in which, in the evening before his performance, Robert-Houdin prepared his "tricks"; in the morning it served as his study and workshop.[19] Center stage was a realm of twilight where, enjoying the doubts and uncertainties attending the fragile form of shared expectation that is willful suspension of disbelief, he practiced his craft. It seems fitting, then, to exit the world of the theater by performing our own bit of scholarly prestidigitation, or rather an old-fashioned bit of bibliomancy. Offering an irrefusable invitation to further scrutiny, a 1906 issue of *L'intermédiaire des chercheurs et curieux,* the French edition of *Notes and Queries,* ran consecutive items seeking information on what had become of Loriot's "meubles automatiques" (automated furnishings), that is, the *table volante,* and in seeming consequence the "trick house" of Robert-Houdin, the Priory.[20] Sit back, relax. What follows is one possible response, beginning with usual and some unusual bits of family drama.

FAMILY DRAMA

Robert-Houdin was perhaps nowhere more charmingly artful than in his own memoir; not everyone was amused. Harry Houdini, whose stage name was inspired by his reading of the *Memoirs of Robert-Houdin,* later wrote the acidulous *Unmasking of Robert-Houdin* (1908), in which he declared his father in magic a pretender, "a mechanician who had boldly filched the inventions of the master craftsmen among his predecessors."[21] The historians of automata Alfred Chapuis and Edouard Gélis write of the memoir that its author was more enchanted by lyricism than by truth, or even verisimilitude.[22] Just as illuminating is Paul Metzner's acknowledgment that "an autobiography, like an automaton, should be a transparently deceptive, but still deceptive, copy of life."[23]

In July 1830, before his public life as a conjurer began, Jean-Eugène married Josèphe Cécile Églantine Houdin, a union that took him to Paris, where her father owned a watch-making business. (It also accounts for his double patronymic, Robert-Houdin.[24]) "It was agreed," Robert-Houdin writes, "that we should live together, and that I should help him in his business."[25] His father-in-law even proved receptive to his scheme of setting up a room in their establishment for the display of mechanical toys and sleight-of-hand tricks. Robert-Houdin was finally free to devote his working hours to contriving mechanical amusements.

His ambitions for this "cabinet" evolved into the program for the Soirées Fantastiques. He went so far as to arrange with an architect to find a suitable theater. But before much progress was made, a reversal ruined his father-in-law's business, along with Robert-Houdin's own expectations. This hardship forced Robert-Houdin to find steady work to support his family, which by this time included three young children. His first step was to reduce dramatically his domestic circumstances, renting modest family lodgings consisting of a room, a cabinet, and a rudimentary kitchen. The largest room served as a common sleeping apartment, and the cabinet served as his workshop. "The proximity of our mutual laboratories," Robert-Houdin writes of the apartment's living and working space, "had also this double advantage, that, whenever my housekeeper was absent, I could watch the *pot-au-feu* or stir a ragout without leaving my levers, wheels, and cogs."[26] His mutual designation of the apartment's living and working areas as "laboratories" recalls the origin of the laboratory itself within the social and material economy of the household.[27] The commercial success of his patented design for an alarm clock that not only sounded the appointed hour but also lit a candle necessitated the addition of another workshop and the hiring of several workmen. He rebalanced the organization of the household in favor of machine production.

This balance would soon be further tipped when a large debt came due, forcing Robert-Houdin to seek a financial remedy in his machines. At the time he was working on a writing automaton, for which he received an advance from the curiosity dealer Alphonse Giroux. Robert-Houdin was happy to retire his household debt, though what made him even happier, he wrote, was "the prospect of devoting myself for a long time to the manufacture of an article satisfying my mechanical taste."[28] The construction of the automata on which house and home depended would take him once again from that house and home. Against the "prayers and supplications of his family," he installed himself in a small room in the Paris neighborhood of Belleville. His reduced set of furniture consisted of a bed, a chest of drawers, a table, and a few chairs. The isolation at first pained him, the company of his wife and children having grown a necessity to him. However, the "automaton, and the various combinations that were to animate it, appeared before me like a consoling vision." Robert-Houdin writes of these automata, "I smile upon them like so many children of my own."[29] When the writing automaton performed for the first time, Robert-Houdin posed the question, "Who is the artist who has given you being?" A push of a button set gears in motion, and the machine traced its creator's signature on a piece of paper. The marvelous display of self-inscription brought tears to Robert-Houdin's eyes.

Robert-Houdin's display of emotion signals the possible incorporation of machines into the domestic drama. What was the nature of Robert-Houdin's (self-)sacrifice? His uncensored regard for his mechanical progeny mixed with a lament for what his family had suffered as a result. Their prayers and supplications having gone unanswered, Robert-Houdin's bachelordom was integral to the conception of his machines and was perhaps better suited to nineteenth-century domesticity than his lonely wife could have known. In their study of the normative dimension of family in the nineteenth century, an institution consecrated by so many quasi-religious rituals of experience and memory, Michelle Perrot and Anne Martin-Fugier write, "Eliminating the family and its domestic theater from private life left two polar opposites: the individual and society. The individual, as Stendhal observed, thrived on selfish curiosity, curiosity necessary if he was to explore the complexities of the emerging public society."[30] The domestic circumstances that Robert-Houdin endured—or secretly enjoyed—at Belleville juxtaposed two forms of interiority: the creative imagination of the individual and the comforts of home. The familiarity of domestic routine was unbearable. The opposition between being subject to mechanism and actively controlling it left others (including family) alienated and at risk. Family life was suspended in the balance; its comfort, if not its very continuity, depended on the successful delivery of his marvelous automata.

Yet did this machine have any feeling for its maker? Another way to pose this question is to ask whether Robert-Houdin learned how to feel from his lifelike machines. As Jessica Riskin argues, nineteenth-century automata makers (Robert-Houdin among them) abandoned the aspirations of their Enlightenment predecessors, whose automata "simulated" life.[31] These simulations, evidenced most notably by Jacques de Vaucanson's automaton duck, were not merely faithful reproductions of life but were themselves the sites of experiment on processes ranging from digestion to cognition. While Robert-Houdin dismissed the savants who were taken in by the claims made by the physician Salomon Reiselius, who created the first "artificial man," his own engagement in "the science, or rather art, of making automata" represented a form of self-experimentation. After several failed attempts to sculpt a head for his automaton from a ball of wax, he finally resolved to look into a mirror, "judging from my own face what features produce expression." Robert-Houdin begs the reader to consider his own surprise upon finding that he had "unconsciously produced an exact likeness of myself."[32] The writing machine was not a prosthesis or artificial extension of his body as much as a proxy: a being that could double for him in society, to gauge its response to his own experimental self. The machine's first act of writing—a facsimile of Robert-Houdin's signature—was tantamount to a signed proxy authorizing it to act in place of its maker.

Robert-Houdin set out to educate his machine or, more precisely, to tune its gears. Gestures, especially automated ones, needed to be perfect for deceptive drama (or drama of deception). In readying his machines for the stage, Robert-Houdin taught himself the mechanics of expectation, belief, and credibility. He notes, "I had taken care to render the mechanism of my writer as perfect as possible, and had set great store on making the clockwork noiseless. In doing this I wished to imitate nature, whose complicated instruments act almost imperceptibly."[33] Yet this very perfection diminished the marvel of his machine. Viewers surmised that the mechanism must be simple; it only required a trifle to produce if it worked so effortlessly. While he was busy tuning his machine, Robert-Houdin attended performances of the celebrated "physicist" Louis Comte in his theater at the Galerie de Choiseul as much to study the tricks as to watch and listen to the audience. He came to the conclusion that it is easier to dupe a clever man than an ignorant one. The ordinary man sees conjury as a challenge to his intelligence and will obstinately seek its manner of working. The clever man, on the contrary, simply enjoys the illusion. The more he is deceived the more he is pleased. Thus Robert-Houdin had the idea of making the clockwork less perfect, so that a whirring sound could be heard. Admiration—for the machine and for its maker—increased with the intensity of the noise: "In this I followed the example of certain actors who overdo their parts in order to produce a greater effect. They raise a laugh, but they infringe the rules of art, and are rarely ranked among first-rate artists. Eventually I got over my susceptibility, and my machine was restored to its first condition."[34]

What other model did he have for fashioning his lifelike automata? It was for the stage of the Soirées Fantastiques that he was educating his marvelous machines. This space of illusion prepared him for his autobiographical passage from home to an initiation into the world of magic. On the stage Robert-Houdin could be his true self: a juggler. Evidently his license to perform depended on his passing himself off as another. The Paris police, which closely monitored the city's theaters and especially its street performers, many of them of foreign extraction, authorized Robert-Houdin's "spectacle of curiosities," noting that its impresario was "neither a mountebank, nor a charlatan, but rather a distinguished man, a savant in the mechanical arts, whose principal goal is to make known to the public his curious masterpieces."[35] Robert-Houdin knew otherwise. Even the most esteemed automata makers were mountebanks and charlatans, he writes. And this was a good thing—they were like himself. In words of high praise, he judged Vaucanson to be an "ingenious trickster" who "laughed in his sleeve at the credulity of the public."[36]

While the tricks Robert-Houdin realized at the Priory were "less prestigious" than those performed on the stage, the latter emerged as the scene for a domestic drama of sorts. His son Émile and his daughter Églantine assisted him on stage, performing alongside Robert-Houdin's mysterious automata. The Louis XV–style set of the Soirées Fantastiques was furnished with undraped tables that better demonstrated that there was nothing to hide. Thus the action was framed within known and reassuring bourgeois life. As one observer notes, this fact intervenes likes a liminal warning: all that is going to happen will be conventional and controlled, all that is going to happen is nothing but an amusement, and no shattering reality will emerge (Figure 4.3).[37] Some were not so comforted. Robert-Houdin writes that audience members would address him letters in which they "severely upbraided the unnatural father who sacrifices the health of his poor child to the pleasures of the public."[38] The writer of these letters, he adds, did not suspect the pleasure they gave him: "After amusing the family circle, I kept the letters preciously as proofs of the illusion I had produced."[39] Was the nature of the illusion one of being a "natural" (meaning kind) father? Or of maintaining a family circle when his own desires were eccentric to it? Or was it a masking of his willingness to sacrifice the well-being of his family to the public?

Robert-Houdin "sacredly kept" the playbill for the first presentation of the Soirées Fantastiques, Thursday, July 3, 1845—a program of "Automata, Sleight-of-Hand, and Magic"—in his private study at the Priory, from which spot he controlled the electrical mechanisms that governed the entire household (Figure 4.4).[40] There he both commemorated his life on stage and continued to produce the rich imaginative terrain of *ailleurs* and *autre temps*. One of the defining rituals of the bourgeois home, to heed historical accounts of private life, was "to supervise the arrangements for private occasions and to signal those occasions with

Figure 4.3. The Ethereal Suspension, first performed in 1847, in which Robert-Houdin appeared to levitate his son, "a stout lad of about six years of age." Jean-Eugène Robert-Houdin, *Confidences d'un prestidigitateur par Jean-Eugène Robert-Houdin: Une vie d'artiste*, vol. 2 (Paris: Librairie Nouvelle, 1859).

effusions of sentiment."[41] This task conventionally fell to the mistress of the household. It was she who at regular intervals convened the family around the dining room table, she who was the "administrator of happiness."[42] At the Priory, Robert-Houdin assumed these roles of supervision and administration through the agency of the building's "mysterious organizations." The ex-conjurer could only finally make himself at home by adultering the norms and forms of family life. The adulterer acts by means of deceit or subterfuge; he is clever, and all who gather near risk being taken in. A suspicious form of hospitality ensues. At his home, Robert-Houdin staged the seductions of mechanical comfort.

THE PRIORY

"Eight o'clock has just struck: my wife and children are by my side. I have spent one of those pleasant days which tranquility, work, and study, can alone secure."[43]

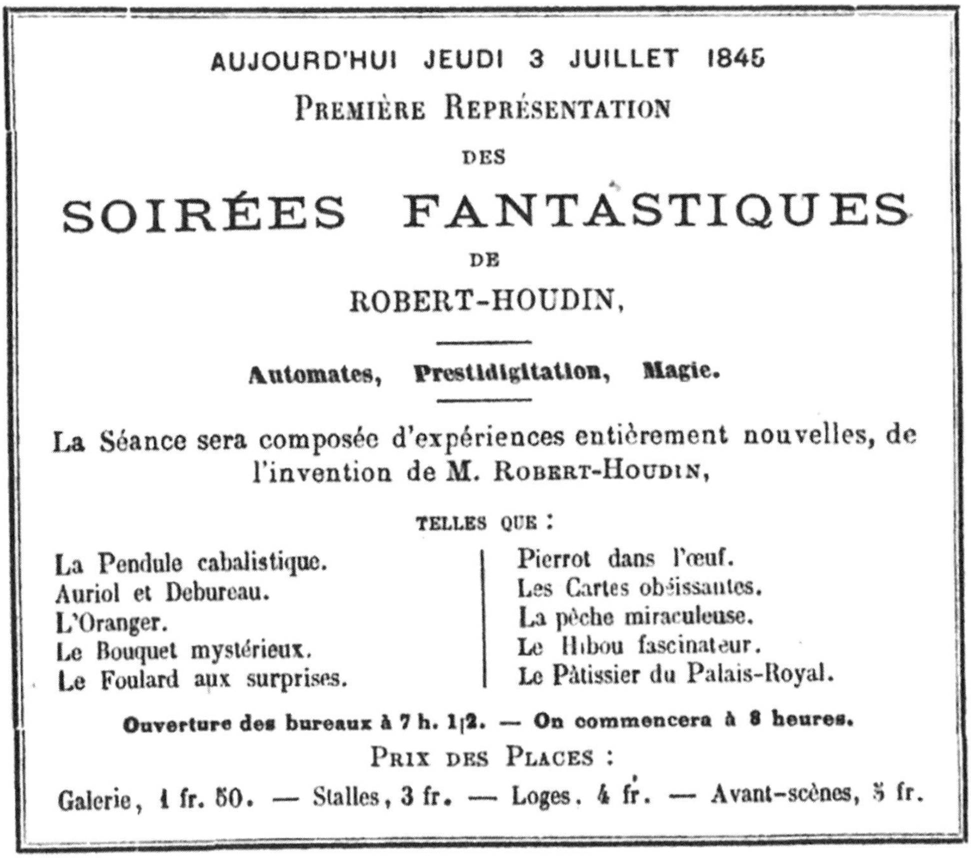

> AUJOURD'HUI JEUDI 3 JUILLET 1845
> Première Représentation
> DES
> # SOIRÉES FANTASTIQUES
> DE
> ROBERT-HOUDIN,
>
> **Automates, Prestidigitation, Magie.**
>
> La Séance sera composée d'expériences entièrement nouvelles, de l'invention de M. Robert-Houdin,
>
> TELLES QUE :
>
> | | |
> |---|---|
> | La Pendule cabalistique. | Pierrot dans l'œuf. |
> | Auriol et Debureau. | Les Cartes obéissantes. |
> | L'Oranger. | La pêche miraculeuse. |
> | Le Bouquet mystérieux. | Le Hibou fascinateur. |
> | Le Foulard aux surprises. | Le Pâtissier du Palais-Royal. |
>
> **Ouverture des bureaux à 7 h. 1|2. — On commencera à 8 heures.**
> Prix des Places :
> Galerie, 1 fr. 50. — Stalles, 3 fr. — Loges, 4 fr. — Avant-scènes, 5 fr.

Figure 4.4. Showbill poster for the first presentation of the Soirées Fantastiques. Jean-Eugène Robert-Houdin, *Confidences d'un Prestidigitateur par Jean-Eugène Robert-Houdin: Une vie d'artiste*, vol. 1 (Paris: Librairie Nouvelle, 1859).

Thus begins Robert-Houdin's memoirs, written from Saint-Gervais, *près* Blois, September 1858. The scene evokes what Hans Robert Jauss, in his reading of Victor Hugo's and Charles Baudelaire's lyrical poetry of 1856, discussed in terms of "la douceur du foyer." Their poetry legitimized and communicated an ideal of interiority; the enclosed space of domestic life represented felicitous images of family, house, city, native land, and the sense of warmth and security. The very words *la douceur du foyer,* Jauss writes, convey in an untranslatable fashion the joy found in repose at the end of the day amid family.[44] It is a scene of contentment, occasionally animated by a visitor bearing tales of elsewhere. Robert-Houdin retired to the Priory to devote himself to scientific research and reflection. Yet the eight o'clock hour irresistibly reminded him of curtain time at the Soirées Fantastiques. On opening night, he recalled, he steeled himself: "Courage! I have my name, my future, my children's fortune at stake: courage!"[45] The ordering of his concerns is telling.

"I am not sorry to abridge these domestic details, which, though personally important to me only possess a very slight interest in my story," Robert-Houdin wrote self-critically of his passing reference to the death of his first wife in 1844, an event that had left him in sole charge of his children.[46] He obviously preferred to discuss his prestigious exploits on stage. Was it discretion or a different motive that kept Robert-Houdin from dwelling on these "domestic details," which in any case may be reverse engineered, as it were, from his design of the Priory? Here was a house run according to his own will and appetites; its function was a display of mastery over a set of circumstances (home life) for the dubious benefit of a captive audience (family and domestics). When eight o'clock sounded, it did so throughout the house, in virtue of an electrically synchronized network, the precise operation of which governed every detail of domestic life. The "domestic details" of the Priory were not unlike the "program" of automata, sleight-of-hand, and magic that Robert-Houdin presented at the Soirées Fantastiques. Rather the Priory's staging of daily life represented an "anti-program," by which Bruno Latour, in an essay on the social gestures brought into being by the design of a particular latchkey, refers to "all devices that seek to annul, destroy, subvert, circumvent a programme of action."[47] The anti-program in question challenged the normative conception of domesticity limned by Robert-Houdin's gesture toward tranquility, work, study, and security.

The Priory's arrangements revealed themselves by turns, inuring its visitors and inhabitants alike to its "hodgepodge" of comfort and control. Like the proscenium that separates theatrical worlds, the portal staged the transition into the Abbey of Tricks. The house was separated from the entrance by a small park crossed by alleys bearing the names of notable personages, among them Vaucanson. This distance, Robert-Houdin offers, explains the necessity for the electrical contrivance he installed at the portal "to play automatically the role of a concierge." Upon arriving at the Priory, one saw:

1. a gate for the entry of carriages,
2. a door on the left for visitors,
3. a letterbox on the right fitted with a balance-beam opening for letters and newspapers.

At eye level at the visitors' door a brass plaque with gold embossed letters bears the name "Robert-Houdin." The sign is extremely useful because there are no neighbors to inform the visitor. Below the plaque, the shape of the small knocker sufficiently indicates its function; but so that there is no doubt, a small gargoyle-like head and two hands of the same nature coming out of the door, as in a pillory, gesture to what is indicated on the plaque below: "Knock." The visitor lifts the hammer according to his fashion, but however feeble the knock, four hundred meters away a bell sounds throughout the house. The ringing, Robert-Houdin hastens to add, is strong enough to be heard but tempered to avoid affronting even the most delicate ear.

The visitor sets the machinery of the Priory in action and alerts its inhabitants to his or her arrival. Though it might not be evident at first, the portal was an automaton of sorts; that is to say, the portal simulated the role played by the *concierge*. As Sharon Marcus has discussed, the person of the *portière* is associated with the power to see into a building. In the case of the Parisian apartment house, the *concierge*—usually a woman—often selected tenants for the landlord and collected rents; within the building, she distributed mail, did housekeeping for some tenants (especially married men), and responded when tenants (who did not have keys to the main door) and visitors rang the bell.[48] When Robert-Houdin lived as a bachelor while constructing his writing automaton, it was the *portière* who brought him his meals; indeed, it was the *portière* who was treated to the first demonstration of the machine. The *portière* "appeared everywhere, in the building's semi-private spaces, in the open space of the street," and her *loge*, located off the building's vestibule or courtyard, was a "space both closed and open at the same time, eminently theatrical . . . propitious for exchanges, for comings and goings."[49] The *loge* is also theatrical space, an extension of the private salon separated from the less elective audience of the *parterre*. With its air of legitimacy, the term was adopted by the impresarios of machines and curiosities who, beginning in the 1780s, staged spectacles in the arcades of the Palais-Royal, where Robert-Houdin's theater had its first home.[50]

The Priory's bell conveyed the sort of information that a *portière* would have gathered. If the bell ceased with the rapping of the knocker, as with ordinary bells, Robert-Hubert explains, then there would be no way to control the opening of the door, and the visitor might approach the Priory unannounced. Instead, the bell did not stop ringing until the lock had operated according to design. To open the lock one simply pushed a button in the vestibule of the house; it functioned like the *cordon* of the *concierge*. When the bell stopped ringing, declared Robert-Houdin, "the servant knows he has succeeded in his task." But this arrangement was still not enough to welcome the visitor properly since he must know that he has been welcomed in. Thus at the same time the lock opened, the name *Robert-Houdin* suddenly disappeared and was replaced with an enamel plate on which the word *Enter!* was written. In response to this unmistakable invitation, the visitor turned an ivory knob and entered by pushing the door, which closed automatically by a spring mechanism. Once the door closed, one could not depart without certain formalities; the door enforced social conventions even as it altered them. On the outside, everything returned to its original state, and the name again replaced the invitation.[51]

Unbeknownst to the visitor, his entry alerted his hosts to his arrival. The host was even alerted to the number and type of visitor (a newcomer, a *habitué*, or an intruder who, unaware of the service entrance, had come through this entrance) by the distinct rhythm of ringing produced by the door as it was being opened and closed. In this respect, the mechanism went "beyond the ordinary laws of mechanics," Robert-Houdin notes, and interpreted the character of the visitor, like a *portière* did. Fearful of arousing the incredulity of his readers, he offers the following explanation of his ability to recognize his visitors at a distance, based on certain infallible acoustic principles. Corresponding to the angle of its swing, the door sent two different rings separated by silent pauses. Thus if one person arrived, he rang, the lock opened, and he entered by pushing the door, which automatically closed behind him. This is what Robert-Houdin calls the "normal opening." The pauses between the rings were all the same interval: *drin . . . drin . . . drin . . . drin* (*drin* is the French onomatopoetic version of "ring"). But, for instance, if several visitors arrived at the portal, the first person opened the door according to the normal manner. According to "the most basic rules of prescribed etiquette," he held the door open for the others. The interval between the first two and the last two rings was proportionate to the number of people who had entered: *drin . . . drin . . . drin . . . drin*. To the well-trained ear the duration of the interval was legible as code; the device thus functioned as a measure of expected social conduct. At the same time, its reliability in the role of *portière* was entirely dependent on guests' conformity to established norms. The portal's design embodied clear expectations about the regularity of human behavior and the likeliness that defined types of people would remain true to type, exhibiting a "particular rhythm."[52]

The timing of the signals also relays whether the visitor is new to the house or has come before. If the visitor knows how the system works, he will not pause to marvel at its action, and once he has rung and the Enter sign appears he will enter the door. The newcomer, by comparison, must take a moment to figure it out; his steps are slower and so, too, the four rings as he tentatively handles the door. The beggar who arrives at the door because he does not know of the service entrance will raise the knocker with hesitation and, instead of seeing someone to open the door, he notes the unusual procedure; he fears something is amiss; he further hesitates to enter. And if he does so the door opens tentatively: *d..r..i..n . . .*

d..r..i..n . . . d..r..i..n . . . d..r..i..n. "It is almost as if we can see this poor devil coming into the house. We go to meet him with certainty. We have never been mistaken." A similar set of procedures was in force at the carriage entrance. The coachmen of the region, Robert-Houdin writes, know "by experience or hearsay" how to open the gates. The coachman gets down from his seat and first enters through the visitors' door. He then finds a key to the gate, the operation of which is indicated in the house with a sign that reads, "The Doors of the Gate Are . . ." followed by "Open" or "Closed." In his eagerness to demonstrate his savoir-faire to his master or his fare, the coachman's is the most rapid of signals: *drin-drin-drin-drin*. This familiarity, tantamount to social credit, earns the esteem of his fare often in the form of a gratuity.[53]

Robert-Houdin's (and his servants') capacity to monitor the comings and goings of the house extended to the operation of the letterbox—the third element of the portal. Its swinging door, too, set off a bell in the house signaling the arrival of newspapers and letters. In fact, the legibility of the code depended on the postman following a prescribed routine: first the newspapers were put in the box and then, following a pause, letters were put in one at a time; thus Robert-Houdin could count the incoming mail from the comfort of his bed. The circuit was reversed for outgoing letters; when a switch was turned in the morning, and when the postman opened the box, instead of sending a signal to the house, the postman heard a bell telling him to come to get the outgoing letters. The operation of the letterbox made more explicit the underlying rationality of the electric concierge: the coding of social, familial, and labor relations. "Family life," Perrot and Martin-Fugier write, "both public and private, was staged according to definite rules. Among the bourgeoisie, fascinated by the court life of old, rules were erected into an elaborate code."[54] The same held for the conduct of domestic labor, upon which the happiness of the home depended.

Traditionally this code was transmitted by manuals that prescribed the moral and social covenant between masters and servants, as Sarah Maza has shown.[55] At the Priory, this code was inscribed in the circuit of so many electric switches and relays. The electric concierge acted as a key, "key" being the device used to tap a signal in telegraphic communication. The "key" may also be understood as a method for decoding the signal that visitors unknowingly transmitted when entering. Unlike Morse code, this code did not form a prearranged interpretive pact between sender and receiver. Only habitués of the household effectuated a "normal opening." Robert-Houdin relates with mild bemusement that the Priory's portal attracted any number of unwelcome visitors who rang the bell in order to see how its mechanism worked. In any case, each signal needed to be responded to in kind. This was especially so for the signals produced from within the house itself, which governed its daily rituals of life and work. The interpretive key to these rituals might in part be found in the pages of nineteenth-century household manuals, the most striking novelty of which, Maza observes, is their marked emphasis on schedules and efficiency; in short they valorized a new managerial regime applied to the home. One manual she cites includes a chapter titled "Service at the Different Hours of the Day"; it concludes a daunting enumeration of tasks with the observation that "a good servant will be better regulated in his habits than the household clock."[56] At the Priory the household clock—the mother-clock, as it was called—further instrumentalized the earlier stated relation between machinery viewed as human and humans managed as machines.

THE MOTHER-CLOCK

Robert-Houdin's mastery of the Priory was nowhere more evident than in the synchronization of all its clocks. The system was first installed to regulate the feeding of his horse. Its groom, he writes, was a thief gifted in the magical art of changing the horse's oats into five-franc pieces. When the groom's "sleight of hand" (*escamotage*) was detected, Robert-Houdin relieved him of his duties and took the matter into his own hands. That is to say, he deployed electricity and mechanics as intelligent auxiliaries. A pendulum clock in his study was connected by electric wire to the stable, situated forty meters from the house. Three times a day, at the clock's signal, a ration of feed was distributed into the horse's stable. Eventually Robert-Houdin installed a burglar alarm for the house itself, which was set to work at midnight, "the thieving hour." The "mother-clock" (*horloge mère*) in Robert-Houdin's private study transmitted the hour to two large dials, one placed on the pediment of the house and the other on the gardener's lodge. These exterior dials indicated the hour to the inhabitants of the neighboring valley and provided the inhabitants of the house "a single and regulating hour."

Thus Robert-Houdin adapted to the home the system of clocks and bells that was at the base of modern regimes of rational management. "Monitors" (both people and machines), time sheets, and clocks with minute dials were all deployed to standardize units of work and pay. In various model factories, "time clocks," devices that at first supervised night watchmen in cities, enforced a new logic of highly divided industrial labor.[57] In his study of modern space-time conceptions, Peter Galison notes that distributed, coordinated precision time spelled each person's access to orderliness, both interior and exterior—to freedom from time anarchy.[58] Freedom from time anarchy, however, entailed (self-)mastery by the clock. At the Priory the mother-clock replaced the mistress of the house, who called the family to the table, where she administered to its happiness; just as crucially it called the domestic staff to order. Ideally the mistress of the house silently and invisibly conducted the harmonious life of the household. "She was to be," Anne Martin-Fugier writes, "like a fairy whose actions one suspects but whom one never sees materially implicated in any given affair." It was as if she waved a "magic wand."[59] In wiring his house, Robert-Houdin made a virtue of the material components of time regulation, and with it, domestic order. Robert-Houdin confides to his readers that the regulator in his study could be manipulated: the hour set ahead or behind depending on when he wanted to take his meals. The hands indicating the hours and minutes were set according to a literal sleight of hand. In his "humble domain," Robert-Houdin was the master of time; he was the deus ex machina of the Priory's domestic drama.

The regulator sounded three different *reveilles* by means of electrical communication. But of necessity, this fact was known only to Robert-Houdin—otherwise his mastery would be compromised. To ensure that the call of the hour was heeded, the bell continued to ring until a button located on the opposite side of the room was depressed. Robert-Houdin conducted life at the Priory from a distance, his will for domestic order hidden behind the face of a clock. Clocks not only set Robert-Houdin's servants to work but the labor of his servants was also unwittingly conscripted in keeping the clocks running. When Robert-Houdin was confronted with the problem of how to reset each day with the weights that drove the machinery that sounded the hour from the small campanile on the Priory's roof, he made use of "lost force" to "automatically carry out this function."[60] Thus he rigged the swinging door in the kitchen on the ground floor with a transmission so that when the servants opened and closed the door as they carried out their duties, they imperceptibly reset the clock. Here was Robert-Houdin's signature sleight of hand: not only did the clock summon the servants to work but it also maximized their labor, or it stole labor from them. Was the fact that this theft went undetected any less remarkable for the minute amount of "lost force" that was ill-gotten? These were the elements of comfort and agreement that Robert-Houdin promised to deliver with "mysterious organization," of which the mother-clock was the chief mechanical embodiment. These were the machines that Robert-Houdin mastered during his elective separation from his family. It must be asked, then, if the comfort and agreement Robert-Houdin conjured for the home was, in fact, comforting and agreeable.

"MYSTERIOUS ORGANIZATIONS"

Let us consider the following two anecdotes: Catherine Fouilloux, who served as a seamstress at the Priory, recounted to Robert-Houdin's biographer the alternately fantastical, comical, or malicious tricks of which she was the "innocent victim." Such was the fate of all credulous souls who came near the magician.[61] Églantine Lemaître Robert-Houdin similarly recalled the theatrical experiments her father conducted in a former dairy on the grounds of the Priory, in which objects—a statue, a bouquet, etcetera—were made to appear and disappear. One time a friend of the family came with her little boy, who was five or six, and Robert-Houdin had the idea of substituting him for one of these objects. The phantom-like apparition of the child produced such an impression that the mother almost fainted.[62] Evidently Robert-Houdin's brand of hospitality—to which family, friends, and domestics alike were subject (wittingly and not)—turned on the equivocal nature of hospitality itself.

Georges Méliès would seem to have caught the trick on film in his *Escamotage d'une dame chez Robert-Houdin* of 1896. The film, the first in which Méliès employed the trick-shot technique of stop-substitution, appears to take place within Robert-Houdin's domestic universe. The scene, rendered in Louis XV style, resembles nothing so much as the stage of the Théâtre Robert-Houdin. Méliès, dressed as a conjurer, is followed onto stage by a woman, played by Jehanne d'Alcy. He places a newspaper on the floor to show that there is no trapdoor and puts a chair on top of it. The conjurer covers the lady in a cloth, waves his hands, removes the cloth, and the lady is gone. Then Méliès waves his hands again and a skeleton materializes in the chair. Astounded by his own deed, he tries to chase the skeleton from the stage. Regaining his composure, the conjurer rushes to cover the skeleton with the cloth, and the lady reappears on the chair.

Who was this lady chez Robert-Houdin? Was she the wife whose death Robert-Houdin considered a "domestic detail"? Was she a macabre embodiment of domestic virtue? Robert-Houdin's home—a hospital for machines—staged a cruel reversal of the expected comforts of home, formerly seen to, if not ultimately governed by, the mistress of the house. Perhaps Méliès's film records, as only film can, the skeletal apparition of the mother-clock through which Robert-Houdin enacted the unaccustomed role of housekeeper. Skeleton clocks, so called because of their pierced parts and minimal chassis, to better reveal the intricacy of their movements, were the signature pieces of nineteenth-century clockmakers. Might not the skeleton that appears chez Robert-Houdin represent the mechanical precisions he brought into the home in the guise of so many disembodied mysterious organizations? His most famous timepiece, in fact, was the "Mysterious Pendulum," a clock that seemed to work in the absence of any mechanism at all.

Seemingly the same principle operated throughout the Priory. "My electric *concierge* leaves nothing to desire," Robert-Houdin writes. "Its service is perfectly precise; it is perfectly dependable; its discretion is unequaled; as for its salary, I doubt it possible to give less to such a perfect employee."[63] Ever discreet and expecting no compensation, Robert-Houdin's electromechanical adjuncts were the vehicle of his secret—as opposed to his private—life. For Robert-Houdin, the production of mechanical beings was the opposite of being reduced to a mechanical mode of existence, a mode at which he chafed first as a copy clerk and later in the routine of domesticity. This was the undetected trapdoor—through which the lady disappears—that served as the template for his Abbey of Traps. Its "mysterious organizations" consisted in nothing more elaborate than Robert-Houdin's skill as an *escamoteur*. This is the term he used for the groom whose petty larceny led him to experiment with rigging the Priory. *Escamoter* can also mean to hide or erase something and, more figuratively, to get out of doing a chore, to slip through the net, or to make time fly. Robert-Houdin's chief evasion was of reality in its most familiar form: domestic life.

While Méliès assumed operation of the Théâtre Robert-Houdin, making it into the stage for his cinematic fantasies, it was Robert-Houdin's grandson, Paul Robert-Houdin, who best recognized the logic of the Priory's mysterious organizations. Mystery may be understood here in its primitive sense as an initiation, a temporary passage, say, from everyday life to the unreal reality of a theatrical performance. An innovator of "sound and light" spectacles, Paul Robert-Houdin traced his own nocturnal art to his grandfather's 1863 experiment illuminating the house with electric lamps. The occasion was his daughter Églantine's first communion, celebrated with the magical fluid of electricity. At the Priory the sacramental elements of communion, community, and communication would be conducted through switches and relays, bells, and other electrically operated signs. He ruled out electric lighting, however, due to its exorbitant cost; he was, after all, a prudent housekeeper.[64] Paul Robert-Houdin drew further inspiration from Fernand Jacopozzi, a "juggler of light," who in 1925 lit the Eiffel Tower, as if with a "magic wand." ("Juggler," of course, is another name for a master of trickery.) Paul Robert-Houdin's own inspiration was to use historic houses as scenes of enchantment; against this backdrop, sound and light effects suggested the presence of "invisible actors." In his crowning success, in the autumn of 1951 he staged a sound and light show at the Château de Chambord, long known as the "magical château" or the "enchanted palace." Christening his spectacle the "Enchanted Evenings" (*Nuits Féeriques*), he held a singular aesthetic goal: "evasion in an unreal milieu which summons emotions, strong and sweet, for which men of today, like their fathers, have the greatest need."[65]

The eight o'clock bell sounds at the Priory. The hour evokes in its master all manner of fond reminiscences. Robert-Houdin yields to them with pleasure: "At times I even mentally transport myself to the stage, in order to prolong them.

There, as before, I ring the bell, the curtain rises, I see my audience again, and, under the charm of this sweet illusion, I delight in telling them the most interesting episodes of my personal life. I tell them how a man learns his real vocation, how the struggle with difficulties of every nature begins, how, in fact—But why should I not convert this fiction into reality?" This was the "reality" of his memoirs, written from the irreal confines of the Priory, *près* Blois. And thus in his memoir Robert-Houdin unburdens himself of the cross he is made to bear, or rather has fashioned for himself. In his retirement he reveals to his reader what he has done, by himself, to his family and the home he has made for them, equipped as it was with mysterious organizations for comfort and agreement. Robert-Houdin thought it only natural, considering his art, that the name Robert the Devil appears in his family tree; but "being the very slave of truth," he writes in the *Memoirs,* he contents himself with stating that his father was a watchmaker.[66] In the mysterious organizations of the Priory, the conjurer has reenchanted domestic life by subjecting it to the electromechanical escapement of the mother-clock and its dependent apparatuses.

NOTES

For a variety of less than mysterious reasons, this essay has had a more than usually prolonged period of gestation. I would like to thank Zeynep Çelik Alexander and John May for their commitment to seeing it into its final state.

1. Jean-Eugène Robert-Houdin, *Confidences et révélations: Comment on devient sorcier* (Paris: Blois, 1868).

2. Program for the opening night of the *Soirées Fantastiques de Robert-Houdin,* July 3, 1845, reprinted in Jean-Eugène Robert-Houdin, *Confidences d'un prestidigitateur par Jean-Eugène Robert-Houdin: Un vie d'artiste,* vol. 1 (Paris: Librairie Nouvelle, 1859), 393. Unless otherwise indicated, citations in the text refer to the U.S. edition of the *Confidences,* published as *Memoirs of Robert-Houdin: Ambassador, Author, and Conjurer,* trans. R. Shelton Mackenzie (Philadelphia: Geo. G. Evans, 1860).

3. Jean-Eugène Robert-Houdin, *Le Prieuré: Organisations mystérieuses pour le confort et l'agrément d'une demeure* (Paris: Michel Levy, 1867), 22.

4. Joan DeJean, *The Age of Comfort: When Paris Discovered Casual and the Modern Home Began* (New York: Bloomsbury, 2010), 1.

5. DeJean, 11.

6. Nicolas Le Camus de Mézières, *The Genius of Architecture; or, The Analogy of That Art with Our Sensations,* trans. David Britt (Santa Monica, Calif.: Getty Center, 1992), 104.

7. Robin Middleton, introduction to Le Camus de Mézières, *The Genius of Architecture,* 45.

8. Le Camus de Mézières, *The Genius of Architecture,* 104.

9. "Tables volantes," *Mercure de France,* July 1769, 208.

10. "Tables volantes," 208; Joseph de La Porte, "Description des tableaux exposés au Sallon [sic] du Louvre," *Mercure de France,* October 1763, 204. See also Katharine Baetjer and Marjorie Shelley, *Pastel Portraits: Images of 18th-Century Europe* (New York: Metropolitan Museum of Art, 2011), 31.

11. "Tables volantes," 210.

12. "Tables volantes," 210.

13. Henry Havard, "servante," in *Dictionnaire de l'ameublement et de la décoration depuis le XIIIe siècle jusqu'à nos jours,* vol. 4 (Paris: Maison Quantin, 1887), 984.

14. Havard, 984.

15. Norbert Eias, *The Civilizing Process: The History of Manners,* trans. Edmund Jephcott (New York: Urizen Books, 1978).

16. Jean-Eugène Robert-Houdin, *Magie et physique amusante* (Paris: Calmann Lévy, 1885), 30.

17. Robert-Houdin, 35.

18. Robert-Houdin, 30.

19. Robert-Houdin, 31.

20. "Meubles automatique" and "Robert-Houdin," *L'intermédiaire des chercheurs et curieux* 53 (June 30, 1906): 953.

21. Harry Houdini, *The Unmasking of Robert Houdin* (New York: Publishers Printing, 1908), 8. Houdini legendarily wrote the exposé after the widow of Robert-Houdin's son Émile denied him an interview in Paris. He subsequently traveled to Blois, where Robert-Houdin's daughter Rosalie also refused to meet him.

22. Alfred Chapuis and Edouard Gélis, *Le monde des automates: Étude historique et technique* (Paris: Chez les auteurs, 1928), 300.

23. Paul Metzner, *Crescendo of the Virtuoso: Spectacle, Skill, and Self-Promotion in Paris during the Age of Revolution* (Berkeley: University of California Press, 1998), 194.

24. Robert-Houdin's father-in-law was engaged in the clock trade, marketing precision astronomical clocks, chronometers, and regulators. For a compelling recent discussion of the Priory and related automated devices in the context of a "clockwork" interpretation of the world, see Jessica Riskin, *The Restless Clock: A History of the Centuries-Long Argument over What Makes Living Things Tick* (Chicago: University of Chicago Press, 2016), 305–7.

25. Robert-Houdin, *Memoirs of Robert-Houdin,* 91.

26. Robert-Houdin, 130.

27. Claire Salomon-Bayet, *L'institution de la science et l'experience du vivant* (Paris: Flammarion, 1978), 378–79.

28. Robert-Houdin, *Memoirs of Robert-Houdin,* 132.

29. Robert-Houdin, 133.

30. Michelle Perrot and Anne Martin-Fugier, "The Actors," in *A History of Private Life,* vol. 4, *From the Fires of Revolution to the Great War,* ed. Michelle Perrot, trans. Arthur Goldhammer (Cambridge, Mass.: Harvard University Press, 1990), 241.

31. Jessica Riskin, "Eighteenth-Century Wetware," *Representations* 83 (Summer 2003): 99.

32. Robert-Houdin, *Memoirs of Robert-Houdin,* 136.

33. Robert-Houdin, 138.

34. Robert-Houdin, 139.

35. Letter from police headquarters, February 27, 1845, cited in Philippe John Van Tiggelen, *Componium: The Mechanical Musical Improvisor* (Louvain-la-Neuve: Institut superieur d'archéologie et d'histoire de l'Art, Collège Erasme, 1987), 216.

36. Robert-Houdin, *Memoirs of Robert-Houdin,* 105.

37. Pierre Jenn, *Georges Méliès cinéaste: Le montage cinématographique chez Georges Méliès* (Paris: Editions Albatros, 1984), 110.

38. Robert-Houdin *Memoirs of Robert-Houdin,* 90.

39. Robert-Houdin, 216.

40. Robert-Houdin, *Confidences d'un prestidigitateur,* 1:393.

41. Michelle Perrot and Anne Martin-Fugier, "Bourgeois Rituals," in *A History of Private Life,* vol. 4, *From the Fires of Revolution to the Great War,* ed. Michelle Perrot, trans. Arthur Goldhammer (Cambridge, Mass.: Harvard University Press, 1994), 261.

42. Perrot and Martin-Fugier, 263.

43. Robert-Houdin, *Memoirs of Robert-Houdin,* 1.

44. Hans Robert Jauss, *Aesthetic Experience and Literary Hermeutics,* trans. Michael Shaw (Minneapolis: University of Minnesota Press, 1982), 263.

45. Robert-Houdin, *Memoirs of Robert-Houdin,* 167.

46. Robert-Houdin, 156.

47. Bruno Latour, "The Berlin Key or How to Do Words with Things," in *Matter, Materiality and Modern Culture,* ed. P. M. Graves-Brown (London: Routledge, 2000), 18.

48. Sharon Marcus, *Apartment Stories: City and Home in Nineteenth-Century Paris and London* (Berkeley: University of California Press, 1999), 42.

49. Marcus, 42.

50. Barbara Maria Stafford, *Artful Science* (Cambridge, Mass.: MIT Press, 1994), 184.

51. Robert-Houdin, *Le Prieuré,* 12.

52. Robert-Houdin, 13.

53. Robert-Houdin, 16.

54. Perrot and Martin-Fugier, "The Actors," 134.

55. Sarah Maza, *Servants and Masters in Eighteenth-Century France: The Uses of Loyalty* (Princeton, N.J.: Princeton University Press, 1983), 322.

56. Maza, 322.

57. Gerhard Dohrn-Van Rossum, *History of the Hour,* trans. Thomas Dunlap (Chicago: University of Chicago Press, 1996), 319.

58. Peter Galison, *Einstein's Clocks, Poincaré's Maps: Empires of Time* (New York: W. W. Norton, 2003), 227.

59. Anne Martin-Fugier, *La bourgeoise: Femme au temps de Paul Bourget* (Paris: Grasset, 1983), 187.

60. Robert-Houdin, *Le Prieuré,* 27.

61. Jean Chavigny, *Le roman d'un artiste: Robert-Houdin, rénovateur de la magie blanche* (Blois: Imprimerie Lhermitte, 1946), 211.

62. Églantine Lemaître Robert-Houdin, "Notes from a Lecture," in *The Magic of Robert-Houdin: An Artist's Life,* vol. 2, by Christian Fechner, trans. Stacey Dagron (Paris: Editions F. C. F., 2002), 401.

63. Robert-Houdin, *Le Prieuré,* 22.

64. Sylvain Lefavrais and Andé Keime Robert-Houdin, "Robert-Houdin: La magie de l'ampoule," *Cahiers de médiologie* 2, no. 10 (2000): 85.

65. Paul Robert-Houdin, *La féerie nocturne des châteaux de la Loire* (Paris: Hachette, 1954), 23.

66. Robert-Houdin, *Memoirs of Robert-Houdin,* 3.

CHAPTER 5

SPECIFYING

The Generality of Clerical Labor

MICHAEL OSMAN

In industrial society, the distinction between immaterial products of the mind and material products of the hand—between art and craft—underlies a hierarchy that has come to organize the modern labor force. In this context, the architect's work could be considered creative or artistic as long as it can be clearly differentiated from the craftsman's labor. This distinction did not always exist, and the role of the architect was not always so certain. Written specifications—instructions written by the architect to the various tradesmen—served as an instrument for formalizing that difference as well as asserting the designer's intellectual product as an organizational guide for the crafts.

Specifications were thus essential in constituting an architectural profession, particularly in the United States around the middle of the nineteenth century, a moment of the nation's greatest industrial expansion. As an instrument of the architect's practice, the specification reinforced an identification of his work as creative and his workplace as a site for clerical as well as intellectual production. In addition, the document helped integrate and formalize processes of construction in an economy that would soon be based on a wide array of machine-made products to be selected by the architect. Once new professional institutions established specifications as the legal basis for any contract, they inherited the force of law and situated the architect in a managerial role over both machine and human labor. The construction of any architectural project could thereby be viewed as the designers' intellectual effort translated into a physical product.

Recently, as many tools of architectural design have become democratized through more widely available digital software, professional organizations and their paperwork, including specifications, have begun to appear less central to securing architects' collective identity as creative. In response to this trend, many have hypothesized that securing cultural power in the future will require a shift in one's engagement toward what has become known as "mass customization." Mario Carpo has described this process as "an essential trait of the new digital environment: mass production and customization can now coexist."[1] Rather than accept the industrial hierarchy of the mind leading the hand, architects and critics convinced of this future argue that digital design will relocate creativity in the collapse of conceptualization into production. The product that results from this new configuration, it is imagined, will be formed through the communication between designers' tools and those of fabricators without the need for such mediating devices as specifications. Advocates for this trend have also argued that as these two formerly separated identities merge into one, professional organizations will be outmoded as they come to serve a bygone social role.

One of the central polemics of this movement is a critique of architectural modernism's professed devotion to standards, that is, the conventions that bind various industries together in the processes of mass production. According to the "file-to-factory" model, the mediating role of standards to mass production will be bypassed by the direct translation of a designer's concept—packaged as a bundle of data—into a so-called nonstandard product. As a central spokesman of this movement, Carpo contrasts the age of identical reproduction that sought to maximize the efficiency of production through standards to a digital future that overcomes standards through the equally efficient production of infinitely differentiated, customized creations.

If the distinctions between art and craft, concept and product, custom and standard are quickly dissolving into digital ether, then it is important to consider their history as they came into being, especially if they established the very preconditions for this potentially massive technical revolution. Because the architectural specification was central to forming the distinctions between the architect's concept and its production in the first place, the history of this instrument should reveal the underlying logic of modern practice before its complete digitalization. It follows, also, that such a history can help test the hypothesis that the purpose of professional organizations will soon be eclipsed as the period of standardized mass production comes to its predicted end.

In the United States, some of the first specifications were written by architects who designed wood-framed buildings around the middle of the nineteenth century. By focusing on this case, my purpose is to identify the function of specifications for a particular form of construction, most common in America, and one that came to exemplify for modernists a salient instance of standardized building at the dawn of its application for mass production. How did various forms of knowledge come to be divided through documents developed for producing wooden buildings? Did standards help establish that division, or were they products of other forces? And why exactly were standards useful in developing architectural specifications? Under what conditions could a distinction between customized and standardized products come into being and, finally, how could that distinction ever cease to exist?

In the first decades of the twentieth century, as workers employed in the construction trades around the world adopted methods from large-scale industry, European architects pointed to the American balloon frame as a technique that had already successfully translated standards into a construction system for nearly a century.[2] According to the German architect Konrad Wachsmann, it was the simplicity of the frame's parts and assembly that had laid the basis for converting houses into industrially produced commodities. Mass-produced materials such as studs, hardware, and paint were central to his understanding of the way labor processes were organized and made more efficient. In *Holzhausbau*, published in 1930, he wrote:

> The American typically buys from a catalogue in which a fixed price is stated—just as for an automobile or any other industrial product.... The building materials are delivered to the construction site carefully packed, sorted, and numbered. All necessary tools, nails, paint, etc., are also provided. Using such exactly-machined materials anyone can, without assistance, assemble and construct his own house.[3]

Wachsmann's reference is to the so-called ready-cut houses, delivered by Sears, Roebuck and Company beginning in 1908. He identified ballooning as this construction system's origin (Figure 5.1). For him, the process of rationalizing the balloon frame through the American building industry served as a precedent for the factory-built wooden houses that he hoped to produce in Germany. By the time Wachsmann published his book, he had already left his job as the chief architect for the industrial house company Christoph & Unmack, established in 1887 in Niesky. While there, he had sought to reorient that firm's production from delivering finished buildings to fabricating a modular system that could be configured according to the client's desires. He thus viewed the American model as a successful example of applying standards to broaden the audience of potential buyers. Albert Einstein's summer house in Caputh, designed by Wachsmann in 1929 for Christoph & Unmack, was one instance of his modular system put into action (Figure 5.2).[4] Later experiments with the so-called Packaged House System, which he developed with Walter Gropius after their move to the United States, pushed house construction into emerging methods of automation. These

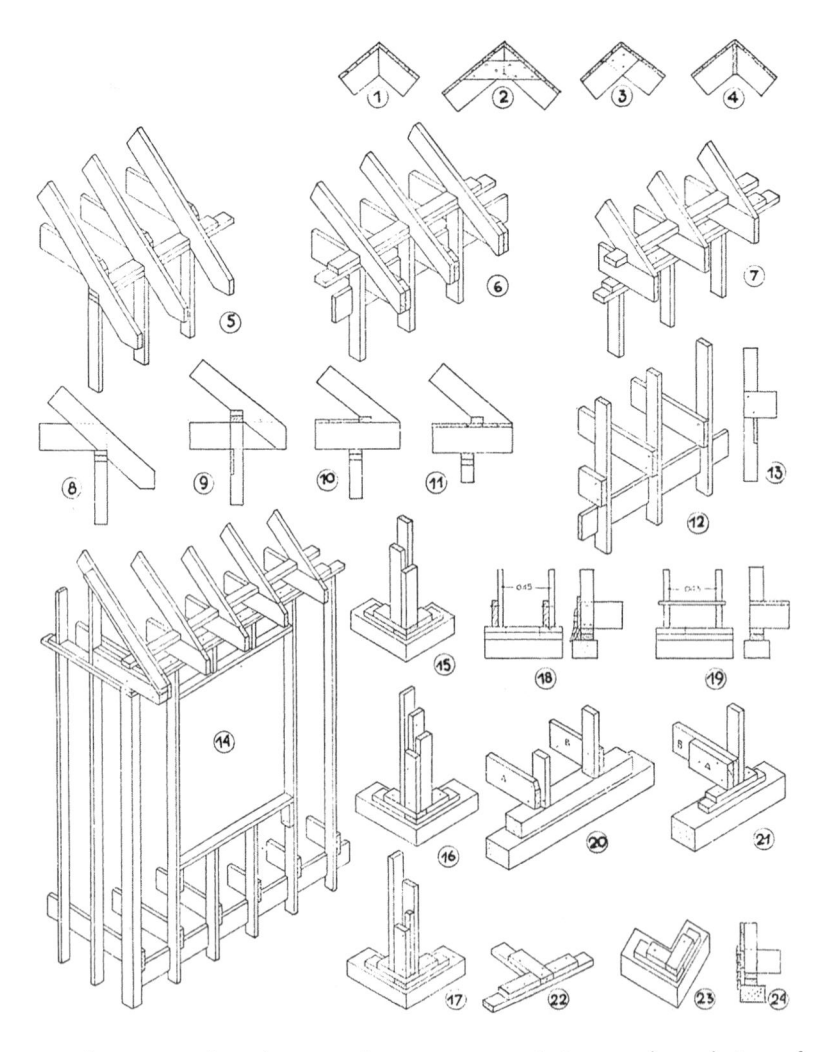

Figure 5.1. These twenty-four drawings illustrate some variations on the techniques for assembling what Wachsmann called "the wood-frame system," 1930. Konrad Wachsmann, *Building the Wooden House,* trans. Peter Reuss (Basel: Birkhäuser Architecture, 1995), 19. Reprinted with permission.

houses signal the apotheosis of the modernist devotion to standards, one with a nearly absurd belief in the capacity of an architect to seamlessly integrate industrial processes into practice.[5]

The architectural historian Sigfried Giedion shared Wachsmann's view that ballooning represented an early instance of construction's translation into an industrial system. Nineteenth-century innovations in the American industries of tool making, automated nail cutting, and lumber milling were central to Giedion's valorization of American ingenuity and were all critical to modern wood-building

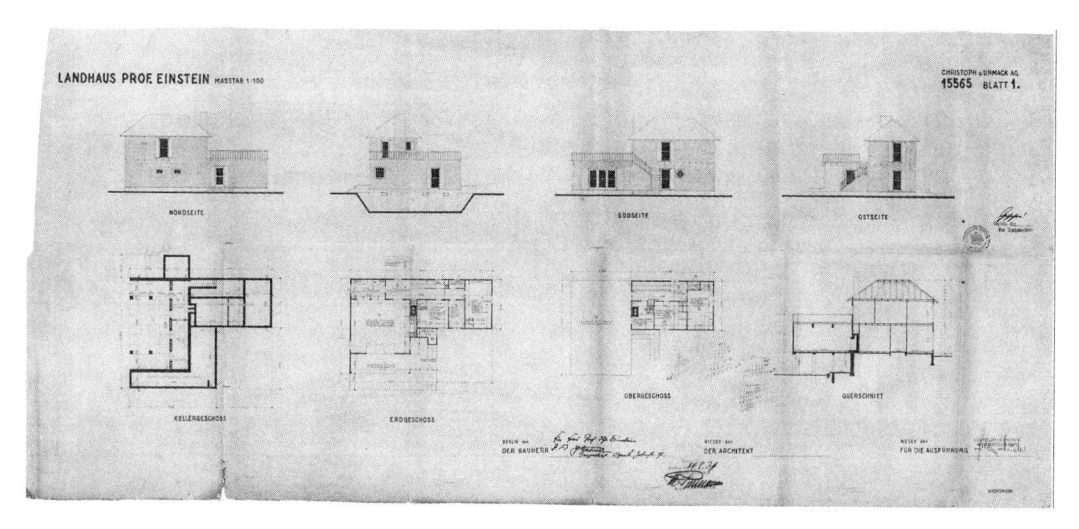

Figure 5.2. Konrad Wachsmann, four elevations, three plans, and a section of Landhaus Prof. Einstein built in Caputh by Christoph & Unmack AG, 1929. Schwielowsee Municipal Archive.

techniques. To his mind, the general emphasis on machinery opened the new nation to more rapid industrialization than its European counterparts by avoiding the lag brought about by the traditional crafts found in those countries. Without the organized resistance of artisans to technological change, by his logic, industrialists could more easily set labor on a scientific basis and standardize practices that would be otherwise embodied in habitual techniques of skilled craftsmen. The seemingly inevitable tendency of large-scale industrial production toward deskilling laborers was, by Giedion's account, enabled by the agreement of factory owners to work through standards.[6] Thus, both Giedion and Wachsmann used the balloon frame as an example of the incipient standardization of construction to clarify and refine modern architecture by foregrounding its attunement to industry. From today's perspective, these ideas appear to have laid the basis for that essential motive of modernism.

But over the span of nearly one hundred years, from the mid-nineteenth to the mid-twentieth century, the structural wooden frame—ballooning included—was never standard. Evidence of its instability is immediately visible in the diagrams drawn by Wachsmann and in the three variations of the wood frame included by Charles George Ramsey and Harold Reeve Sleeper in their *Architectural Graphic Standards,* published in 1932. The illustrations were originally distributed by the National Lumber Manufacturers Association in an effort to promote industry standards, beginning around 1920. The drawings were standardized in their graphic representation, but each frame varied from the others in its details.

Based on the list of distinguishing parts and their assembly, the diagrams were titled "balloon," "braced," or "western" (Figure 5.3).[7] The long history of wood frames is a litany of regional differences in the methods of construction as well as elemental parts. Ted Cavanagh, a historian of wood construction, has shown a general trend toward the technical convergence of the frame from its numerous traditional craft techniques, based in the builders' European origins.[8] Still, differences in this resulting type remain necessary as builders respond to ongoing shifts in industrial methods for producing lumber parts and nails, the means of their delivery, and updates to their tools for assembly.[9]

Due to the widely accepted modernist emphasis on the industrial standardization of the balloon frame, little attention has been placed on the way the frame served to mediate architects' knowledge of construction and that which remained with builders. The frame did not come into existence with its own internal standards in materials or in their assembly. Further, professional organizations were not preconfigured with the power to develop contractual relationships around a standardized frame. Rather, it is the history of specifications in architectural practice that reveals how the frame could be defined as both a conceptual and material object through the mediation offered by this form of paperwork. Architectural

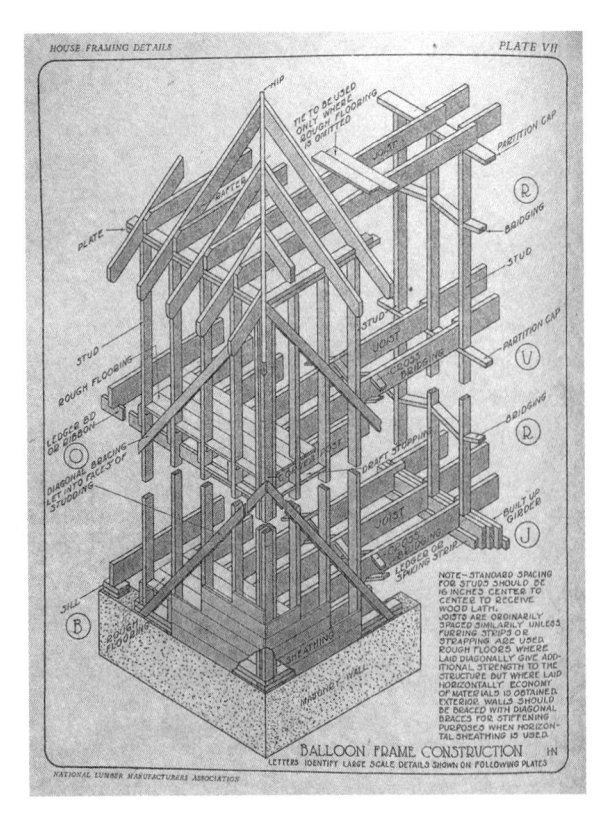

Figure 5.3. Drawings of (a) balloon-frame construction, (b) braced-frame construction, (c) and western-frame construction. National Lumber Manufacturers Association, *House Framing Details* (Washington, D.C.: National Lumber Manufacturers Association, 1929).

b

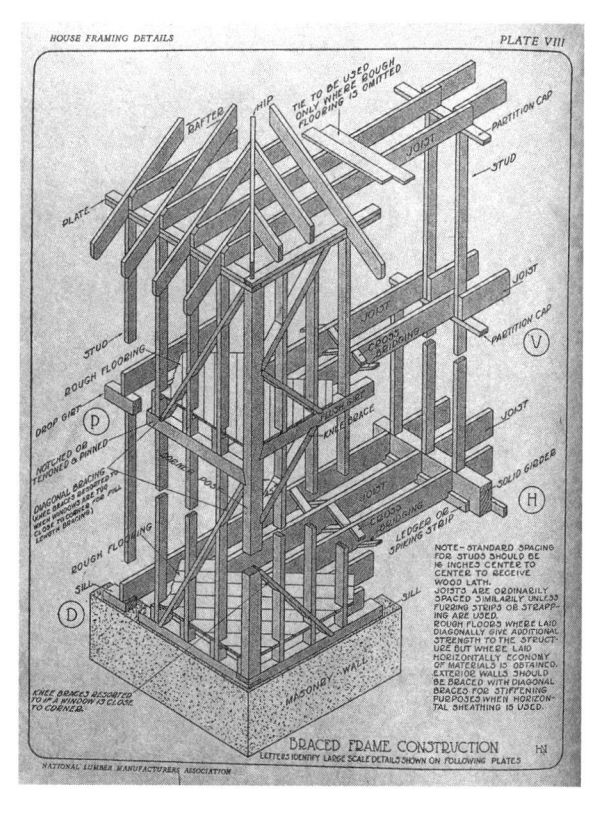

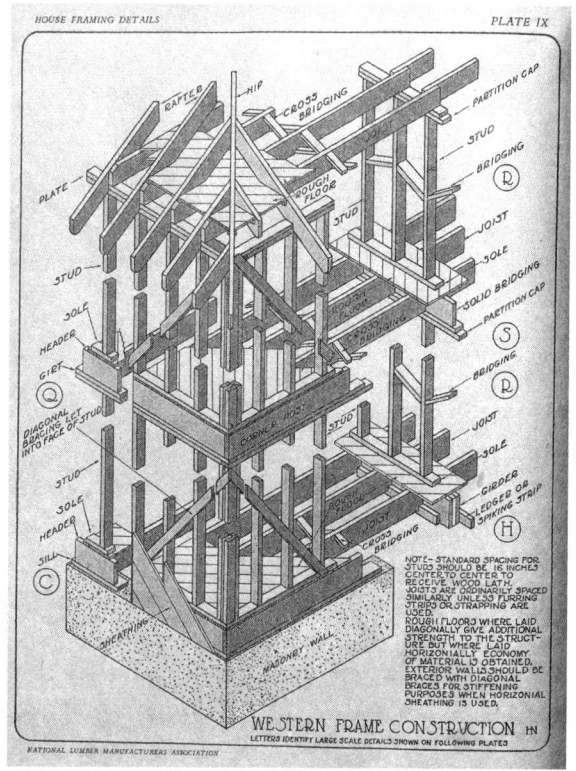

c

professionals, in other words, incorporated specifications in order to more clearly identify their role as intellectual producers in the context of that rapidly industrializing nation.

As we shall see, with the architectural specification, the balloon-frame technique could be codified. The professional status of architects relied on this codification to maintain an association of their work with producing theoretical knowledge. Writers who produced instructions for making balloon-framed buildings in pattern books—which many builders would have probably ignored—sought to establish a distance between the labor of design and that of construction. Further, control over certain aspects of the frame's construction were left beyond the purview of architects, not included in their written instructions, and thus remained unregulated by legal contracts. This allowed for incremental changes to be made to the frame, retaining only general descriptions, and therefore omitting those slight differences from the history of architectural design. I use the term *general* rather than the modernist preference for *standard* to emphasize specifications' capacity to allow for changes in techniques of industrial production or regional differences in executing a design. For my purposes, *generality*—much like genus when compared to species—helps explain the similarities in many buildings built over one hundred years while still allowing for their infinite number of disparities. As specifications allowed architectural production to be identified with theoretical knowledge, generalizing a craft technique also gave force to the association of an architect's labor with creativity. Creativity, in other words, was secured through clerical work. The document's effect on the frame is therefore not immediately evident from detailed surveys of houses, barns, and churches built in the United States during this time. Rather, to understand its role in the process of building construction, we must turn to the historical changes in the status of that paperwork as it secured a social relation between art and craft in the middle of the nineteenth century.

Notably, specifications were developed long before nineteenth-century American architects and builders worked on the design and construction of wooden frames. As Tilo Amhoff and Katie Lloyd Thomas have shown, written instructions were used to direct the building trades as early as the middle of the eighteenth century in England, and similar documents existed elsewhere even earlier.[10] In his work on the reproduction of text and images in architectural theory, Mario Carpo reminds us that before plans for buildings were transmitted in images, they were often reproduced through a process of oral transmission, which can be interpreted as another form of architects' instructions.[11] But once techniques for building construction became widely disseminated through the publication of nineteenth-century instructional manuals, specifications took on two important functions for practicing architects: they identified the source of an architectural design with an expert author and they invested that author with the power to control the construction process from a distance. The relatively late formation of the architectural profession in the United States, in the 1850s, and the slow adoption of documents for practice allowed the specification to be manipulated by a group of emerging American architects as an interface—a mode of communication but also a boundary—between the intellectual labor of designing buildings and the physical demands of managing materials and labor on an industrializing construction site.[12]

Outside their role in building construction, according to a law guiding English patents formulated in 1718, specifications would be required as supplements to drawings. James Puckle's design for a machine gun was an early example of an invention that required "an instrument in writing" to indicate its practical method of operation (Figure 5.4). This precedent formed a particular legal relation between word and image that carried over into patent law in the United States.[13] Beginning in the 1790s, American tool builders wrote specifications for their patents to describe machines that mass-produced everything from cotton thread to nails to lumber.[14] As Giedion keenly observed, collections of these patents made it possible to understand broad historical shifts in the knowledge that shaped early American industries. For example, it is possible to see a shift around the 1820s, as lumber-milling and nail-cutting machines were powered by steam rather than human or natural sources of power. In such cases, specifications helped explain details that were not immediately evident in the drawing, they bound an invention to its inventor, and situated it as an improvement to other related patents, thereby explaining its value as a product of creative labor.

Writing specifications for architecture, like those for patents written by an inventor, ensured the final physical object would conform to the design, beyond its description in the drawings. It thereby further confirmed the authorship of the architect—as a creator of ideas—and forced the contractor to accept the terms of his design before beginning the process of constructing a building. On the other hand, specifications for buildings were different from patents because they also formalized the sequence for the object's assembly and often included a bill of materials with cost estimates for industrially produced parts. Thus, beyond connecting the drawing to the architect-as-author, the specification also gave the client and the builder a basis from which to predict and negotiate the cost of construction.

The difficulty of controlling any aspect of construction around the middle of the nineteenth century becomes evident with a quick glance at the various methods used by manufacturers of building materials to market their products. Nails,

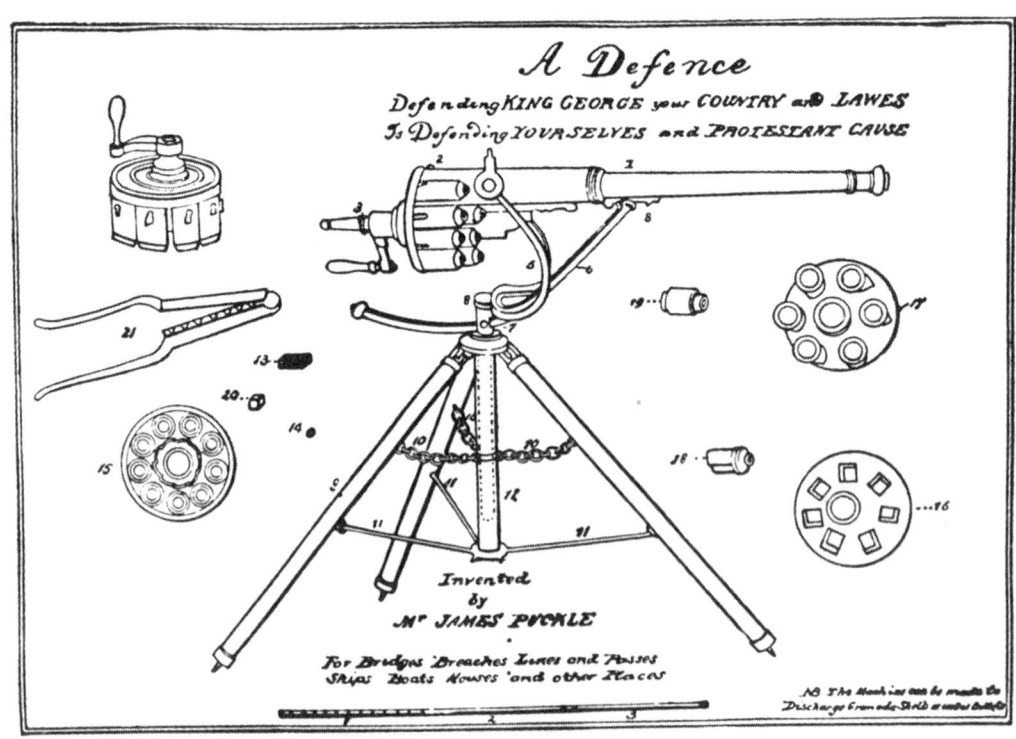

Figure 5.4. James Puckle, Drawing and Specifications for a Portable Gun, 1718. Patent no. 418 (1718); European Patent Office, GB171800418.

for example, were priced by their pennyweight, a unit that was based on varying increments of length and, once the industry moved from metal plate to wire, a set of corresponding gauges. These changes made predicting the cost of nails, often the most expensive material involved in house construction, difficult to calculate and often incorrect.[15] Lumber merchants used even more complex techniques to calculate prices for their product from the sizes of logs based on equations called "log rules," related to the diameter and length of a log. Tabulations based on these equations were collected in "Ready Reckoners," books used by merchants to estimate the price of the parts purchased from a mill and sold to a contractor for a given job, whether a house or a boat.[16] These sources of data, with their variations in units and inevitable errors in calculation, were the only link between industrial producers, merchants, and builders. To maintain a profitable business, a builder would need to accommodate the variability in prices according to a geographic region or resulting from different methods for milling wood or cutting nails.

Builders who sought to expand their business were thus not only invested in methods for assembling wood parts with nails, they must have also sought to know about the availability of these elements in different regions and relied on various printed sources to predict their prices. Based on the massive proliferation of balloon-frame buildings in the 1850s, it is clear that the published data helped builders construct a similar frame in different regions of the country by purchasing similar parts at similar costs, assembled similarly.

From this limited survey of early nineteenth-century practices related to wood construction, it is clear that the relations between producers, merchants, and builders depended heavily upon regional associations. If Wachsmann imagined a background for producing the balloon frame as an already integrated system of mass production, this was still far from the case at the end of the nineteenth century and was never fully realized in the twentieth century, even by such large corporations as Sears & Roebuck. Rather, relationships between builders and industry required establishing conventions to organize the building trades as well as the emerging interest of professional architects to formalize their forms of organization. With specifications, relationships between an architect's design, the activities of the builder, and his sources for materials could appear integrated, at least from a distance—that is, we could say that they were made general. These documents do not immediately give evidence of industrial integration but more clearly mark a fundamental transformation in the American architect's self-description. That is, in them we see the development of methods for managing the value of architectural design as separate from the construction business.

Before specifications became an official instrument in American architectural practice, contracts and drawings were the only methods for directing the builder's work. For example, a contract written in 1799 between the architect Benjamin Henry Latrobe and the builder responsible for executing the marble work of the Bank of Pennsylvania stipulated that all drawings should be followed strictly (Figure 5.5). If a failure resulted from a discrepancy from the physical execution of the architect's drawings, fault in the construction would be assigned to the builder; otherwise the liability would land on the architect.[17] But there was no legally binding way to stipulate the process of construction beyond the contract and the drawings; these decisions were left entirely to the builder. Without specifying the process of assembly or the materials for construction, the written contract and the legal power it carried always relied on the drawings. This situation often allowed builders to interpret the architect's drawings against the designer's intentions.

Based on his experience in England, Latrobe expressed his frustration with the lack of legal recourse for an architect working in the United States.[18] In the case

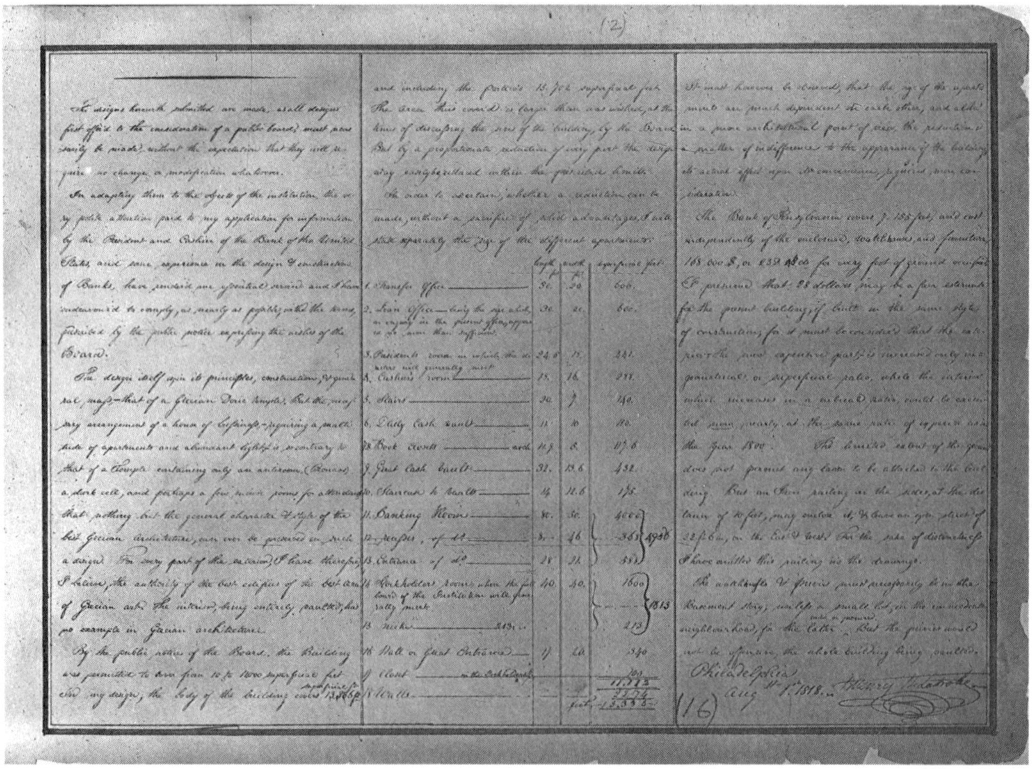

Figure 5.5. Benjamin Henry Latrobe, contract for the Bank of Pennsylvania without specifications, 1818. Library of Congress, Benjamin Henry Latrobe Papers, ADE—UNIT 2546, no. 15 (D size) [P&P].

of wood-framed buildings, according to Mary Woods, this compromised power was more extreme because the early nineteenth-century architects were rarely involved in such projects. Particularly when houses were to be built from wood, they were usually produced by master builders who were called "mechanics."[19] There remain some records from the early nineteenth century that reveal the means these tradesmen employed. By the 1830s, as Dell Upton has shown in some detail, builders began collecting images and texts in pattern books with the aim of publicizing their skills in realizing a range of designs. These books also served to conventionalize knowledge of various construction techniques, but they did not include ballooning.[20] Those who published pattern books eventually included specifications. From a selection of these books, written by both builders and architects, it is possible to illustrate changes in the form of that document and the various authors' hopes for its anticipated effect.[21]

Asher Benjamin's popular book *The Architect; or, The Practical House Carpenter,* issued seventeen times between 1830 and 1857, described the five classical orders to instruct carpenters on the proportions of their details (Figure 5.6). The title's lack of differentiation between architect and carpenter makes explicit the still-unresolved professional status of architects. There were no specifications included in the book, another sign that the difference between theoretical and practical knowledge had not yet been divided between a building's design and its construction. The book included some rudimentary instruction in geometry to help craftsmen lay out trusses, but among these basic lessons Benjamin made no reference to construction systems that used mass-produced parts.[22] While apocryphal stories trace the balloon frame's origins to the period in which Benjamin's book was first published, its absence among those pages indicates that either he was unaware of the technique or that he did not consider it relevant to an audience of builders primarily interested in the proportions of classical ornaments.[23]

One early American pattern book to include specifications was Richard Upjohn's *Rural Architecture,* published in 1852, five years before he cofounded the professional organization known as the American Institute of Architects (AIA).[24] The book illustrated four of his designs: a wooden church, a chapel, a schoolhouse, and a parsonage. None were given a specific location beyond their rural surroundings, depicted in the perspective drawings. The stated purpose for his book was to provide designs for "cheap but still substantial buildings" for the nation's westward expansion. These designs were devised to broaden the influence of an already successful New York–based practice. The book thus indicates a significant investment in identifying the architect's professional status: it staged a relationship between design, its graphic representation, and written specifications, making it

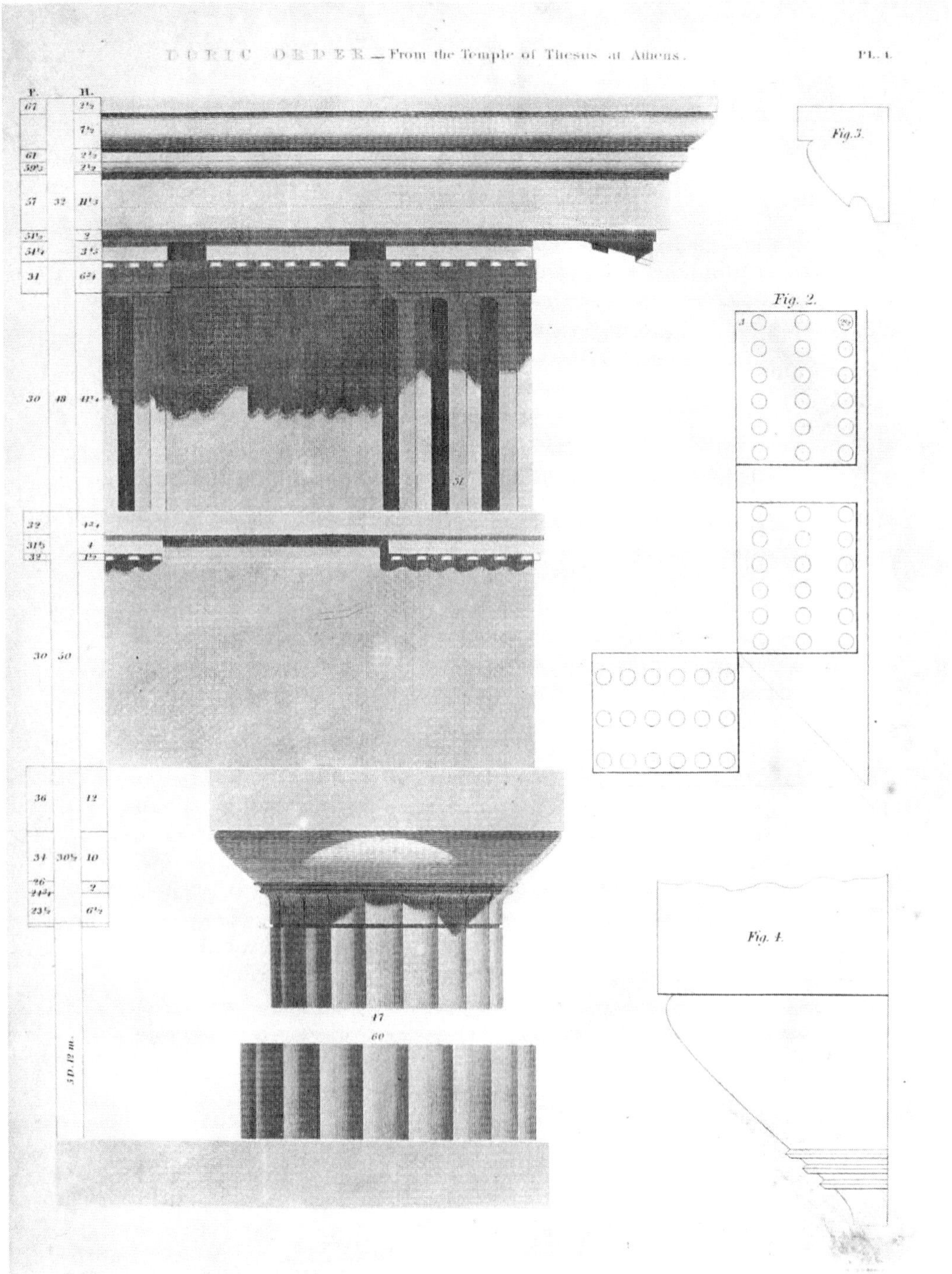

Figure 5.6. Doric order from the Temple of Thesus at Athens. Asher Benjamin, *The Architect; or, The Practical House Carpenter* (1830; repr., Boston: Sanborn, Carter, Bazin, 1847).

possible to imagine a system for transmitting one's design over a distance while still maintaining some control over the outcome.[25]

Upjohn's specifications listed, in the most general terms, the materials and labor required to execute each of his designs. As an example of his approach to generality, the kind of timber to be used for framing for his designs would, in his words, "be determined by the resources of the section of the country in which the building is to be erected. Generally, pine is to be preferred, if it can be had at as low prices as other timber."[26] This kind of openness would become increasingly common as specifications were written by architects who directed builders from across the continent in order to allow substitutions of materials based on their availability. Furthermore, drawings of wood framing were included only where Upjohn felt that they were necessary to execute the intended design, such as in the tower and spire of the church or the gables of the chapel (Figure 5.7). No such drawings were made of the parsonage; decisions regarding its framing would be left to the builder, as long as he followed the instructions written in the specifications. Thus, unlike Asher Benjamin's book, Upjohn's publication was not

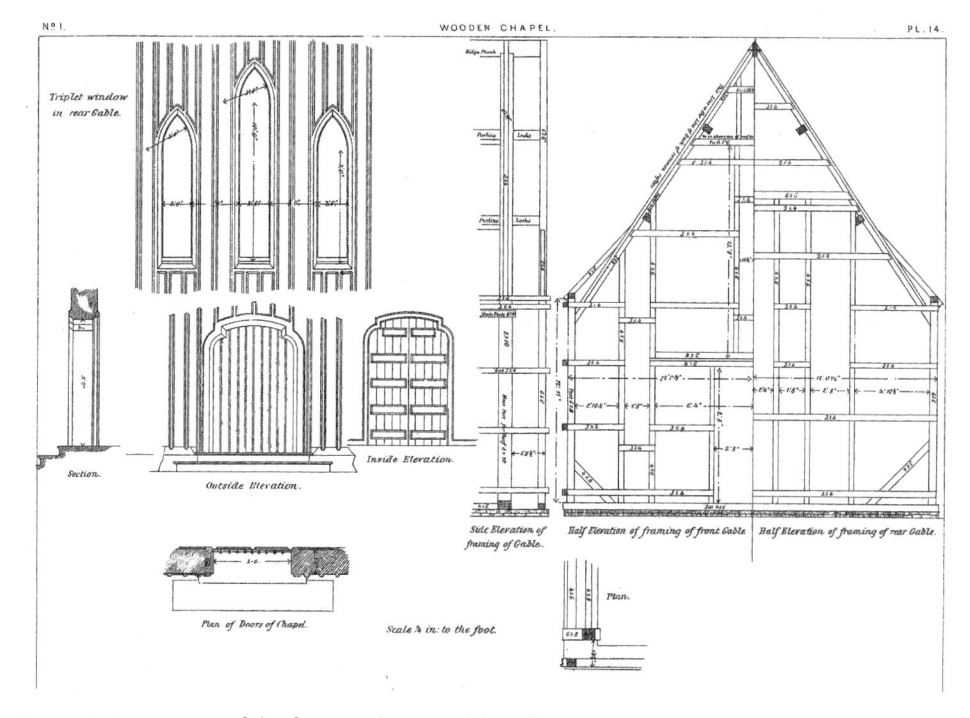

Figure 5.7. Framing of the front and rear gables of a wooden chapel. Richard Upjohn, *Rural Architecture: Designs, Working Drawings, and Specifications for a Wooden Church and Other Structures* (New York: G. P. Putman, 1852).

intended to provide training to carpenters; rather, by developing a uniform written language for directing each of the various trades involved in building construction, it extended the architect's influence over a distance, and helped mark the difference between his expertise and that of the builder.

Specifications were also included in Edward Shaw's 1854 book, *The Modern Architect,* an updated version of his *Rural Architecture* of 1843. Trained as a contractor and builder, Shaw viewed the publication of this book, his third, as proof that he had fully transformed from a craftsman into an architect. The evolution in his identity was the result of developing expertise in what he called the "theoretical practice and science of Architectural Drawings and Plans, both ancient and modern." Moreover, the book's wide dissemination, Shaw explained, would allow every carpenter to shift his identity, as he had, and become "his own master." This message can be read in the allegorical frontispiece of the book, which illustrates an implied transfer of knowledge and status from the seated man, an architect with a top hat and coat, instructing carpenters dressed in vests standing beside a drawing (Figure 5.8). Another craftsman, sawing a piece of lumber for the partially completed building in the background, works to realize the design found on the drawing under discussion. While the carpenters stand beside the architect to watch him perform the value of his knowledge with the classical instruments of compass and rule, behind him sits an open box of carpenter's tools, some chisels, a drill, and an axe, propped on the box resting on its head beside a plumb line. By comparison to the craftsman's unwieldy materials, the architect's tools fit in his palms and the folio of drawings at his feet are testament to his modern authorial identity. As a gentleman with "theoretical practice and science," he is free from the toil of construction, and his mobility allows him to instruct rather than work with his hands: he has earned the self-determining power of theoretical knowledge.[27]

Shaw displayed his mastery of architecture's history with his designs for "Grecian Doric" houses, ornamented with details found on "the Athenian Temple of Minerva." At the same time, amid descriptions of the plates, specifications intricately divided the labor for his designs' construction. The work was described with tasks, named either according to the object-to-be-produced (i.e., "foundation-walls," "windows," "doors," "stairs") or by a set of specific techniques (i.e., "underpinning," "framing," "flooring," "furring," "sheathing," "lathing and plastering," and "warming"). The text on "framing" was written as a staccato procession of parts and dimensions.

> First floor, plank, two by twelve inches. Trimmers, three by twelve inches; floor plank, sixteen inches from centre to centre. Second floor, two by eleven inches; the

Figure 5.8. Frontispiece of Edward Shaw, *The Modern Architect; or, Every Carpenter His Own Master [. . .]* (Boston: Dayton & Wentworth, 1854).

second and attic, distance as on the first floor; frame partitions fitted for twelve-inch nailings. Studs, three by four inches; proper trusses and doorjambs; the roof framed with trusses to support covering; joists not exceeding seven feet for the bearing.[28]

Unlike the teleological narrative that moves from medieval oral descriptions to Renaissance orthographic drawings and to the eventual standardization of architecture through mass production, here images appear to be insufficient for transmitting the necessary information, so verbal description must accompany them. Instead of a technological upgrade from oral to visual transmission of design, the information is packaged to extend the didactic power of an image through text.

Against Upjohn's rather general specifications, Shaw explicitly referred back to architectural drawings in order to allow the reader—presumably a builder aspiring to become an architect—to interpret the plans with an exact sense of their required labor and material cost. Shaw must have assumed his builder-readers already had technical knowledge of terms related to construction, which he never defined, as well as the general shape of a wooden carcass, which he never drew. Notably, during the time between the publication of *Rural Architecture* and *The Modern Architect*, a distance between the architectural professional and the builder had emerged, and Shaw's specifications sought to bridge this gap. Practical knowledge of construction, in his view, could mix with the theoretical knowledge of architectural representation and historical reference to create a smooth social transition from the status of a builder to that of an architect.

We have seen that Benjamin's book did not distinguish between the professional architect and the builder and that Upjohn and Shaw used specifications to identify the tools of art and those of craft. But none of these books specifically mentioned the technique of ballooning. Only with William E. Bell's 1857 publication, *Carpentry Made Easy; or, The Science and Art of Framing*, did an author explicitly focus on identifying and codifying this technique, but Bell paid little attention to either the history of architecture or its professional status. In fact, while Bell referred to himself as an "architect and practical builder," his book included no architectural designs and gives no evidence of his participation in professional practice. Instead, most of the pages are dedicated to formalizing carpentry techniques in order to disseminate them to "those who are devoted to the Mechanic Art and Amateurs who have felt the necessity of a faithful guide in house-building and other structures."[29] The method used for writing this "faithful guide" was to invent what he called a "science of carpentry," meaning he applied mathematical principles—mostly geometric—to describe the layout of a frame. The entire first part of the book was thus dedicated to solving thirty-one algebraic and geometric propositions with theorems, giving carpenters' methods more rigor.

For the second part of the book, Bell produced the earliest published drawings of balloon frames along with instructions enumerating the required tasks for construction (Figures 5.9, 5.10, 5.11). The drawings represent three variations of a wooden carcass without finishes—one story, one and a half stories, and two stories—and the instructions give dimensions of the members and their sequence of nailing. He did not call these specifications, however, because they did not relate to the construction of an architectural design. Bell's book offered craftsmen a method for assembling generic frames and did not connect ballooning to the architectural profession or to emerging systems of mass production. Its purpose was, instead, to tie craft to mathematical universals and shift builders from rules of thumb to what he called "geometrical reasoning."[30] The book thus codified the frame as an object of theoretical knowledge, separated from embodied know-how transferred from master to apprentice. The urge toward rationalization did not result in Bell securing intellectual property, and it was still a far cry from the modernist myth of the balloon frame as an early integration of the American building industry. With Bell, the frame had been theorized but not yet generalized.

Beginning in January 1860, the architect George E. Woodward, owner of a professional office and publishing house for architectural books in New York, described the balloon frame in a series carried by *The Cultivator and Country Gentleman*. The journal was guided by the motto "to improve the soil and the mind," and his contributions sat comfortably among the other articles dedicated to rural topics, including methods for feeding sheep, building corn barns, and new varieties of potatoes. To explore the balloon frame's history, as an architect might, Woodward turned to a letter by the builder Solon Robinson, on "How to Build Balloon Frames," read at the American Institute and the Farmers' Club of New York in 1855.[31] But the frame's history stopped there; Woodward could not extend much beyond this firsthand account. So, after echoing the procedures outlined by Robinson, he concluded that the frame was simply a technique without an author. "The Balloon Frame belongs to no one person," he wrote. "Nobody claims it as an invention, and yet in the art of construction it is one of the most sensible improvements that has ever been made."[32] Craft was common property—an improvement, not an invention—meaning that the frame was neither patented nor patentable and it was not modern in the sense that it did not replace manual labor with that of machines. Rather, Woodward's interest in the technique was its potential value as part of his professional cache of knowledge. Translating this craft into knowledge added value to both his practice and his publication.

Beyond his work as the head of an architectural office, Woodward operated a shop at 151 Broadway in New York City, where he sold popular books on architecture. These included such authors as John Claudius Loudon and Andrew Jackson

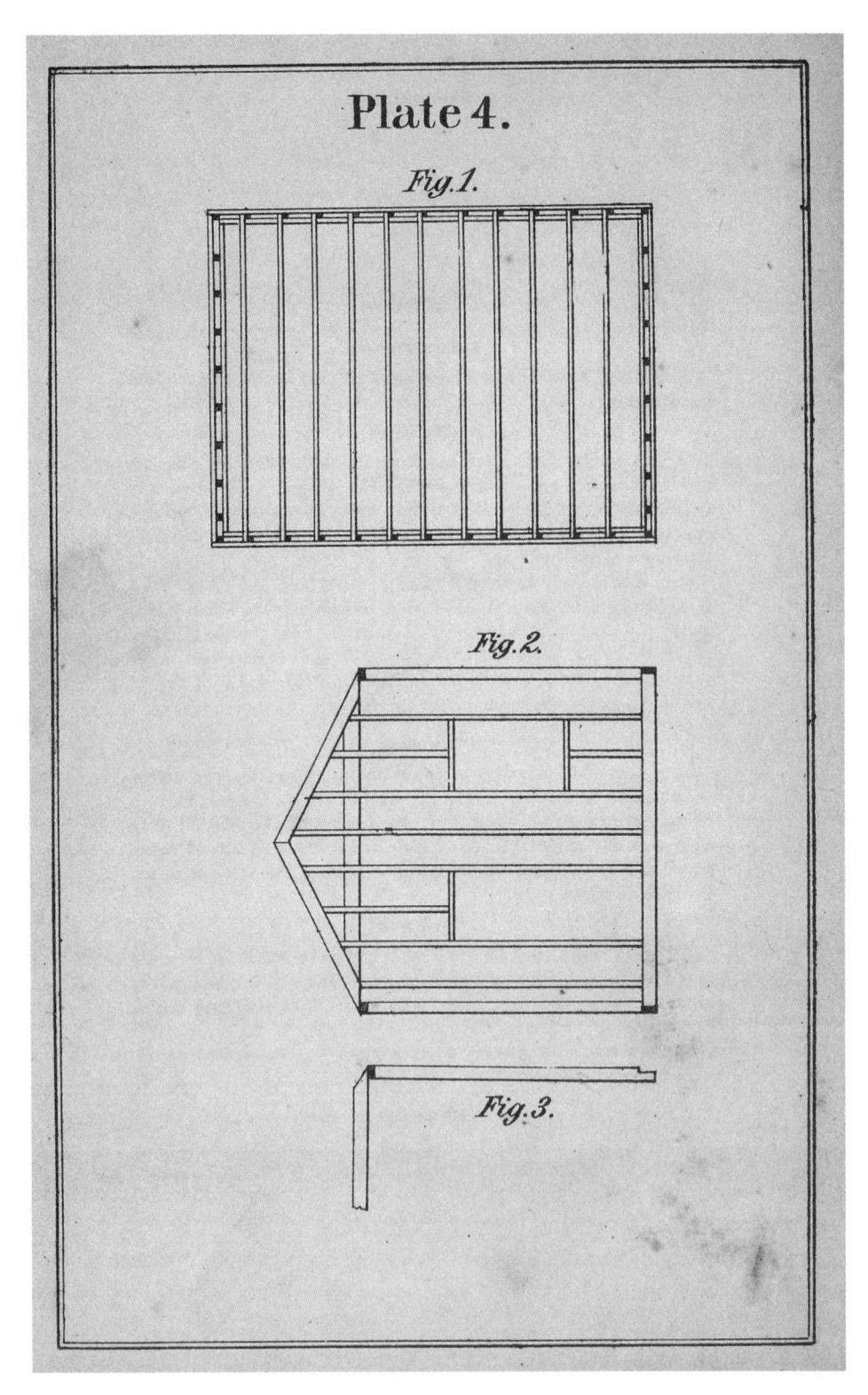

Figure 5.9. One-story balloon frame. William E. Bell, *Carpentry Made Easy; or, The Science and Art of Framing, on a New and Improved System* (Philadelphia: J. Challen & Sons, 1857), plate 4.

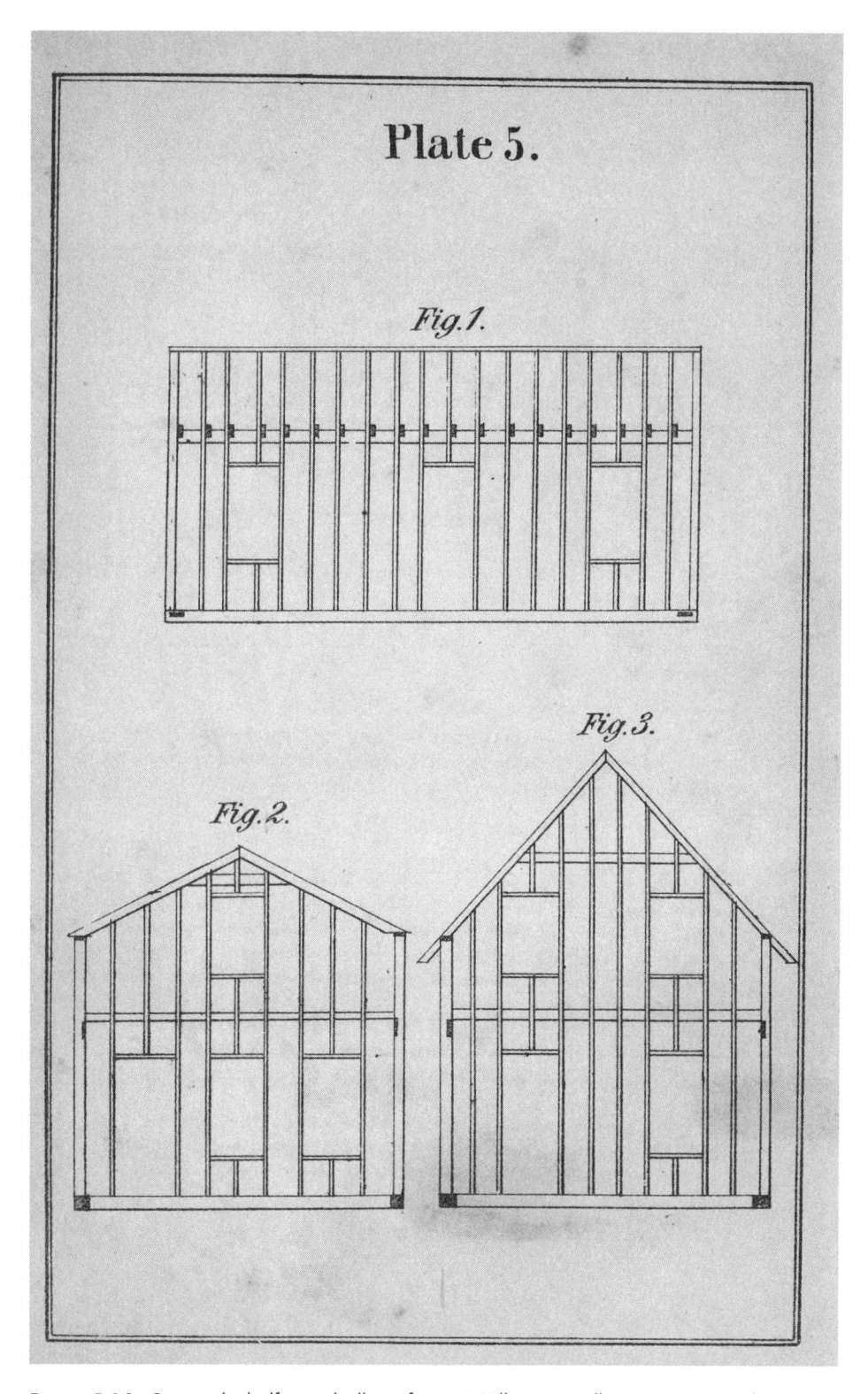

Figure 5.10. One-and-a-half-story balloon frame. William E. Bell, *Carpentry Made Easy; or, The Science and Art of Framing, on a New and Improved System* (Philadelphia: J. Challen & Sons, 1857), plate 5.

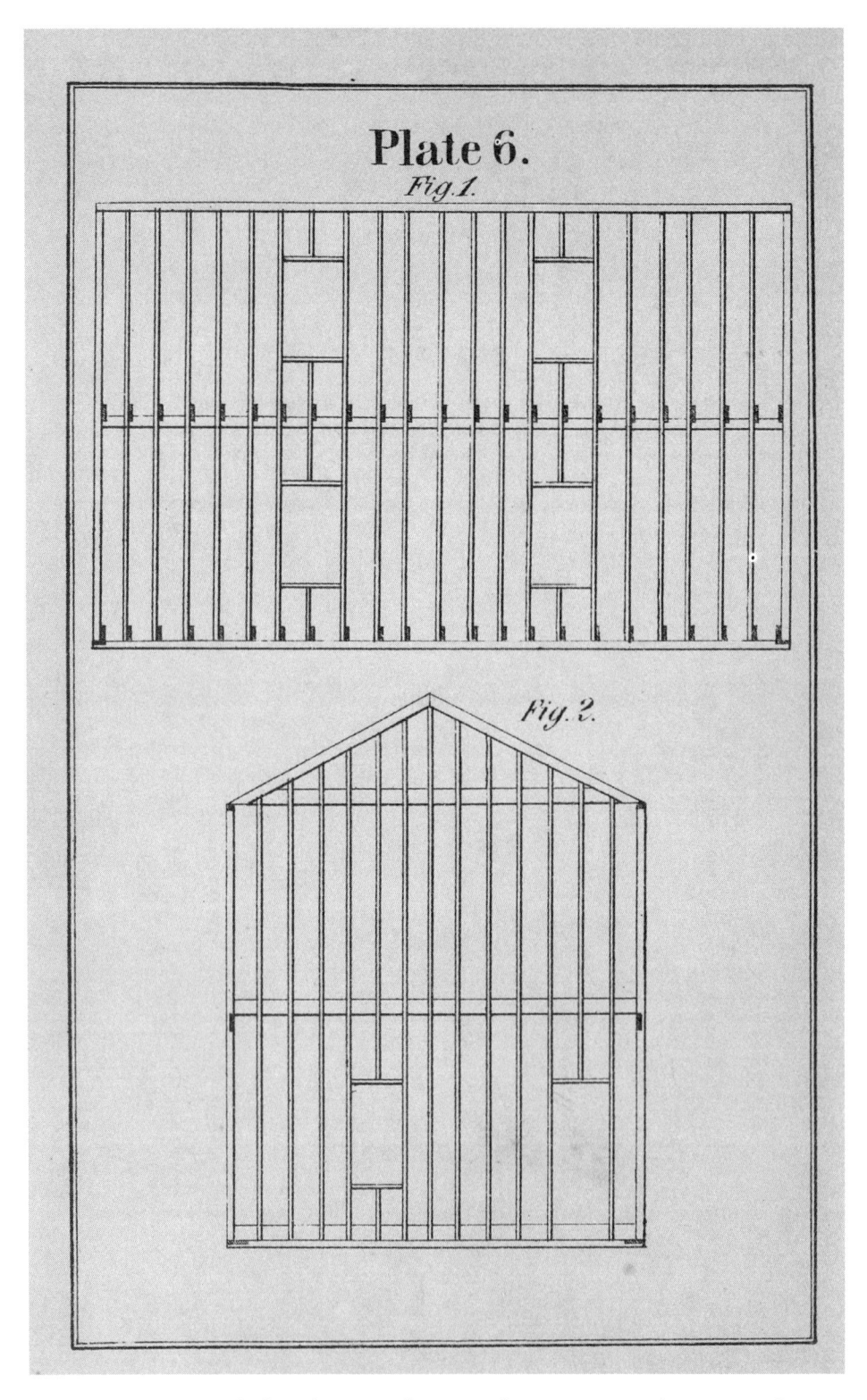

Figure 5.11. Two-story balloon frame. William E. Bell, *Carpentry Made Easy; or, The Science and Art of Framing, on a New and Improved System* (Philadelphia: J. Challen & Sons, 1857), plate 6.

Downing, but he also sold treatises on carpentry. The shop allowed him to promote his own books, such as *Woodward's Country Homes,* which he published in 1865, compiling much of the series he had written for *The Cultivator.*[33] As the final section of the book, much like a technical appendix, the description was narrative and not identified as specifications for realizing the book's illustrated designs. The drawings and descriptions of the balloon frame were therefore included to imply that *any* of the thirty designs illustrated in the preceding pages could be built similarly with this system. Exceeding both Robinson's procedural description and Bell's geometric rules, Woodward drew the balloon frame in a partial "isometrical perspective" and followed with details to illustrate the "manner of nailing," the "manner of splicing," and the "manner of tying" such a structure (Figure 5.12). The isometric drawing included an end wall with a few studs beyond, and the drawings that followed were diagrams of various intersections found in the frame.

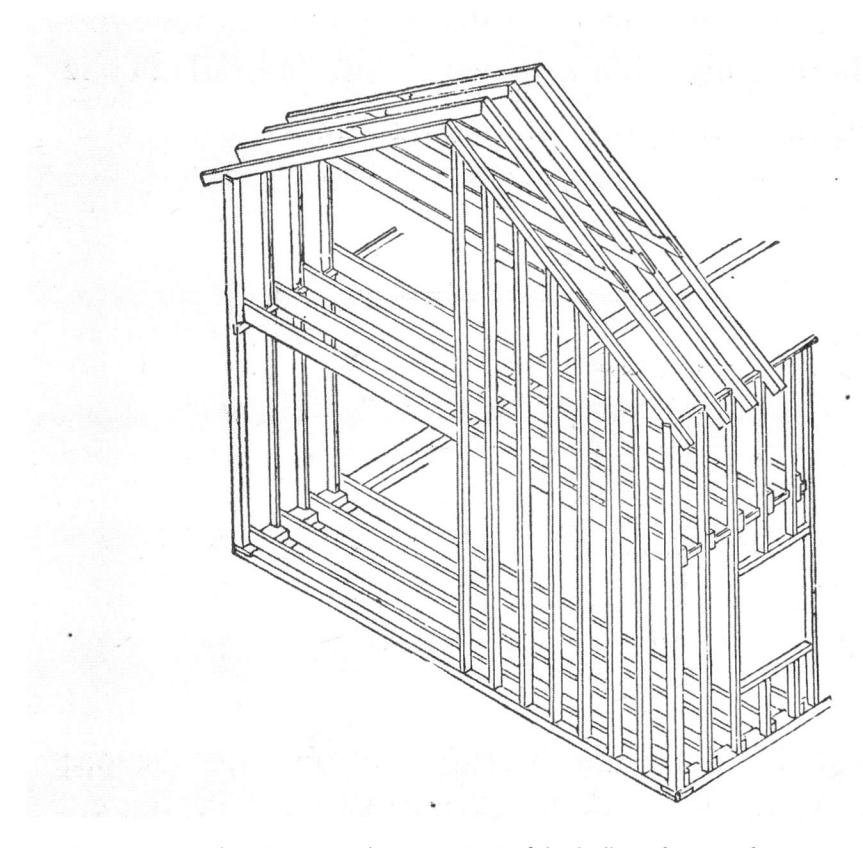

Figure 5.12. This "isometrical perspective" of the balloon frame is far more complex than that published in *The Cultivator* in 1860. Here, framing for a window is included as well as a second floor. George Woodward, *Woodward's Country Homes* (New York: Woodward, 1865), 153.

Together this combination of text and images established ballooning as a system that could be applied to a building of nearly any plan and as high as three stories.

In 1869 Woodward published *Woodward's National Architect* with Edward G. Thompson, a more extensive monograph with a title that implied a corresponding geographic extension of influence across the continent with designs for "country, suburb, and village." In this case, carpenters', masons', and plumbers' specifications were appended to three of the nineteen fully elaborated house designs. These texts helped guide the reader who might choose to realize a design by cross-referencing plans with sections, exterior and interior details, and bills of materials. Woodward insisted that "the forms of specifications given are such, that they may be adapted to any of the designs, so that full and final estimates can be obtained from local builders."[34] Thus, while each set of drawings was specific to the design for a house, the specifications were written generally so that they could be used selectively, edited at will, and adapted to the particularities of a region. This generality was invaluable to the professional architect: the specification held sources of information together and positioned the design as a point of convergence for builders' practical knowledge, the materials they required, and the infrastructures of the surrounding context. In other words, the specification was an element of office infrastructure that functioned more effectively when it was flexible rather than overly rigid.

While such architects as Woodward produced specifications that generalized designs for their wide distribution throughout the nation, owners of large-scale industries expanded the capacity of their plants to mass produce materials for construction. But regional differences in the availability and quality of these materials still greatly affected the activities of local builders. This variability did not produce problems until the widespread influence of pattern books with specifications such as *Woodward's National Architect* were being widely circulated. How could Woodward predict the cost of a house design if he had no knowledge that the average cost of lumber in Amherst, Massachusetts, was twice that of Appleton, Wisconsin?

To address this concern, Elisha Charles Hussey, who had worked for Woodward and later shared his architectural office, published *Home Building*. Hussey traveled across the continent in 1875 to gather "the facts" related to building materials and their costs from "about 400 places from New York to San Francisco." He published forty-two designs with cursory drawings while the specifications were "extended and elaborated" to identify regionally available materials and information on their technical limits. Hussey's emphasis on specifications—as opposed to his designs—reveals the persistent difficulty of producing a seamless translation between design and construction. Most builders, he explained, simply did not know where to find the materials specified by an architect or how to estimate their prices. His extended fact-based specifications thus helped release the architect from the obligation of producing a "detail recital of how a house should be mechanically constructed, how large the timbers should be, of what nature the brick, stone, wood and other material should consist, and how used; . . . which the average contractor or mechanic is already best informed."[35] The information published in *Home Building* cannot be categorized as either theoretical or practical knowledge; rather, its value was the capacity it offered architects to distance art from craft with now readily available reference information that allowed for their mutual distinction. Hussey's book and his work for Woodward indicate a general trend in architectural offices toward data collection. Once they were arranged in the tabular form found in Hussey's book, these singular facts transformed into data. Over the following decades, more clerical positions would be dedicated to arranging paperwork and managing the distribution of office tasks to incorporate such data into the final outputs of a professional architect. This shift indicates the mutually reinforcing form of architectural work as both clerical and creative. Despite the seeming antagonism of qualitative design ideas to the quantitative world of industrial data, architects became increasingly enmeshed in the bureaucracy of paperwork precisely to clarify the place of their work in industrial society.[36]

As evidence of this transition, consider the difference between the plans of two large architectural practices: Burnham and Root's Chicago offices in the Rookery Building from 1890, and Albert Kahn's Detroit offices in the Marquette Building from 1918 (Figures 5.13, 5.14). Burnham's office was outfitted with a gymnasium for the gentlemanly architect and a small library that included a mix of books on classical buildings and technical manuals related to modern materials and structure. There was also a central area for clerks, bookkeepers, typewriters, and a telephone. The scene of the office appears to our eyes as generally social and studio-like. By contrast, twenty-five years later, in Kahn's office the quantity of space devoted to paperwork was far greater. No gymnasium or library were available for the workers. One room was dedicated entirely to storing specifications and another for the typists who produced them. These rooms were positioned between one of the two drafting rooms and the designers' office, possibly chosen as a convenient location for communication—an interface between the conceptual work of design and the integration of data related to the industrially produced construction materials.[37]

The increasing emphasis placed on writing specifications in architectural offices became a central concern for the professional press. In 1906 the Architectural Record Company established *"Sweet's": Indexed Catalogue of Building Construction* with specifications for various materials, written in a condensed form

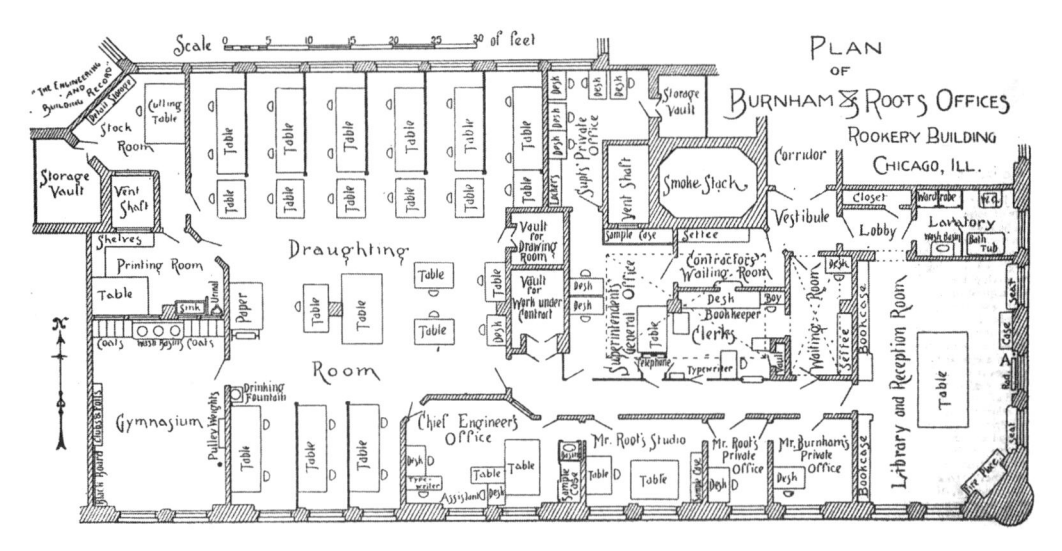

Figure 5.13. Plan of Burnham and Root's office in the Rookery Building in Chicago. *Engineering and Building Record,* January 11, 1890.

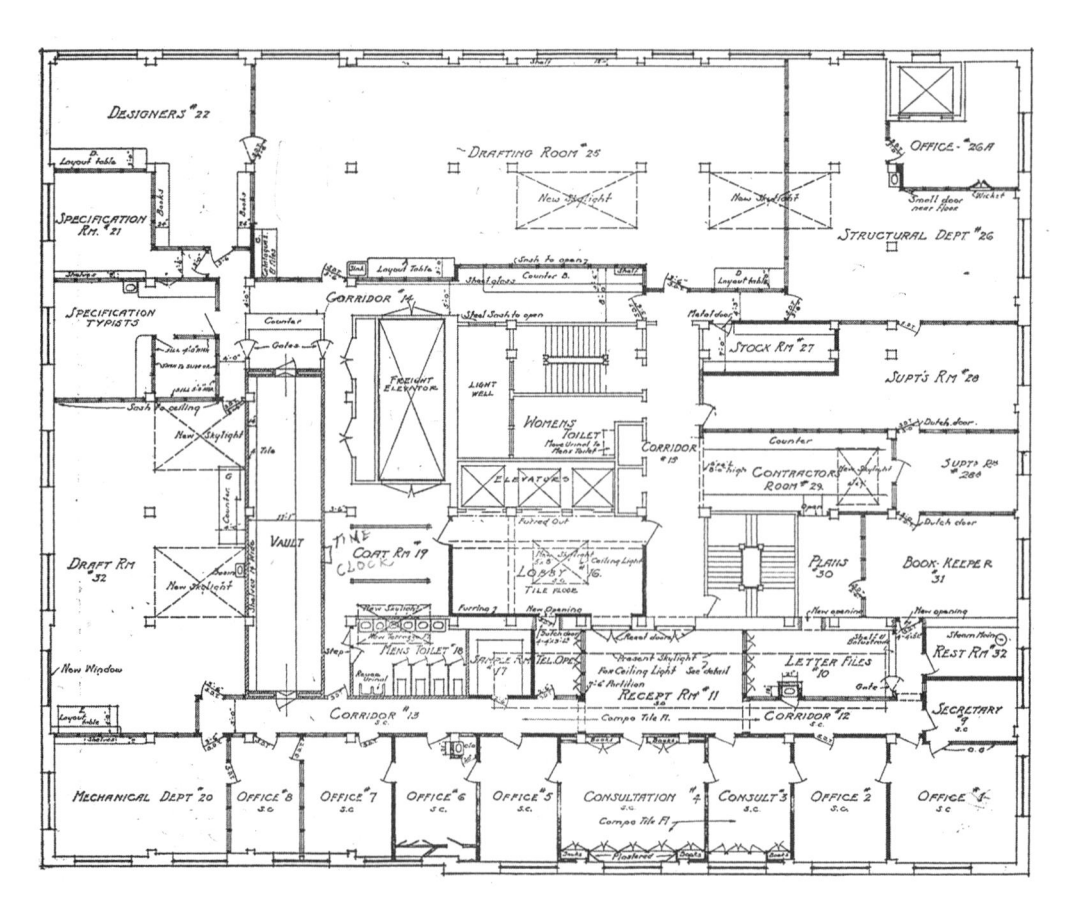

Figure 5.14. Plan of the offices of Albert Kahn in Detroit, Michigan. George Baldwin, "The Offices of Albert Kahn, Detroit, Michigan," *Architectural Forum* 29 (1918): 126.

to solve what the architect Thomas Nolan called the "catalogue problem." In his experience, every attempt had been made to accommodate the onslaught of information coming from industry: "arrangements of shelves, bookcases, pasteboard boxes, filing cases, patent binders, filing cabinets, cases of drawers, indexing schemes and 'index-rerums.'" Nolan believed the solution to be a reference work that indexed and arranged all that information in a single format.[38] The early history of the catalog, as Andrew Shanken has shown, was dedicated to making clerical office work as efficient as possible.[39] A similar impulse drove the *Architectural Review* to include a monthly column called "The Specification Desk" in its journal *Pencil Points* devoted to clerical work.[40] The discussion in that column focused on bringing standards to the language of specifications, especially after the legal status of these documents was established by the AIA as a "Contract Document."[41] In parallel to the modernist dogma that "standard" industrial products would bring architecture into synchrony with its time, professional architects found the language of standards—and standard language—immediately applicable to the types of clerical work they now found fundamental to their office routine.

Always attracted to the problem of standards in architectural practice, Harold Reeve Sleeper followed his *Architectural Graphic Standards* with a massive guide to the clerical worker simply titled *Architectural Specifications* in 1940. Based on his experience in Frederick Ackerman's office and a survey of nearly sixty others, Sleeper reformatted the specialized knowledge of specification writers into a collection of forms that could be used as specifications in which he provided blank spaces to be filled in according to a project's needs. For example, each of the images from *Architectural Graphic Standards* of balloon, braced, or western frames could now be paired with such a form to specify the materials from which the structures would be built. Rather than give any further specificity in images, Sleeper transformed the once strategic use of generality into a visual element in the form's arrangement. But Sleeper's reference book on specifications did not have the same uptake in professional offices as his book of graphic standards. Anticipating the difficulty, he admitted that his book would "not automatically enable [the architect] to write a good specification"; this would require "the knowledge, experience, and common sense required to interpret by means of the written word."[42] Changes in the processes of materials production and assembly often overwhelmed his attempt to standardize the language and composition of specifications. Even his integration of blanks did not prove flexible enough for the type of generality required of the clerical worker.

For more than a decade, beginning in 1932, the architect Don Graf initiated a more expansive project than Sleeper's and challenged the dominance of the Sweet's catalog by developing a new office infrastructure to incorporate the vastly proliferating and shifting data from industry. Graf introduced a set of binders in which architects would collect the most up-to-date information on building products, called *Data Sheets*. Although they were based on published advertising found in the monthly journal, Graf wrote that the sheets were "not advertising in the usual sense of the word—but rather helpful facts on actual products of merit, presented to save your time."[43] Manufacturers sponsored the free distribution of a data sheet that contained information on each of their products, formatted to fit in one of the provided binders. These sheets could be updated as the products themselves changed or the best practices of their application were revised. The sheets were organized within categories related to the products, such as "A. Materials in General" and "B. Structural Design," while others were more abstract, such as "C. Mathematics" or "D. Planning." So open and flexible was this system that it proved too difficult for Graf to manage. During World War II, as industries scaled up and greatly expanded the number of products brought to market, a data deluge tested the capacity of the *Data Sheets* infrastructure. "As a result of the multiplication of material and equipment items," Graf wrote, "the architect spends a larger and larger percentage of his business time in the consideration of products. . . . In a very real sense, architecture is spelled P-R-O-D-U-C-T-S. . . . Yet, with the added complexity of the building market, no steps have been taken to render the architect's selection of suitable products easier."[44] Graf noted that the Producers' Council had estimated that an average architectural office received seventy-four pages of direct-mail advertising per day. Unable to grapple with the quantity, Graf moved from the infrastructure of data sheets to the transmission of individual facts given in narrative form. His monthly column, now called "Building Product Facts," published an abbreviated synopsis of changes in industry.

As a regular collection of updates for his readers, Graf's summaries explicitly relinquished the obligation of managing industrial data to a new set of institutions. In 1948 the specification writers of government agencies founded the Construction Specification Institute (CSI) and produced a universal format for construction specifications with sixteen major divisions of work. The guidelines for writing specifications, as established by the CSI, were eventually called the "MasterFormat" and have recently been translated into software.[45] MasterFormat is updated every other year to reflect the expanding number of techniques developed for the construction industry. Building information models, also known as BIM, are now instantly synchronized to this process of technical obsolescence: part of the function of a BIM model is to automate and automatically update the process of specifying materials and construction techniques, integrating these changes into the data that has come to represent a building's design. I am not referring here to the automation of a process that replaces handwork with the work of machines as in the wood houses designed by Konrad Wachsmann; I mean the automation of processes through which connections are made between different forms of labor and their particular forms of knowledge, that is—industrial data, the management of construction schedules, and updates to numerous other variables.[46]

After the mid-nineteenth century, the hierarchy between designers and builders in architectural projects in the United States relied on the integration of clerical labor into the office workflow. The expanding scope of that work exceeded the capacity of any architect's office, and it soon overwhelmed the profession. As Graf had anticipated with his binders, building data required an infrastructure of perpetual renewal and growth. Yet the significance of the specification can still be found in the habits and language of architectural design, a practice that cannot exist without the clerical work that situates it in industrial society.

This is perhaps most clearly visible in the somewhat offhand comments written by the electrical engineer Douglas Engelbart. In his text *Augmenting Human Intellect,* prepared for the Information Sciences Division of the U.S. Air Force in 1962, Engelbart selected the architectural professional as an example of the soon-to-be-computerized office worker. Some have seen his words as prophetic of the digitalization of design—a set of tasks that had yet to be automated. But the choice of an architectural office for his analysis may have less to do with what was yet to come than with what had already happened to any given workday in that context.[47] After one hundred years of proliferating paperwork in professional practice, the architectural office must have appeared to Engelbart as an unusually stable combination of creative and clerical tasks. Indeed, the reliance of human creativity on the increased capacity for data processing with computers appears to motivate his text. I quote these passages at length, then, to emphasize the number of times Engelbart returns to specifications, catalogs, and handbooks as the bases for developing and evaluating the architect's "dreamed up" building design.

> Let us consider an "augmented" architect at work. He sits at a working station that has a visual display screen some three feet on a side; this is his working surface, and is controlled by a computer (his "clerk") with which he can communicate by means of a small keyboard and various other devices.
>
> He is designing a building. He has already dreamed up several basic layouts and structural forms, and is trying them out on the screen. . . . Now he enters a reference line with his "pointer" and the keyboard. Gradually the screen begins to show the work he is doing—a neat excavation appears in the hillside, revises itself slightly, and revises itself again. . . . Ignoring the representation on the display, the

architect next begins to enter series of specifications and data—a six-inch slab floor, twelve-inch concrete walls eight feet high within the excavation, and so on. When he has finished the revised scene appears on the screen. A structure is taking shape. He examines it, adjusts it, pauses long enough to ask for handbook or catalog information from the "clerk" at various points and readjusts accordingly. He often recalls from the "clerk" his working lists of specifications and considerations to refer to them, modify them, or add to them. These lists grow into an ever-more-detailed, interlinked structure, which represents the maturing thought behind the actual design.[48]

Engelbart's vision of the augmented architect's practice was based on acknowledging the data infrastructure that subtends any building design. As decisions move back and forth from design to specification, they could be updated in real time by the computer—that is, Engelbart's automated "clerk." This was not the vision of total standardization imagined by the modernists; nor did it anticipate the ideology of mass customization.

Engelbart described the potential synchronization of clerical labor into the architect's workflow. The creative process of architectural design, which had been successfully distanced from the practical knowledge of building construction, could now be undergirded by the increasingly invisible ground of industrial data. Data would not be circulated through software in order to *overcome* specification. Rather, the computer's capacity to manage data allowed the architect to expand the reach of such clerical aspects of office work into even more aspects of a design. The distance between design and construction, and the corresponding difference between theoretical and practical knowledge, would not be eclipsed. The specification, in Engelbart's vision, emerged from a set of mediating instruments that linked databases to the architect's creative process. Database systems designed in the 1970s replaced the data sheets that architects accumulated in their offices at midcentury. Their real-time integration into BIM, then, has only further clarified the hybrid nature of architectural design, where creativity relies on the generality afforded by such clerical instruments of practice as the specification.

Now that industrial variability is updated invisibly to most users; we see neither the process of total standardization nor the fulfillment of an ideology known as mass customization. The modern myth of the standard and its corollary in the nonstandard appear to be category errors that have been held over from the shared cultural memory of modernism.[49] The difference between theoretical and practical knowledge is now mediated by automated systems charged with producing generality out of the uncontrollable processes that, in combination, produce seemingly endless new specificities.[50]

NOTES

1. Mario Carpo, "Review: Architectures Non Standard," *Journal of the Society of Architectural Historians* 64, no. 2 (June 2005): 234. See also Mario Carpo, *The Alphabet and the Algorithm* (Cambridge, Mass.: MIT Press, 2011); Frédéric Migayrou and Zeynep Mennan, eds., *Architectures non standard: Exposition présentée au Centre Pompidou, galerie sud, 10 décembre 2003–1er mars 2004* (Paris: Centre Pompidou, 2003); Bernard Cache, *Earth Moves: The Furnishing of Territories* (Cambridge, Mass.: MIT Press, 1995).

2. An exhibition at the Canadian Centre for Architecture reviewed the European sense of America's modernity. The catalog was published as Jean Louis Cohen, *Scenes of the World to Come: European Architecture and the American Challenge, 1893–1960* (Montreal: Canadian Centre for Architecture, 1995).

3. Konrad Wachsmann, *Holzhausbau* (1930), translated by Peter Reuss as *Building the Wooden House* (Basel: Birkhäuser Architecture, 1995), 19. Wachsmann relied on photographs taken by Richard Neutra published in the same year in his book, *Amerika: Die Stilbildung des neuen Bauens in den Vereiningten Staaten* (Vienna: Anton Schroll Verlag, 1930).

4. Michael Grüning, *Der Wachsmann-Report: Auskünfte eines Architekten* (Berlin: Verlag der Nation, 1986).

5. Herbert Gilbert, *The Dream of the Factory-Made House: Walter Gropius and Konrad Wachsmann* (Cambridge, Mass.: MIT Press, 1984).

6. Sigfried Giedion, *Space, Time, and Architecture: The Growth of a New Tradition,* 5th ed. (Cambridge, Mass.: Harvard University Press, 1969), 335–54. For his views on American ingenuity, see also Sigfried Giedion, *Mechanization Takes Command* (Oxford: Oxford University Press, 1948), 46–75.

7. See the three axonometric drawings in Charles George Ramsey and Harold Reeve Sleeper, *Architectural Graphic Standards* (New York: Wiley Press, 1932); National Lumber Manufacturers Association, *Frame Construction Details* (Chicago: National Lumber Manufacturers Association, 1920).

8. Ted Cavanagh, "Dream or Dilemma: The Unconscious Construction of the Modern House," *Journal of Architectural Education* 70, no. 2 (2016): 300–310.

9. Balloon frames are no longer widely used, as a result of the constraint on the vertical dimension of the stud that now is milled to fit on a flatbed truck. Most wood-framed houses are currently built with a technique known as "platform framing." For the early history of timber-framing techniques, see Dell Upton, "Traditional Timber Framing," in *Material Culture of the Wooden Age,* ed. B. Hindle (Tarrytown, N.Y.: Sleepy Hollow Press, 1981), 35–93. For a close study of the origins of ballooning, see Paul E. Sprague, "The Origin of Balloon Framing," *Journal of the Society of Architectural Historians* 40, no. 4 (December 1981): 311–19; and Paul E. Sprague, "Chicago Balloon Frame: The Evolution during the 19th Century of George W. Snow's System for Erecting Light Frame Buildings from Dimension Lumber and Machine-Made Nails," in *The Technology of Historic American Buildings: Studies of the Materials, Craft Processes, and the Mechanization of Building Construction,* ed. H. Ward Jandl (Washington, D.C.: Foundation for Preservation Technology for the Association for Preservation Technology, 1983), 35–53.

10. Tilo Amhoff and Katie Lloyd Thomas, "Writing Work: Changing Practices of Architectural Specification," in *The Architect as Worker: Immaterial Labor, the Creative Class, and the Politics of Design*, ed. Peggy Deamer (London: Bloomsbury, 2015), 121–43. See also Tilo Amhoff, "'Except Where Herein Otherwise Directed': Building with Legal Documents in Early Nineteenth-Century England," *arq: Architectural Research Quarterly* 16, no. 3 (2012): 238–44.

11. Mario Carpo, *Architecture in the Age of Printing: Orality, Writing, Typography, and Printed Images in the History of Architectural Theory*, trans. Sarah Benson (Cambridge, Mass.: MIT Press, 2001), 23–41.

12. My main source for the history of the American architectural profession is Mary N. Woods, *From Craft to Profession: The Practice of Architecture in Nineteenth-Century America* (Berkeley: University of California Press, 1999).

13. On the conventions of patent drawings, see William J. Rankin, "The 'Person Skilled in the Art' Is Really Quite Conventional: U.S. Patent Drawings and the Persona of the Inventor, 1870–2005," in *Making and Unmaking Intellectual Property: Creative Production in Legal and Cultural Perspective*, ed. Mario Biagioli, Peter Jaszi, and Martha Woodmansee (Chicago: University of Chicago Press, 2011), 55–75.

14. John Leander Bishop, *A History of American Manufactures from 1608 to 1860* (Philadelphia: Edward Young, 1868).

15. Amos J. Loveday Jr., *The Rise and Decline of the American Cut Nail Industry: A Study of the Interrelationships of Technology, Business Organization, and Management Techniques* (Westport, Conn.: Greenwood Press, 1983); Charles E. Edgerton, "The Wire-Nail Association of 1895–96," *Political Science Quarterly* 12, no. 2 (June 1897): 246–72.

16. See, for example, John Marston Scribner, *The Ready Reckoner: For Ship Builders, Boat Builders, and Lumber Merchants* (Rochester, N.Y.: G. W. Fisher, 1866); and Oliver Byrne, *Byrne's Timber and Log Book: Ready Reckoner and Price Book, for Lumber Dealers and Ship Builders* (New York: American News Company, 1878).

17. Edward C. Carter, ed., *The Correspondence and Miscellaneous Papers of Benjamin Henry Latrobe*, vol. 1, *1784–1804* (New Haven, Conn.: Yale University Press, 1984), 131.

18. J. Meredith Neil, "The Precarious Professionalism of Latrobe," *AIA Journal* (May 1970): 67–71.

19. Woods, *From Craft to Profession*, 19–20.

20. On the history of these books as they relate to the architectural profession, see Dell Upton, "Pattern Books and Professionalism: Aspects of the Transformation of Domestic Architecture in America, 1800–1860," *Winterthur Portfolio* 19, nos. 2/3 (Summer–Autumn 1984): 107–50. See also Daniel D. Reiff, *Houses from Books: The Influence of Treatises, Pattern Books, and Catalogs in American Architecture, 1738–1950* (University Park: Penn State University Press, 2000).

21. In the United States, this publishing practice began with Andrew Jackson Downing. See, for example, Andrew Jackson Downing, *Cottage Residences; or, A Series of Designs for Rural Cottages and Cottage Villas [. . .]* (New York: Wiley and Putnam, 1844).

22. Asher Benjamin, *The Architect; or, The Practical House Carpenter* (1830; repr., Boston: Sanborn, Carter, Bazin, 1847). On Benjamin's influence, see Vincent J. Scully Jr.,

"Romantic Rationalism and the Expression of Structure in Wood: Downing, Wheeler, Gardner, and the 'Stick Style,' 1840–1876," *Art Bulletin* 35, no. 2 (June 1953): 121–42. See also Florence Thompson Howe, "More about Asher Benjamin," *Journal of the Society of Architectural Historians* 13, no. 3 (October 1954): 16–19; and Jack Quinan, "A Bibliography of Writings by and about Asher Benjamin," *Journal of the Society of Architectural Historians* 38, no. 3 (October 1979): 254–56.

23. For example, on St. Mary's Church in Chicago, see Giedion, *Space, Time and Architecture*, 347.

24. Richard Upjohn, *Rural Architecture* (1852; repr., New York: Da Capo Press, 1975). For specifications extracted from realized buildings, see William H. Ranlett, *The Architect: A Series of Original Designs, for Domestic and Ornamental Cottages and Villas [. . .]* (New York: Dewitt & Davenport, 1855). For an example of a book with specifications, organized around the various building trades, see Samuel Sloan, *The Model Architect: A Series of Original Designs for Cottages, Villas, Suburban Residences, etc. [. . .]* (Philadelphia: E. S., 1852).

25. Judith S. Hull, "The 'School of Upjohn': Richard Upjohn's Office," *Journal of the Society of Architectural Historians* 52, no. 3 (September 1993): 281–306.

26. Upjohn, *Rural Architecture*, 1.

27. Edward Shaw, *The Modern Architect; or, Every Carpenter His Own Master [. . .]* (Boston: Dayton and Wentworth, 1854), 3n.

28. Originally from Edward Shaw, *Rural Architecture: Consisting of Classic Dwellings, Doric, Ionic, Corinthian and Gothic, and Details Connected with Each of the Orders [. . .]* (Boston: James B. Dow, 1843), 75, reprinted in Edward Shaw, *The Modern Architect*, 73.

29. William E. Bell, *Carpentry Made Easy; or, The Science and Art of Framing, on a New and Improved System [. . .]* (Philadelphia: J. Challen & Sons, 1857), 3.

30. Bell, 12.

31. A summary of the letter is given in "Cheap Houses," *Burlington Tri-weekly Hawk-eye*, February 3, 1855, 2.

32. George E. Woodward, "Balloon Frames, IVth Article," *The Cultivator and Country Gentleman* 16, no. 1 (July 5, 1860): 18.

33. Michael McCordie, "Review: *Woodward's National Architect* by George E. Woodward, Edward G. Thompson," *Journal of the Society of Architectural Historians* 37, no. 1 (March 1978): 54.

34. George E. Woodward and Edward G. Thompson, *Woodward's National Architect* (New York: Geo. E. Woodward, 1869).

35. Elisha Charles Hussey, *Home Building: A Reliable Book of Facts, Relative to Building, Living, Materials, Costs, at about 400 Places from New York to San Francisco* (New York: Leader & Van Hoesen, 1876), 204.

36. Michael Osman, "Regulation through Paperwork in Architectural Practice," in *Modernism's Visible Hand: Regulation and Architecture in America* (Minneapolis: University of Minnesota Press, 2018), 165–89.

37. George Baldwin, "The Offices of Albert Kahn, Detroit, Michigan," *Architectural Forum* 29 (1918): 126.

38. Thomas Nolan, "Introduction," *"Sweet's": Indexed Catalogue of Building Construction* (New York: Architectural Record Company, 1906), ix

39. Andrew M. Shanken, "From the Gospel of Efficiency to Modernism: A History of Sweet's Catalogue, 1906–1947," *Design Issues* 21, no. 2 (Spring 2005): 28–47.

40. "The Specification Desk" was first published in *Pencil Points* 1–2 (July 1920): 23.

41. Ralph E. Hacker, "The Use of a Standard Specification," *Pencil Points* 8, no. 7 (July 1927): 451–53; Edward M. Bridge, "Architectural Specifications," *Pencil Points* 8, no. 9 (September 1927): 581–82. For a good summary of these discussions, see Goldwin Goldsmith, *Architects' Specifications—How to Write Them* (New York: John Wiley & Sons, 1935).

42. Harold Reeve Sleeper, *Architectural Specifications* (New York: John Wiley & Sons, 1940), vii.

43. Don Graf, "Facts at Your Fingertips," *Pencil Points* 16, no. 5 (May 1935): 78.

44. Don Graf, "Introducing a New Service for Pencil Points Readers," *Pencil Points* 25, no. 4 (April 1944): 79.

45. In 1975 the CSI established MasterFormat, a standard numbering system for organizing specifications and other written information for commercial and institutional building projects in the United States and Canada.

46. See, for example, Frank Boukamp and Burcu Akinci, "Automated Processing of Construction Specifications to Support Inspection and Quality Control," *Automation in Construction* 17, no. 1 (November 2007): 90–106.

47. See Molly Wright Steenson, *Architectural Intelligence: How Designers and Architects Created the Digital Landscape* (Cambridge, Mass.: MIT Press, 2017), 10–11.

48. Douglas C. Engelbart, *Augmenting Human Intellect: A Conceptual Framework* (Menlo Park, Calif.: Stanford Research Institute, 1962), 4–5.

49. Mario Carpo, *The Alphabet and the Algorithm* (Cambridge, Mass.: MIT Press, 2011).

50. Paolo Tombesi, "On the Cultural Separation of Design Labor," in *Building (in) the Future: Recasting Labor in Architecture,* ed. Phil Bernstein and Peggy Deamer (New York: Princeton Architectural Press, 2010), 117–36.

CHAPTER 6

POSITIONING

Architecture of Logistics

JOHN HARWOOD

These places, spread out everywhere, yield up and orient new spaces: they are no longer temples, but rather the opening up and the spacing out of the temples themselves, a dis-location with no reserve henceforth, with no more sacred enclosures—other tracks, other ways, other places for all who are there.

—Jean-Luc Nancy, "Of Divine Places," trans. Michael Holland, in *The Inoperative Community* (1991)

Now all around Sedan, from all the lost positions—Floing, the plateau of Illy, the Garenne woods and the valley of the Givonne, the Bazeilles road—a panic-stricken flood of men, horses and cannon was pouring towards the town. This fortress, on which they had had the disastrous idea of depending, was proving to be a terrible snare, a shelter for fugitives, a sanctuary into which even the bravest men let themselves be lured in the general demoralization and panic. Behind those ramparts they imagined they would at last escape from the terrible artillery which had been thundering for nearly twelve hours; all conscience and reason had fled, the animal had run away with the human and there was nothing left but the mad rush of instinct stampeding for the hole in which to go to earth and sleep.

—Émile Zola, *The Debacle* (1892)

THE ARCHITECTURE OF POSITION

Toward the beginning of *The Stones of Venice*, John Ruskin neatly divided architecture in two. Architecture's purpose is either "to hold and protect something," which he called the "Architecture of Protection," or it is to "place or carry something," which he named the "Architecture of Position."[1] Readers of even the twentieth-century abridged American edition of Ruskin's nearly 500,000-word masterpiece of perverse erudition will recall that he had much more to say about the former than the latter. The architecture of protection, he held, is the aim of the greatest properly architectural achievements, provided that it is produced with the proper moral orientation and sound rationality required; yet Ruskin did spare some words for the architecture of position.

> This is architecture intended to carry men or things to some certain places, or to hold them there. This will include all bridges, aqueducts, and road architecture; lighthouses, which have to hold light in appointed places; chimneys, to carry smoke or direct currents of air; staircases; towers, which are to be watched from or cried from, as in a mosque, or to hold bells, or to place men in positions of offence, as ancient movable attacking towers, and most fortress towers.[2]

The theme reappears in the tenth chapter of book 1, in a tantalizing passage on towers (in which he promises a freestanding study on the subject, one of the few things Ruskin never wrote), and in several other passages both before and after the partition.[3] With each of these passages, however, it is possible to detect both the logic of Ruskin's division of architecture and to deduce from that logic a progressive conceptual split in architectural thought, dating from the early nineteenth century, which has only recently begun to be bridged by a renewed engagement with the problem of *movement*.[4]

As is familiar to most architectural readers of *The Stones of Venice,* Ruskin posited the "Architecture of Protection" as proceeding first from a general cultural attitude (including religion, the prevailing organization of labor, and other customs), and next from a deliberate exploitation of structural principles (such as the bonding of stones in a wall, and the statics of arched openings). Through some contortions of ex post facto rationalization and embracing an anachronism similar to that at the core of the architectural ideas of A. W. N. Pugin, Ruskin argued forcefully for a modern commitment to a renewal of gothic architecture as a means for producing a unified and morally correct culture.

The architecture of position, on the other hand, proceeds entirely from instrumental needs for movement or its temporary cessation. *Carrying* and *holding*: the division between protection and position that Ruskin describes is analogous to the division between these architectures' status as *media*.[5] The architecture of protection (re)presents meaning through symbols—whether the sculptural and ornamental, or the more subtle traces left in the structure by the hands of the builders—whereas the architecture of position functions as a baser mode of communication.

The former structures history by rendering monuments that can be organized taxonomically in order to establish tidy tautologies about the unity of cultures at various locations in time and space. The latter is simply bound by an instrumental challenge to the limitations of time, presentist and consequently rapidly obsolesced. The architecture of position is little more than a vessel, one whose qualities are interiorized and closed, dehumanized and almost without history precisely because it is so preoccupied with speed.[6] Today, we would name this latter architecture an architecture of *logistics*.

The phrase *architecture of logistics* appears to be so very nearly an oxymoron and a tautology that it would seem difficult to justify. Yet this essay is an effort to insist that something called an "architecture of logistics" not only exists in the most literal and technical sense but is also among the most pressing matters of concern for any architect, theorist, or historian who is keen to understand the rapid transformations currently taking place in architecture, urbanism, and landscape.[7]

Allow me to explain. What is meant by "architecture" ought to be plain enough—the generalized body of knowledge that allows for the production of expertly produced designs for buildings, among many other products of human industry. "Logistics" requires further theorization here, but before turning to a more direct discussion of logistics, its history and theory, and its rapidly transforming relationship to architecture, it will be useful to spend a bit more time with Ruskin's division and its unfortunate and confusing consequences for subsequent architectural thought.

Again and again throughout *The Stones of Venice* and elsewhere, Ruskin ascribes to the architecture of protection the quality of *immediacy*.[8] As Marshall McLuhan noted in his early book-cum-"mosaic" *The Gutenberg Galaxy,* and in his later work via quoting Ruskin himself at length, gothic architecture could be seen to have the capacity to produce divine truths through the exploitation of the aesthetic logic of the grotesque. This is not, McLuhan makes plain, a result of the grotesque as an ugly, rough, or—to borrow Ruskin's term—"savage" approach to rendering images on the page or in stone; rather, the key characteristic of the grotesque is the parataxis of symbols. Paradoxically, precisely by eliding the connective tissue of the grammar and syntax of perspectival representation and naturalism, the hard juxtaposition of metaphors, icons, and images characteristic of, say, a tympanum bas-relief on a medieval church, the viewer could achieve access to genuine illumination. Such a hypothesis does not survive any rigorous contemporary media theoretical analysis, which would insist on McLuhan's crypto-Catholic commitment to art as an immediate medium capable of revealing the world as it really is—what McLuhan called the "counterenvironment."[9]

Nevertheless, just as in the mid-twentieth-century effort to rationalize and universalize aesthetics by means of information theory, McLuhan's neo-Ruskinian grotesque served as a mode of reading that could exploit the "gaps" between images in order to produce associations and syntheses in the mind of the viewer that are not present in the images themselves, thus leaping over the phenomenal boundaries of the senses and breaking out of the tyranny of the linearity of print technologies.[10] McLuhan famously relied heavily on his idiosyncratic but close readings of William Shakespeare's *King Lear* and James Joyce's *Ulysses* in order to foreground this tension within print culture, as works that seemed in important ways to work against the grain of the book as a "medium." In relation to architecture, however, there is a similar structure to the problem, and it is important not to slip into the mysticism that characterizes the Christological/eschatological operations that McLuhan/Ruskin set in motion.[11]

Ruskin was very plain—even if his reasons remain partially obscure—that any consideration of the new material substrata of architecture in the industrializing nineteenth century was beyond the pale.[12] The alloyed materials of the mines and factory production—the metals that less than a generation after his death in 1900 would become the historical subject of a new essentialist materialism championed by art historians—were not the stuff of serious architecture.[13] Indeed, the very fact that these corrupt products of the industrial capitalist order alienated the worker from his (Ruskin spoke largely in "hises," unless he was lecturing women on proper comportment or valorizing feminine beauty in allegorical terms) labor was likely the reason for a willful blindness. It was far more important to Ruskin to get on with the (equally modern) business of turning back time in a vain effort to recapture a fictive lost past.[14]

Ruskin's great French rival in reframing the legacy of medieval art and architecture for contemporary theory, Eugène-Emmanuel Viollet-le-Duc, had less trouble engaging with the problem of architecture created for the purpose of lodging and transporting; however, he chose a specific disciplinary ground on which to engage the matter. One finds little on the architecture of warehouses or rail stations in the *Dictionnaire* (his famous effort to systematize knowledge on the history of what really counts as "architecture" and the "decorative arts"), but in his military treatise-cum-children's novel *Annals of a Fortress,* Viollet-le-Duc makes explicit the need to consider architecture in purely logistical terms. In the afterword to the novel, cleverly framed as a report from a fictional French artillery officer written in response to the shameful defeat at the hands of the Prussians in 1872, it is demonstrated that the offensive firepower of modern artillery has rendered the fortress—which, in a militarized jargon version of Ruskin's "architecture of position," he names the *enceinte de préservation*—permanently obsolete.

In the hands of Viollet-le-Duc's contemporary, Émile Zola, this principle became a mechanism through which to analyze not only the military but also the cultural crisis of late nineteenth-century France. For Viollet-le-Duc, the architecture of warfare in the future would need to become a newly imagined *enceinte de combat* characterized by a temporary manipulation of the ground (earthworks), facilitating incessant repositioning of firepower.[15] This insight has rendered *Annals* into a classic reference work for military theorists, but for further insight into the antitypological and protean character of the architecture of position, it is necessary to establish some baselines of military logistical history and theory.

A PRIMER ON MILITARY LOGISTICS

Logistics has a rather odd history, and a stranger theory. Like architecture (and most anything), the phenomena the term gives a name to predate the name itself, and its origins are equally ancient and obscure. Historians have not even been able to agree on its etymology. Its first modern theoretician, Antoine-Henri Jomini—Napoleon's quartermaster and the author of the only real rival in the nineteenth century of Carl von Clausewitz's *Vom Krieg (On War)*—in his *Précis de l'art de la guerre* (1838), claims that the word is "derived, as we know, from the title of the *major général des logis* (translated in German by *Quartiermeister* [until recently rendered literally as 'quartermaster' in English]), an officer whose duty it formerly was to lodge and camp the troops, to give direction to the marches of columns, and to locate them upon the ground."[16] Later, predominantly American, authors trace the term further back. The U.S. Army "primer" on the logistics states instead that

> the word "logistics" is derived from the Greek adjective "logistikos" meaning "skilled in calculating." The first administrative use of the word was in Roman and Byzantine times when there was a military administrative official with the title "Logista." At that time the word apparently implied a skill in the science of mathematical computations. Research indicates that the first use of the word with reference to an organized military administrative science was by the French writer, Jomini, who, in 1838, devised a theory of war upon the trinity of strategy, ground tactics, and logistics. The French still use the words "logistique" and "loger" with the meaning "to quarter."[17]

This polite exchange over a gap of more than a century is surprisingly characteristic of the scholarship on logistics. First developed as a theoretical and descriptive term for the newly incorporated business of supplying armies (and navies and marines), logistics developed rapidly from the Napoleonic era into a systematic body of theory regarding the ability to *lodge*, or *house*, people/things/personnel/matériel across a temporal matrix that extends much further than the conventional "schedule" of construction drawings or navigational cartography that had existed already for several centuries in the West.

It has always been necessary in any culture to move things and people from here to there in order to accomplish some end, so it is perhaps germane at this junction to note that in repeating a call for an increased attentiveness to (and method for addressing in critical terms) logistics, one risks reinforcing a trope of the extant literature on the subject that is particularly empty. Indeed, the first thing one notes about logisticians is their tendency to complain that they are neglected.

> That Logistics has received so little academic attention and is so little mentioned in the literature of war is readily explained.
>
> Strategy is to war what the plot is to a play; Tactics is represented by the role of the players; Logistics furnishes the stage management, accessories, and maintenance. The audience, thrilled by the action of the play and the art of the performers, overlooks all of the cleverly hidden details of stage management.[18]

The class politics of this false sense of grievance should be plain to readers of this or any other essay (the hero/bully once again shoves the good guy/nerd into the locker of history), but lest the point be missed, the logistical enterprise relies from the first on a rhetorical invocation of a need to appropriate control of quartering (housing) from the working class to the (emergent, novel) managerial class.[19] Later historians and theorists of military logistics (such as the odious but erudite Martin Van Creveld, who is largely responsible for the growth in the past forty years of the historiography of logistics) note over and over, following Jomini, that it is a sharply limited and delimited art. Its potential efficiencies are forever over the horizon, because "theory and practice are nowhere so far apart as in the field of war."[20] In short, precisely because of the complexity of exchanges between various elements of the system, the speed of the functioning of the system is only a fraction of the top speed of the fastest element in the system (e.g., the railroad in the U.S. Civil War, or the gasoline-powered truck introduced halfway through World War I).[21] In short, logistics is usually theorized ex post facto, and proceeds historically and instrumentally as a matter of practical experience, trial and error, and rules of thumb—art as much as or more than science.

Nevertheless, in this very contentious subfield of military history and theory, all authors appear to agree upon the necessity for a *logistical model* that operates according to the idealistic logic of efficiency that is the foundation for what would become present-day game theory, operations research, and heuristic programming. In the words of the most influential theorist of logistics of all time, George C. Thorpe, even if it is true that "problems in logistics are problems in uncertainty rather than displaying the regularity of events in the physical sciences" because they involve the interactions between a vast number of participants with a wide range of choices available to them, a

> consideration of pure Logistics cannot be complete without some reference to a theory of preparing the parts of the organization for efficient operation. Efficiency of the parts is required.
>
> Efficiency may be said to be the power that accomplishes a designed work; as the state of possessing adequate knowledge for the performance of a duty; as the ratio of effect produced to the energy expended in producing it. The outstanding essentials appear to be: *power* and *knowledge* as subjective; *task* as objective. The subjective conditions must be proportioned to the objective requirements; that is to say, the quantity and quality of power and knowledge to be possessed by functionaires [sic] in the military machine must be measured and provided to meet the requirements of the task.[22]

That is to say, each component or element of the system can, on its own, be optimized, improving the performance of the system as a whole.[23] This particulate view of systems inherent to logistical knowledge marks it out as a separate discipline from holistic (if also stridently instrumental) fields such as systems theory and its derivatives, such as ecology.

Insofar as military theorists of logistics are concerned with architecture at all, they universally consider it, however unwittingly, in Ruskin's terms as an architecture of position. Buildings are in the first instances *depots* of various types, places where men and matériel are deposited to await future movement or use. The simplest depots are *dumps,* little more than holes in the ground where troops could deposit food, fodder, and ammunition during, before, or after fighting to extend the life of a line of supply and increase their capacity for movement, or as longer-term hedges intended to supply a protracted retreat. More sophisticated depots such as tented or tilt-up field hospitals are not fortified encampments; yet they do, from an early date, often have relatively ordered plans for the distribution of equipment on their interiors, a plan facilitating the flow of wounded bodies and caregivers through the structure, and an intimate relationship to the vehicles (horse-drawn carts but later trucks, boats, planes, and helicopters) that can carry them and their contents away from the theater of war at speed. The most sophisticated depots in twentieth-century warfare were the vast warehouses that organized and distributed the thousands of unique items required to supply forces operating in four out of the five possible "mediums of fighting: the land surface, the water surface, the air, the subterranean, and the submarine" (war in outer space still remains a fantasy, despite the logistical emplacement of orbital satellites, but an eminently realizable one).[24] In this schema, the pattern of the historical development of the depot is, of course, entirely parallel and coeval with the development of building (and perhaps even architecture) in general, as Le Corbusier plainly acknowledged in the opening salvos of *Vers une architecture*.[25]

What is exposed in reviewing the architectural historical literature—and, more broadly, literatures attending to the rapidly multiplying "cultural techniques" of movement—is that an architecture of position rarely corresponds in any meaningful sense to conventional architectural theoretical tropes such as "type," "typology," "tectonics," "order," and so on. Instead, one finds in the historical record a persistently informal set of architectonic improvisations. As the historian David M. Henkin shows in his study *The Postal Age*, the relatively rigorous logistical machinery of the nineteenth-century postal system in the United States was at first housed in improvised furniture, small additions to houses and minor public buildings, then slotted into a broad array of extant aspects of the urban environment long before receiving the attentions of professional architects concerned with anachronistically providing logistical depots and termini with a representational architecture (usually derived from a tortured transposition of conventions from traditional religious architecture).[26] This kind of phenomenon, so common to the architectural history of modernity, plainly illustrates that the *remediation* of an architecture of position into an architecture of protection is part of a more or less chaotic *process* that is distended across an amount of time incommensurate with the speed at which the infrastructural systems of logistics operate, and that this process is littered with missteps.[27] Strange, then, that so much of the rhetoric in both logistical and architectural circles should be oriented around a logic and vocabulary of *immediacy*.

"REAL TIME" AND THE MEDIA OF IMMEDIACY

What is shocking about the discourse of immediacy is how thoroughly divorced it is from the explicit and tacit acknowledgment in logistical discourse that war is slow. Although in treatises on strategy and tactics it is not uncommon to read the rhetoric of instantaneity—terms and phrases like *Blitzkrieg*, C3, autonomous drone, Star Wars, and so on—these are absent in the logistical framework. In business and military institutions, then, there is a kind of schizophrenia with regards to the problem of *distance over time,* or *speed* (as opposed to the classical and modern problem of thinking the space-time relationship in physics and metaphysics[28]). What divides these two mentalities is the answer to an ontological question regarding physics: whether or not the matériel, personnel, and weapons move *through* anything. In short, it is a question of *media.*

The aforementioned Thorpe, who even in a theoretical discussion intended to address the matter of "pure logistics" as opposed to the practical humdrum, theorized this problem explicitly and characteristically from a logistical point of view when he pointed out that before one could determine the particular character of a given logistical setup, the quartermaster would need firm knowledge of the material state of the theater of war or "business."

> At the same rate in which we find modern war losing its mystery and chivalry, we find it ranging itself in close alliance with industry of the commercial kind, from which war is acquiring "business methods." The lessons of every war of the past hundred years have emphasized the importance of the business factor. As the nation at peace is a hive of industry, so the state at war is a nation in arms—every individual with a part to perform either in the actual fighting or in providing means for fighting. To be efficient, in this great task, there must be "team-work." The tasks to be performed must be classified and the performers distributed to the various classes of work in such manner as to eliminate duplication and waste. This is almost exclusively the province of Logistics.[29]

The admission of the inevitable "duplication and waste" that structurally prevent a logistical setup from achieving the velocity of its fastest element by binding it to its slowest runs counter to all attempts to theorize a dromological theory of war, whether by generals or rather credulous leftist critics such as Paul Virilio.[30] The military dream of immediacy is but one such dream.

Another crucial insight that Thorpe's analysis provides—if only obliquely—is his alignment of "business methods" with the need to encroach upon military practice as a means of facilitating "team-work." Despite his efforts at fixing a rigorous theory of logistics, Thorpe here shows that the corporate body is a form of *improvisation.* The specific form of a corporate body—military or paramilitary, such as the industrial titans of logistics of his day, including the nascent United States Railroad Administration, General Electric, or CTR (later IBM)—is shaped not by a positive statement of program, as the legal language of charters might lead one to believe, but rather a response to a perceived logistical inefficiency (e.g., corruption, delay of supply, defeat, or any other form of what economists term "deadweight loss").[31] In the language of logistics, inefficiency is the mother of efficiency, and a contingent set of corporate structures are the primary media through which efficiency may be achieved.

Nowhere is the deliberately obfuscating ideological rhetoric of instantaneity more apparent than in the ubiquitous term *real time*. Taken to signify "immediacy," real time is the effect of the operations of, in the words of Bernard Stiegler, "technics as time."[32] Even the most cursory examination of any actual technical apparatus that is said to produce events taking place in real time—e.g., telephone calls, computerized financial transactions, and "instant" messaging—reveals that all such apparatuses are in fact dependent, in the first instance and the last, on the technical principle and limit of *delay*. Like a film or a ticker tape, real-time technologies seem to operate as a seamless and regular flow yet in fact are radically discrete, and require a mechanical or electronic apparatus in order to reorganize and regulate their movement. In light of this simple observation, the relevant but not primary question of speed is revealed. The requisite speed of a real-time system is not "the speed of light" or "absolute speed"; rather, and simply, the requisite speed is *faster than the fastest human being's apperceptive apparatus*. Just as the film unspools and races past the lens faster than the eye can capture the individual photographs on its surface and process each as a *framed* object, any real-time system needs only to dupe the sensoria—and, more importantly, the *apperceptive* capacity—of the human beings who are its functions and functionaries.

There are any number of examples of such "real-time" technologies that one might take to illustrate the point; yet one text that has so far eluded the attention of most architectural historians and theorists is Paul Baran's 1962 RAND Corporation report, "On Distributed Communications Networks."[33] Media archaeologists, particularly those who are at pains to produce an ontology of "time criticality," are keen to mine such texts as this for their manifold contradictions.[34] This is, of course, admirable, and just plain common sense; yet questions linger regarding the precise question of how such delays might *matter*, in any sense familiar to a reader versed in materialism.

Baran was a Polish-born electrical engineer who, having worked for Eckert-Mauchly Computer Company and Hughes Aircraft before settling into a post at the RAND Corporation, became a pioneer in the field of computer networks.[35] His particular brief at RAND was to develop a "survivable" or "hardened" communications system for the U.S. Department of Defense and its various branches—one that would be able to function in the wake of a massive nuclear attack. As such, Baran's work is exemplary in that it reflects—in the crystal-clear language of the engineer—the frustrated desire for instantaneity and its techno-ideological effects.

Baran's research in the service of "survivability" began, like all information and communications theory, from the well-established information-theoretical premise of *redundancy*.³⁶ Instead of the redundancy of code and the new electronic means for furthering the degree of redundancy in the transmission of a given message against the withering effects of noise, Baran placed special emphasis on the "redundancy of connectivity." In other words, he was less concerned with the hardware and more concerned with the way it was set up. The proper apparatus could, he argued, be accomplished through the construction of "distributed" as opposed to "centralized" or "decentralized" communications infrastructure (Figure 6.1). Provided that a perfect or near-perfect system of switching—that is, one that was maximally flexible and performed its work instantaneously, what Baran called the "'hot potato' heuristic routing doctrine"—could be developed at a technical level (which, for Baran, involved the invention of new kinds of software as well as hardware), such a distributed arrangement could protect the military's communications systems. This he demonstrated using a set of Monte Carlo simulations of hypothetical heavy bombings of various distributed network designs, concluding that "if n [the number of maximally interconnected switches] is made sufficiently large, it can be shown that highly survivable system structures can be built—even in the thermonuclear era."³⁷

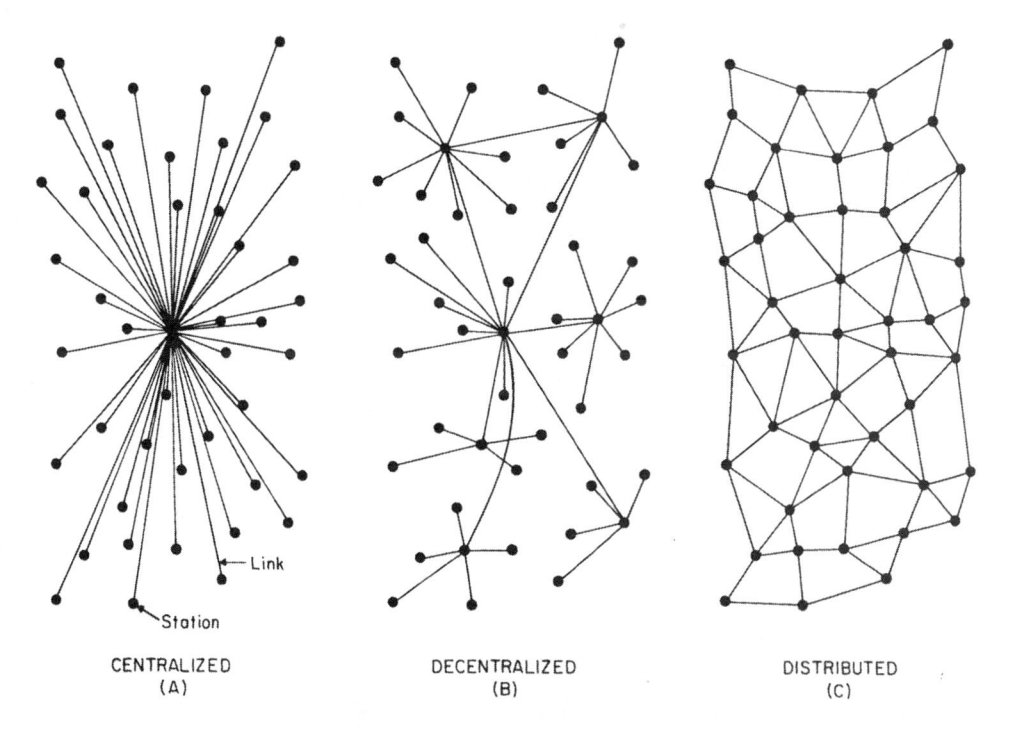

Figure 6.1. Centralized, decentralized, and distributed networks. Paul Baran, "On Distributed Communications Networks," November 1962.

The point stands, but only up to another point. As Baran noted, his proposed switching system did not, in fact, exist, and could not, in theory or practice, be built. Because of the use of packet switching, which required delays in order to aggregate and then transmit data, such a network could only provide networked connections in "quasi-real-time."[38] What mattered instead was the *economy* of the system that would be built, using the ideal of perfect switching as a paradigm for the development of technologies that were just good enough. This economy operated at two levels. First, there was the game-theoretical level, which justified Baran's and RAND's decision to make his research public, thus guaranteeing its effectiveness as a deterrent to his counterparts in the USSR. As he put it in a brief statement on nascent "future systems": "We will soon be living in an era in which we cannot guarantee the survivability of any single point. However, we can still design systems in which system destruction requires the enemy to pay the price of destroying n of n stations."[39] Such a price was never a matter of serious inquiry, to the continued consternation of all who worry about such things.

At a second level, however, the minimax language of operations research allowed Baran to state the problem of producing survivability as an optimization of the dollar cost of producing high-speed packet switching technologies in a distributed network with the media effect of *apparent* instantaneity: "There would be no physical real-time connection between the transmitting and receiving end. But, I felt that would be okay; if the transmission data rate was high enough, *the user would be fooled by the illusion that the real-time connection existed.*"[40] By keeping this switching system operating at a delay of under one second of "simulated real world time," Baran sketched out a conceptual plan for what would become ARPANET and the internet.[41]

The explicitness of the oxymoronic logic is, at a first reading, astonishing. "Simulated," "real"; "real," "world"; "world," "time"—all these tensions and oppositions are used to produce a "simulated . . . time" that at once produces real effects in the "world" and makes absolutely necessary the application of this new form of "time" to the entire "world" as a necessary, willful, and yet deceitful requirement. Yet this duplicity should not be as surprising as it appears to be. In fact, this non- or even antidialectical form of reasoning has provided the technical character and characteristics of our communications technologies for millennia.

Drawing upon the work of Harold Innis, Jack Goody, McLuhan, Friedrich Kittler, and many others, Brian Rotman has recently argued forcefully that these paradoxes of temporality proceed from the very structure of the alphabet. More important for the purposes of this essay than Rotman's argument regarding the end of alphabetism and its consequences is a corollary argument that is developed throughout his trilogy on mathematics, the alphabet, and writing: that human beings fix or embody temporal phenomena—themselves passing, in motion, and temporary—precisely in order to allow them to *endure and move* in the world as instruments.[42] Their seeming permanence—orders preserved in archives, invoices, cartographies, even memoirs—is always produced in the service of a temporal instrumentality that is itself only (con)temporary and contingent.

MEDIA ARCHITECTURES

To take but one example of a "building type" or "typology" (both terms have their serious flaws, despite their currency, as we shall see), railroad depots can serve as an instructive example of how our understanding of a properly logistical architecture can be enriched by producing a historical and technical frame that would be attentive to its status as a depot within a distributive network. A crudely formalist and materialist pocket history of the railroad station quickly reveals the strangeness and syncretism of its architecture, and yet our histories of these buildings have been and remain preoccupied with the building's ornamental programs or the tautology of arguing that their presence is evidence of modernity.

Let us take the only train station to receive full monographic scrutiny from an architectural historian, London's immortal Paddington Station, as an example.[43] Steven Brindle's living history of the terminus of the line linking London to Bristol from its first, quite simple instantiation in 1835 to its postmodern reworking in the twenty-first century is remarkable for many reasons (not least of which is its actual impact on the preservation scheme for several archaeological discoveries during the latter-day expansion of the station). But more to the point here, Brindle's account departs from every other architectural historical analysis of railroad stations because of its painstaking documentation and reconstruction of the working method of the station's primary designer—the engineer, architect, and naval architect Isambard Kingdom Brunel (1806–59)—in its two primary nineteenth-century versions.

Brindle documents—occasionally down to the *minute,* as the rapidly churning engines of industry produced, razed, and produced again—the complex's history, and there is no need to rehearse the details here. What is plainly shown, however, through Brunel's original sketches and archaeologically reconstructed plans, is the way in which Brunel allowed the demands of the trains, their tracks, and their switches to determine the *parti* of each architectural installation in the complex. Buildings were slotted in between curving tracks, or allowed to straddle the tracks entirely, each situated and shaped to fulfill a particular logistical function: the storage and distribution of goods between rail and cart, the temporary housing of passengers and their effects (on quays and in waiting rooms and in hotel rooms alike), the temporary housing of engines and rail cars, the sorting of mail, police stations, administrative offices, taxi stands, and more. Brunel's early designs for Paddington left much of the space of the station open to the surrounding streets, with minimal architectural mediation between rail and pavement, but even then, the jumble of programs that needed to be brought into some kind of order was enormous (Figure 6.2). Thus we see that the architecture of position—at least as it is articulated in a logistical monument such as Paddington—is one of perpetual improvisation, in which some aspects (the train tracks and switches, the chutes and cubbies for sorting mail) are worked out at a high degree of technical resolution, whereas conventional architectural elements are left as open and as flexible as possible in response.[44] Indeed, the architect of record on the project in its early

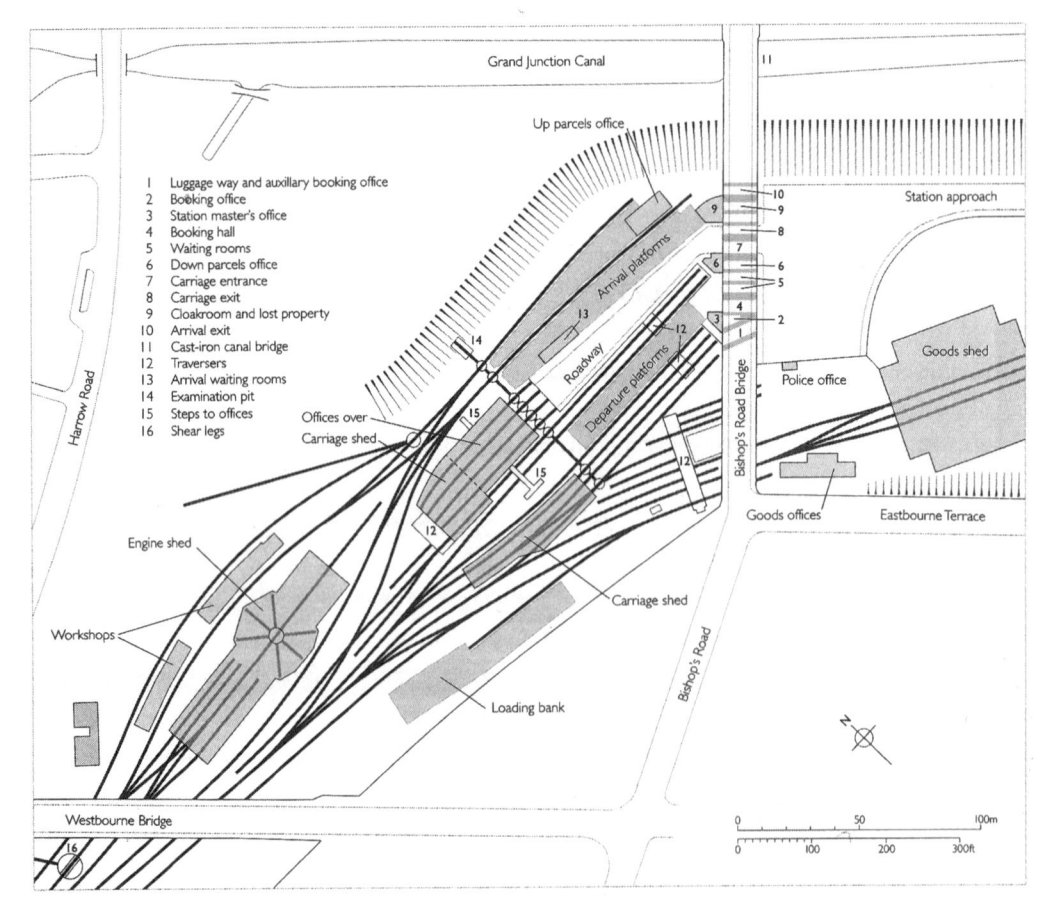

Figure 6.2. Reconstructed plan of Paddington Station in 1845, based on I. K. Brunel's original designs and historical articles from *Great Western Railway Magazine*. Steven Brindle, *Paddington Station: Its History and Architecture*, 2nd ed. (Swindon: English Heritage, 2013), 20.

stages, Matthew Digby Wyatt—who, incidentally, was also a critic who attacked Ruskin for his refusal to embrace industrial and logistical culture—was left to coordinate the decorative and ornamental schemes of additional designers such as Owen Jones and Alfred Stevens, alongside providing some sculptural flourishes of his own. He certainly was not entrusted by Brunel to comprehend the logistical system itself (Figure 6.3).[45]

Beyond the *parti* and its relation to the rail network itself, the true significance of the architecture of position demands attention to the seemingly small and insignificant technical detail. For instance, the engineering team of William J. Wilgus and Frank J. Sprague—who worked out the highly complex logistics of the new Grand Central Terminal in midtown Manhattan in the early twentieth century—was only able to make possible the construction of tens of massive high-rise hotels and office buildings surrounding the station because it was able to perfect, through an ingenious act of inverting the section, the electrical third rail.[46] Not only did this do away permanently with the need for a massive train shed and complex ventilation systems (which did not really function anyway); it also allowed the trains to *loop through* the terminal rather than move forward and reverse, without the need for constantly shunting engines, trucks, and cars. Moreover, the volume of traffic into and out of the terminal could be more than trebled by superimposing one level of tracks over another, forever transforming the massive development of yet another business district within metropolitan New York (Figures 6.4, 6.5, 6.6).

Before turning to a discussion of the contemporary demands on architectural history to these questions, it must be stressed that careful attention to the materiality of logistical architecture serves as a vital counter to the mendacious tendency to imagine communication as immediate and immaterial.[47] The tendency to imagine *metaphor*—which, as Marshall McLuhan and many others have stressed, carries one thing from where it is to where it is going—as something purely symbolic or abstract carries with it a shockingly dangerous attitude toward the world. As numerous materialist theorists, critics, and historians of media have rightly claimed, the seemingly ethereal experience of push-button ordering a commodity from, say, Amazon involves setting into perpetual motion people and things within the most massive infrastructural apparatus ever built.[48]

A PROVISIONAL CONCLUSION: LOGISTICAL MONUMENTS AND CONTEMPORARY ARCHITECTURAL HISTORY

Military culture's utter neglect of architecture conceived of as anything other than an ad hoc vessel and an unfortunately necessary adjunct to a larger and more dynamic process (i.e., the depot) is the mirror image of architectural history,

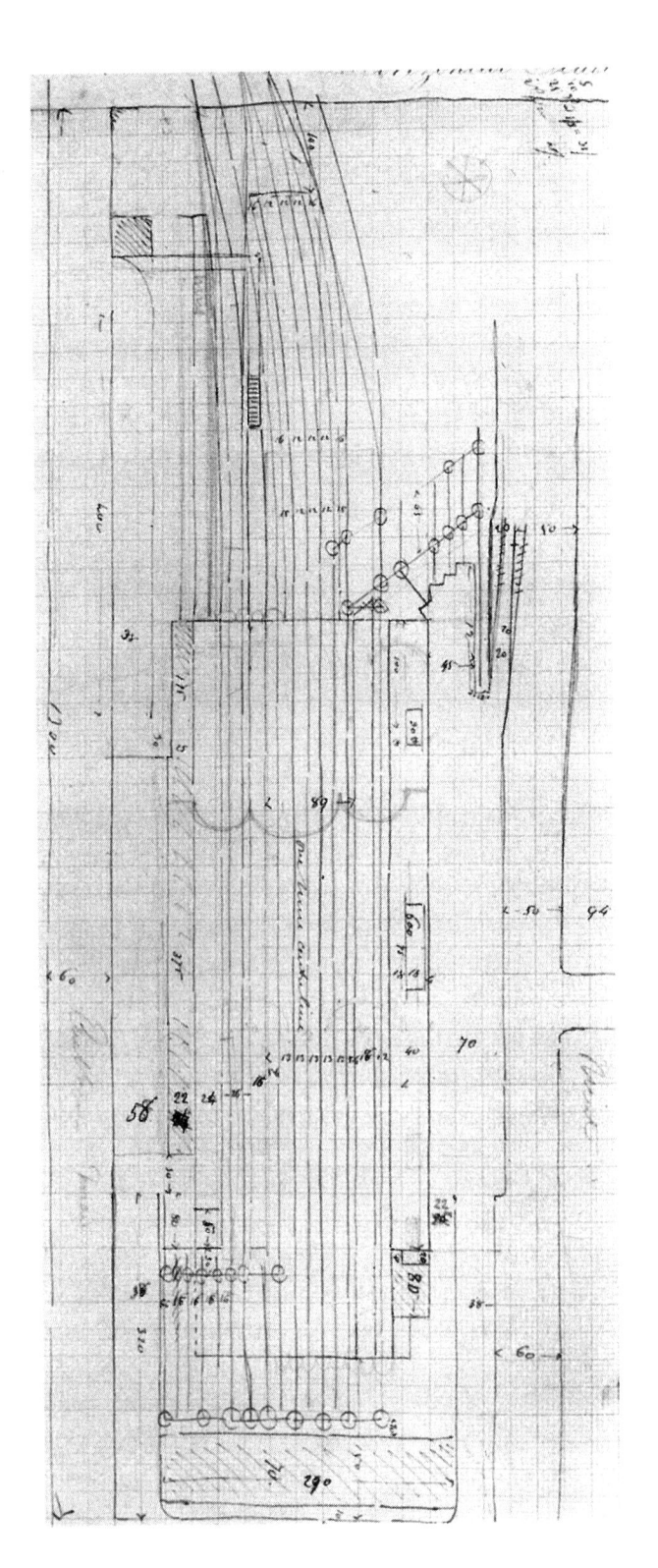

Figure 6.3. I. K. Brunel, plan sketch of the new Paddington Station showing how the architectural organization of the program is derived from the track and switch layout, December 1850. University of Bristol Brunel Collection, DM 162/8/1/1, large sketchbook 3, folio 13. Courtesy of the Brunel Institute, a collaboration of the SS Great Britain Trust and the University of Bristol.

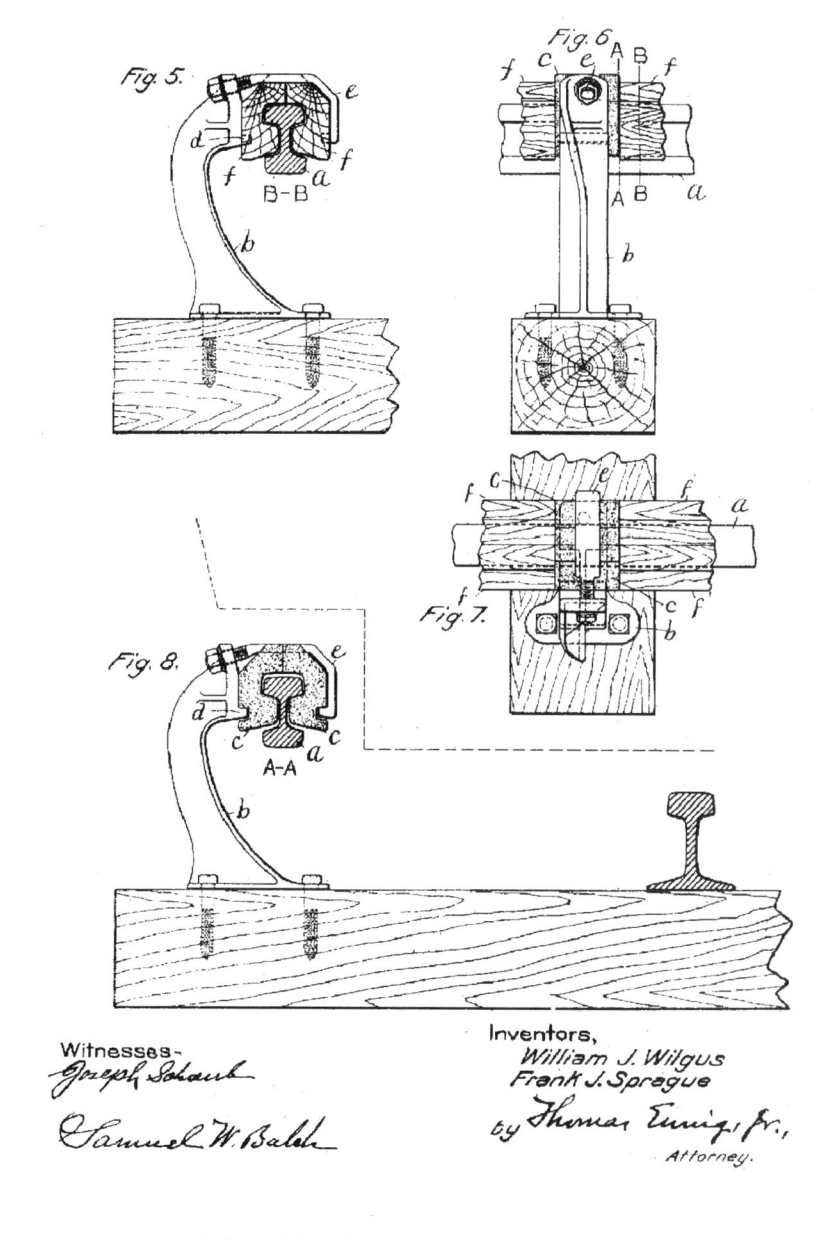

Figure 6.4. Section and plan of the "third rail." W. J. Wilgus and F. J. Sprague, Third Rail, U.S. Patent 908,180, application filed May 27, 1905, patented December 29, 1908.

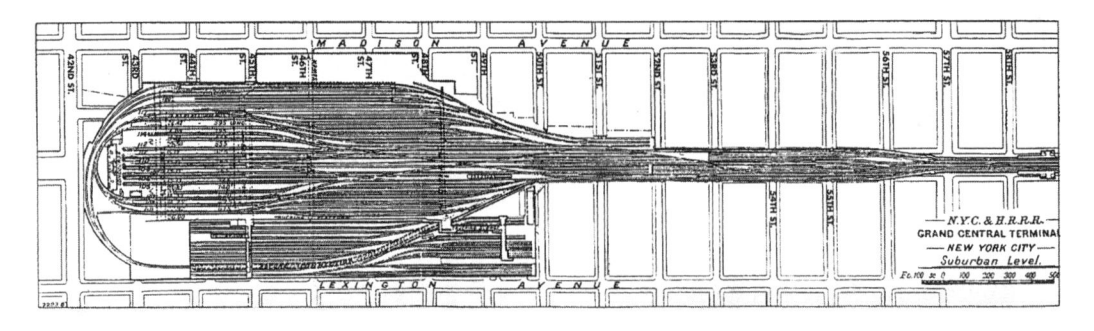

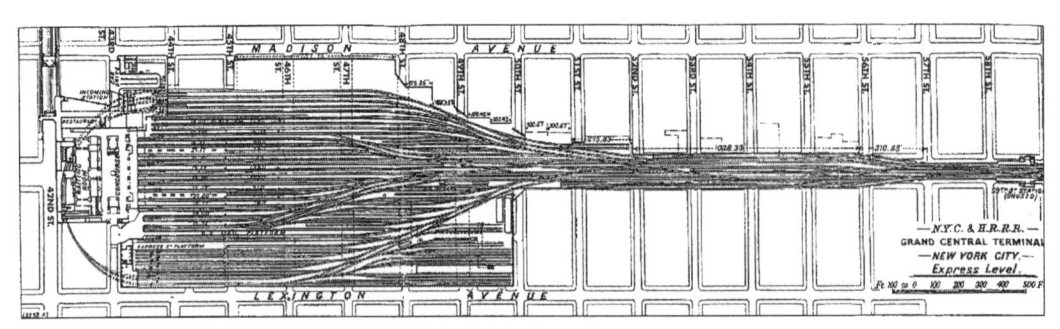

Figure 6.5. Schematic plans showing lower (suburban) and upper (express) track levels and "run around track" or "balloon loop." W. J. Wilgus, Grand Central Terminal, New York, 1904–14. Wikimedia Commons.

Figure 6.6. Warren & Wetmore, Grand Central Terminal, New York, 1904–14. Perspective section diagram showing all relevant passenger areas and train lines. "Monumental Gateway to a Great City," *Scientific American* 107, no. 23 (December 7, 1912): 484.

which has likewise nearly always avoided substantive discussion of the architecture of position. The old Pevsnerian saw to the effect that "a bicycle shed is a building, Lincoln Cathedral is a piece of architecture" can be taken as the *reductio ad absurdum* of this elitist and anachronistic attitude.[49] One might parse Nikolaus Pevsner's statement in an ingenuous effort at critique: If Lincoln Cathedral is a piece, what is the whole? If neither were built by architects, how does architecture exist independently of human agency? Yet this would be to focus on a purely negative critique rather than to attempt the aim of this essay, which is to point to the potential of a positive project for contemporary architectural historiography.

I propose reconstructing a bibliographic framework that may prove useful to contemporary architectural historians who are at pains to address the pressing problems of historicizing vernacular, logistical, scientific, and infrastructural buildings and systems. This bibliography cannot be constructed in full here, but the other essays in this volume indicate clearly that a model could be provided worthy of criticism and redesign in the service of an architectural history capable of wrestling the architecture of position, lodging, and timing back into the frame of contemporary architectural historiography.

Happily, there is already strong work now available and currently progressing within and around architectural history that could serve as the roots of a viable countercanon. This countercanon would include works on naval and military architecture: say, Christopher Drew Armstrong's crucial reassessment of the work of Julien-David LeRoy, Keith Mallory and Arvid Ottar's somewhat dated *Architecture and War*, Virilio's *Bunker Archaeology*, and Larrie D. Ferreiro's recent and magisterial (and largely unread by conventional architectural historians) *Ships and Science*.[50] One would need to add the most significant works on corporate architecture: Antoine Picon's studies of the intersections of architecture and engineering in the eighteenth century; Carl W. Condit's entire oeuvre; Reyner Banham and Manfredo Tafuri's ideologically divergent critiques of the office building; Carol Krinsky's pioneering work on Rockefeller Center; Jean-Louis Cohen's work on World War II; Reinhold Martin's string of extraordinary books on the topic from *The Organizational Complex* to *Utopia's Ghost* and *Urban Apparatus*; Keller Easterling's pioneering polemical research culminating in the recent *Extrastatecraft*; and a younger generation of historians such as Michael Osman, Gretta Tritch Roman, and Jesse LeCavalier, who have attempted even more explicit descriptions of logistical systems as the basis for architectural and urban innovation from genuinely critical perspectives.[51] One could add the sophisticated historians of science who have diagrammed the complex corporate concatenations of the U.S. National Laboratory System, the intricacies of big and small science alike, and so on. Art historians have also been on board, as Matthew C. Hunter's recent work (some of which is in this volume) as an author and editor has shown far better than I could summarize in the form of a truncated bibliographic essay. The point of asking for such a bibliography, though, is to press mediacy and position back into the center of architectural debate by invoking—nay, echoing—the calls of a surprisingly vast archive of material, authors, and technicians who have insisted that the logistical is the modern and vice versa.

In concluding his 1890 lecture on the "great architectural problem" facing contemporary architects, John Wellborn Root was more straightforward. After some broad generalizations regarding classical and neoclassical architecture and walking the students at the Art Institute of Chicago through the exigencies of planning a modern twelve-story office building, he turned to a sustained argument regarding the need to reorient the entire matter of architectural design around the technical—and therefore logistical—demands of the building type, especially the need to accommodate a number of complex circulatory systems. Throughout, he stressed that such problems could only be solved through a strictly rational coordination of what would soon be rearticulated in the minimax equations of operations research: "The utmost economy is employed, not a useless pound being admissible."[52] What is more surprising about Root's remarks, however, is his frank willingness to discard the solemnities that so characterized Ruskin's bias toward the ecclesiastical, monarchic, academic, and (putatively secular) civic architecture of protection. For Root, such tropes were for the weak.

> To other and older types of architecture these new problems are related as the poetry of Darwin's evolution is to other poetry. They destroy indeed much of the most admirable and inspiring of architectural forms, but they create forms adapted to the expression of new ideas and new aspects of life. Here, vagaries of fashion and temporary fancies should have no influence; here the arbitrary dicta of self-constituted architectural prophets should have no voice. Every one of these problems should be rationally worked out alone, and each should express the character and aims of the people about it.[53]

The seduction of the invocation of *poesis* that tectonic discourse inaugurated in the nineteenth century as a justification of conservative cultural values validating architects' work in the service of capital is here invalidated. The raw, technical fact of the architects' duty, for figures such as Root (and a long genealogy of architects and their firms stretching before and after the summer of 1890), is that the architecture of lodging and of position—of logistics—is the primary object of the architect's concern. The refusal to theorize or historicize that concern is dangerous.

Root concluded his lecture with a final and pointed illustration: a schematic plan and section of the foundation of a prototypical office building (Figure 6.7).

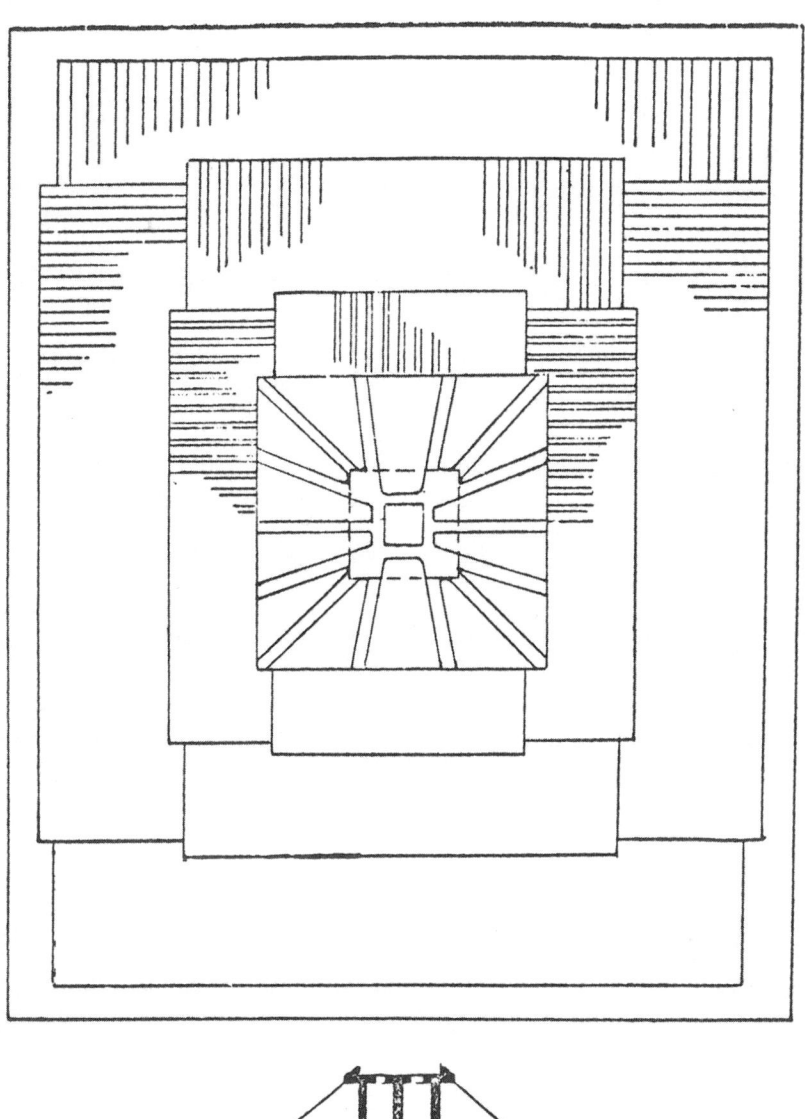

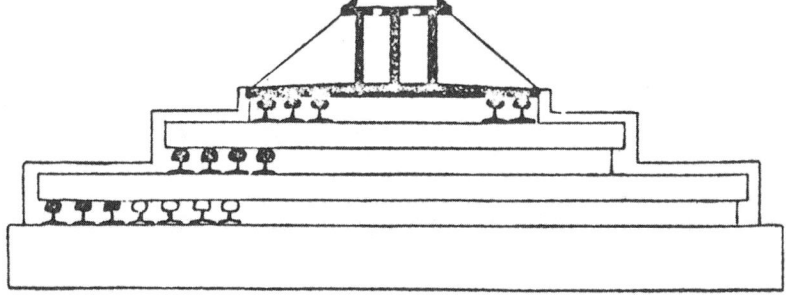

Figure 6.7. Schematic plan and section of the foundation of a prototypical office building, ca. 1890. John Wellborn Root, "A Great Architectural Problem," *Inland Architect and News Record* 15, no. 5 (1890): 71.

The plan and section are not technical diagrams that would serve as engineering or construction specifications; rather, they are rhetorical. The rails of train tracks and elevator shafts are shown as the basis for the office building. The structural and logistical elements are, in the eyes of a technocratic architect at the end of the nineteenth century, essentially one.

What is at stake should be clear: bicycle sheds (and their larger depot cousins) are far more important than we as architectural historians once dared to believe. Lurking underneath the styled surfaces of buildings are material conditions operating, in "real time," on architecture from the inside out.[54] There is much work to do, but perhaps we might well conclude this brief essay by taking slight liberties with the old logistical saw "For want of a nail . . . ," credited to Benjamin Franklin: for want of a history, the theory was lost; for want of a theory, the critique is lost; for want of a critique, architecture was lost, washed away by a tide of infrastructural projects indifferent to its willful anachronism.[55]

NOTES

Epigraphs: Jean-Luc Nancy, "Of Divine Places," trans. Michael Holland, in *The Inoperative Community*, ed. Peter Connor (Minneapolis: University of Minnesota Press, 1991), 150; Émile Zola, *The Debacle*, trans. Leonard Tancock (London: Penguin, 1972), 296.

1. John Ruskin, *The Stones of Venice*, abr. and ed. J. G. Links (New York: Hill and Wang, 1960), 40.

2. Ruskin, 40.

3. Aside from the obvious reference one could make here to the vast literature on the skyscraper that would begin to flower in the late nineteenth century, the more direct heir to Ruskin's injunction to study the tower can be found in Sidney Toy's classic *Castles: A Short History of Fortifications from 1600 B.C. to A.D. 1600* (London: William Heinemann, 1939), esp. chaps. XIV and XVI.

4. Ironically, Ruskin's hero Thomas Carlyle, in his satirical novel *Sartor Resartus: The Life and Opinions of Herr Teufelsdröckh, in Three Books* (1831; repr., London: Cassell, 1904), anticipated the need to theorize movement as a quintessential aspect of modernity, despite his general pessimism that such a feat could be accomplished. Perhaps the first effort to synthesize a theory in architectural discourse that would bring the Platonic solids of orthographic representation with the paradigmatic transportation technologies of modernity is Le Corbusier's *Vers une architecture* (Paris: Les Éditions G. Crès et Cie., 1923), which provocatively demands a new mode of vision capable of capturing the complexity of logistical phenomena such as the steamship, airplane, and automobile as opposed to "eyes that do not see."

5. John Durham Peters, in *The Marvelous Clouds: Toward a Philosophy of Elemental Media* (Chicago: University of Chicago Press, 2015), argues for much the same operation of remembrance of the medial status of the elements; see esp. chap. 3, "The Fire Sermon,"

which treats a broad array of ancient and recent attempts to retheorize the hearth and vessel as containers of space and matter.

6. Ironically, sometime in the intervening ninety years of English history, Ruskin's hasty and convenient settlement became a moral principle of architectural history and theory, even for those who sought to conserve the dying embers of a vanguardist movement that the English themselves had done little enough to promote. Nevertheless, logistical monuments such as factories (e.g., the Fagus plant) and the aestheticization of logistical networks (e.g., the Townscape movement) were still required to populate the canon of an architectural history based on the exploitation of "modern materials" such as steel, concrete, and glass. See Nikolaus Pevsner, *Pioneers of the Modern Movement from William Morris to Walter Gropius,* 4th ed. (New Haven, Conn.: Yale University Press, 2005).

7. During the advent of the internet in the late 1980s and early 1990s, historians concerned with understanding the so-called information revolution worked to recover the deep history of telecommunications and management techniques in the eighteenth and nineteenth centuries. See, e.g., Lisa Bud-Frierman, ed., *Information Acumen: The Understanding and Use of Knowledge in Modern Business* (New York: Routledge, 1994); and in particular Martin Campbell-Kelly, "The Railway Clearing House and Victorian Data Processing," and Jo-Anne Yates, "Evolving Information Use in Firms, 1850–1920: Ideology and Information Techniques and Technologies," both in Bud-Frierman, *Information Acumen,* 27–74. This line of inquiry has spawned a rich array of studies since, e.g., Lisa Gitelman and Geoffrey B. Pingree, eds., *New Media, 1740–1915* (Cambridge, Mass.: MIT Press, 2004); M. Michaela Hampf and Simone Müller-Pohl, eds., *Global Communication Electric: Business, News and Politics in the World of Telegraphy* (Frankfurt: Campus Verlag, 2013); David M. Henkin, *The Postal Age: The Emergence of Modern Communications in Nineteenth-Century America* (Chicago: University of Chicago Press, 2006), esp. chap. 3, "Playing Post Office: Mail in Urban Space."

8. Ruskin's desire for immediacy was the unambiguous result of his ambivalent reading—inherited from his "master," Thomas Carlyle—of German idealist aesthetics, combined with a Protestant conviction in the legibility of the "book of the world." Unlike Carlyle, who preferred irony and satire as a means of outwardly rejecting the naïve immediatic theories of Johann Wolfgang von Goethe and reform pedagogues such as Johann Heinrich Pestalozzi while embracing a pessimistic view of truth derived from the work of Immanuel Kant (see Carlyle, *Sartor Resartus*), Ruskin instead turned increasingly away from the tactics of ekphrasis and realism and retreated instead into a method of idiosyncratic encyclopedism in order to preserve the possibility of the transparency of the world to the human soul. The best insight into Ruskin's method is provided by the index to *Fors Clavigera: Letters to the Workmen and Labourers of Great Britain,* 4 vols. (Boston: D. Estes, 1900), compiled by an unnamed employee of Ruskin toward the end of his life.

9. Perhaps the most familiar articulation of this strange concept is Marshall McLuhan, "The Invisible Environment: The Future of an Erosion," *Perspecta* 11 (1967): 161–67. See also Marshall McLuhan, *Through the Vanishing Point: Space in Poetry and Painting* (New York: Harper & Row, 1968); Marshall McLuhan, *The Gutenberg Galaxy: The Making of Typographic Man* (Toronto: University of Toronto Press, 1962).

10. On information theory, see Abraham Moles, *Théorie de l'information et perception esthétique* (Paris: Denoël, 1973); and Orit Halpern, *Beautiful Data: A History of Vision and Reason since 1945* (Durham, N.C.: Duke University Press, 2014). This effort to exploit the gaps between images is the result of an under- or negatively theorized dream, identified by Claude Shannon as "the noiseless channel," a frictionless communications system that could produce whole rather than atomized significance. The best critique of this synesthetic dream remains Friedrich Kittler's in *Discourse Networks 1800/1900*, trans. Michael Metteer and Chris Cullens (Stanford: Stanford University Pres, 1990).

11. See McLuhan, *The Gutenberg Galaxy*, 265.

12. Ruskin, *The Stones of Venice*, 45: "A wall has been defined to be an even and united fence of wood, earth, stone, or metal. Metal fences, however, seldom, if ever, take the form of walls, but of railings; and, like all other metal constructions, *must* be left out of our present investigation" (emphasis added).

13. I have attempted a latter-day assault on this point of view. See John Harwood, "On Wires; Or, Metals and Modernity Reconsidered," *Grey Room* 69 (Winter 2018): 108–36.

14. In this sense, Ruskin demonstrates that he had thoroughly absorbed the modernist anachronism of the manifesto, a genre of theoretical writing that invokes history precisely in order to combat the determinism of nineteenth-century historicist logic. In other words, he is in ample and diverse company in being credulous about the possibility of reversing history in order to restart it again. See Jacques Derrida, *The Specters of Marx: The State of the Debt, the Work of Mourning, and the New International*, trans. Peggy Kamuf (New York: Routledge, 1994), chap. 5.

15. Eugène-Emmanuelle Viollet-le-Duc, *Annals of a Fortress*, trans. Benjamin Bucknall (Boston: James R. Osgood, 1876).

16. Baron Henri de Jomini, *Précis de l'art de la guerre* (Paris: Anselin, 1838), translated by G. H. Mendell and W. P. Craighill as *The Art of War* (Philadelphia: J. B. Lippincott, 1862), 252. Note the date of the American translation—the crisis of the U.S. Civil War appears to have given a boost to popular and technical publications on logistics alike, much as treatises on aeronautical warfare appeared in greater numbers during the Spanish Civil War and World War II. Jomini's fate as a lesser-known theorist, of course, was due to the French losses in Russia and during the Hundred Days. See also the complete edition of Carl von Clausewitz, *On War*, ed. and trans. Michael Howard and Peter Paret (Princeton, N.J.: Princeton University Press, 1976).

17. Col. Felix J. Gerace (Commandant, Headquarters, United States Army Logistics Management Center, Fort Lee, Virginia), "Logistics, Management, Information" training pamphlet, May 1965, reprinted in James A. Huston, *The Sinews of War: Army Logistics, 1775–1953* (Washington, D.C.: Office of the Chief of Military History, United States Army, 1966), 691–701.

18. George C. Thorpe, *Pure Logistics: The Science of War Preparation* (1917; repr., Washington, D.C.: National Defense University Press, 1986), 2.

19. Something quite like this dynamic is clearly a motivation for the development of Karl Marx's late thought, which is ultimately centered on producing a critique of bourgeois theories of money and capital, the so-called primary "media" of "distribution" and

"exchange." See Karl Marx, *Grundrisse,* trans. Martin Nicolaus (London: Penguin, 1973), 233: "Money in its final, completed character now appears in all directions as a contradiction, a contradiction which dissolves itself, drives towards its own dissolution. As the *general form of wealth,* the whole world of real riches stands opposite it."

20. Martin Van Creveld, *Supplying War: Logistics from Wallenstein to Patton,* 2nd ed. (New York: Cambridge University Press, 2004), 261. After its initial publication in 1977, *Supplying War* drew the scrutiny of many critics; perhaps the most comprehensive critical review is provided in John A. Lynn, "The History of Logistics and *Supplying War,*" in *Feeding Mars: Logistics in Western Warfare from the Middle Ages to the Present,* ed. John A. Lynn (Boulder, Colo.: Westview Press, 1993), 9–27.

21. Creveld, *Supplying War,* 261: "Compared to ordinary life, waging war is like trying to walk in water: anything that seems easy suddenly requires a much greater effort, and every movement is slowed down."

22. Thorpe, *Pure Logistics,* 89.

23. This Whiggish trend from experimental tinkering toward "systems-thought" in twentieth-century military-industrial-academic institutions is a leitmotif of most histories and theories of logistics; however, authors sanguine about the possibility of a holistic solution to logistical problems are rare outside of the relatively lightweight discourse of business management theory. On the latter, see Keller Easterling, *Extrastatecraft: The Power of Infrastructure Space* (New York: Verso, 2014), chap. 4, which provides a strident critique of the main lines of scholarly and popular discourses on systems-building.

24. Thorpe, *Pure Logistics,* 4. On war conducted in the various theaters ranging from the terrestrial to the aquatic, aerial, and extra-atmospheric, see Paul Virilio, *War and Cinema: The Logistics of Perception,* trans. Patrick Camiller (London: Verso, 1989); Augustin M. Prentiss, *Civil Air Defense: A Treatise on the Protection of the Civil Population against Air Attack* (New York: McGraw-Hill, 1941); Paul N. Edwards, *The Closed World: Computers and the Politics of Discourse in Cold War America* (Cambridge, Mass.: MIT Press, 1996); Thomas Pynchon, *Against the Day* (London: Penguin, 2006); and John Harwood, "The Other End of the Trajectory: Danger Zones," *Grey Room* 54 (Winter 2014): 80–116.

25. Le Corbusier, *Vers une architecture,* vii–xi.

26. David M. Henkin, *The Postal Age: The Emergence of Modern Communications in Nineteenth-Century America* (Chicago: University of Chicago Press, 2006), chap. 3, "Playing Post Office: Mail in Urban Space." On the transposition of tropes from temple architecture to wholly different architectural programs, see Charles Belfoure's rather silly but essentially correct *Monuments to Money: The Architecture of American Banks* (Jefferson, N.C.: McFarland, 2005).

27. Daniel M. Abramson makes this case in his magisterial *Building the Bank of England: Money, Architecture, Society, 1694–1942* (New Haven, Conn.: Yale University Press, 2005), which concludes with the almost tragic remaking of the bank's headquarters in the 1930s.

28. See Max Jammer, *Concepts of Space: The History of Theories of Space in Physics,* 3rd ed. (New York: Dover, 1993), esp. the introduction, and chaps. 1, 4, and 5.

29. Thorpe, *Pure Logistics,* 30.

30. The most recent American theorist of a fully automated and autonomous lighting war was none other than the former (two-time) U.S. secretary of defense Donald Rumsfeld, who not only "modernized" the U.S. military's organizational structure globally in 2002 but also developed the doctrine of *preemption* in order to eradicate terrorism. On Rumsfeld's and others' techniques of preemption, see Andrew Cockburn, *Kill Chain: The Rise of the High-Tech Assassins* (New York: Henry Holt, 2015). For Virilio's theory of dromology and his characterization of the transformation of the media of warfare, see in particular Paul Virilio, *Popular Defense and Ecological Struggles* (New York: Semiotext(e), 1990), which offers his most direct statements on the literal apparatus of war as opposed to its representational techniques.

31. An excellent window into the provisional nationalization of American logistical corporations during the crisis of the U.S. entry into World War I is provided by the Records of the United States Railroad Administration in the National Archives, accessed May 2, 2017, https://www.archives.gov/research/guide-fed-records/groups/014.html#14.1. The fluidity with which bureaucrats, political figures, businessmen, and military leaders exchanged positions in the reshuffling of the entire industrial system of the United States is convincingly narrated in Huston, *The Sinews of War.*

32. The fragmentation of time and the transposition of memories under the terms of modern technics is critiqued powerfully in Stiegler's work. See Bernard Stiegler, *Technics and Time,* vol. 1, *The Fault of Epimetheus,* trans. Richard Beardsworth and George Collins (Stanford: Stanford University Press, 1998), 212–14, on the question of "the now"; and Bernard Stiegler, *Technics and Time,* vol. 2, *Disorientation,* trans. Stephen Barker (Stanford: Stanford University Press, 2009), 63: "As always, *epimetheia* means: delay because of speed. The contemporary *what* has frequently been defined by its speed. If speed, as advancement, has always been an essential attribute of technics, of the technical, then in the age of the letter, it is a question of delay as deferred time. Today, technical speed must confront this delay. . . . 'Real time' is . . . an apparent displacement, and the resistant reactions it incites result from a mute sense of the menacing possibility of an *in-différance.*"

33. Paul Baran, "On Distributed Communications Networks" (RAND Corporation paper for the First Congress of the Information Systems Sciences [MITRE Corporation and U.S. Air Force Electronic Systems Division], November 1962). This article was rewritten, greatly expanded, and republished many times, appearing in a series of 1964 RAND Corporation reports and in a condensed form in *IEEE Transactions on Communications Systems* 12, no. 1 (March 1964): 1–9.

34. A rather far-flung circle of such media archaeologists has formed around the work of Wolfgang Ernst. See Ernst's essay on method, "Media Archaeography: Method and Machine versus History and Narrative of Media," in *Media Archaeology: Approaches, Applications, and Implications,* ed. Erkki Huhtamo and Jussi Parikka (Berkeley: University of California Press, 2011), 239–55. For an alternative, more theoretically developed approach to the same topic, see Bernhard Siegert, *Relays: Literature as an Epoch of the Postal System,* trans. Kevin Repp (Stanford: Stanford University Press, 1999), in particular chap. 2, "On Time (Registered Letter I)," in which Siegert states the case for considering the basic contradictions at the root of real-time systems, which I attempt to carry forward here with

regard to more recent technical systems: "On the threshold of modern authorship, the body of a scholar interconnected with the postal system dreamed of optimizing its interconnection.... As an ideal, it both failed to recognize and camouflaged the situation: it displayed perfection in the form of obsolescence" (23).

35. On Baran, see RAND's own biography, "Paul Baran and the Origins of the Internet," accessed September 11, 2013, http://www.rand.org/about/history/baran.list.html.

36. Claude E. Shannon, "A Mathematical Theory of Communication," *Bell System Technical Journal* 27, no. 3 (July 1948): 379–423.

37. Baran, "On Distributed Communications Networks" (RAND Corporation paper), 18.

38. Baran, "On Distributed Communications Networks," *IEEE Transactions on Communications Systems* 12, no. 1 (March 1964): 9. At the time Baran published his research, he did not use the term *package switching* (he called packages "message blocks"); the now-ubiquitous term *package switching* is attributed by Baran himself to Donald W. Davies of the British National Physical Laboratory, who coined the term in 1965.

39. Baran, 9.

40. Paul Baran, "The Beginnings of Packet Switching: Some Underlying Concepts," *IEEE Communications Magazine* 40, no. 7 (July 2002): 43.

41. On the biopolitical implications of the use of packet switching, see Alexander R. Galloway, *Protocol: How Control Exists after Decentralization* (Cambridge, Mass.: MIT Press, 2004).

42. Brian Rotman, *Becoming beside Ourselves: The Alphabet, Ghosts, and Distributed Human Being* (Durham, N.C.: Duke University Press, 2008).

43. Rail stations have been the subject of a sizeable literature in architectural history, beginning with Carroll L. V. Meeks's classic *The Railroad Station: An Architectural History* (New Haven, Conn.: Yale University Press, 1956), and with significant entries by Carl W. Condit and Steven Brindle (see below). However, the incessant and perverse desire to analyze stations for their apparent formal qualities rather than their organizational logic is plainly reflected in Meeks's argument that the railroad station is a result of an aesthetic ideology. See Meeks, *The Railroad Station*, chap. 1, "The Nineteenth Century Style: Picturesque Eclecticism." To Meeks's credit, the book contains lasting insights into the planning of early railroad stations; see, e.g., his analysis of César Daly's and I. K. Brunel's efforts to regularize the *partis* of depots and termini (29–41).

44. The perversity of reading the railroad station as a type, in any other than a technical and logistical sense, proceeds at least in part from the confusion that prevails regarding the ontology of the corporation. Any novel form of incorporation is always a fiction of immediacy complicated by a need for producing corporate forms as a means of improvisationally overcoming transaction costs. See John Harwood, "Corporate Abstraction," *Perspecta* 46 (2013): 218–47.

45. See Steven Brindle, *Paddington Station: Its History and Architecture*, 2nd ed. (Swindon: English Heritage, 2013), 35–50.

46. Although one might wish for a greater depth of analysis, the contributions of Wilgus and Sprague are properly noted in Carl W. Condit, *The Port of New York: A History of*

the Rail and Terminal System from the Grand Central Electrification to the Present (Chicago: University of Chicago Press, 1981); and Peter Pennoyer and Anne Walker, *The Architecture of Warren & Wetmore* (New York: W. W. Norton, 2006), 78–109.

47. A beautiful and moving refutation of communication as dematerialized is offered by Mark Goble in *Beautiful Circuits: Modernism and the Mediated Life* (New York: Columbia University Press, 2010), esp. chap. 1, "Pleasure at a Distance in Henry James and Others."

48. See Jesse LeCavalier, *The Rule of Logistics: Walmart and the Architecture of Fulfillment* (Minneapolis: University of Minnesota Press, 2016); Nicole Starosielski, *The Undersea Network* (Durham, N.C.: Duke University Press, 2015); and, for a scathing overview of the perversions of labor and real estate engendered by the on-demand, real-time logistics of twenty-first-century America, see Corey Pein, *Live Work Work Work Die: A Journey into the Savage Heart of Silicon Valley* (New York: Metropolitan Books, 2018).

49. Nikolaus Pevsner, *An Outline of European Architecture,* 7th ed. (Harmondsworth, UK: Penguin, 1963), 15.

50. Christopher Drew Armstrong, *Julien-David Leroy and the Making of Architectural History* (New York: Routledge, 2012); Keith Mallory and Arvid Ottar, *The Architecture of War* (New York: Pantheon Books, 1973); Paul Virilio, *Bunker Archaeology,* trans. G. Collins (New York: Princeton Architectural Press, 1994); Larrie D. Ferreiro, *Ships and Science: The Birth of Naval Architecture in the Scientific Revolution, 1600–1800* (Cambridge, Mass.: MIT Press, 2007).

51. See, in particular, Michael Osman, *Modernism's Visible Hand: Architecture and Regulation in America* (Minneapolis: University of Minnesota Press, 2018); Gretta Tritch Roman, "The Reach of the Pit: Negotiating the Multiple Spheres of the Chicago Board of Trade Building in the Late Nineteenth Century" (PhD diss., Pennsylvania State University, 2016). Condit's work on "the Chicago School" of office building design is his best known among students of architectural history today, but the more relevant work by Condit for continuing to renovate histories of the architecture of position is *The Port of New York*.

52. John Wellborn Root, "A Great Architectural Problem" (lecture delivered to the architecture class of the Art Institute of Chicago, June 1890), published in *Inland Architect and Architectural Record* 15, no. 5 (June 1890): 67–71, and reprinted in John Wellborn Root, *The Meanings of Architecture: Buildings and Writings by John Wellborn Root,* ed. Donald Hoffmann (New York: Horizon Press, 1967), 130–142 (quote on 142).

53. Root, *The Meanings of Architecture,* 142.

54. See Geoffrey C. Bowker and Susan Leigh Star, *Sorting Things Out: Classification and Its Consequences* (Cambridge, Mass.: MIT Press, 2000), 323: "The invisibility of infrastructure makes visualization or description difficult. The metaphors we reach for to describe infrastructure are ironic and somehow childish. We speak of 'way down in the underwear,' 'underneath the system,' or use up-down metaphors such as 'runs under,' or 'runs on top of.'"

55. See Kenneth Macksey, *For Want of a Nail: The Impact on War of Logistics and Communications* (London: Brassey's, 1989), xiii, which quotes Franklin's maxim in full: "For want of a nail, the shoe was lost—for want of a shoe, the horse was lost—for want of a horse the rider was lost—for want of a rider the battle was lost."

CHAPTER 7

REPEATING

Cybernetic Intelligence

ORIT HALPERN

"Real time," "internet time," "run time": there is a seemingly endless vocabulary in our present for describing time in digital networks. What makes this surplus of language remarkable, however, is the stunning homogeneity of temporal modes being described. All this creative description refers, in one way or another, to notions of temporality as the self-referential product of network behavior. Time in contemporary discourse emerges from *within* systems. There are many temporalities, but none of them are outside technical networks. The corollary to this obsession with temporality as a self-produced and modulated process is a concern about stasis or nontime. Jamming, blocking, sabotaging, or otherwise "stopping" the network are all understood as usually negative (or at least destructive) acts. Such interruptions are often couched in a language of stupidity, psychosis, terror, opacity, and failure. Systems incapable of constantly assimilating change, variation, and difference are also systems that lack in contemporary parlance "resilience," "smartness," or "intelligence." This chapter will interrogate this relationship between temporality and reason in cybernetics to explain contemporary concerns about data visualization, ubiquitous computing, and "smart" networks. The argument is that cybernetic concerns about managing the flow or circulation of information are intimately linked to ideas of networked intelligence and "smartness." The topography of this relationship is not simple. Cyberneticians compressed psychoanalytic ideas of reason and unconsciousness with machine logic and systems thinking to make the environment itself a medium for cognition.

Arguably stasis and (ir)rationality have long been linked in discussions about the potential, and risk, of computationally networked systems. Writing to the cybernetician Norbert Wiener in 1952, the anthropologist Gregory Bateson, for example, explicitly correlated repetition with automatism and stasis with psychosis. He wrote about the "paranoidal" behavior of that most rational of Cold War institutions, the RAND Corporation.

> What applications of the theory of games do is to reinforce the players' acceptance of the rules and competitive premises, and therefore make it more and more difficult for the players to conceive that there might be other ways of meeting and dealing with each other. . . . I question the wisdom of the static theory as a basis for action in a human world. The theory may be "static" within itself, but its use propagates changes, and I suspect that the long-term changes so propagated are in a *paranoidal* direction and odious.[1]

What makes Bateson's comment unique, even fascinating, is its appropriation of psychoanalytic concerns with memory time, and death drive to propagate a rather new idea of intelligence. Bateson slides between game theory and paranoid and "odious" concepts of psychology without question. In doing so, he also compresses subjects and psychologies with systems, players, and generally "action" in a human world. By deduction, the forms of rationality being described do not belong to isolated minds or even centralized corporations but to networked and collective entities unified through processes and protocols (in the case of game theory).

There is also a temporality to this circuit. Bateson correlates "static" (atemporal) games with paranoid schizophrenia to signify a condition that induces autonomous and automatic repetition, culminating in potentially genocidal violence (nuclear war in this case)—a "paranoidal direction." Bateson is not referring here to human illness or disability; rather, he is discussing systemic behaviors. He fears that the performance of past data paraded as prophecy will produce only repetition without difference. In a stunning inversion of psychoanalytic concerns, Bateson recognizes that the ubiquity of computational logics makes distance impossible to achieve, as implied by the invocation of paranoia, a pathology making spatial differentiation impossible—the patient cannot differentiate their subjectivity from an external environment; they are, one might say, "too close" to the world by being in it.[2] As such, Bateson argues, paranoia induces violence, not as a result of any misdirected object choices or imagined enemy Others—game theories have no such formulations within them—but as the result of performing and repeating commands without interpretation, by generating enemies from within the process of play rather than finding enemies outside the game.

In fact, it is precisely the lack of imagination, or even futurity, that defines this condition. Bateson foresees a total war without desire; there is no projection of love or hate onto the enemy. There may not even be an object-enemy, only a circuit. The form of war being invoked is a war of subtraction, a war *without* difference, desire, and—most critically—time.

For Bateson, however, machines, like people, can desire and imagine, just as they can fail to do so. At stake is not the question of how the time (this imagined futurity) of a machine is different from that of a person but rather how one produces circuits that induce change without repetition.

The problem, according to Bateson, with "static" models is not so much a problem with computation per se as an approach to the human world. It is a problem of training, a question of how machines or people might adjust, change, and learn about the world; to be able to learn becomes the marker of intelligence and the inverse, paradoxically, of rationality. Rationality, in its "pathological" formulation, lacks any history, or perhaps even any temporality. Like the Freudian unconscious, for Bateson RAND's decision-making apparatus lacks temporal organization or signification. The circuit simply repeats. The corollary to this comprehension of rationality as psychotic but atemporal is that learning is associated with the time of evolution and change.

These ideas of temporality and rationality permeated cybernetics, a science that compressed older sciences of the human with an embrace of stochiastic processes and probability inherited from physics. Norbert Wiener, for example, specifically invoked the relationship between Bergsonian "vitalist" and Newtonian "mechanical" and "deterministic" temporalities in defining this new science. Wiener argued in *Cybernetics* that our age of complex automata and feedback systems exists in an active Bergsonian "vitalist" time, which is to say a temporality that is nonreversible and probabilistic (the past and the future are always interpenetrated through conditions of potentiality). This "vital" time that animates networks, like living organisms from within, makes the entire distinction between vital and mechanical "relegated to the limbo of a badly posed question."[3]

Wiener's invocation of Bergson, however, is complicated by a recognition that cybernetic forms of feedback and temporality posed fundamental problems for representation, meaning, and reason. It was by way of Sigmund Freud, the exemplar of a previous century's sciences, that Wiener implied the impossibility of describing a world in its totality, of ever rendering "reality" legible. Wiener displaces earlier modernist concerns with documenting the unconscious or mechanical objectivity, to embrace stochiastic processes and uncertainty. Instead, he argued, we are faced with an "incomplete determinism," an operative lack that cannot enter description but can produce something else—a self-referential and probabilistic form of thought.

> One interesting change that has taken place is that in a *probabilistic* world we no longer deal with quantities and statements which concern a specific, real universe as a whole but ask instead questions which may find their answers in a large number of similar universes.... This recognition of an element of incomplete determinism, almost an *irrationality* in the world, is in a certain way parallel to Freud's admission of a deep irrational component in human conduct and thought.[4]

This form of probabilistic thought that emerged at the turn of the last century would now, in Wiener's work and that of his compatriots in the information sciences, be connected with theories of messages. Wiener was comfortable with acceding that the universe in its plurality may never be known. This accession, however, was only made to allow for the possibility that—within far more localized situations in the future—chance might yet be contained by way of technology.

Viewed from a historical distance, Wiener and Bateson make clear that the time of the network and ideas (and practices) of agency, knowledge, power, and governance are intimately linked. Wiener's challenge moves from the "discovery" of indeterminacy to using this unknowability and "irrationality" to create many forms of machines. These statements mark a historical transition from the concept of temporality as the limit to human knowledge and the absolute site of a reality outside inscription or representation to today's "real time," a technical process, a time emanating from inside networks, a superficial design problem prompting concerns neither about subjectivity or objectivity but rather over logistics and management. If for figures such as Henri Bergson and Sigmund Freud time was understood as the absolute limit to, or expression of, human subjectivity and in turn they posited a time (or timelessness) of a reality unconscious in nature and inaccessible to science, in the cybernetic world there is no unconscious or "present" to discover, only a new ambition to produce self-referential systems that can learn and change. This switch from real to "real" is also a transformation in epistemology from the search for truths in an external world to the search for internal consistency variables and operability within our networks.

But if today we live in a world always focused on the performative (and always deferred) future—the next version, the next demo, the next interaction—problems of historical temporality, memory, and change continue to trouble our machine dreams. For both cybernetics and postwar psychoanalysis, amnesia, psychosis, and temporality were the mechanism for both producing violence and reformulating subjectivity, consciousness, and, as numerous historians of science have suggested, reason and learning.[5] I want to depart from accounts of Cold War rationality, however, by demonstrating its "psychotic" and circuitous underbelly. Cybernetic concerns with temporality and intelligence produced rationality as an emergent, dynamic, and constantly differentiating entity, a rationality that took different forms in different locations.

So how are we to contemplate this time of the network from within the machine? In this chapter, I examine the early work of cyberneticians on neural nets and machine memory in order to examine how ideas about temporality and memory were key to reconfiguring cognition and rationality in a manner that "anticipates" contemporary architectures of networks and discourses of "smartness" in complicated ways. It is particularly the cybernetic relationship to temporality and engagement with and against psychoanalysis that shaped new models of time in circuits fundamental to the reformulation of intelligence as rational, producing a new epistemology of pragmatic behavioralism, embodied and affective logic, and nonliberal agents. These are all concepts that continue to inform contemporary practices in fields ranging from neuroscience to finance to urban planning.[6] It is my contention that a troubled and troubling relationship between logic, history, and memory animates our machines and digital networks, driving a dual imaginary of instantaneous analytics and collective intelligence while encouraging the relentless penetration of media technologies into life through a frenzy to record and store information.[7] These practices arguably underpin the ongoing penetration and interweaving of computation and life, to support what many theorists label "biopolitics," but not without also birthing some new problems and possibilities that could serve as sources and inspirations for thinking and imaging alternative technological futures.[8]

THE LOGICAL CALCULUS OF THE NERVOUS NET

To begin contemplating contemporary concerns with both time and intelligence, it may be worth momentarily asking what concepts of memory and intelligence were introduced by cyberneticians after World War II. As is well documented, cybernetics emerged from work at the Radiation Lab at the Massachusetts Institute of Technology on antiaircraft defense and servomechanisms during World War II. Norbert Wiener, working with the MIT-trained electrical engineer Julian Bigelow and the physiologist Arturo Rosenblueth, reformulated the problem of shooting down planes in the terms of communication—between an airplane pilot and the antiaircraft gun. These researchers postulated that under stress, airplane pilots would act repetitively and display algorithmic behaviors analogous to servomechanisms, and therefore be amenable to mathematical modeling and analysis. This understanding allowed for all entities to be "black boxed" so as to be studied behaviorally and statistically.[9]

In 1943, inspired by this idea that machines and minds might be thought together through the language of logic and mathematics, the psychiatrist Warren

McCulloch and the logician Walter Pitts at the University of Illinois at Urbana-Champaign decided to take quite literally the machinelike nature of human beings. The pair would later go to MIT in 1952 at Norbert Wiener's behest.[10] Their article "A Logical Calculus of Ideas Immanent in Nervous Activity," appearing in the *Bulletin of Mathematical Biophysics,* has now come to be one of the most commonly referenced pieces in cognitive science, philosophy, and computer science. In their article, McCulloch and Pitts outlined a series of moves by which neurons could be made equivalent to logic gates, and therefore "thought" could be made materially realizable from the physiological actions of the brain. These moves reformulated psychology but they also demonstrated a broader transformation in the constitution of evidence and truth in science.[11]

The model of the neural net put forth in McCulloch and Pitts's article has two characteristics of note that are critical in producing our contemporary ideas of rationality.[12] The first claim is that every neuron firing has a "semiotic character"; that is, it may be mathematically rendered as a proposition.[13] To support this claim, McCulloch and Pitts imagined each neuron as operating on an "all or nothing" principle when firing electrical impulses over synaptic separations; that is, the pair interpreted the fact that neurons possess action potentials and delays as equivalent to the ability to effect a discrete decision. This effect affirms or denies a fact (or activation). From this follows the claim that neurons can be thought of as signs (true/false) and nets as semiotic situations, or communication structures (just like the structured scenarios of communication theory) (Figures 7.1, 7.2).[14] This discrete decision (true or false, activate or not) also made neurons equivalent to logical propositions and Turing machines.

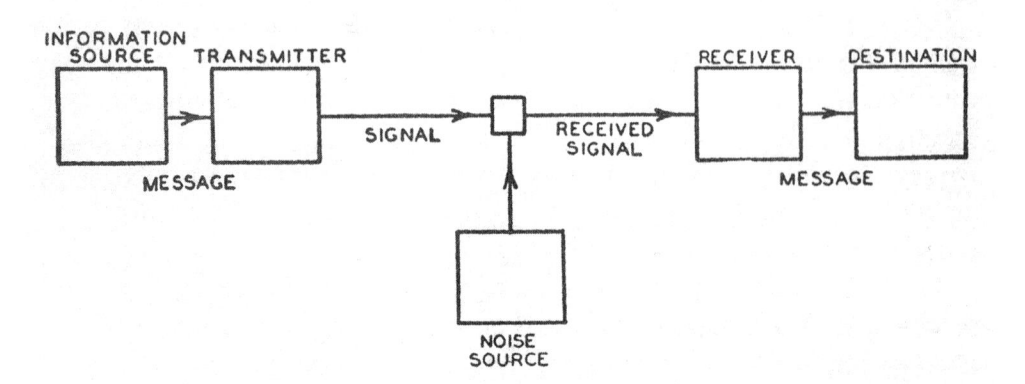

Figure 7.1. Schematic diagram of a general communication system. Claude Elwood Shannon, *The Mathematical Theory of Communication* (Urbana: University of Illinois Press, 1949), 3.

FIGURE 1

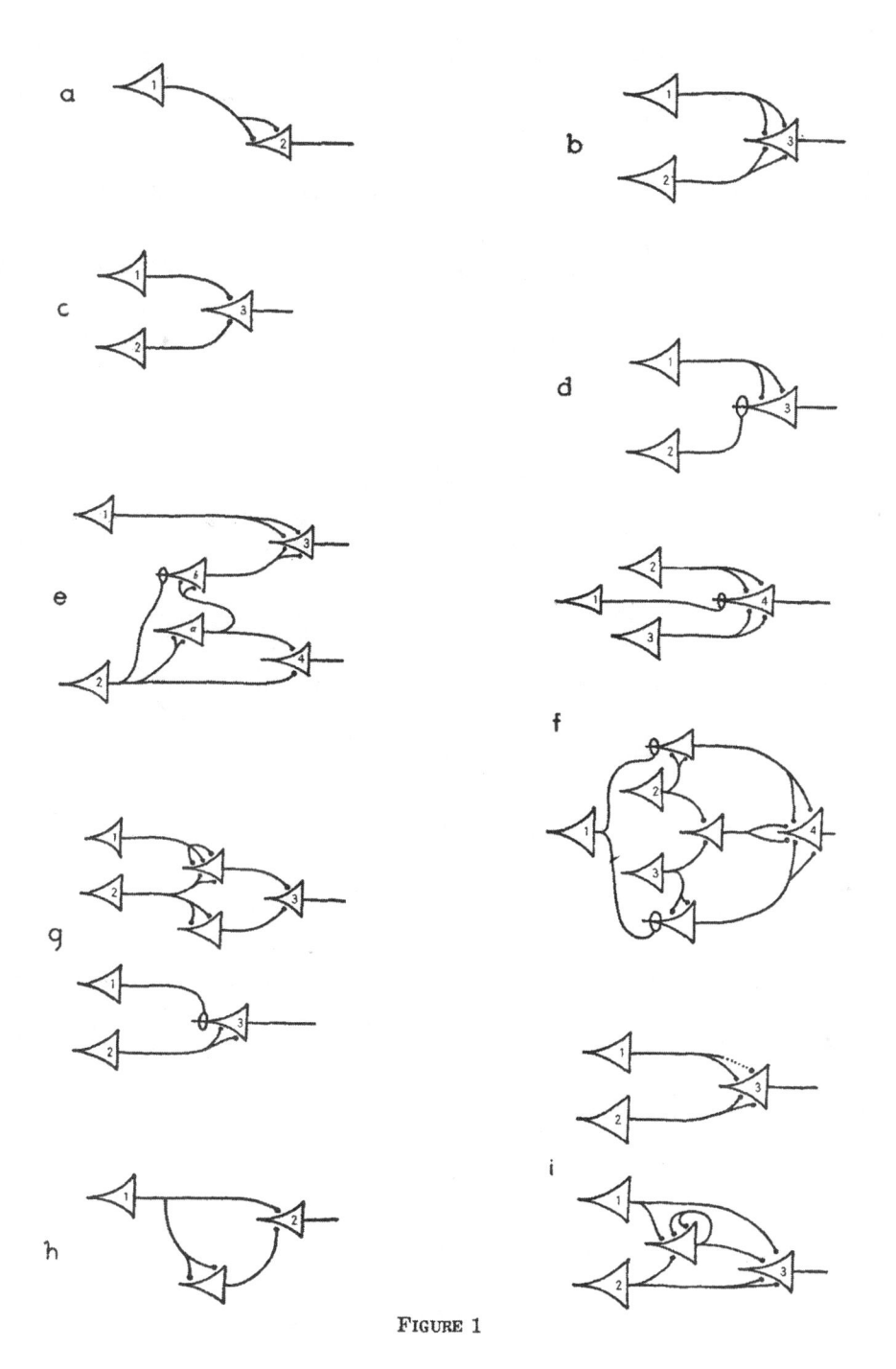

Figure 7.2. Neural net structures expressing the indeterminacy of the past, since signals may come through a number of different routes. Warren S. McCulloch and Walter H. Pitts, "A Logical Calculus of Ideas Immanent in Nervous Activity," *Bulletin of Mathematical Biophysics* 5 (1943): 130. The single memory neuron discussed is indicated by (i).

The second element of the model that is important here is the adoption of a strictly probabilistic and predictive temporality. Neuronal nets are determinate in terms of the future (they are predictive) but indeterminate in terms of the past (Figure 7.2). In the model, given a net in a particular time state (T), one can predict the future action of the net (T+1) but not the past action. From within the net, one cannot determine which neuron fired to excite the current situation.

McCulloch offered as an example the model of a circular memory neuron activating itself with its own electrical impulses. At every moment, what results as a conscious experience of memory is not the recollection of the activation of the neuron but merely an awareness that it *was* activated in the past, at an indeterminant time. The firing of a signal, or the suppression of firing, can only be known as declarations of "true" or "false"—true if there was an impulse or false if there was no firing—not an interpretative statement of context or meaning that might motivate such firing.

Within neural nets, at any moment, one cannot know *which* neuron sent the message, *when* the message was sent, or *whether* the message was the result of a new stimulus or merely a misfire. In this model the net cannot determine with any certitude whether a stimulus comes from without or from within the circuit, whether it is a fresh input or simply a recycled "memory." Put another way, from within a net (or network) the boundary between perception and cognition, the separation between interiority and exteriority, and the organization of causal time are indifferentiable. McCulloch and Pitts's brilliance was that instead of thinking of this as a disadvantage for the capacity of a neural net, they saw it as an advantage. They ended on a triumphant note, announcing an aspiration for a subjective science. "Thus our knowledge," they wrote, "of the world, including ourselves, is incomplete as to space and indefinite as to time. This ignorance, implicit in all our brains, is the counterpart of the abstraction which renders our knowledge useful."[15] If subjectivity had long been the site of inquiry for the human sciences, now, perhaps, it might—in its very lack of transparency to itself, its incompleteness—become an explicit technology.

PSYCHOSIS AS RATIONALITY

McCulloch went even further to propose that logic was not reasonable but *actually* psychotic. He proudly announced that the nature of computing is analogous to a psychotic mind.

> What we thought we were doing (and I think we succeeded fairly well) was treating the brain as a Turing machine; that is, as a device which could perform the

kind of functions which a brain must perform if it is only to go wrong and *have a psychosis.*[16]

Speaking at a conference in Pasadena, California, on circuits and brains and addressing a room of the most prominent mathematicians, psychologists, and physiologists of the day, McCulloch sought to provoke his respectable audience by offering them a seemingly counterproductive analogy. Finite state automata—those models of calculative and computational reason; the templates for programming; the very seats of repetition, reliability, mechanical, logical, and anticipatable behavior—might be "psychotic" just as brains can sometimes be. However, McCulloch, while trained as a psychiatrist, was *not* discussing psychosis in relation to patients in mental clinics. Rather, he was responding to a famous paper delivered by the mathematician John von Neumann on logical automata.[17] The psychiatrist did not argue about the essential characteristics, the ontology, of machines or minds. He recognized that computers were not the same as organic brains. The question of equivalence was not at stake.

What *was* at stake was a set of methodologies and practices in the human sciences, statistics, and engineering, the epistemology, if we will, that might build new machines—whether organic or mechanical. And the answer, both McCulloch and von Neumann provided, was to develop a new form of logic, an epistemology they labeled "psychotic" *and* "rational." Such an epistemology, they argued, might make processes usually assigned to analytic functions of the brain, perhaps associated with consciousness and psychology, amenable to technical replication.

McCulloch and Pitts were explicit that their work was a *Gedankenexperiment,* a thought experiment that produces a way of doing things, a methodological machine. Cheerily, McCulloch admitted that this was an enormous "reduction" of the actual operations of the neurons.[18] He further elaborated, "But one point must be made clear: neither of us conceives the formal equivalence to be a factual explanation. *Per contra!*" At no point should anyone assume that neural nets were an exact description of a "real" brain.[19] In fact, nets were not representations; they were methodological models and processes.[20] McCulloch and Pitts discussed this logical reasoning as an experiment, a machine perhaps like the ones described by Gilles Deleuze and Félix Guattari in *A Thousand Plateaus,* that does not describe a reality but helps scientists and engineers envision new types of brains and machines, and challenge what scientists thought they knew about how mental processes work.

Reductive or not, the pair had, therefore, established that a capacity for logic and very sophisticated problem-solving might emerge from small physiological units such as neurons linked up in circuits. In doing so, and by way of exploiting the amnesia of these circuits, McCulloch and Pitts were able to make neural nets analogous to communication channels and shift the dominant terms for dealing with human psychology and consciousness to communication, cognition, and capacities. Their conception of the neural net informs a change in attitudes to psychological processes that makes visible an epistemological transformation in what constituted truth, reason, and evidence in science.

Let me outline this new epistemology briefly here. It rests on three important points that are seemingly unimportant alone but significant when recognized as joining a history of logic, engineering practices, and the human sciences in a new assemblage. The first is that logic is now both material and behavioral, and agents can be an- or non-ontologically defined or "black boxed." The second is that cybernetic attitudes toward the mind rest upon a repression of all concerns about documentation, indexicality, archiving, learning, and historical temporality. And, third, the temporality of the net is preemptive: it always operates in the future perfect tense but without necessarily defined endpoints or contexts.[21] If nets are about T+1, the past is indeterminate. McCulloch regularly argued against caring about the actual context, or specific stimulus that incited trauma in patients, or systems.[22] Together these points meant that rationality could be redefined as both embodied and affective and that good science was not the production of certitude but rather the account of chance and indeterminacy. For neural net researchers, the question that turned out to be determining was not whether minds are the same or different as machines but rather, as anthropologist Joseph Dumit has put it, "What difference does it make to be in one circuit or another?"[23] As he argues, cybernetics does not ask what a mind or machine is but rather what could one *do* with a mind (or a machine), what one can do with different types of networks or circuits.

CONTROL, MEMORY, AND COMPUTING

Having inserted the logic of the machine into the brain, this model was then fed back into the design of machines. The model of the cycling memory neuron, in fact, directly refracts an earlier concept of control in the Turing machine (and would later become the model for memory in von Neumann's architecture for EDVAC).[24] Control in the Turing machine is the head that "reads" the program from memory and then begins the process of executing it according to the directions in the memory. On the one hand, control directs the next operation of the machine. On the other hand, control is directed by the program. The control unit, or the reading head in a Turing machine, is directed by the tape that it is reading from memory, not the reverse. Control is that function that will read and act upon this retrieved data, inserting the retrieved program or data into the run of the machine. Such machines do not operate in a top-down fashion but in feedback loops between storage, processing segments, and the interface for input and output. In his 1946 report on building a computing machine, the *ACE Report,* Alan Turing reiterated that only the possession of memory "give[s] the machine the possibility of constructing its own orders; i.e. there is always the possibility of taking a particular minor cycle out of storage and treating it as an order to be carried out. This can be very powerful."[25] If there is a feature that allows computers to act in uncanny and unexpected ways, it is this surprising capacity to change the pattern of action by way of insertion of a program from storage. Control in computers is like reverberating circuits in brains, and both are defined, in psychoanalysis, as psychotic insofar as they involve receiving memories without history (Figure 7.2).

Therefore this redefinition of rationality demanded a reconsideration of what "control" might mean. In most contemporary scholarship, control was correlated with prediction, knowing the future, and the ability to command in the military sense.[26] In their famous book *Planning and Coding of Problems for an Electronic Computing Instrument,* Herman H. Goldstine and von Neumann introduced flow charts and circuits for stored-program computers (Figure 7.3). However, in describing their circuits they wrote, "We propose to indicate these portions of the flow diagram of C by a symbolism of lines oriented by arrows. Second, it is clear that this notation is incomplete and unsatisfactory."[27] In other words, control is not definable; its operable imagining and its explicit definition are incommensurate. But rather than treat this failure in representation as a problem, this threshold became a technological opportunity; this emergent space between the definable and the infinite provided the contours of the engineering problem—an opportunity to turn from logic to technology.

Significantly for us, McCulloch and Pitts inverted the problem posed by the original negative proof of the *Entscheidungsproblem* that is the Turing machine. If throughout the nineteenth and earlier twentieth centuries an army of mathematicians and philosophers struggled to infinitely extend the limits of logical representation to which the Turing machine is a negative proof, demonstrating the impossibility of fully representing all statements in first-order logic, then McCulloch and Pitts had a different epistemology and frame.[28] Accepting that there were many things that could not be known or computed, McCulloch inverted the question that Turing had posed. If instead of seeking an absolute reasonable foundation for mathematical thought that other logicians and mathematicians— including Gottlob Frege, Kurt Gödel, David Hilbert, Bertrand Russell, Alfred North Whitehead, and Alan Turing—had attempted, McCulloch and Pitts chose to ask

202   ORIT HALPERN

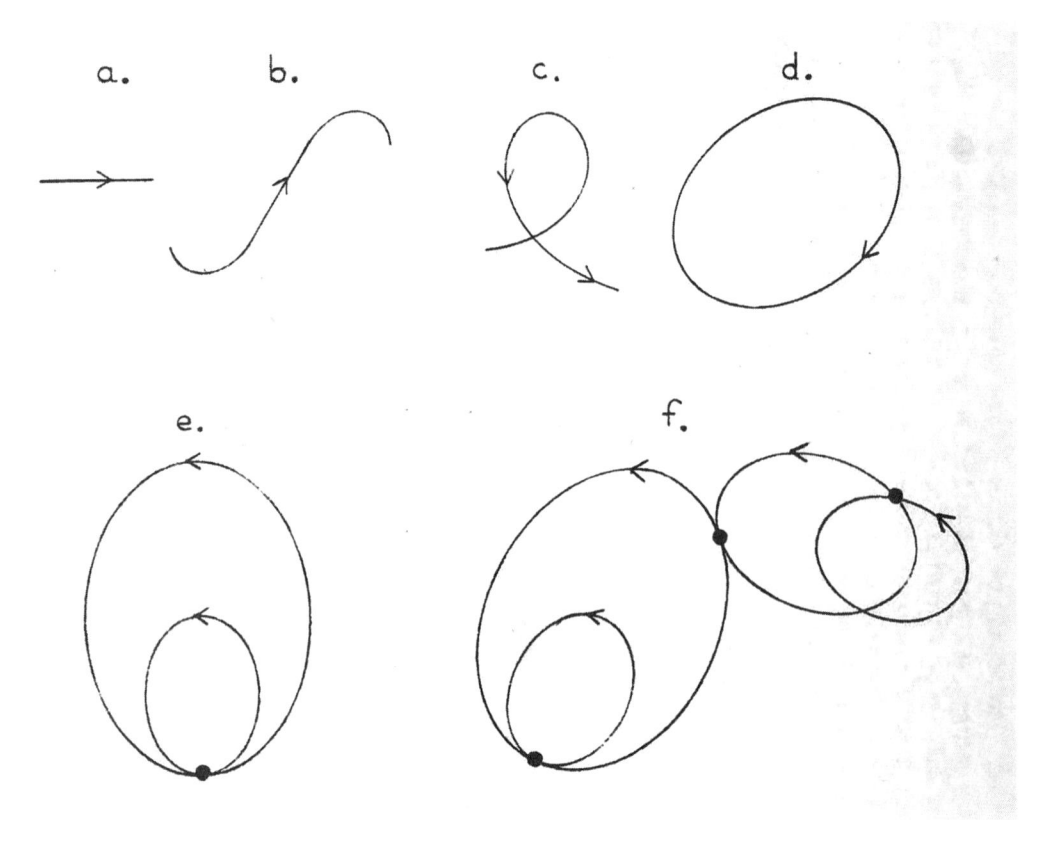

Figure 7.3. Diagrams of "C." Herman H. Goldstine and John von Neumann, *Planning and Coding of Problems for an Electronic Computing Instrument*, part II, *Report on the Mathematical and Logical Aspects of an Electronic Computing Instrument*, vol. 1 (Princeton, N.J.: Institute for Advanced Study, Princeton University, 1947), 6.

instead: What if mental functioning could now be demonstrated to emanate from the physiological actions of multitudes of logic gates? What could be built? Not: What could be proven? The problem could be inverted from seeking the limits of calculation to examining the possibilities for logical nets. What had been an absolute limit to mathematical logic became an extendable threshold for engineering. McCulloch implied we should turn instead to accepting our partial and incomplete perspectives, our inability to know ourselves and make this "psychosis," in his words, an "experimental epistemology."[29]

RATIONAL NETWORKS

Such experiments were central to reformulating older, liberal ideas of agency and consciousness. As numerous historians of science have demonstrated, cybernetic and communicative concepts of the mind were part of a broader shift at the time in concepts of reason, psychology, and consciousness.[30] They informed everything from finance and options trading equations to environmental psychology and urban planning programs (such as those by Kevin Lynch and later MIT's Architecture Machine Group and the Media Lab headed by Nicholas Negroponte), from the political science models of Karl Deutsch at Harvard to the "bounded rationality" introduced by Herbert Simon and widely considered the foundation of contemporary finance. The postwar social sciences were repositories of these techniques that transformed what had once been questions of political economy, value production, and the organization of human desire and social relations to problems of circulation and communication by way of a new approach to modeling intelligence and agency.[31]

This rationality is also sensible and, perhaps, even affective: a situation that considerably revises dominant understandings of digital and computational mediums as distancing, disembodied, or abstract. And if it is one of the dominant assumptions in the study of modern history and governance that liberal subjectivity and economic agency are defined as a logic guided by a reason separate from sense, then these discourses mark a clear contrast.[32] The historian of science Lorraine Daston reminds us that we would do well to recall that those things today considered virtuous and intelligent—such as speed, logic, and definitiveness in action—were not always so. She is explicit: rationality in its Cold War formulation, despite the insistence of technocrats, policy makers, and free-market advocating economists, is not reason as understood by Enlightenment thinkers, liberals, or even modern logicians.[33]

If this is true, then our financial instruments, markets, governments, organizations, and machines are rational, affective, sensible, and preemptive but not reasonable. To recognize the significance of this thinking in our present, it might help to contemplate Brian Massumi's definition of "preemption." Preemption, he argues, is not prevention; it is a different way of knowing the world. Prevention, he claims, "assumes an ability to assess threats empirically and identify their causes." Preemption, on the other hand, is affective; it lacks representation; it is a constant nervous anticipation, at a literally neural if not molecular level, for a never fully articulated threat or future.[34]

Within ten years from the end of the war, cyberneticians moved from working on antiaircraft prediction to building systems without clear endpoints or goals, and embracing an epistemology without final objectives, or perhaps objectivity (even if many practitioners denied this). Nets, taken as systems, are probabilistic scenarios, with multiple states and indefinite run times even if each separate neuron can act definitively. In cognitive and early neuroscience, the forms of knowledge being espoused were always framed in terms of experiment, never definitive conclusions. "Experimental epistemologies," as McCulloch put it, came to mean that there are never final facts, only ongoing experiments.

The human and social sciences based on this logic thus made operative the unknowable space between legibility and emergence and turned it into a technological impulse to proliferate new tools of measurement, diagrams, and interfaces. At the limits of this analysis is the possibility that emergence itself has been automated. As the theorist Luciana Parisi puts it, cybernetics takes hold of the space between infinity and logic and makes it the very site of technical intervention, the very site to proliferate algorithms into life.[35] If cybernetics initially sought to control the future, now control itself became the unclear site of emergence, an indefinable state that was part of networks operating in the future without full definition or information about endpoints or pasts. The problem of how to act under conditions of uncertainty, or how to define a man or a machine, instead became a pragmatic mandate and a focus on process. Instead of asking what a circuit, a neuron, or a market is, human scientists and cyberneticians turned to asking: What do circuits do? How do agents act?[36] By creating an ongoing opportunity to entangle calculation and life at the level of nervous networks and by correlating the nervous system with the financial and political system, they displaced discourses of subjectivity and objectivity for a focus on process and experiment.

TIME, AUTOMATA, AND PSYCHOANALYSIS

What, then, is at stake in the cybernetic reformulation of reason in terms of "psychosis"? It is perhaps no surprise that psychosis might offer the possibility of producing a logic "spoken" directly by nerves, or that it should be related to computational machines and digital mediums. Friedrich Kittler has already suggested that the initial effect of psychoanalysis was the externalization of the psyche and its incorporation into larger discursive networks. In delineating the "discourse network of 1800" from the "discourse network of 1900," Kittler specifies the latter as being concerned with an obsession with the minute, unimportant, and indiscriminately recorded, which characterized the nascent media technologies of the time.[37] Therefore Freud's obsessive concern not with the obviously scripted "events" but with slips of the tongue, minute details, and so forth advanced a larger technical assemblage obsessed with delivering recorded and stored events, detached from any clear referential relation to an external, and meaningful, "reality."[38]

But cybernetic invocations of psychoanalysis and psychosis complicate the seamless extension of the 1900 discourse network into the present. As Mary Ann

Doane has framed it, in psychoanalysis it is consciousness that produces historical temporality. The unconscious in Freud's essay "The Interpretation of Dreams" is, according to Doane, "a vast storehouse of contents and processes that are immune to the corrosive effects of temporality."[39] Memory records everything. Psychoanalysis's disciplinary fantasy is the total representation and cataloging of this repository, a task that drove the disciplinary enterprise but which even Freud understood as impossible.

In psychoanalysis the residue of this vast archive of experience was consciousness. Consciousness was simply the visible and articulable symptom of this memory, a memory that was now "out there" and outside representation but whose excesses of information could overwhelm and incapacitate the subject. Consciousness was the filter, the translation zone, that allowed the organism to function and produced a teleological and functional temporality—a temporality not of infinitude and flow but of marked events and history. Consciousness and its related measurable and historical time were thus antithetical to memory, although protective of the organism. Consciousness, by this logic, was a barrier to accessing the moment of impression—the present, or (again) the "real." As a discipline, psychoanalysis wanted to overcome this barrier to representation but could not.[40]

Psychotics resist any efforts at organizing time and space. For the cultural historian Eric Santner, paranoid schizophrenia for psychoanalysts of the early twentieth century demonstrated the "drive dimension of signification." Santner argues that this psychotic rhythm of mechanical sounds (telecast and circulating as hallucinations and visions) repeats without concern for meaning or context but only as "expression of genuine feeling."[41] By extension, the subject has neither a clear future nor past; nor can it delineate a circular repetitive cathexis emerging from within the system from a new stimuli coming from without. For a subject that lacks a stable ego or consciousness, memory and projection (or futurity) thus become the same. The memory cycles of psychotics, the temporality of neural nets, and the control structure of a Turing machine are all therefore remarkably similar.

For psychoanalysis, psychosis therefore appeared resistant to any "talking cure"; paranoid schizophrenia was a pathology that demonstrated the subjective heart of psychoanalysis while refusing the assertion of narrative and signification that designated the authority of the analyst over the analysand. The possibility of language as a drive that produces real effects equivalent to desire but without clarity in object choice was both stunningly proximate to the psychoanalytic project and threatening to scientific ideals of knowledge and practice. To cite Roger Caillois, there is a mimetic excess to these states in which the subject is "consumed" by the environment, unable to delineate the boundaries between the self and others.[42]

Such proximities—between the doctor and the patient, the mind and the body, and desire and knowledge—Freud found troubling.

Cyberneticians, on the other hand, attempted to displace these questions of both difference and time by problematizing accumulation and not memory's inaccessibility and representability. Time emerged from within the system, but without consciousness there was no demand to recuperate historicity or narrative. Lacking concern with representation, or translation, cyberneticians built systems fundamentally dedicated to action and not description. Temporality, here, was not the supplement but the substrate for producing different circuits. If in psychoanalytic formulations of mind and time, memory and trauma were the result of impressions that entered the organism from an outside world only to be stored in an incoherent virtual interior space of the unconscious, in cybernetics there was no external world; all times and traumas emerged from within systems whose space is indefinite but whose temporal dimensions are always circumscribed.

For McCulloch, Pitts, and their many interlocutors in the emerging cognitive and social sciences of the time, psychoanalytic concerns with pathology, normalcy, and, in fact, the time of consciousness were displaced. If for Freud the "occult returned in the form of the erotic," for cyberneticians, and especially McCulloch, the occult returned in the form of a self-referential machine whose locus was never aimed at a desire for an external, other-demanding redirection but instead became a self-referential and self-generating world.[43] The anthropologist and ethnographer Gregory Bateson made this reorganization of the terms of desire into algorithm explicit.

> Classical Freudian theory assumed that dreams were a *secondary* product, created by "dream work." Material unacceptable to conscious thought was supposedly translated into the metaphoric idiom of primary process to avoid waking the dreamer. And this may be true of those items of information which are held in the unconscious by the process of repression. As we have seen, however, many other sorts of information are inaccessible to conscious inspection, including most of the premises of mammalian interaction. It would seem to me sensible to think of these items as existing *primarily* in the idiom of primary process, only with difficulty to be translated into "rational" terms. In other words, I believe that much of early Freudian theory was upside down. At that time many thinkers regarded conscious reason as normal and self-explanatory while the unconscious was regarded as mysterious, needing proof, and needing explanation. Repression was the explanation, and the unconscious was filled with thoughts which could have been conscious but which repression and dream work had distorted. Today we think of

consciousness as the mysterious, and of the computational methods of the unconscious, *e.g.,* primary process, as continually active, necessary, and all-embracing.[44]

Bateson thus radically externalized the unconscious. His statement implies that science now had a new technique—"computational methods" of the unconscious—not only to account for the behavior of individuals but to be "all embracing," extendable to systems, ecologies, and organizations. He went so far as to label these unconscious and computational methods "algorithms of the heart, or, as they say, of the unconscious."[45] Bateson's statements suggest a transformation of psychological inquiry and concern from the conscious to the unconscious and the displacement of what had once been a source of vexing scientific concern and a limit to knowledge (mainly the recognition of the subjective nature of human perception and consciousness) into a "method" and an "algorithm."

This "love" that is now algorithmic speaks to the frenzy to insert responsiveness and interactivity into our environments and networks today. Our "love" can now be met, immediately, through the actions of our circuits, actions now defined within the rubrics such as "personalization," "responsiveness," "logistics," and "enterprise management" that drive ever greater interaction with and through our machine systems. If time for psychoanalysis always emanated from within the operations of the mental apparatus, this "discovery" could now become technically realized in communication networks.

At stake in the emergence of psychotic logic, therefore, was the stability of older histories of objectivity, truth, and documentation. But also up for negotiation were the terms of encounter between bodies and subjects. These questions of authority and intimacy, however, were deferred. Instead of asking about the contents of memory and unconsciousness, cyberneticians asked about the organization of the circuit and the flow of information through communication channels. By the mid-1960s, the centrality of consciousness or even unconsciousness as tools to model human behavior, subjectivity, and society had been increasingly replaced in cybernetically informed human sciences with a new set of discourses and methods, those that made "algorithm" and "love" speakable in the same sentence and explicitly correlating psychotic perspective with analytic logic. Cyberneticians sought to make the very space between rationality and reason, or the unconscious and conscious, amenable to logical, perhaps mathematical, representation. The impossibility of visualizing this process—an impossibility already faced by Freud in his turn to dream work, now attached to a language of channels, circuits, and communication—could be reformulated into calculative and statistical technologies that underpin a continuing frenzy of data visualization, personalization, and analytics. Time as the exterior to science or truth became "time" in the mode of "real-time," a self-referential and system-generated temporality that makes computing and life synonymous.

MEMORY AS A CYCLICAL MACHINE

As any user knows, however, no system is seamless: our actions occasionally return to haunt us; our networks constantly suffer "jams," disruptions, and collapses. Imagined operations are never realized, and imagined projections and practices often diverge. Having been displaced from the algorithmic rationality of the network, the older terms of consciousness, reason, and desire would return in cybernetics under the guise of visualization, time, and memory. At the famous sixth Macy Conference, "Circular Causal and Feedback Mechanisms in Biological and Social Systems," held in 1949 in New York City, the immediacy and temporality of the televisual came to replace the older conceptions of tapes, photographs, and films. McCulloch opened the event with a beacon and a warning. He offered the example of a new type of tube, in development at Princeton and similar to a cathode ray tube, that beamed onto a screen on which items were stored. The persistence of the "memory" of the beam was temporary and had to be refreshed. Memory was thus increasingly problematized in terms of the relations between its dynamic and stable elements and storage. McCulloch viewed this idea of a cycling or scanning memory as offering the possibility of miniaturizing and expanding machine memory.[46]

McCulloch's second example was a warning from John von Neumann: even the entire number of neurons in the brain, according to a calculation, could not account for the complexity of human behavior and ability. McCulloch reported the finding that "the performance of the army ant . . . is far more complicated than can be computed by 300 yes or no devices."[47] But this was not to say that these capacities needed to be understood as illogical or analog. Rather, McCulloch turned to another model that might retain the logical nature of the neurons but still account for the capacity to learn and behave at scales beyond the comprehension of computation.

The answer, coming through a range of discussions about protein structure and memory within cells, involved refreshing information in time. Wiener argued that "this variability in time here postulated will do in fact the sort of thing that von Neumann wants, that is, the variability need not be fixed as variability in space, but may actually be a variability in time." The psychologist John Stroud at the same conference offered the example of a "very large macro-organism called a destroyer." This military ship had endless "metabolic" changes of small chores throughout the day but still retained the function of a destroyer. This systemic stability, despite internal differentiation and cycling, became the ideal of agency and action in memory.[48]

McCulloch and Stroud went on to present understandings of memory in terms of an opposition between perfect retention of all information with retroactive selection and memory as a constant active site of processing of information for further action, based on internal "reflectors" or "internal eyes." "We may," they stated, "need only very tiny little reflectors which somehow or other can become a stimulus pattern which is available for this particular mode of operation of our very ordinary thinking, seeing, and hearing machinery. This particular pattern of reflectors is what I see as it were with my internal eyes just as what I see when I look at a store window, is a pattern on the retinal mosaic."[49] Mental processes were equated here with processing data and pattern seeking, but it was internal "eyes" from within the psychic apparatus that allowed a self-reflexive apparatus for deferring decisions and agency. The mind here emerged from multiple time systems operating between the real-time present of reception and circulating data and memory in time: a cyclical "refreshing" as in a television screen system, where change and differentiation—between the organism and the environment as well as between networks—became possible through the delay and reorganization of circuits from within the organism. The problems of computational representation, the initial problems that were faced in mathematical and logical representations of intelligence, were no longer organized with a language of conscious and unconscious, discrete and infinite, reason and psychosis but were reorganized through new terms of vacillating temporalities between immediacy and reflexivity.

THEORIZING THE NERVOUS NETWORK

I opened this chapter by arguing that cybernetics and affiliated communication and human sciences aspired to the elimination of difference in the name of rationality and that they operated with a dream of self-organizing systems and autopoietic intelligences produced from the minute actions of small, stupid, logic gates, a dream of a world of networks without limit, focused eternally on an indefinite and extendable future state. I also invoked Bateson's concerns about self-referential violence: the worry that in the real-time obsession to entangle life with calculative logics, learning—and, by extension, thought itself—would be automated in such a way as to lead to violent harm and, perhaps, the destruction of the world. Bateson articulated a problem that Jacques Lacan too would visit: how to encounter difference, in time or in subjects, within the cybernetic circuit.[50] This issue of encounter was also a question of change, learning, and ultimately survival. Systems must be able to evolve, change, and differentiate if the circuit is not to repeatedly consume the world and eventually realize "death."

Bateson, involved in family therapy and addiction treatment programs, also offered one of the more compelling models and practices for rethinking the mind: the model of the "double bind" devised to explain psychic suffering, addiction, and other maladjusted and compulsive behaviors. In 1954 Bateson wrote to McCulloch concerning his research in schizophrenic communication. The pair had met at the Macy Conferences, and it was McCulloch who had assisted Bateson in receiving funding to develop the theory of the double bind and gain the support to study schizophrenia as a "communication" disorder. In the letter Bateson wanted McCulloch's opinion on the validity of his theory that "the syndromata of schizophrenia are describable as pathologies in the use of those signals which should identify the 'language games' in Wittgenstein's sense; and that the etiology of schizophrenia goes back to infantile learning in which the relevant traumata have patterns reminiscent of type confusion."[51] At stake in this discussion was the relationship between logic and memory. The disease reenacted "patterns" from earlier in life, like a child, and did so in the manner of a logical "game." In short, the pattern repeated in the circuit but without historical forms of temporality or diegetic.

In a conference in 1969 at the National Institute of Health, Bateson further elaborated on this problem of a circuit that repeats without change. He offered an example to demonstrate his ideas of both psychology and treatment. He discussed a research project conducted with porpoises trained at U.S. Navy research facilities to perform tricks and other trained acts in return for fish. One day, he recounted, one of the porpoises was introduced to a new regimen. Her trainers deprived her of food if she repeated the same trick. Starved if she repeated the same act but also if she did not perform, the porpoise was caught in a double bind. This experiment was repeated with numerous porpoises, usually culminating in extreme aggression, and a descent into what from an anthropomorphic perspective might be labeled disaffection, confusion, and antisocial and violent behavior. Bateson with his usual lack of reservation was ready to label these dolphins as suffering a paranoid form of schizophrenia. The anthropologist was at pains, however, to remind his audience that these psychotic animals were acting rationally. In fact, they were doing exactly what their training as animals in a navy laboratory would lead them to do. Their problem was that they had two conflicting signals. The poor animals, having no perspective on their situation as laboratory experiments, were naturally breaking apart, fissuring their personalities (and Bateson thought they had them) in efforts to be both rebellious and compliant but above all to act as they had been taught. Bateson argued this was the standard condition for humans in contemporary societies.

Having established the mechanisms that led to a decentered and multiple subject, Bateson commenced to articulate the dangers and possibilities of this condition. He recalled how, between the fourteenth and fifteenth time of demonstration, one of the porpoises "appeared much excited" and for her final performance gave an "elaborate" display, including multiple pieces of behavior, of which four were "entirely new—never before observed in this species of animal."[52] These were not solely genetically endowed abilities, then, but were learned, the result of an experiment in time. This process in which the subject, whether a patient or a dolphin, used the memories of other interactions and other situations to transform their actions within the immediate scenario was represented as the site of innovation.[53] The porpoise's ego (insofar as she may have had one) was sufficiently weakened to develop new attachments to objects in her environment through the memories of her past and of other types of encounters. This rewired network of relations was what was held to lead to emergence through the recontextualization of the situation within which the confused and conflicted animal found itself.

Bateson ended in triumph, having now successfully made the psyche intersubjective and simultaneously amenable to technical appropriation via family therapy.[54] The productivity of a schizoid situation rested for Bateson on the discovery made by both communication theory and physics that different times could not communicate directly to one another. Only *temporal differences* resisted circulation from within the definition of communication that was being put forward here. Bateson applied this understanding liberally to animals. In cybernetic models, the ability of an entity to differentiate itself from its environment and make autonomous choices was contingent on its ability to simultaneously engage in dangerous spatial proximities with other entities and its ability to achieve distance from them in time.

At stake in the negotiation over the nature of networks and the timescale of analysis was nothing less than how to encounter difference—whether between individuals, between value in markets, or between vast states during the Cold War. A question that perhaps started in psychoanalytic concerns over psychosis and the excessive proximity between patients and analysts had now found technical realization in cybernetics. For cyberneticians the problem of analog or digital (otherwise understood as the limits between discrete logic and infinity; the separation between the calculable and the incalculable, the representable and the nonrepresentable; and the differences between subjects and objects) was transformed into a reconfiguration of memory and storage.

It is this transformation that continues to inform our multiplying fantasies of real-time analytics while massive data storage infrastructures are erected to ensure the permanence and recyclability of data. While the time of neural nets and communication theories is always preemptive, it also depends on a shadow archive haunting the speculative network, an endless data repository whose arrangement and visualization might return imagination and agency to subjects. These wavering interactions—between the networked individual and the fetish of data—continues to preoccupy us in the present, speaking through our contemporary concerns with data mining, search engines, and connectivity. The relationship between rationality and control drives the ongoing penetration and application of media technologies as the result of an imperative to seek consciousness through better visualization and collective intelligence through the collaboration of many logical, but hardly reasonable, agents. Architecturally these dual desires incarnate themselves in a proliferation of interfaces and a fetish for visualization and interactivity, merged with an obsession to amass and store data in huge systems of data centers and server farms. What had first been articulated as a problem of memory and time has now become a compulsion for analytics.

This condition only becomes inevitable, however, if we ourselves descend into the logic of immediate and real-time analytics. We must avoid this conclusion and this condition. Like Bateson's porpoise, torn between reactionary return and self-referentiality, we are forced to ask about the other possibilities that still lie inside our machines and our histories. Deferral, difference, "man's waiting": these were all also discovered within cybernetics. As Donna Haraway and many other feminist and queer theorists have noted, cybernetics permits dangerous proximities and alternative recombinations within space while posing simultaneous threats of homogenization; the trick is to vacillate between the immediate and the deferred, to reject the laws of the binary order that ignore what cybernetics first brought into the world, which is the decentering of our egos, and to develop the ability to recognize that our consciousness and subjectivities are in lag to the world and are comprised through our interactions with others.[55] Control can mean prediction, but cybernetics also revealed that control is about probability, unknowability, and alterity. Control is about both the limiting and the producing of potentialities for future actions within systems.

The cycles of the porpoise thus reenact the telling of cybernetic history where ideas of control and rationality are often overdetermined in their negative valence, and the inevitability of the past to determine the future is regularly assumed. Perhaps the hope is in the very machinery that was imagined into being through the cybernetic circuits—systems that can both recognize and disavow their history, for which memory and archiving remain at tense and productively incommensurable distances, incarnated in a drive to accelerate the speed of speculation while intensifying the infrastructure for data gathering and storage, all supported by a nervous rationality that is constantly multiplying from within. As psychoanalysis later learned from cybernetics, computation and control may yet not be about determinism but rather about chance: the impossibility of knowing the future or the past and the radical possibility to affiliate with others, to build new machines, to build new worlds . . . those that have not yet arrived.

NOTES

1. Gregory Bateson to Norbert Wiener, September 22, 1952, MC22, box 10, folder 155, p. 2, Norbert Wiener Papers, Massachusetts Institute of Technology.

2. For an elaboration of this psychoanalytic theory of spatial closeness and internally induced differentiation in schizophrenia, see Victor Tausk, "On the Origin of the 'Influencing Machine' in Schizophrenia," in *Incorporations,* ed. Jonathan Crary and Sanford Kwinter (New York: Zone Books, 1919), 542–69.

3. Norbert Wiener, *Cybernetics: Or Control and Communication in the Animal and the Machine* (New York: John Wiley and Sons, 1948), 44.

4. Norbert Wiener, *The Human Use of Human Beings: Cybernetics and Society* (1954; repr., New York: Da Capo, 1988), 7, 11.

5. Paul Erickson, Judy L. Klein, Lorraine Daston, Rebecca Lemov, Thomas Sturm, and Michael D. Gordin, *How Reason Almost Lost Its Mind: The Strange Career of Cold War Rationality* (Chicago: University of Chicago Press, 2013).

6. There is a significant body of work concerning cybernetics and the human and social sciences; for example, see Andrew Pickering, *The Cybernetic Brain* (Chicago: University of Chicago Press, 2010); Steve Heims, *The Cybernetics Group* (Cambridge, Mass.: MIT Press, 1991); Rebecca Lemov, "Hypothetical Machines: The Science Fiction Dreams of Cold War Social Science," *Isis* 101, no. 2 (2010): 401–11; N. Katherine Hayles, *How We Became Posthuman: Virtual Bodies in Cybernetics, Literature, and Informatics* (Chicago: University of Chicago Press, 1999); and Jean Pierre Dupuy, *The Mechanization of the Mind: On the Origins of Cognitive Science* (Princeton, N.J.: Princeton University Press, 2000).

7. For other discussions about time and memory in cybernetics and early computing, see Wendy Hui Kyong Chun, "The Enduring Ephemeral, or the Future Is a Memory," *Critical Inquiry* 35, no. 1 (Autumn 2008): 148–71; and Orit Halpern, "Dreams for Our Perceptual Present: Temporality, Storage, and Interactivity in Cybernetics," *Configurations* 13, no. 2 (2005): 283–319.

8. There is a large literature assuming the direct intensification of computation and calculation over life in many fields; for a sampling, see Friedrich A. Kittler, *Gramophone, Film, Typewriter* (Stanford: Stanford University Press, 1999); Paul Virilio, *The Vision Machine* (Bloomington: Indiana University Press, 1994); Tiziana Terranova, *Network Culture* (London: Pluto, 2004); Fred Turner, *From Counterculture to Cyberculture: Stewart Brand, the Whole Earth Network, and the Rise of Digital Utopianism* (Chicago: University of Chicago Press, 2006); and Reinhold Martin, *The Organizational Complex: Architecture, Media, and Corporate Space* (Cambridge, Mass.: MIT Press, 2003).

9. Peter Galison, "The Ontology of the Enemy: Norbert Wiener and the Cybernetic Vision," *Critical Inquiry* 21, no. 1 (1994): 228–66; Hayles, *How We Became Post-Human*. See also Arturo Rosenblueth, Norbert Wiener, and Julian Bigelow, "Behavior, Purpose and Teleology," *Philosophy of Science* 10, no. 1 (1943): 18–24.

10. Lily E. Kay, "From Logical Neurons to Poetic Embodiments of Mind: Warren McCulloch's Project in Neuroscience," *Science in Context* 14, no. 4 (2001): 591–94.

11. Warren S. McCulloch and Walter H. Pitts, "A Logical Calculus of Ideas Immanent in Nervous Activity," in *Embodiments of Mind*, by Warren S. McCulloch (Cambridge, Mass.: MIT Press, 1965), 19–38.

12. The model has been reviewed elsewhere; here I am briefly outlining the work with a focus on epistemology. See Kay, "From Logical Neurons"; and Tara Abraham, "(Physio) Logical Circuits: The Intellectual Origins of the McCulloch-Pitts Neural Networks," *Journal of the History of the Behavioral Sciences* 38, no. 1 (Winter 2002): 3–25.

13. The logic used in the article was taken from Rudolf Carnap, with whom Pitts had worked.

14. McCulloch and Pitts, "A Logical Calculus," 21–24.

15. McCulloch and Pitts, 35.

16. John von Neumann, "The General and Logical Theory of Automata," in *Papers of John von Neumann on Computing and Computer Theory*, ed. William Aspray and Arthur Burks (1948; repr., Cambridge, Mass.: MIT Press; Los Angeles: Tomash, 1986), 422 (emphasis added). For more on automata theory, see also William Aspray, *John von Neumann and the Origins of Modern Computing* (Cambridge, Mass.: MIT Press, 1990).

17. Von Neumann, "The General and Logical Theory of Automata," 391–431.

18. The pair had derived their assumptions about how neurons work on what, by that time, was the dominantly accepted neural doctrine in neurophysiology. Using the research of Spanish pathologist Santiago Ramón y Cajal, who first suggested in the 1890s that the neuron was the anatomical and functional unit of the nervous system and was largely responsible for the adoption of the neuronal doctrine as the basis of modern neuroscience, and the work of Cajal's student Lorento de Nó on action potentials and synaptic delays between neurons and reverberating circuits, McCulloch and Pitts had the neurological armory to begin thinking neurons as logic gates. Santiago Ramón y Cajal, *Texture of the Nervous System of Man and the Vertebrates* (New York: Springer, 1999); McCulloch, *Embodiments of Mind*.

19. McCulloch and Pitts, "A Logical Calculus," 22.

20. Joseph Dumit, "Circuits in the Mind" (unpublished manuscript, April 2007, in author's possession).

21. See also Halpern, "Dreams for Our Perceptual Present."

22. See, for example, interviews on the treatment of soldiers coming from World War II done in Britain, where McCulloch steadfastly spoke against narrative therapy and proactively promoted drug treatment to rewire circuits in the brain. British Broadcasting Corporation, "Physical Treatments of Mental Diseases," radio transcript, July 23, 1953, Warren S. McCulloch Papers, B.M139: series III, box 64, American Philosophical Society, Philadelphia, Penn.

23. Dumit, "Circuits in the Mind," 7.

24. John von Neumann, "First Draft of a Report on the EDVAC," Contract No. W-670-ORD-4926 between the United States Army Ordnance Department and the University of Pennsylvania (Philadelphia: Moore School of Electrical Engineering, June 30, 1945). Von Neumann confessed that the McCulloch/Pitts model had influenced him in conceiving machine memory. The Electronic Discrete Variable Automatic Computer (EDVAC) was one of the first electronic computers; it was binary and was a stored-program computer.

25. A. M. Turing, "Proposal for Development in the Mathematics Division of an Automatic Computing Engine (Ace) (1946)," in *A. M. Turing's Ace Report of 1946 and Other Papers*, Charles Babbage Institute Reprint Series for the History of Computing, ed. B. E. Carpenter and R. W. Doran (Cambridge, Mass.: MIT Press, 1986), 21.

26. See also Galison, "The Ontology of the Enemy"; and Paul N. Edwards, *The Closed World Computers and the Politics of Discourse in Cold War America* (Cambridge, Mass.: MIT Press, 1997).

27. Herman H. Goldstine and John von Neumann, *Planning and Coding of Problems for an Electronic Computing Instrument*, part 2, *Report on the Mathematical and Logical Aspects of an Electronic Computing Instrument*, vol. 1 (Princeton, N.J.: Institute for Advanced Study, Princeton University, 1948), 157.

28. Compare A. M. Turing, "On Computable Numbers, with an Application to the Entscheidungsproblem," *Proceedings of the London Mathematical Society*, 2nd ser., 42, no. 1 (1936): 230–65; Bertrand Russell, *The Principles of Mathematics* (New York: Routledge, 2009); Erich H. Reck, ed., *From Frege to Wittgenstein: Perspectives on Early Analytic Philosophy* (Oxford: Oxford University Press, 2002); Rebecca Goldstein, *Incompleteness: The Proof and Paradox of Kurt Gödel* (New York: W. W. Norton, 2005); Kurt Gödel, *On Formally Undecidable Propositions of Principia Mathematica and Related Systems* (New York: Basic Books, 1962); Alan Mathison Turing, *The Essential Turing: Seminal Writings in Computing, Logic, Philosophy, Artificial Intelligence, and Artificial Life; Plus the Secrets of Enigma*, ed. Jack Copeland (New York: Oxford University Press, 2004); and Carpenter and Doran, *A.M. Turing's Ace Report of 1946 and Other Papers*.

29. McCulloch, *Embodiments of Mind*, 359.

30. Erickson et al., *How Reason Almost Lost Its Mind*.

31. See Orit Halpern, *Beautiful Data: A History of Vision and Reason* (Durham, N.C.: Duke University Press, 2014), chapter 3. See also Herbert Simon, "A Behavioral Model of Rational Choice," *Quarterly Journal of Economics* 69, no. 1 (1955): 99–118; Hunter Crowther-Heyck, *Herbert A. Simon: The Bounds of Reason in Modern America* (Baltimore: Johns Hopkins University Press, 2005); and Herbert A. Simon, *Economics, Bounded Rationality and the Cognitive Revolution* (Northhampton, Mass.: Elgar, 1992).

32. See Donald A. MacKenzie, *An Engine, Not a Camera: How Financial Models Shape Markets* (Cambridge, Mass.: MIT Press, 2006), on rationality; and Jonathan Crary, *Techniques of the Observer: On Vision and Modernity in the Nineteenth Century* (Cambridge, Mass.: MIT Press, 1990), for a discussion of mediation, reason, and observation that supports my critique of dominant histories.

33. Lorraine Daston, "The Rule of Rules, or How Reason Became Rationality" (public talk, University of California, Berkeley, March 25, 2011, transcript in author's possession).

34. Brian Massumi, "Potential Politics and the Primacy of Preemption," *Theory & Event* 10, no. 2 (2007): 4.

35. See Luciana Parisi, *Contagious Architecture: Computation, Aesthetics, Space* (Cambridge, Mass.: MIT Press, 2013).

36. Dumit, "Circuits in the Mind."

37. Kittler, *Gramophone, Film, Typewriter*, 3.

38. Friedrich Kittler, *Discourse Networks 1800/1900*, trans. Geoffrey Winthrop-Young and Michael Wutz (Stanford: Stanford University Press, 1990).

39. Mary Ann Doane, "Freud, Marey, and the Cinema," *Critical Inquiry*, no. 22 (1996): 316.

40. Doane, 316. See also Mary Ann Doane, *The Emergence of Cinematic Time: Modernity, Contingency, the Archive* (Cambridge, Mass.: Harvard University Press, 2002).

41. Eric Santner, *My Own Private Germany* (Princeton, N.J.: Princeton University Press, 1996), 35.

42. Roger Caillois, "Mimicry and Legendary Psychasthenia," trans. John Shepley, *October* 31 (Winter 1984): 16–32.

43. Pamela Thurschwell, "Ferenczi's Dangerous Proximities: Telepathy, Psychosis, and the Real Event," *Differences* 11, no. 1 (1999): 150–78.

44. Gregory Bateson, *Steps to an Ecology of Mind* (Chicago: University of Chicago Press, 2000), 135–36.

45. Bateson, 139.

46. Claus Pias, ed., *Cybernetics: The Macy Conferences*, vol. 1 (Berlin: Diaphanes, 2003), 31.

47. Pias, 31.

48. Pias, 35.

49. Heinz von Foerster, ed., *Cybernetics: Circular Causal and Feedback Mechanisms in Biological and Social Systems: Transactions of the Sixth Conference* (New York: Josiah Macy Jr. Foundation, 1950).

50. "Cybernetics [is about] chance . . . that it seeks to contain by way of laws of the binary order. . . . In keeping on this frontier the originality of what appears in our world in the form of cybernetics, I am tying it to man's waiting . . . to the chance of the unconscious. . . . At this point we come upon a precious fact revealed to us by cybernetics—there is something in the symbolic function of human discourse that cannot be eliminated, and that is the role played in it by the imaginary." Jacques Lacan, *The Seminar of Jacques Lacan*, book II, *The Ego in Freud's Theory and in the Technique of Psychoanalysis, 1954–1955*, ed. Jacques-Alain Miller, trans. Sylavana Tomaselli, with notes by John Forrester (New York: W. W. Norton, 1991), 296–300.

51. Gregory Bateson to Warren McCulloch, November 29, 1954, Warren S. McCulloch Papers, Mss.B.M139: series I. Correspondence, box 2, American Philosophical Society, Philadelphia, Penn.

52. Bateson, *Steps to an Ecology of Mind*, 278.

53. On the relationship between schizophrenia, creativity, difference, and genius, see Irving Gottesman, *Schizophrenia Genesis: The Origins of Madness* (New York: W. H. Freeman, 1991); Shoshana Felman, *Writing and Madness* (Stanford: Stanford University Press, 2003); and Sander Gilman, *Difference and Pathology: Stereotypes of Sexuality, Race, and Madness* (Ithaca, NY: Cornell University Press, 1985).

54. Bateson, *Steps to an Ecology of Mind*, 278.

55. Donna Haraway, "A Cyborg Manifesto: Science, Technology, and Socialist-Feminism in the Late Twentieth Century," in *Simians, Cyborgs, and Women: The Reinvention of Nature* (New York: Routledge, 1991), 149–81.

AFTERWORD

Architecture in Real Time

JOHN MAY

At its inception, this project was in part motivated by what appeared to be an ongoing and deepening crisis of architectural representation. First, entire regions of contemporary architectural reasoning appeared obviously disturbed by a subtle but palpable discursive confusion, which resided not at the level of logical analysis (closed systems are always internally rational) but was buried much deeper, in the raw, preconceptual substrate from which the contemporary architectural mind fashions an understanding of itself and its world. Having strained to digest and incorporate the capacities and contradictions of contemporary scientific civilization—that is, having (explicitly) reframed *urbanism* as *environmentalism* and (tacitly) recast *autonomy* as *automation*—the design fields seemed (and still seem) unable to articulate, even for themselves, the material and epistemic conditions under which they labor. The entire critical-conceptual framework of postwar architectural discourse, it seemed, had evaporated (not because it was proven wrong; it was simply *rendered obsolete* by technical transformations beneath its language), taking with it even those theoretical postures that define themselves through opposition to that framework. So-called disciplinary debates had become, in most cases, episodes in an ongoing theater of historical reenactment: shadowboxing matches between semantic anachronisms.[1] (The words *digital* or *ecological,* for example, by covering over and stupefying massive and delicate tectonic shifts in lived life, now obfuscate far more than explicate, subsisting within our language as shiny but hollow vagaries.)

This condition is intensified by a more generalized ambivalence regarding the modern technosciences—principally the sciences of mind and environment but also the vast catalog of managerial practices that lean upon those sciences for guidance and legitimacy (environmental management and control engineering, urban planning, building sciences, etc.). After the twentieth century, those fields are no longer able to deny or explain away their own objective pasts and must now speak from both sides of their mouths, often condemning and promoting one another in the same breath.[2] Ultimately, these realities belong to a generalized condition of contemporary existence that can only be grasped through a project of extended philosophical-historical reflection that patiently exposes to view the elaborate technical underside of contemporary architectural reasoning, such that it might be made to see beyond and outside itself, if only ever partially and incompletely.

In tandem with this first set of conditions (the erosion of our language), architects must now also confront on a daily basis the fact that forms of visualization specific to technoscientific practices have come to dominate—and now literally *precede*—architecture's own historically embedded forms of representation (viz., parallel and perspectival orthographics). This dominance has had the destabilizing effect of initiating a kind of perpetual amateurism into the field, because by the time a specific technical routine has been mastered, it is already outdated. Worse still, architects are suspended in this state of breathless amateurism at exactly the moment when we are trying to assert, more forcefully than ever, our status as technoenvironmental cultural experts.

THREE AXIOMS × THREE FORMATS

Two questions run sideways across the project but nonetheless provide entry to our central concerns. First, how have processes of *technical imaging*—scanning, sensing, modeling, rendering, repeating, positioning, specifying, etcetera—so rapidly and thoroughly displaced our entire internal history of representation as the primary site of reasoning and experimentation? And second, what are the effects and consequences of this rapid displacement, for our thought, and for our interventions in the world around us?

What follows is neither a history nor a theory of architectural images but a brief philosophical description of *architecture after imaging*.[3] First, in order to clear away a series of confusions and misconceptions inherited from the historical legacy of humanism, we will consider three speculative axioms on technical life.

> **Axiom 1: There are no pretechnical forms of thought.** There are no ways of thinking that remain isolated from technical acts, no ideas or dreams or fears or desires insulated from the characteristics of a given technical age. The notion that ideas exist apart from their technical formation (in the brain or "the mind") is one of the most pervasive fallacies of modern life.

Even our oldest forms of thought and expression—many of which were pre-linguistic (ideographic, pictographic, cuneiform, etc.)—involved thoroughly technical-gestural acts of marking, inscribing, and engraving (Figure A.1).[4] Seen from an anthropological view, technical life is inseparable from processes of *hominization*—inseparable, that is, from the very processes by which a group of animals learned to think of themselves as human subjects distinct from an objective world. This paleo-ontological view, which asserts that life is always lived by means other than life—that is, by way of technical organs ("objects")—is what establishes *technics* as a conceptual category distinct from so-called technology (a term that will not be used here).[5]

Axiom 2: Nothing technical is ever merely technical. There are no "minor technicalities"—or rather, all technicalities are tethered, in some way or

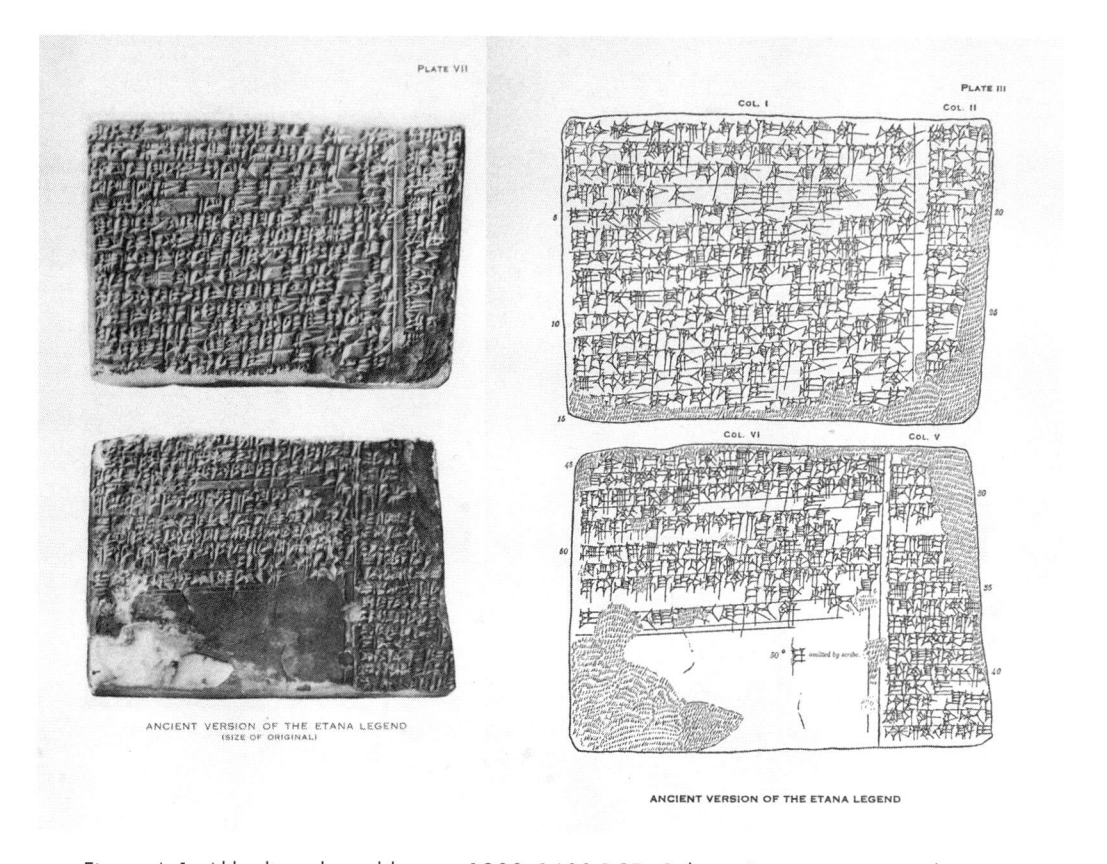

Figure A.1. Akkadian clay tablet, ca. 1900–1600 BCE. Column 2 contains a partial version of the ancient Sumerian Legend of Etana written in cuneiform. Albert Clay, *A Hebrew Deluge Story in Cuneiform, and Other Epic Fragments in the Pierpont Morgan Library* (1922), plates III and VII.

another, to the deepest regions of consciousness. All technicalities warrant historical and philosophical reflection because we can discover hidden aspects of ourselves and our thought in even the most seemingly mundane technical routines. New descriptions of those aspects will never amount to a "solution" to any specific life problem because life's technical immersion is not a problem to be solved but rather a condition to be continually re-understood—which is to say that the best philosophies of technics are, strictly speaking, useless.

Axiom 3: The specific conception of time embedded in a technical system is inseparable from the forms of thought and imagination it makes possible or impossible. Distinct technical ages are bound up with distinct conceptions of time. Technics contain specific models of time, which resonate with lived life. From an anthropological view, all technics are an externalization of programs: gestural-mental routines for living life. For our purposes here, all technics may be regarded as mnemo-technics: storehouses of the cumulative knowledge and wisdom we now refer to as "culture," whose memory exceeds the lifespan of the finite individual. In the processes of externalizing memory (which, in their accumulation, form cultures), the storage speed of the medium—its speed of inscription or recording, and its retentional duration—is decisive for the forms of consciousness with which it is associated. The structural pace with which any respective technical system allows us to record our thoughts and actions is inseparable from the ways of life it makes possible or impossible.[6]

These three axioms can be driven sideways through the three categories of visual depiction that supposedly define contemporary architectural culture: drawings, photographs, and images. Architecture today seems uninterested in distinguishing between these three, or at the very least seems unable to parse their ambiguities with any consistency. Far from indicating the permanence, exchangeability, or "resurgence" of any one category, the slippages between them are symptomatic of a chronic confusion, throughout the design fields, rooted in basic category errors concerning the enmeshment of life, thought, and technique. In place of that ambiguity, let us establish certain minimum technical criteria to define each category.

Drawing: What is architectural drawing? First, drawings consist of hand-mechanical gestures that inscribe or deposit geometric, rule-bound (syntax-bound) marks into or onto a seemingly stable surface. Hand-mechanical depiction is static: once drawn, drawings do not move. At base, "architectural drawing" refers to acts of geometric gesturing *always* aided by mechanical tools, always in some way mechanized, such that the gesture itself belongs to a synchronization between the hands and various externalized organs (straightedges, compasses, squares, etc.) (Figure A.2). Even "freehand" drawing (sketching) always involves the becoming-mechanical, through practice, of hand movements in relation to a tool. In both cases, gestures become predictable, regular, controlled, and approximately repeatable; their coordination is mechanistic.

Photograph: Seen technically, all photography is a form of *heliography*: the writing of the sun. Photography always involves the *organ-ized*—that is, coordinated by mechanisms (Figure A.3)—exposure of a chemical "first substance" to "the action of light." The photograph is thus always a chemical-mechanical (or *chemomechanical*) visual format, depicting "without any idea

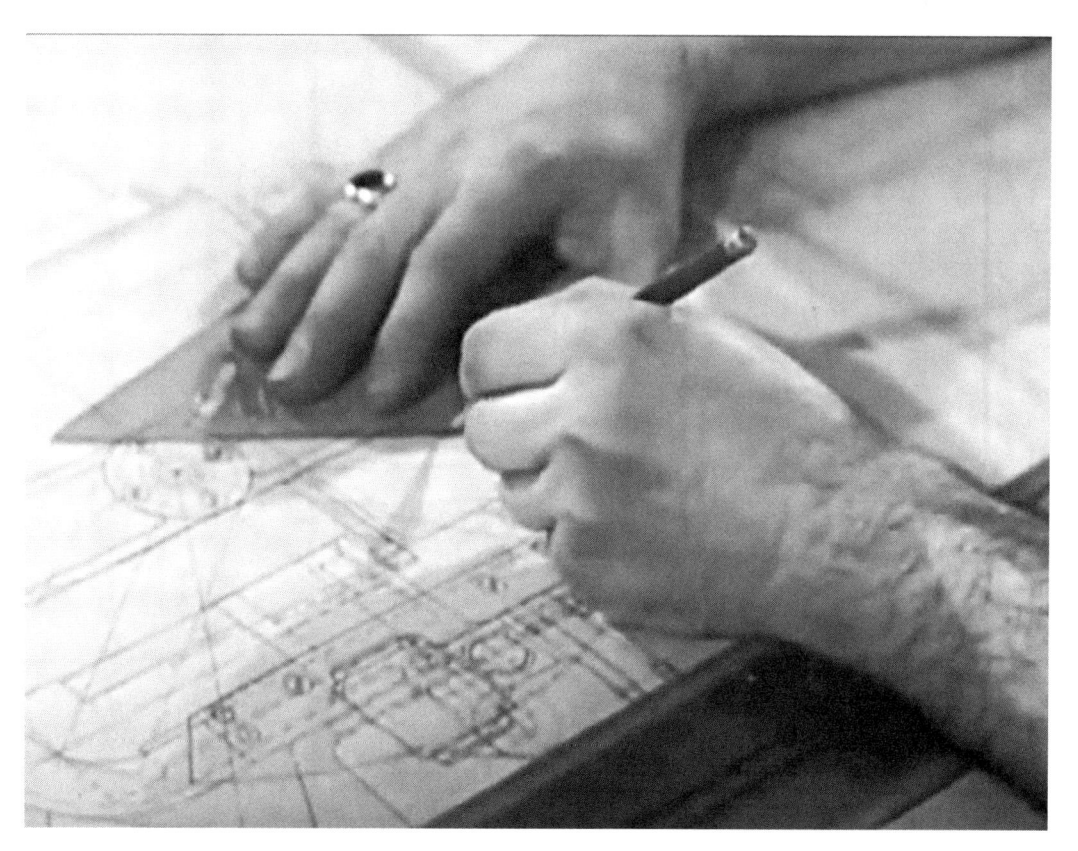

Figure A.2. Orthographic gesturing. Film still, "The Language of Drawing," *Mechanical Drawing Series,* produced by the McGraw-Hill Book Company, 1948.

of drawing... the most detailed views, the most picturesque scenery."[7] Despite its capacity to depict a visual scene nearly instantaneously, the invention of photography amounted to a regression in the domain of visual mathematiziation. Whereas the constructed perspective drawing was a thoroughly mathematical depiction (drawings were geometric arrangements of geometric quantities), the mathematics of a photograph always remains locked deep within its chemical composition—in the formulas and equations expressing that composition. The photograph offers no empirical surface for immediate calculation; it must be labored over if quantities are to be extracted from it. It was precisely this regressive weakness that stimulated, during the twentieth century, the gradual coalescing of a new format—the electrical image—from technical domains unrelated to the practice of photography; from electrical engineering, telegraphy, and physiological optics.

Image: Too much has been said of images—historically, aesthetically, politically. But nontechnical definitions are no longer helpful for architecture, so let us offer an extremely specific definition: in our lives, imaging is a form of photon detection. Unlike photographs, in which scenic light is made visible during chemical exposure, all imaging today is a process of detecting energy emitted by an environment and chopping it into discrete, measurable electrical charges called signals, which are stored, calculated, managed, and manipulated through various statistical methods. Images are thus the outputs of energetic processes defined by *signalization,* and these signals, in their accumulation, are what we mean when we say the word *data*.

Images are always already data, and all imaging is, knowingly or not, an act of data processing. It is precisely the *energetic* basis of all imaging that, from Paul Gottlieb Nipkow onward, opened up the possibility of forms of screen movement that were not predicated on the rapid mechanical succession of cinematic still photographs (film) but on the *exponentially* more rapid transmission of electrical signals. In other words, images are inherently dynamic, and our tendency to think of them as fixed is likely related to the psychological residue of drawings and chemical photographs. Because signals are energy transmitted from detectors to storage formats, signalization is inseparable from telematics: the electrical transmission of images (or, more precisely, of the data comprising any image).[8] As a storage format, images are always already quantified, always already mathematized. This cannot be overemphasized: in every instance that follows, the term *image* refers only to this very narrow (but now thoroughly ubiquitous) telematic technical format.

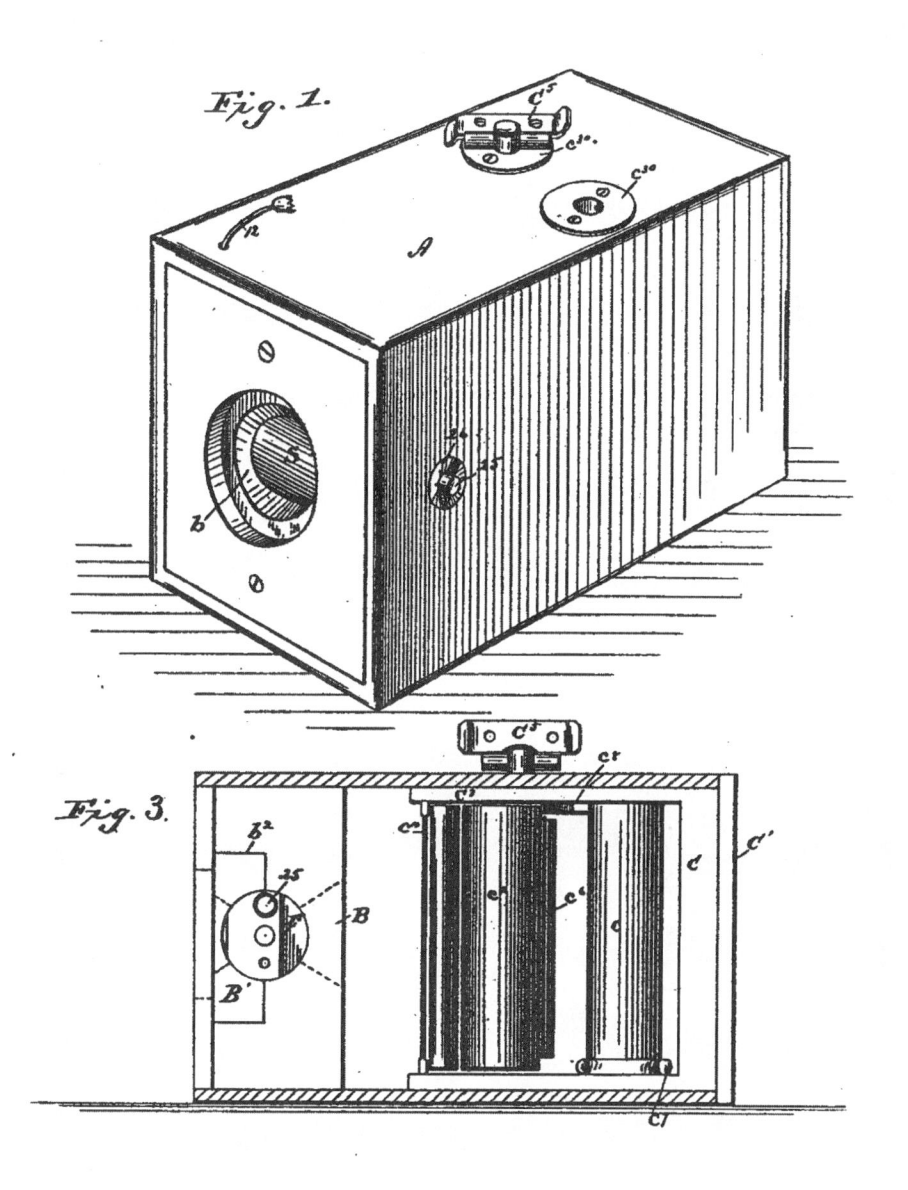

Figure A.3. Mechanisms of a camera. George Eastman, Camera, U.S. Patent 388850, filed March 30, 1888, and issued September 4, 1888.

In imaging, the labor-calculating processes that typified drawing and photography are collapsed into a single automated process that takes place behind or below the threshold of perception, through miniaturization (pixilation) and/or instantiation ("real timing" and telematics). Calculability and visibility are made coextensive through a process of automated, signalized "mathematization," in which the world and a specific statistical view of it are made to merge indistinguishably.[9]

Photo-*graphy* and photon-*detection* are held apart from one another as technical categories by this fundamental and unbridgeable epistemic abyss between heliography and bolometry; between photography as written light and imaging as detected energy; between Nicéphore Niépce's *View from the Window at Le Gras* (ca. 1826–27) (Figure A.4) and John Logie Baird's telescan of Oliver Hutchinson (1926). For this very simple, technical reason, photographs and images have virtually nothing in common with one another—nothing, that is, aside from a visual resemblance that has led us to equate two completely incompatible technical formats,

Figure A.4. Nicéphore Niépce, *View from the Window at Le Gras,* ca. 1826–27. This heliographic image, taken in Saint-Loup-de-Varennes, France, is the oldest camera photograph in existence. Wikimedia Commons (manually enhanced version).

belonging to two competing epistemic visions of the world. Images are far more closely related to spreadsheets and statistical formulas than to photographs, whose chemical composition obscures their underlying mathematical structure. Photographs, never immediately calculable, remain thoroughly visual; images, structurally calculable, are only apparently visual.

Drawing, photograph, image: three distinct and utterly incompatible forms of memory and storage. Drawings are a hand-mechanical, geometric storage format; photographs are chemical-mechanical storage (granular and molecular but not at all geometric); images are a statistical-electrical storage format. Because technics are, at base, coincident with cultural memory itself—because all techniques are ways of recording, storing, and retrieving thoughts and systems of knowledge that exceed the finitude of any single individual life—these three different formats realize three distinct mass psychologies, producing and reproducing forms of consciousness within the cultures that continually (mostly habitually) engage with them.

Through the succession of technical regimes, one format can gradually—or, more often, suddenly—eliminate not only a previous format (as in technical obsolescence) but also an entire mode of storage and its attendant forms of thought, imagination, and consciousness. Put simply, technical succession makes impossible previous ways of thought and life and makes possible other ways of thought and life.

WHAT ORTHOGRAPHY WAS

As Robin Evans has noted, "It would be possible . . . to write a history of Western architecture that would have little to do with either style or signification, concentrating instead on the manner of working."[10] Seen from an anthropological view, orthography is a geometric gesture that arranges marks into legible (repeatable and recognizable) lines and texts. Etymologically, *ortho-graphy* means something like "straight scratching," or more precisely *correct* scratching/digging/inscribing.

For the orthographer, the world *was* geometry, as both text and drawing. All orthography, written or drawn, was a form of "linear graphism": a technics in which thought was structured by rule-bound lines with beginnings and ends. Orthography produced a framework for conceptual exactitude and brought the notion of literacy into the world, because within any orthographic system, one must learn to read its meanings by way of syntactical rules and conventions. Orthographic gestures brought fundamentally new objects and objectives into the world.

Orthographic reasoning transformed a preconceptual visual world of mythical markings, always arranged in a nonlinear, associative fashion, into linear depictions of the world. In a very real, practical way, "history" and orthography were coemergent, not simply because texts and lines allowed for the recording and archiving of events but more profoundly because the character and speed of that recording and archiving capacity produced a historical sensibility in which the past was tied to the future. "Writing consciousness should be referred to as *historical consciousness* . . . for it is not as if there were a historical consciousness capable of expressing itself in various codes, writing being one of them; rather writing, this linear alignment of signs, made historical consciousness possible."[11]

There was in fact a quiet tension within orthography between two competing visions of the world. In the first vision (alphanumeric handwriting), geometric gestures structured by "the device of linearity" represented the audible and phonetic world, thus placing speech and text at the center of thought (Figure A.5): "Written language, phoneticized and linear in space, becomes completely subordinated to spoken language, which is phonetic and linear in time. . . . The whole of [the] human linguistic apparatus becomes a single instrument for expressing and preserving thought."[12]

In the second vision (orthographic drawing), geometric gestures structured by the laws of scale and proportion represented the silence of lived spatial experience, thus placing form and materiality at the center of thought. In other words, we find a rupture near the birth of orthography, within geometry itself, between speech and silence, text and architecture. Drawing (like musical notation) emerged as a kind of nonalphabetic orthography—a writing of space and form—while writing itself progressed as a kind of alphabetic drawing, in which ideal geometries were pieced together to form alphanumeric characters.

If we reflect back on architecture's orthographic past, we can see that it contained two forms of historical consciousness simultaneously, resonating with one another across time: the first belonging to the written texts of architectural treatises, manifestoes, and architectural history; the second belonging to drawn lines of architectural orthography. In other words, although there is a historical sensibility conveyed in the texts of architectural history and theory—and a crucial one—it is a sensibility that nonetheless remains thoroughly discursive; it belongs to the textual side of orthography. Architectural orthography, on the other hand, contained within itself a historical sensibility that, because it was essentially pre- or extradiscursive, sat on an altogether different register, constituting a silent form of communication within and between drawings themselves. It was a sensibility that resided in the technical substrate of architectural intuition, in hand-mechanical gestures that, although they changed over time, remained relatively

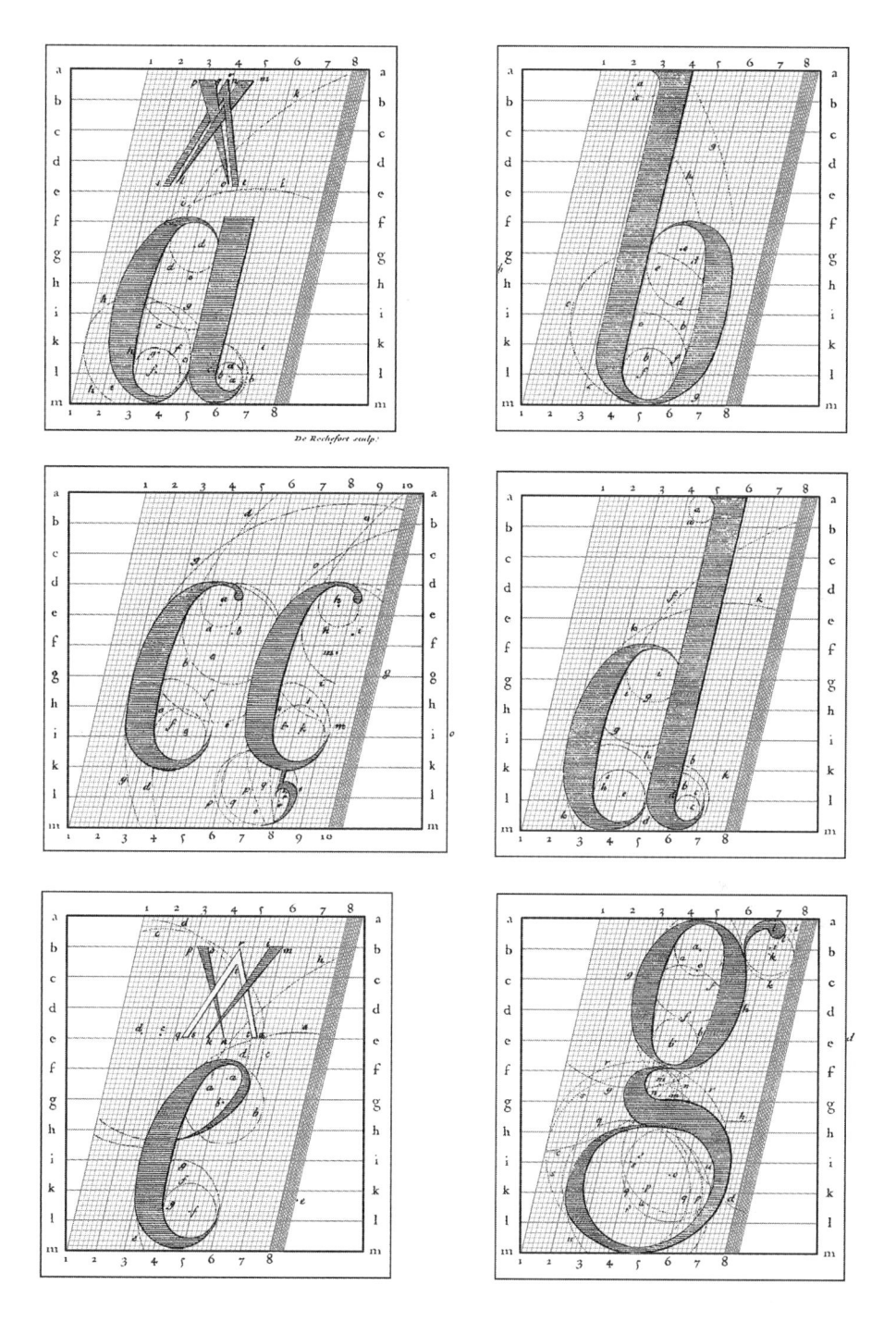

Figure A.5. The construction of oblique letters for the Romain du roi (King's roman), one of the first mathematically defined typefaces, commissioned in 1692 by Louis XIV for exclusive use by the Imprimerie royale. *Descriptions des Arts et Métiers, faites ou approuvées par messieurs de l'Académie Royale des Sciences* (Paris, 1761–88).

stable. Like textual grammars and syntaxes, drawing's rules and conventions developed and changed rather slowly; orthography was defined far more by an adherence to tradition (as technical memory) than by any rejection of it.

This correspondence between past and present, embedded in the technics of the orthographic drawing, established a deep connection between architectural experimentation and historical reasoning. In orthography, all future architecture was "drawn out from" architecture's past—this is the logic of the precedent, which carried in its technical-gestural structure the geometric inheritance of past instances of order, proportion, symbolic expression, and so on.[13] Thus the act of drawing was always an act of drawing the historical present, and the drawing itself (in its labor time) was a "stage" of history—not the textual-phonetic history of historians but the silent tectonic history of architecture past.

The fact that for many thousands of years prior to the emergence of orthographic writing time was conceived of as a circle or cycle is proof that we are not born thinking linearly or historically.[14] We trained this way of thinking into ourselves and our cultures by way of orthographic media: texts, drawings, and other forms of notation. It follows from this that cultures can train themselves *out* of linear, historical thinking—and we are currently doing just that, through our immersion in postorthographic surfaces.

POSTORTHOGRAPHY: IN REAL TIME

If the world of the orthographer was simultaneously a text and a drawing, the world of the postorthographer is simultaneously an image and a model—an *electrical* image and an *electrical* model, signally mapped onto one another. Because all signalization requires the materialization of a statistically managed signal-to-noise ratio, all postorthographic image-models are probabilistic in their underlying logic.

Put in the most basic terms: if orthography was predicated on linear historical time, materialized in texts, drawings, and mechanical clocks, postorthographic technical systems now enmesh our work in "real time," materialized in signals and image-models. Unlike historical time, which was predicated on technical regimes and gestures that continually related present and future to the past, real time relates the present to all possible futures at once (or at least as many as can be recorded and computed). Real time is the time of statistical thought, in which futures knowable and unknowable are posed simultaneously, some more calculably probable than others, but all possible. This probabilistic conception of time is fundamentally different from the linear, mechanical conception that structured orthography.[15] Our models contain *simulations* of all possible future drawings—

using the "Make2D" command is not at all the same as drawing an orthographic plan. What we see on postorthographic surfaces is simulated representation—electrical simulations of the orthographic formats that once represented the world (Figure A.6). But unlike drawing, imaging does not want to be a representation of the world; it wants to be a presentation of the world—an automatic and perceptually up-to-date, real-time model of the world.

Models are images that "refresh" at a speed anterior to perception, and just as we no longer write but instead *process* words (by manipulating the electrical signals that govern simulated alphanumeric text on screens), we also no longer draw but instead process images. Images do not and cannot make drawings; they can only make more images, some of which we "print" by electromechanically depositing material (ink, starch, plastic, concrete, etc.) with a speed and precision unimaginable to any orthographer.

The always-present experience of all calculably possible future states—which is the logic of real-time modeling—is a very different imaginative framework than the orthographic imagination, which always drew on (traced, overlaid, re-presented) the past to "project" the future. We see this difference in the kinds of evidence that are now used to justify architectural form. If the graphic language of historical precedent was once used to legitimize architectural objects, we now use the imagery and language of real-time data: images of performance, efficiency, fidelity, and control (Figure A.7).[16]

Figure A.6. Image-model and simulated orthography, 2017. Autodesk Revit promotional image.

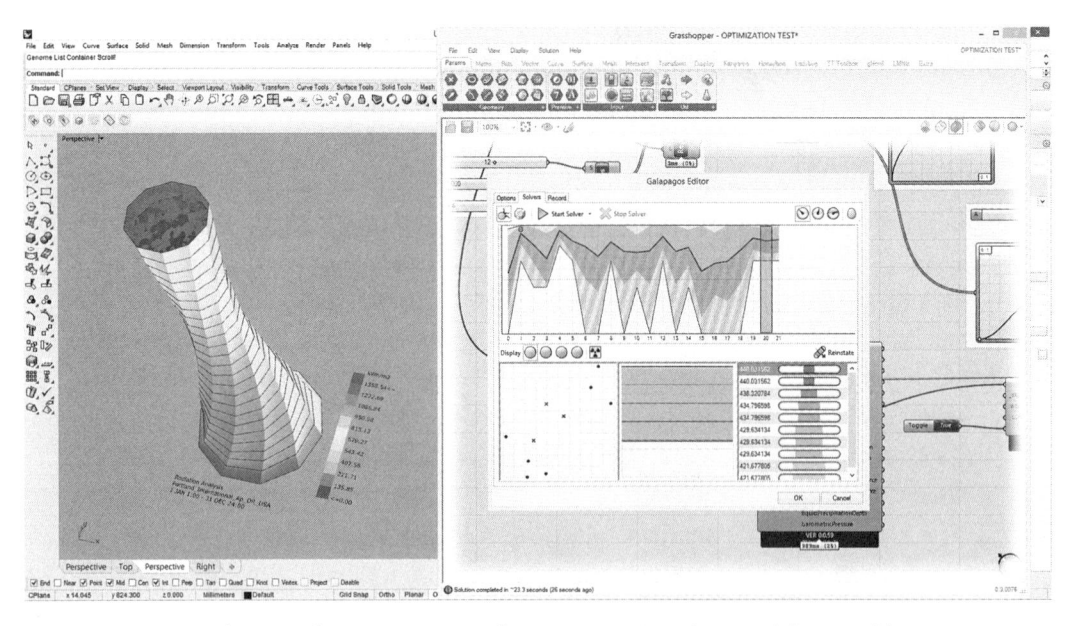

Figure A.7. Galapagos form optimization fitness test in Grasshopper/Rhino. Public instructional image by Stephen Gonzales, "Ladybug + Galapagos Solar Radiation Optimization," May 15, 2015, https://gonzalesarch.wordpress.com/.

It might be imagined that this technical succession was a purely negative event—the erasure of one set of routines and gestures by another. But in hindsight, can we now finally say what it has meant for architecture to use the word *digital* (or now, *postdigital*)? It has meant, and still means, *pseudorthography*. Pseudorthography is not at all "fake" but instead indicates the residual psychology of orthography laboring in the absence of its own technical-gestural basis—a pathology in which *familiarity,* that crucial element of comprehension, is preserved as a coping mechanism in the face of unfamiliar conditions.[17]

Postorthography is thus a condition in which our thought and imagination are strung between two competing forces, one waxing, the other waning. On one side, we struggle to retain whatever remnants of the orthographic we can still remember—line weight, precedent, tectonics. To the extent that this mentality imagines itself laboring over a drawing ("computer aided" or otherwise)—to the extent that it imagines the act of drawing as *still possible*—we are in the presence of pseudorthography. Far from extinct, pseudorthography retains dominance over a current generation of younger practitioners who have recently and emphatically declared their allegiance to an imagined "culture of drawing."[18]

At the same time, we blissfully immerse ourselves in the telematic ubiquity of the present, producing our "drawings" in telematic image formats and advertising ourselves on telematic social platforms whose technical structures bear no relation to drawing, and which want nothing more than to forget drawing, writing, and history in favor of real-time imagery.

Some architects imagine that drawings are still needed to build buildings, and that this indexical connection has preserved orthography as the solid center of our practices. But in a technical sense, we have not used a drawing to build anything in decades. Everything is now built from simulated orthography (images), with its attendant forms of transmission, duplication, repetition, and instantaneous modification—all of which have coalesced into a form of telematic managerialism unknown to orthography.

The psychological-gestural residue of orthography is disappearing from an architectural culture that is becoming ever more indistinguishable from telematic life. Lines "drawn" by computers, or by the nostalgic hands of architectural minds whose very oxygen *is* telematic imagery, can never again amount to drawing, because the age of orthography has drawn to a close, Friedrich Kittler's own final words its epitaph: "Only that which can be switched, can be."[19]

AUTOMATION; OR, THE POLITICS OF (VERY) LARGE NUMBERS

The city was an *orthothesis*: an orthographic idea-object born of the continual interplay between writing and drawing. It was the shared geometric basis of those two technical gestures that served as a platform for the *polis,* where politics was a fluid field established between the discourse of written laws, constitutions, decrees, dissent, and the silence of drawn plans, sections, elevations, and surveys.[20]

During the emergence of "digital architecture"—over the course of roughly the past three decades—architecture's principal political debates surrounded the erasure of the city by something called urbanism. Out of this came the idea that the visible, physical, and material dimensions of collective life were ceding political primacy to its invisible, electrical, topological, and ecological aspects. Today we can declare that process complete.[21] And so, while there is an everyday politics of urban life—a politics of protest and dissent—that must be enacted and preserved, it would nonetheless be a fallacy to see this everyday politics as the primary terrain of political *theorization*. The primary terrain is now imaging, which, by infusing itself throughout all of life, is driving us exponentially deeper into what Alain Desrosières has called the "politics of large numbers," where the managerial calculus of probabilities finds new forms of sociovisual expression every day (Figure A.8).[22]

Imaging places the fact of *automation* at the center of our lives but not in ways relatable to our historical traditions. The methods of automation that emerged

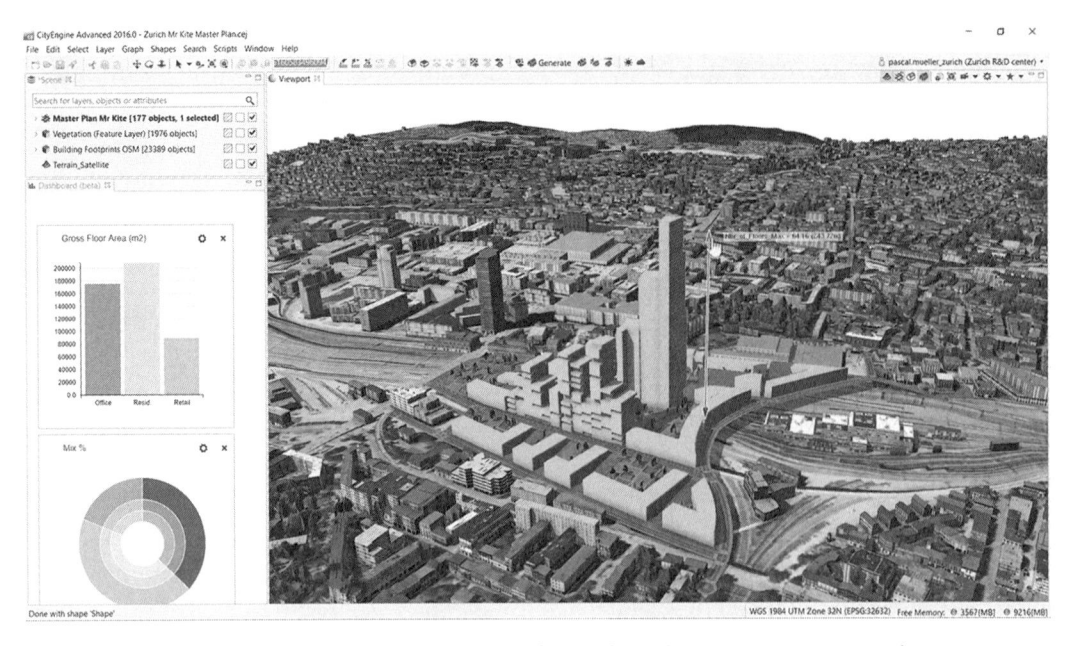

Figure A.8. Esri CityEngine, "3D Modeling Software for Urban Environments," with "Computer Generated Architecture [CGA] shape grammars" and real-time Geographic Information Systems (GIS). ESRI CityEngine promotional image.

during the age of orthography belonged to the technical logic of mechanization—the essence of which, we know from Sigfried Giedion, consists in "endless rotation," producing a geometric translation of energy and force (Figure A.9).[23] During the later phases of that technical age, machines employed electricity only as a continuous source of rotational power. In signalization—understood broadly as the ongoing project of converting all of lived experience into discrete, measurable, calculable electrical charges (signals)—automation is released from the prison of endless rotation and moves into thinner realms, into the topological and electrical, in processes concealed from perception by their size and speed. Unlike machines, signalized apparatuses know only the logic of discretization, whose translation of force relies on an electrical communication among their parts. The two are conjunctive: mechanization aimed to automate manual labor, and signalization now aims to automate the mental processes that can be made to control automated manual processes (isn't this what we mean today when we say "parametric"?).

The radical difference between imaging and previous forms of simulation is that what imaging simulates is not specific ideas or thoughts but rather *thinking itself*. Thus in signalization we are always confronted with the fact that simulated thinking is much faster than previous forms of thinking with respect to an

Figure A.9. Workers on the first moving assembly line, at the Ford Highland Part plant, put V-shaped magnets on Model T flywheels to make one-half of the flywheel magneto, 1913. Henry Ford in collaboration with Samuel Crowther, *My Life and Work* (Garden City, N.Y.: Garden City, 1922).

expanding range of "non-routine mental activities."[24] To achieve this speed we make a simple exchange: we trade the historical consciousness of hand-mechanical orthography for the statistical consciousness of the real-time image-model. In a deeply technical sense, we leave behind the time of historical thought, where all contemplation and reflection found a home. As it replaces orthographic consciousness, the technics of real-time production is removing the labor time in which architecture used to ruminate on the possibilities and consequences of its forms for life and is thereby eliminating all previous political and ethical questions from architectural reasoning. In other words, the so-called crisis of tectonics induced by computation is in fact a restructuring of all previous political, moral, and existential reasoning.

The electrical automation of postorthography is, however, in no way thoughtless. It simply reformats acts of thinking, displacing them to different arenas. Automation has never been a simple matter of passing labor from humans to machines; it has always involved the enmeshment of consciousness and gestural habituation within processes that are internal neither to the organic nor to the machinic but instead reside within both categories simultaneously. It has always relied on deeply practical "theories of organic extension," best understood through a "biological philosophy of technique."[25] It has always involved, in other words, the concretization of technical objects, which are not objects at all but rather points of genesis at which thoughts and repetitive gestures codetermine one another, giving rise to new physiological processes and new lived experiences. Under the technical conditions of real time, *signalization takes command*, and in doing so it organizes and initiates an exhaustive reformation of all previous thought and language whose result is an entirely new orientation toward the world.

Somewhat contemporaneous with the transition from mechanization to signalization, we find another, equally definite event: the movement from a deterministic to a probabilistic world picture.[26] The most decisive conceptual event of twentieth-century physics was the discovery that the world is not deterministic. Similarly, the most decisive event in modern biology was the substitution of probabilistic populationism for deterministic essentialism.[27] In both cases, probabilistic thought laid bare the unrecoverable limitations within any deterministic conception of the physical world. This epistemic division *seems* to map neatly onto the mechanization-signalization divide and seems in some ways to confirm its veracity. We cannot know. And in any case, such questions are meaningful only insofar as they are unanswerable.

When we speak of statistical thinking today, we do so in the following way: *Although the causal chain of the physical world is no longer defined by perfect, reversible continuity, it is nonetheless subject to statistical regularities, as expressed by probabilities; predictive causal relationships prevail within large, diverse masses despite the chance character of certain individual phenomena. Statistical reasoning ignores the messy reality of the individual instance by attending to processes that can be applied to generality.*[28]

Probabilistic reasoning in general gained acceptance as a means of rationalizing decisions under conditions of uncertainty; which is to say, probability theory aimed to standardize opinions regarding how best to draw inferences about the future from past experience. In its earliest applications, "probability theory was to native good sense what a telescope or spectacles were to the naked eye: a mechanical extension designed along the same basic principles as the original. Thus the entire historical arc of the emergence of probability and statistical thinking is at base a history of first, the mechanization of, and later the signalization of, inference."[29] Through these procedures the classical category of "generality" was quietly but thoroughly transformed into the mutable notion of *mass phenomena*. From that moment forward the primary technical goal was to make *immediately visible* the statistical analysis of mass phenomena.

We can ask: What exactly does probabilistic reasoning want from technics? The answer is deceptively simple: it wants more, always more. What we find when we gaze at contemporary statistical images is that their technical recordings are never thick enough, can never be acquired fast enough nor processed fast enough. Probabilistic reasoning wants to believe that the body of observational data upon which it operates has been acquired at a rate and volume worthy of being considered an instantaneous record of reality. The past is fine, but it is far more difficult to thicken than the present, and in any case it is nearly always in the wrong format.

We now see electrostatistically, which bears tremendous consequences for our thought. At the very least, it marks a decisive rupture in the treatment afforded to the act of historical reflection, and toward the concept of "the past" more generally. If determinism was nourished by the idea of a thick historical record of events that might be fast-forwarded in the name of predictive certainty, probabilistic reasoning thrives on the dream of an instantaneous and complete recording of the always-present moment in the name of calculable uncertainty.

TELEMASIS

Insofar as the world seeps into and wells up within us in secret and mostly unseen ways—through techniques and routines, through institutions and habits—our work now finds itself swept up in an immense cultural experiment called imaging. If our technics are always already pulled taut between life and thought, if they are a fact in the world while also being a vision of that world, then we should regard as self-delusional any architectural culture that disregards the philosophical dimensions of its own technical practices.

The question of how exactly architecture today designates things or conditions as either *natural* (viz., "organic," "essential," "innate," "dynamic," "generative," "emergent," etc.) or *unnatural* (viz., "built," "artificial," "machinic," "constructed," "political," "historical," etc.) emerged as one of the principal anchors binding the various branches of this project. Because this question nearly always, in architectural practices, takes the form of technoscientific visualizations, the "neonaturalism" we have described—this often elegant mixture of technical acumen and philosophical oblivion, in which *signalization* displaces *signification* as the primary epistemic mortar in architectural reasoning—is as much image as concept.[30] We might even be justified in hyphenating those terms; perhaps neo-naturalistic reasoning is best understood as a rapidly growing repertoire of technical *image-concepts* (building information models, tool paths, brain scans, thermal maps, geographic-information systems, ecological performance models, etc.) in which discursive concepts are reduced to commands.

Image-concepts do not merely make specific claims about "nature"; deep down in the details of their technicality they make more generalized philosophical claims about *the nature of nature.* They silently posit an entire cosmological theory of life in every scene (in general, that the world is a statistical object and is therefore best understood as an ever-growing body of electrical data). We have provisionally named this condition "neonaturalism." It is an event entirely beyond good or evil but one for which our fields are philosophically and politically unprepared.

Complicating this account, however, is a somewhat distinct consideration concerning our contemporary use of images, which has only been roughly outlined here: a rapid transition from an age of representation to one of presentation.[31] In other words, perhaps what appeared at first glance to be a "crisis of representation," in which our technical capabilities have drastically outpaced our ability to conceptually re-present reality, is in fact not the case at all. And perhaps this concept we have called "neonaturalism"—by which we indicated the passage from an evidentiary regime rooted in historical signification to one rooted in electrical signalization (data-as-information)—is in fact precisely wrong when viewed from *inside* our contemporary technical systems.

Unlike historical time, which was concerned with representing the past as a way of *determining the future,* real time presents all possible futures at once (or at least as many as can be counted, computed, and parametrized) as a way of *managing the present.* Perhaps, in a purely technical sense, there can be no "crisis of representation" within the technics of real-time presentation, and we are not so much entering a new evidentiary paradigm as moving beyond any recognizable conception of evidence.

Put differently: what we have been calling *neonatural representation* may well be a kind of brief transition phase on the way to *autonatural presentation*—one in which an older, presignalized technics of data (viz., "paperwork"[32]) gradually cleared away signification and, in doing so, laid the psychological groundwork for a condition in which all the old *significant* questions (ontological, epistemological, metaphysical) are now preemptively superseded by a technics that always immediately presents the world as a field of data without bounds. As that world emerges, the old gap between representation and intervention—the gap in which concepts such as *evidence, objectivity, precedent,* and *history* made their home—recedes further and further from view, as more and more forms of presentation take up residence behind or below ocular perception.[33]

Within the gaze of presentational, real-time technics, the very concept of "crisis" is (automatically, by design) excluded; it is not so much *erased* as simply *deleted*, in a gesture "illuminating and eliminating itself like night."[34] It remains to be seen whether real-time principles like simultaneity and instantaneity can be made to bear any resemblance to history, or whether the managerial image-concepts of presentational intervening can somehow take the place of the countless "historical-philosophical images of the future" that animated not only the political philosophy of progress but also the substrate of historical reasoning more generally.[35]

What, then, is an image in our time, if fully recognized *as an image*? It is our field of experimentation and our field of politics. It is the technical format in which experimental lives—lives consciously lived differently from our own—might one day find not only their form but possibly, hopefully, their political expression within a new statistical literacy capable of navigating the conditions of telematic culture.

Do we not already see in images? When we see a thing, a scene, an experience, do we not already now see it *first* as transmissible? Telematic lives are lives constantly animated from a distance.

Going forward, architecture will effortlessly shed the historical consciousness of orthography. It cannot possibly hold. Scanning, sensing, rendering, specifying, projecting, touching, swiping, scrolling, selecting, filtering, cropping, resizing, zooming, channelizing, compressing, tagging, batching—in short, image processing—are not the minor expressions of technical systems external to thought or instrumentalizable techniques with known or controllable affects (Figure A.10). They are the gestural basis of an entire consciousness that, for now, continues to refer to our practices as *architecture* but will soon loosen and forget that name if architecture stubbornly clings to "the pieties of essentialism and persistence" and confuses "longevity with profundity."[36]

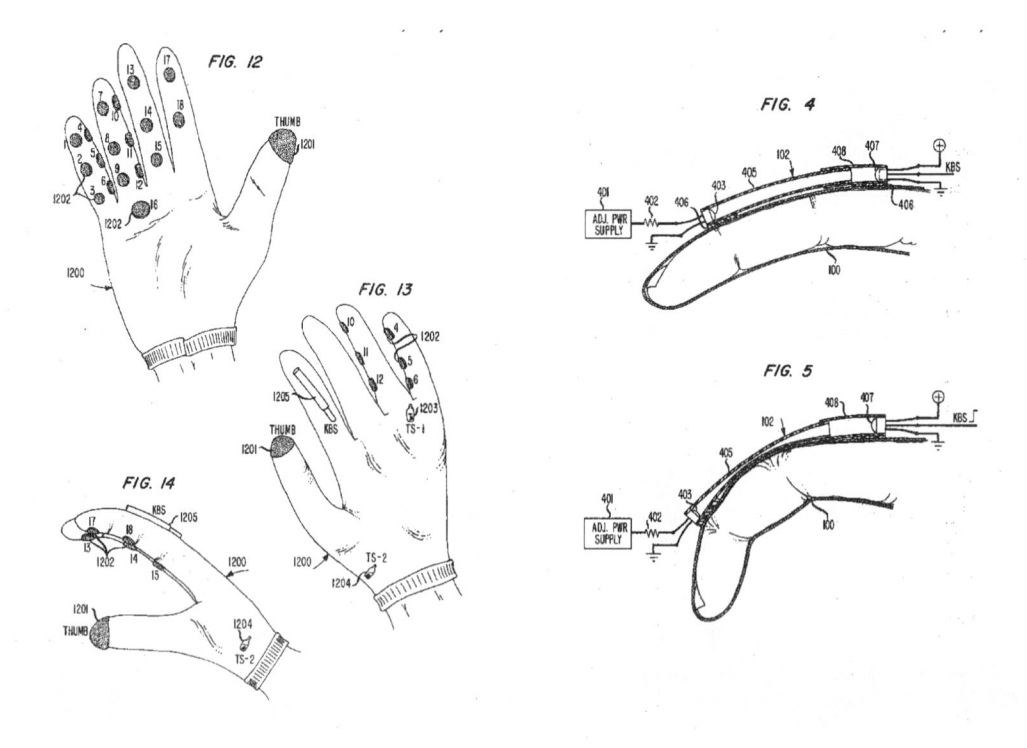

Figure A.10. Postorthographic gestural technics. Gary J. Grimes, Digital Data Entry Glove Interface Device, U.S. Patent 4414537 A, filed September 15, 1981, and issued November 8, 1981.

NOTES

1. See John May, "The Logic of the Managerial Surface," *Praxis* 13 (2013): 116–24; and Zeynep Çelik Alexander, "The Core That Wasn't," *Harvard Design Magazine,* no. 35 (Fall/Winter 2012): 84–89.

2. "If we were previously concerned with externally caused dangers (from the gods or nature), the historically novel quality of today's risks derives from internal decision.... Science is one of the causes, the medium of definition, and the source of solutions to risks.... In the reciprocal interplay between risks it has helped to cause and define, and the public critique of those same risks, techno-scientific development becomes contradictory." Ulrich Beck, *Risk Society: Towards a New Modernity* (London: SAGE, 1992), 155.

3. My position throughout this exploration is that the word *digital* has, through overuse and generalization, lost all sense and meaning, and that we will have to rely on other words, other concepts, to describe the world anew. Certainly the remarkable "Archaeology of the Digital" project at the Canadian Centre for Architecture (CCA) has gone some way to recover this lost meaning during a specific moment in architectural thought, but as will become clear, the present description of computational images diverges from that project in fundamental and irreconcilable ways.

4. See André Leroi-Gourhan, *Gesture and Speech,* trans. Anna Bostock Berger (Cambridge, Mass.: MIT Press, 1993); and Jean Bottéro, *Mesopotamia: Writing, Reasoning, and the Gods* (Chicago: University of Chicago Press, 1992).

5. Leo Marx, "Technology: The Emergence of a Hazardous Concept," *Technology and Culture* 51, no. 3 (July 2010): 561–77.

6. I am drawing heavily here on Leroi-Gourhan's analysis of programming in *Gesture and Speech* but also Bernard Stiegler's reading of that work in his own *Technics and Time* volumes. It is impossible to adequately acknowledge here the full debt owed by the present essay to that body of work. The third axiom, for example, is a reduced condensation of Stiegler's central thesis: "Technics, far from being merely in time, properly constitutes time." Bernard Stiegler, *Technics and Time,* vol. 1, *The Fault of Epimetheus,* trans. Richard Beardsworth and George Collins (Stanford: Stanford University Press, 1998), 27.

7. Louis Jacques Mandé Daguerre, "Daguerreotype," in *Classic Essays on Photography,* ed. Alan Trachtenberg (New Haven, Conn.: Leete's Island, 1980), 13.

8. Signalization and telematics are in fact so entwined that the project to realize the electrical image as a transmissible form of visual information was motivated by the desire during World War II to transmit scenic military information instantly and automatically (which is to say, electronically), much like telegraphy had already "instantized" discourse by transforming its content into (signalized) information.

9. On the "mathematization of nature," see Edmund Husserl, *The Crisis of European Sciences and Transcendental Phenomenology,* trans. David Carr (Evanston: Northwestern University Press, 1970), 9, 23–59; and Michael Lynch, "The Externalized Retina: Selection and Mathematization in the Visual Documentation of Objects in the Life Sciences," *Human Studies* 11, no. 2/3 (1988): 201–34.

10. Robin Evans, "Translations from Drawing to Building," *AA Files* 12 (Summer 1986): 16.

11. Vilém Flusser, *Does Writing Have a Future?,* trans. Nancy Ann Roth (Minneapolis: University of Minnesota Press, 2011), 7.

12. Leroi-Gourhan, *Gesture and Speech,* 210.

13. To give a simple example, Le Corbusier was famously obsessed with Moisei Ginzburg's Narkomfin Building, and reportedly even traced its plans while developing his conception of the Unité d'habitation. See Jean-Louis Cohen, *Le Corbusier and the Mystique of the USSR: Theories and Projects for Moscow, 1928–1936* (Princeton, N.J.: Princeton University Press, 1992), 23.

14. "Primitive thought appears to take place within a temporal and spatial setting which is continually open to revision.... The fact that verbal language is coordinated freely with graphic figurative representation is undoubtedly one of the reasons for this kind of thinking.... The thinking of agricultural peoples is organized in both time and space from an initial point of reference—*omphalos*—round which the heavens gravitate and from which distances are ordered. The thinking of pre-alphabetic antiquity was radial, like the body of a sea urchin or the starfish." Leroi-Gourhan, *Gesture and Speech,* 211.

15. See John Harwood and John May, "If We Wake Up to Find We Have Been Too Well-Trained," in *Architecture Is All Over,* ed. Esther Choi and Marrikka Trotter (New York: Columbia Books on Architecture and the City, 2017).

16. See John May, "Under Present Conditions Our Dullness Will Intensify," *Project* 3 (Spring 2014); and Zeynep Çelik Alexander, "Neo-naturalism," in "New Ancients," ed. Dora Epstein Jones and Bryony Roberts, special issue, *Log,* no. 31 (Spring/Summer 2014): 23–30.

17. Seen in this way, the CCA's "Archaeology of the Digital" project might equally be understood as a genealogy of the last orthographers—a generalized biography of an orthographic consciousness struggling to persist within a technics that had no use for it, and for which it in turn had no language, as it searched to resolve its previous world with this new technics that had completely destabilized its sense of reality.

18. For example, see Sam Jacob, "Drawing in a Post-Digital Age," *Metropolis* 36, no. 8 (March 2017): 76–81; and "New Ancients," ed. Dora Epstein Jones and Bryony Roberts, special issue, *Log,* no. 31 (Spring/Summer 2014).

19. Friedrich Kittler, *Draculas Vermächtnis: Technische Schriften* (Leipzig: Reclam, 1993), 182.

20. Jean-Pierre Vernant, *Myth and Thought among the Greeks* (New York: Zone Books, 2006), 202–7.

21. See Sanford Kwinter, *Requiem for the City at the End of the Millennium* (New York: Actar, 2010), 58; and May, "The Logic of the Managerial Surface."

22. See Alain Desrosières, *The Politics of Large Numbers: A History of Statistical Reasoning,* trans. Camille Naish (Cambridge, Mass.: Harvard University Press, 2002).

23. "The difference between walking and rolling, between the legs and the wheel, is basic to all mechanization." Sigfried Giedion, *Mechanization Takes Command: A Contribution to Anonymous History* (New York: Oxford University Press, 1948), 47.

24. Carl Benedikt Frey and Michael A. Osborne, "The Future of Employment: How Susceptible Are Jobs to Computerisation?," *Technological Forecasting and Social Change* 114 (January 2017): 254–80.

25. Georges Canguilhem, "Machine and Organism," trans. Mark Cohen and Randall Cherry, in *Incorporations,* ed. Jonathan Crary and Sanford Kwinter (New York: Zone Books, 1992), 61.

26. See Gerd Gigerenzer, Zeno Swijtink, Theodore Porter, Lorraine Daston, and Lorenz Kruger, *The Empire of Chance: How Probability Changed Science and Everyday Life* (New York: Cambridge University Press, 1989); Ian Hacking, *The Taming of Chance* (New York: Cambridge University Press, 1990); and Morris Kline, *Mathematics; The Loss of Certainty* (New York: Oxford University Press, 1980).

27. Ernst Mayr, *The Growth of Biological Thought: Diversity, Evolution, and Inheritance* (Cambridge, Mass.: Harvard University Press, 1982), 45–47.

28. See Theodore Porter, *The Rise of Statistical Thinking, 1820–1900* (Princeton, N.J.: Princeton University Press, 1986).

29. Gigerenzer et al., *The Empire of Chance,* 286–88.

30. On neonaturalism, see Alexander, "Neo-naturalism"; and May, "The Logic of the Managerial Surface."

31. "In the current moment, there is another kind of image-making that's becoming very important, that [is . . .] neither an "ideal," nor "mechanical," nor "expert-altered" image. The surgeon, the electronics fabricator, or somebody working with toxic materials—they're all using the image to manipulate something. I think that images actively used as part of manipulation mean we are no longer concerned with *re-presentation*, but rather with *presentation*. [Now] images are a part of the primary intervention into the world. . . . We are no longer wondering if our re-presentation of the thing matches something out there. Today, more and more, we want images that do things. An evidentiary image is no longer sufficient for many scientists. We want images that help us organize information, that are accessible, that may not be a copy of something 'out there' at all. . . . Images become tools, like a video-monitor image used by a distant doctor to conduct tele-surgery. When images are there to cut, fold, connect, manufacture, their purpose is to help us do things beyond the classical task of categorizing and confirming. In that world, which is more engineering or surgery or sampling, the fundamental question is not, as with the classic from particle physics: 'Does this exist?' Instead, it's: 'Does our evidence demonstrate to a reasonable probability that there are particles of the type that we've described?'" Peter Galison, quoted in "The Lives of Images: Peter Galison in Conversation with Trevor Paglen," *Aperture,* no. 211 (2013): 36–37. For an extended treatment, see Lorraine Daston and Peter Galison, *Objectivity* (New York: Zone Books, 2008).

32. See Ben Kafka, *The Demon of Writing: Powers and Failures of Paperwork* (New York: Zone Books, 2012).

33. See Peter Galison and John May, "The Revelation of Secrets: Peter Galison and John May on Artifacts of Surveillance, Part I and II," in *Scandalous,* Thresholds 43, ed. Nathan Friedman and Ann Lui (Cambridge, Mass.: SA+P Press, MIT, School of Architecture + Planning, 2015), 136–267.

34. Michel Foucault, *The Birth of the Clinic: An Archaeology of Medical Perception* (London: Routledge, 1973), 195.

35. Reinhart Koselleck, *Critique and Crisis: Enlightenment and the Pathogenesis of Modern Society* (Cambridge, Mass.: MIT Press, 1988), 9.

36. Evans, "Translations from Drawing to Building," 15.

Contributors

LUCIA ALLAIS is associate professor of architecture at Columbia University, author of *Designs of Destruction: The Making of Monuments in the Twentieth Century*, and an editor of the journal *Grey Room*.

ZEYNEP ÇELIK ALEXANDER is associate professor in the Department of Art History and Archaeology at Columbia University. She is author of *Kinaesthetic Knowing: Aesthetics, Epistemology, Modern Design* and an editor of the journal *Grey Room*.

EDWARD A. EIGEN is senior lecturer in the history of landscape and architecture at the Harvard University Graduate School of Design. He is author of *On Accident: Episodes in Architecture and Landscape*.

ORIT HALPERN is associate professor of sociology at Concordia University and author of *Beautiful Data: A History of Vision and Reason since 1945*. She is also director of the Speculative Life Research Cluster, a laboratory bridging the arts, environmental sciences, media, and the social sciences.

JOHN HARWOOD is associate professor of architecture in the John H. Daniels Faculty of Architecture, Landscape, and Design at the University of Toronto. He is author of *The Interface: IBM and the Transformation of Corporate Design, 1945–1976* (Minnesota, 2011) and an editor of the journal *Grey Room*.

MATTHEW C. HUNTER is associate professor in the Department of Art History and Communication Studies at McGill University in Montreal. He is author of *Painting with Fire: Sir Joshua Reynolds, Photography, and the Temporally Evolving Chemical Object* and *Wicked Intelligence: Visual Art and the Science of Experiment in Restoration London* and an editor of the journal *Grey Room*.

JOHN MAY is assistant professor of architecture at the Harvard University Graduate School of Design and founding partner, with Zeina Koreitem, of MILLIØNS, an award-winning Los Angeles–based design practice.

MICHAEL OSMAN is associate professor and director of the Critical Studies MA/PhD programs at UCLA Architecture and Urban Design. He is author of *Modernism's Visible Hand: Architecture and Regulation in America* (Minnesota, 2018).

Index

Page numbers in italics refer to figures.

Abbey of Traps, 123
Abbey of Tricks, 103, 116
ACE Report, 201
Ackerman, Frederick, 155
aesthetics, 28, 189n4; experience, 36n15; geometric, 12; of incompletion, 31–33; information theory and, 166; Kantian, 76; machine, xv, xxiin31
agency, x, *33*, 60, 114, 181, 194, 202–3, 209, 212
AIA. *See* American Institute of Architects
air pump, 9, 51, *52*
Alberti, Leon Battista, 5, 36n12, 47, 49
algorithms, 91, 204, 206, 207, 208; ray-casting, 28; ray-tracing, 28; rendering, 28, 31; shading, 28
Althusser, Louis, x, xi, xixn2
American Institute of Architects (AIA), 141, 155
Amhoff, Tilo, 136
analog, 208, 211; digital and, xxiin32
analogy, 53, 199; identity and, 44n100; modeling and, 69n77
analysis, x, 84, 86; historical, 175; logical, 219; mathematical, 195; media theoretical, 165; statistical, 96n7

analytics: compulsion for, 212; data, 207; instantaneous, 195; real-time, 211, 212
Annals of a Fortress (Viollet-le-Duc), 166, 167
Anschauungsunterricht, 82, 84
anthropocentrism, 75, 76
"Archaeology of the Digital" project (CCA), 240n3, 242n17
Architect, The (Benjamin), 141
Architectural Graphic Standards (Ramsey and Sleeper), 133, 155
Architectural Record Company, 153
Architectural Review, 155
Architectural Shades and Shadows (McGoodwin), 1, 20
Architectural Specifications (Sleeper), 155
Architecture and War (LeRoy, Mallory, and Ottar), 181
Architecture Machine Group, 203
"Architecture of Position" (Ruskin), 164
"Architecture of Protection" (Ruskin), 163–64
Architecture of the Well-Tempered Environment (Banham), xiv
Arch of Titus, 7
Armstrong, Christopher Drew, 181

ARPANET, 174
artillery, 163, 166
Art Institute of Chicago, 182
Arvo, James: work of, *30*
Aspen Movie Map, 31, 43n93
"Atelier, L'" (Hertenberger), *19*
Augmenting Human Intellect (Engelbert), 157
Aurangzeb, 48
automata, 112–13, 193, 204–8; making, 111, 112
automation, 112, 131, 233–37; autonomy and, 219; electrical, 236; imaging and, 233–34
axioms, formats and, 220–24, 226–27

Bachelard, Gaston, 32
Bacon, Francis, 51
Baird, John Logie, 226
Bakewell, Frederick Collier, 79, 81
balloon frame, 134, *134*, 136, 139, 152, 159n9; drawings of, 147, 151; history of, 147; isometrical perspective of, *151*; mass production and, 147; one-and-a-half story, *149*; one-story, *148*; two-story, *150*
Banham, Mary, xiv
Banham, Reyner, xvii, xviii, 181; Giedion and, xiv; guesswork of, xxiin29; technics and, xv
Bank of Pennsylvania, 140; contract with, *140*
Baran, Paul, 172–73, 174, 189n38
Bateson, Gregory, 191, 206, 207, 211; double bind and, 210; McCulloch and, 210; porpoise and, 212; psychoanalytic concerns and, 182; self-referential violence and, 209; static games and, 192, 193; total war and, 192–93
Baudelaire, Charles, 115
Bauhaus, 82, 90–91
Beaux-Arts, 20, 26, *26*, 40n65. *See also* École des Beaux-Arts

Beaux-Arts architect, vignette of, *16*
behavior, 118, 200, 211; algorithmic, 195; anticipatable, 199; antisocial, 210; complexity of, 208; network, 191; paranoidal, 192; transformations of, 108
Bell, William E., 146; balloon frames and, 147, *148, 149, 150*
Bénard, Émile: palace by, *17*
Bender, John, 9
Benjamin, Asher, 141, 143, 146
Bergson, Henri, 193, 194
Bibliothèque Sainte-Geneviève, 18
Bilbao Museum, xv
Bildung, 84, 90, 91, 99n51
BIM. *See* building information modeling
biopolitics, 189n41, 195
black boxed, 31, 195, 200
Boring, Edward, 87
Bötticher, Karl, xiii
Boullée, Etienne-Louis, 12
Boyle, Robert: air pump by, 9, 51, *52*
braced frame, 134, *135*
Brindle, Steven, 175
British East India Company, 47
Brunel, Isambard Kingdom, 175, 176, 177, 189n43; design by, *176*; sketch by, *178*
Brunelleschi, Filippo, 49
builders, 131, 139, 141, 144
building information modeling (BIM), 50, 156, 158
"Building Product Facts" (Graf), 156
Bulletin of Mathematical Biophysics, 196
Bunker Archaeology (Virilio), 181
Burnham and Root (firm), 153; plans for offices of, *154*

Caillois, Roger, 205
calculation, 213n8, 226, 237; sensations and, 37n28
Calgary Central Library, 32; design for, *2*
Callendar, Craig, 57
calligraphic hodgepodge, *104*

Index

camera: mechanisms of, *225*; movements of, 32
camera obscura, 77, 78, 92, 98n27
Canadian Centre for Architecture (CCA), xixn1, 159n2, 240n3
CAPTCHA technology, 88
Caravaggio, naturalism and, 49
Carbonnel, Maurice, 25
carpenters: architects and, 144; methods of, 146; tools of, 144
Carpentry Made Easy (Bell), 146
Carpo, Mario, 5, 130, 136; Alberti and, 36n12, 47
cartography, 25, 38n30, 39n47, 168
Cartwright, Nancy, 47
Cavanagh, Ted, 134
Chambers, Ephraim, 49
Chapuis, Alfred, 110
Charles II, King, 49
Château de Chambord, 123
Christoph & Unmack, 131
Church of Sainte Geneviève, 9–10
Church of Saint Solemne, 103
Church of Saint-Sulpice, 12; northern tower of, *13*
circuits, 192, 193, 195, 198, 199, 200, 201, 204, 206, 209, 210, 212; language of, 207
"Circular Causal Feedback Mechanisms in Biological and Social Systems," 208
Clausewitz, Carl von, 167
clay tablet, Akkadian, *221*
Clere, Richard: model by, 49, *50*
Clere, William: model by, 49, *50*
clockworks, 103, 230
cognition, 6, 25, 59, 191, 195, 198, 200
Cohen, Jean-Louis, 181
Cohen, Jonathan, 57
Cold War, 192, 194, 203, 211
collage, 22, 25
comets, modeling, 57, 58
communication, 91, 123, 130, 137, 153, 174, 177, 200, 203, 210; affiliated, 209; centralized/decentralized, 173; electrical, 234; frictionless, 186n10; language of, 207; materialities of, 78; refutation of, 190n47; schematic diagram of, *196*; theory, 172, 196, 211
community, 6, 123; computer programming, 28; scientific, 33
computation, 91, 207, 208, 213, 213n8, 240n3; architectural history of, 44n98
Computer Generated Architecture (CGA), 234
computer graphics, 25, 27, 28, 30, 155
computers, 215n24; network of, 77; stored-program, 201, 215n24
computing, 27, 200–202; digital, 26; early, 213n7
Comte, Louis, 112
Condit, Carl W., 181, 190n51
Confidences et révélations (Robert-Houdin), 103; title page of, *104*
connectivity, 90, 173, 212
consciousness, 92, 199, 205, 206, 207, 208, 209, 212, 222; agency and, 202–3; gestural habituation and, 236; historical, 228; orthographic, 235, 242n17; statistical, 235
construction, 146; building, 137, 144; business, 139; house, 139; process of, 140; schedules, 157; sites, 131, 137; techniques for, 136–37, 141; trades, 131; wood, 139
Construction Specification Institute (CSI), 156, 162n45
"Contract Document" (AIA), 155
control, 200–202, 212, 213, 231; comfort and, 105–9
Convent des Cordeliers, 11
copy electric telegraph, *81*
counterenvironment, 165
craft, art and, 129, 130
Crystal Palace, xv
CSI. *See* Construction Specification Institute

Cultivator and Country Gentleman, The (Woodward), 147, 151
customization, mass, 130, 158
cyberneticians, 191, 195, 203, 206, 207, 211
cybernetics, xvii, 91, 191, 193, 194, 200, 204, 209, 211, 212, 213, 213n6, 216n50
Cybernetics (Wiener), 193

d'Alcy, Jehanne, 122
d'Alembert, Jean Le Rond, 54, 106
Darwin, Charles, 182
Daston, Lorraine, 66n43, 203
data: collecting, 153, 212; display/raster-type, *75*; fetish of, 212; industrial, 153, 157, 158; as information, 238; memory and, 209; personalization, 207; presignalized technics of, 239; processing, 209; quantitative, xvi; real-time, 231; recyclability of, 211; retrieving, 201; storage of, 212; term, 224; transmission, 174
data mining, 212
Data Sheets, 156
death drive, 192
Debacle, The (Zola), 163
decoration, 14, 22, 106, 166
DeJean, Joan, 105
Deleuze, Gilles, 199
de Montespan, Madame, 105
de Pompadour, Madame, 105
depots, 169, 170, 189n43
Derrida, Jacques, 6, 36n15
des Combes, Eric de Broche, 1, 2
design, 141; architectural, 129, 136, 137, 139, 157, 182; automation of, 20; experiential basis of, 15; model, 49–50; network, 173; programs, 28; standardization of, 36n12; structural, 156; visual transmission of, 146
design course, exercise from, *94*
Desrosières, Alain, 233
determinism, 186n14, 193, 194, 213
Deutsch, Karl, 203

Dewey, John, 4
diagrams, 92, 133, 134, 151, 201, 204; technical, 184
Dickinson, Emily, 107
Dictionnaire (Viollet-le-Duc), 166
Diderot, Denis, 54, 106
digital, ix, xv, 4, 25, 30, 31, 33, 211, 219; analog and, xxin32; digitalization, 130, 157; genealogy of, xixn1; term, 232, 240n2
Dilthey, Wilhelm, 4, 88, 90, 91, 92
discourse, 204; American, 77; architectural, xxiin33, 46, 219; Enlightenment, x; Germanic, 77; instantized, 241n8; logistical, 170; progressive, 36n15
Discourse XIII (Reynolds), 47
discretization, 77, 79, 95
dissection, xvii, 84, 88
distribution, 152, 153, 156, 169, 175; media of, 186n19
Doane, Mary Ann, 204–5
Doric order, *142*; shadow of, *3*
dots: perceptual organization of, *88*; virtual, 24
double bind, model of, 210
Downing, Andrew Jackson, 147, 151
drawings, 25, 224, 227; architectural, 26, 46, 140, 144, 223; axonometric, xiv; building and, 233; construction, 168; culture of, 232; freehand, 91, 223; geometrical, 39n44; hand-mechanical, 222–23; isometric, 151; models and, 50; orthographic, 146, 228, 230; perspective, 141; standardized, 134
dromology, 171, 188n30
Duhem, Pierre, 51, 53, 56, 65n36
Dumit, Joseph, 200
Durand, Jacques-Nicolaus-Louis, 14, 39n48

Easterling, Keller, 181
Eastman, George: camera of, *225*
Eckert-Mauchly Computer Company, 172
École des Beaux-Arts, 2, 12, 14, 15

École Polytechnique, 9, 14
ecology, xvi, 169, 207, 219, 233
education, ix, 84, 99n51; artistic, 82; visual, 90–91
EDVAC. *See* Electronic Discrete Variable Automatic Computer
efficiency, 169; images of, 231; logic of, 169
Ehrenzweig, Anton, 92, 93, 95
Eiffel Tower, xv, 123
Einstein, Albert, 131
Eisenman, Peter, 46
Electronic Discrete Variable Automatic Computer (EDVAC), 200, 215n24
"Elements of Scientific Modeling" (Frigg), 59
Elowitz, Michael B., 45, 56, 61
enceinte de combat, 167
enceinte de préservation, 166
Encyclopédie (Diderot and d'Alembert), 54
Engelbart, Douglas, 157, 158
engineering, 45, 200, 201; control, 219; creativity, 30; electrical, 224; structural, 9
engineers: sensation/calculation and, 37n28; software, 31
Enlightenment, 37n25, 38n37, 53, 92, 111, 203
Entscheidungsproblem, 201
epistemology, xvi, 28, 54, 195, 199, 201, 203, 239; experimental, 202, 204; foundationalist, xviii; Helmholtzian, 92; relational, 38n37; shadow, 37n25; transformation of, 194
Erfahrung, 4
Ernst, Wolfgang, 74, 96n12
Escamotage d'une dame chez Robert-Houdin (Méliès), 122
escamoter, 123
Esri CityEngine, work of, *234*
essentialism, 236, 239
Ethereal Suspension, performance of, *114*
Evans, Robin, 227

experience, 96n12; always-present, 231; as completeness, 6; concept of, xvi; as constructed, 5–6; digital, 31; experiment and, 9; provisional theory of, 31; as received, 5–6; spatial, 228; term, 4, 32; unity of, 86; working theory of, 33
Experiential Technologies Laboratory (ETL), 31–32
experimentation, 9, 45, 220, 239
Extrastatecraft (Easterling), 181

fabrication, 47, 49, 243n31
familiarity, 111, 119; cognitive, 43n93; as coping mechanism, 232
Ferreiro, Larrie D., 181
Flächenbild, 82
flywheels, assembling, *235*
Ford Highland Part plant, *235*
formalism, 84, 90–91, 95, 101n82; brand of, 82; engineering, 45; mathematical, 59
formats, axioms and, 220–24, 226–27
forms: experiments with, *89;* teaching, 84
Forty, Adrian, 50
Foucault, Michel, xi, 97n19
Fouilloux, Catherine, 121–22
framework, 181, 219, 227; disciplinary, 95; imaginative, 231; logistical, 170
framing, 143, *143,* 144, *151;* platform, 159n9
Franklin, Benjamin, 184, 190n55
Frege, Gottlob, 201
French Academy of Sciences, 11
Freud, Sigmund, 193, 194, 205, 206
Frigg, Roman, 58, 61, 69n83, 70n94; modeling and, 60; on model systems, 69n87; pretense theory and, 61; work of, 59
Furètiere, Antoine, 49
future, 167, 174, 193, 198, 200, 201, 203, 204, 205, 228, 230, 231, 237, 239; determining, 212, 213, 238; digital, 130; performative, 194; technological, 195

Gainsborough, Thomas, 49
Galapagos form optimization fitness test, 232
Galerie de Choiseul, 112
Galileo, 6
Galison, Peter, 66n43, 91, 120
game theory, 91, 169, 174, 192
Gedankenexperiment, 199
Gehry, Frank, xv
Gélis, Edouard, 110
General Electric, 171
generality, 136, 143, 152, 155, 158, 236, 237
Geographic Information Systems (GIS), 234, 238
geometry, 4, 6, 7–8, 14, 18, 33, 146, 147, 223, 224; arithmetic and, 5; descriptive, 8; Euclidian/non-Euclidian, 35n10; transformation of, 37n20
Gesamtbild, 81–82
Gestalt, 87, 88, 91, 92, 96n3
Gestalten, 76
Gestaltung, 84
gesturing, 223; hand-mechanical, 228; orthographic, *223*
Giedion, Sigfried, xiii, xvii, xviii, xxiiin44, 234; American ingenuity and, 132–33; patents and, 137; tectonic trajectory and, xiv; tectonic unconscious and, xv; Wachsmann and, 132
Giere, Ronald, 57
gift of screws, 107
Giroux, Alphonse, 110
GIS. *See* Geographic Information Systems
Gödel, Kurt, 201
Godfrey-Smith, Peter, 56, 67n58
Goethe, Johann Wolfgang von, 66n42, 86, 185n8
Goodman, Nelson, 57
Goody, Jack, 174
Google Earth, 31, 32
Gordon, Peter, 33
Gottschaldt, Kurt, 87–88
Gouraud, Henri, 28

"Graded Washes of Watercolor" (Harbeson), *21*
Graf, Don, 155, 156, 157
Grand Central Terminal, xvii, 177; section diagram of, *180*
Grasshopper/Rhino, Galapagos form optimization fitness test in, *232*
Great Model, 49, *50*
Greenberg, Clement, 95
Gropius, Walter, 90, 131
Guattari, Félix, 199
Gutenberg Galaxy, The (McLuhan), 165
Gyan Vapi mosque, 48

Hacking, Ian, x, 63n10, 97n19; modeling and, 47, 51; on natural science, 45–46
hacks, 31, 43n95
handwriting, alphanumeric, 228
Haraway, Donna, 212
Harbeson, John F., 20; illustration by, *21*
Hastings, Warren, 47
Haussmann, Georges-Eugène, 10
Heidegger, Martin, 33
heliography, 223, 226, *226*
Helmholtz, Hermann von, 78, 79, 86, 92
Henkin, David M., 170
hermeneutics, 75, 79, 95, 96n12
Hertenberger, Claude: illustration by, *19*
"High Quality Physically-Accurate Visualization of the September 11 Attack on the World Trade Center, A" (Rosen, Popescu, Hoffmann, and Irfanoglu), *34*
Hilbert, David, 201
Hildebrand, Adolf von, 81, 82, 92; relief by, *83*
historiography, xiii, 168, 181
history, 203, 230, 239; architectural, xvi, 76, 144, 177, 181–82, 184, 185n6, 190n51, 228; cybernetic, 212; intellectual, 76; military, 167, 168; technical, 76
Hodges, William, 47, 48, 54, 64n15; painting by, *48*
Hoffmann, Christopher: work of, *34*

Index

Holland, Michael, 163
Hollerith system, 75
Holzhausbau, 131
Home Building (Hussey), 152, 153
Homer, 54
Hooke, Robert, 49, 51; experiment of, 57, 58
hospitality, 105, 114, 122
Houdin, Josèphe Cécile Églantine, 110
Houdini, Harry, 109, 125n21
"How to Build Balloon Frames" (Robinson), 147
Hughes Aircraft, 172
Hugo, Victor, 115
humanities, 90, 95, 102n86
Humboldt, Wilhelm von, 90
Husserl, Edmund, 4, 6, 32, 36nn14–15, 44n104
Hussey, Elish Charles, 152–53
Hutchinson, Oliver, 226
Hymen relief (Hildebrand), 83

IBM, 28, 75, 171
identity, 130; analogy and, 44n100; collective, 129
ideology, 189n43; idea and, x
image-making, 6, 243n31
image-models, 230, *231*, 235
images, 1, 20, 77, 233, 239; collecting, 141; contemporary use of, 238; electrical, 224, 230; evidentiary, 243n31; video-monitor, 243n31; visual, 227
imagination: architecture of, 69n82; historical, 44n106
imaging: architecture after, 220; automation and, 233–34; simulation and, 234; technical, 220
imitation, 53–56
immediacy: real time and, 170–75; reflexivity and, 209
incompletion, aesthetics of, 31–33
Industrial Age, xv
industrialization, 133, 136

industrial process, 132, 134
Industrial Revolution, xv, 51, *53*
industrial society, 153, 157
industry, 130, 165; large-scale, 152; standards, 31, 133
inefficiency, 171–72
infinity, logic and, 204, 211
information, 155, 158, 204, 205, 209; collecting, 12, 195; military, 241n8; organizing, 243n31; signalized, 241n8; sources of, 152; storing, 77; theory, 42n83, 166; visual, 241n8
Information Age, xv
Information Sciences Division (U.S. Air Force), 157
infrastructure, 157, 170, 177; data storage, 211; invisibility of, 190n54
Innis, Harold, 174
instantaneity: media effect of, 174; rhetoric of, 172
integration, 27, 91, 139
intelligence, 191, 194; collective, 195; modeling, 203; representation of, 209
intermédiaire des chercheurs et curieux, L', 109
International Business Machines Corporation, 75
International Congress of Photogrammetry, 24
Interospectionists, 87
"Interpretation of Dreams, The" (Freud), 205
intervention, 46, 53, 58, 204, 220, 239, 243n31
Irfanoglu, Ayhan: work of, 34
isometrical perspective, *151*

Jacopozzi, Fernand, 123
Jardin du Luxembourg, 11
Jauss, Hans Robert, 115
Javal, Louis Émile, 84; saccadic movements and, 86
Jomini, Antoine-Henri, 167, 168

Jones, Owen, 177
Joyce, James, 166

Kahn, Albert, 153; plans for offices of, *154*
Kant, Immanuel, 66n43, 185n8; modeling and, 47, 53, 54, 55, 62; *Nachahmung* and, 61, 66n44; *Nachfolge* and, 56, 61; on work of genius, 54; works of, 53–54
Kapp, Ernst, xi, 76
Karnak, 31, 32
Kepes, György, 91, 92
King Lear (Shakespeare), 166
Kirk, David: work of, *30*
Kirsch, Russell A., 74
Kittler, Friedrich, xi, 174, 204, 233
knowledge, 56, 158, 206; cumulative, 222; instrumentalization of, xvi; logistical, 169; monetization of, xvi; politics of, 62; power and, 169; scientific, 55; as subjective, 169; theoretical, 144
Krafft-Ebing, Richard von, 82
Krinsky, Carol, 181
Kritik Der Urteilskraft (Kant), 53
Kuhn, Thomas, 61, 62
Kunstform, xiii

Laboratory Life (Latour), 55
labor: clerical, 157, 158; creative, 137; hierarchy, 40n59; intellectual, 137; machine and, 129; mechanical, 105; organization of, 164; process, 131, 226; structural/instrumental form of, xiii
labor movements, architectural culture and, 20
Labrouste, Henri, 22; restoration by, 15, 18, *18*
Lacan, Jacques, 209
landscape, xvi, 15, 165; absence of, 32
Larkin Administration Building, xiv
Latour, Bruno, 9, 38, 55, 116
Latrobe, Benjamin Henry: contract by, 140, *140*
Laugier, Marc-Antoine, xiii

Le Camus de Mézières, Nicolas, 106
LeCavalier, Jesse, 181
Le Corbusier, 22, 184n4, 191, 241n13
Legend of Etana, *221*
Leibler, Stanislas, 45, 56, 61
Leroy, Julien-David, 12, 181
L'Eveille, Stanislas, 9
Levy, Arnon, 61, 69n83
Lincoln Cathedral, 181
linear graphism, 5, 227
lines: operational, 5; respect for, 35n9; shadows and, 4–5, 27, 36n14
logic, 195, 199, 211, 219, 230; calculative, 209; computational, 192; embodied/affective, 195; history of, 200; memory and, 210; organizational, 189n43; psychotic, 198, 207; symbolic, 77
"Logical Calculus of Ideas Immanent in Nervous Activity, A" (McCulloch and Pitts), 196
logic gates, multitudes of, 202
logistics, 175, 177, 182, 186n16, 190n48, 207; historiography of, 168; language of, 171; military, 167–70; nationalization of, 188n31; problems in, 169; scholarship on, 167; theories of, 165, 169, 187n23
London Central School of Arts and Crafts, design course exercise from, *94*
Loriot, Antoine-Joseph, 106, 107, 109
Loudon, John Claudius, 147
Louis XIV, 229
Louis XV, 105, 108
lumber, 139, 143, 144, 152, 153
Luxigon, 1, 2, 32
Lynch, Kevin, 203
Lynn, Greg, 32

machine, 76, 103, 195, 203; human labor and, 129; intelligence, 27
machine gun, design for, 137, *138*
Macy Conferences, 208, 210
make-believe: science and, 61–62; social environment of, 60

Mallory, Keith, 181
Marcus, Sharon, 117
Marquette building, 153
Martin, Reinhold, 181
Martin-Fugier, Anne, 111, 119, 121
Marx, Karl, xi, 76, 186n19
Marx, Leo, xii
Massachusetts Institute of Technology (MIT), 91, 92, 195, 196
mass production, 63n9, 146; balloon frame and, 147; standardized, 130
Massumi, Brian, 203
master-and-slave dialectic, x, xi
master builders, xv, 141
MasterFormat, 156, 162n45
material conditions, xi, 9, 110, 200
materialism, 166, 172
materials, 134, 156, 185n6; bills of, 152; building, 137, 139, 153; mass-produced, 131; toxic, 243n31
mathematics, 5, 6, 156, 174, 199, 201
mathematization, 2, 36n14, 224, 226
Maza, Sarah, 119, 120
McCulloch, Warren, 195–96, 199, 200, 201, 202, 206, 208, 209, 214n18, 214n22; Bateson and, 210; logic and, 198
McGoodwin, Henry, 1, 20, 22, 30; drawings by, 2, *3*, 4
McLuhan, Marshall, xi, 166, 174, 177, 185n9; counterenvironment and, 165; media and, 76
mécanicien, 106, 108
mechanical arts, concepts of, 54
mechanization, xviii, 234, 242n23; signalization and, 236
Mechanization Takes Command (Giedion), xiv, xvii
media, 164, 171; digital, 4; graphic, 9; mechanical, 22; orthographic, 230; theory, x
media archaeology, 76, 172, 188n34
Media Lab, 203
Méliès, Georges, 122, 123

Memoirs of Robert-Houdin (Robert-Houdin), 109, 124
memory, 192, 194, 198, 200–202, 205, 206, 212; cultural, 158; as cyclical machine, 208–9; data and, 209; externalizing, 222; logic and, 210; machine, 195, 208; persistence of, 208; possession of, 201; storage, 74, 211; technical, 230; understandings of, 209
Mercure de France, 106, 107, 108
Merleau-Ponty, Maurice, 32
metaphors, xviii, xxiiin46, 98n27, 165, 177, 190n54; philosophical, 77
metaphysics, x, 5, 171, 239
Metzner, Paul, 110
Meydenbauer, Albrecht, 22
Mies van der Rohe, Ludwig, xiii, 22
military, architecture and, 40n57, 177
Millon, Henry A., 49, 65n27
Mimesis as Make-Believe (Walton), 60
Mitchell, W. J. T., 55
model description, 57, 58, 61
modeling, xii, 45, 48–49, 54, 63n11, 67n45, 67n58, 70n94; analogy and, 69n77; architectural, 55, 62, 63n7; comet, 57, 58; computational, 66n42; elements of, *59*; Enlightenment and, 53; illustrations and, 50; *imitatio/emulatio* and, 49; industry and, 53; instrumentality of, 49; locating, 46–47; as make-believe, 60; philosophical literature on, 56; power and, 55; process of, 58–59; scientific, 60; theoretical potential of, 62
models, 231, 238; cardboard, *29*; copying, 54; describing, 61; digital, 42n80; drawings and, 50; electrical, 230; fictionality of, 56; group of, 59–60; as ideological, 51; internal construction of, 70n94; interpreting, 56; logistical, 168–69; machine-like, 62; mathematical, 195; messiness of, 59; natural sciences and, 50; products of genius, 53; speculation

on, 46; studying, 69n87; term, 48–49, 51, 63n8
model systems, 58–59, 69n87
Modern Architect (Shaw), 144, 146; frontispiece from, *145*
modernism, xiii, xiv, 22, 40n65, 76, 130, 133, 158
modernity, 15, 76, 95, 184n4; American, 159n2; formlessness of, 91; linear graphic representation and, 5; pendulum of, 82; reflexive, xvii
Modern Movement, xiii, xv
Moholy-Nagy, László, 90, 91
Monte Carlo simulations, 173
monuments: logistical, 177, 181–82, 184; photographic archives of, 24; rebuilding, 41n70; recording, 41n74; rendering, 165
Morgan, Mary S., 47, 56
morphology, xvii, 56, 88
Morrison, Margaret, 56, 59
Morse, Samuel, 81; telegraphic notation by, *80*
Morse code, 79, 81, 119
mother-clock, 120–21
movement, 15, 24, 57, 78, 79, 82, 122, 169, 172, 184n4, 236; camera, 32; cultural techniques of, 170; hand, 223; problem of, 164; saccadic, *86*, 87; screen, 224
Müller, Johannes, 78, 98n28
Müller-Lyer diagram, 92, *93*
Mumford, Lewis, xii, xvii, xviii, xxiiin44; neotechnic phrase of, xxiiin43; selfhood and, xi; technics and, xxiin30
mysterious organizations, 114, 121–24
"Mysterious Pendulum," 122
mythologies, 47–51, 53

Nachahmung, 53–56, 61, 66n44
Nachfolge, 53–56, 61, 66n44
Nancy, Jean-Luc, 163
Napoleon, 167
narcissism, 53

narratives, ix, 6, 205, 206; tectonic, xiii; teleological, 146
National Institute of Health, 210
National Lumber Manufacturers Association, 133
naturalism, 8–9, 49
natural sciences, xvi, 45–46, 51, 90; models and, 50
nature, 51; imitation of, 47; mastery over, xxiiin44; nature of, 238
Negroponte, Nicholas, 203
neoclassicism, 15, 28
neonaturalism, 238
nervous-electric transmission, theory of, 79
nervous system, 77; theorizing, 209–13
nets, 203; action of, 198; logical calculus of, 195–96, 198, 202; neural, 198, 200; neuronal, 198; as semiotic situations, 196
networks, 77, 173, 194, 200, 211; behavior, 191; centralized, *173*; communication, 207; decentralized, *173*; digital, 191, 195; discourse, 204; distributed, *173*; logistical, 185n6; nervous, 204; oscillatory, 45; problems for, 208; rational, 202–4; smart, 191; speculative, 212; technical, 191
neural net, 195; structures, *197*
Neurath, Otto, xviii–xix
neurons, 77, 196, 198, 203, 204, 214n18
neuroscience, xvi, 195, 214n18
New Bauhaus, 91
New Criticism, 95
Newell, Martin, 28
Newton, Isaac, 54, 193
Nguyen, James, 61, 69n83, 70n94
Niépce, Nicéphore, 226; image by, *226*
Nipkow, Paul Gottlieb, 78, 79, 88, 224; myth of, 98n32
Nipkow disk, 71, 84, 87
Nolan, Thomas, 155
Nordau, Max, 82
Notes and Queries, 109

objectivity, 193, 194, 204, 207, 239
object lesson, 82, 84
oblique letters, construction of, *229*
"Of Devine Places" (Nancy), 163
"On Distributed Communications Networks" (RAND Corporation), 172
ontology, 239; historical, x, 76, 97n19
oral transmission, process of, 136
organisms, 45, 209
Organizational Complex (Martin), 181
organ projection, xi, 76, 236
"Origins of Geometry, The" (Husserl), 6
ornamentation, xiii, xxin24, 141, 144, 164, 175, 177
orthography, 227–28, 230, 231, 234, 242n17; architectural, 228; hand-mechanical, 235; nonalphabetic, 228; parallel/perspectival, 220; psychology of, 232, 233; simulated, *231*
Osman, Michael, xvi, 181
Others, enemy, 192
Ottar, Arvid, 181

Packaged House System, 131
Paddington Station, 175, 176; reconstructed plan of, *176*; sketch of, *178*
"Palace for the Exhibition of Fine Arts, A" (Bénard), *17*
Palais Royale, 108, 117
Palladio, Andrea, 7
parallelism, 74, 77, 96n5, 97n22
Paris, 36n18, 103, 113; aerial photograph of, 22; architectural experiences of, 15; urban survey of, 10, 12
Parisi, Luciana, 204
parti, 175, 177, 189n43
Pascal, Blaise, x, xixn2
patents, 137
pattern books, 141
pattern seeking, 209
pedagogy, 5, 20, 82, 84
Pencil Points, 155
Pensées (Althusser), x

perception, 84, 198, 231; model of, 92; ocular, 239; scale of, 25
perceptual organization, 88
Pérez-Gómez, Alberto, 5, 6, 35n10
performance: images of, 231; models/ecological, 238
Perrot, Michelle, 111, 119
Pestalozzi, Johann Heinrich, 84, 185n8; curriculum of, *85*
Pevsner, Nikolaus, 181
phenomenology, 6, 31, 32, 33, 43n96, 86
Phong, Bui Tuong, 28
photoconductive properties, 79
photogrammetry, 25–26; machines, *24, 25*; as mechanical rendering, 22, 24–25; Renaissance surveyors and, 22; stereo, 25; traditional, 24–25
photography, 20, 25, 223–24, 227; aerial, 41n74; horizontal, 22; single-point, 24
photon-detection, *226*
Photoshop, 20
physics, 56, 171, 211, 236
physiology, 82, 199, 202
Pitts, Walter, 196, 198, 199, 200, 201, 202, 206, 214n13, 214n18
planning, 156, 184; exigencies of, 182; practice/science of, 144; urban, 195, 220
Planning and Coding of Problems for an Electronic Computing Instrument (Goldstine and von Neumann), 201
Plan Voisin (Le Corbusier), 22
plaster cast, shadows and, *23*
politics, 62, 203, 204, 233, 235, 239; class, 168
Pompeii, reconstruction of, 26–27, 42n80
Pompeii (film), 27
Popescu, Voicu: work of, *34*
populationism, 236
porpoise, xvii, 210, 211, 212
Porter, Theodore M., 6
Port of New York, The (Condit), 190n51
position, architecture of, 163–67, 177
positivism, xvi, 56

Postal Age, The (Henkin), 170
postorthography, 230–33, 236; gestural technics, *240*
power, 137; knowledge and, 169; modeling and, 55; rhetorical, xiv; as subjective, 169
Précis de l'art de la guerre (Clausewitz), 167
preemption, 188n30, 203
presentation, 238–39, 243n31
pretense theory, 60, 61
Priestly, Joseph, 51, 53
Prieuré, La (Robert-Houdin), 105
Priory, 103, 113, 114–20, 122, 123, 124, 125n24; comfort/control at, 105–9; domestic drama of, 121; hospitality at, 105; mother-clock at, 120–21; portal at, 105, 117
probability theory, 74, 236–37
Problem der Form, Das (Hildebrand), 81
Producers' Council, 156
production, 4, 8; industrial, 22, 133, 136, 139, 155; intellectual, 129; real-time, 235; standardization of, 36n12
products: building, 156; concept and, 130; material/immaterial, 129
progress, political philosophy of, 239
projection, 36n16, 49, 77, 87, 192–93, 205, 208; organ, xi, 76, 236
prosthetic extension, using, 24, 26
psychoanalysis, 194, 195, 204–8, 212–13; cybernetic invocations of, 204–5
psychology, 84, 86, 192, 199, 203, 207; descriptive, 90; experimental, 82; Gestalt, 87, 88, 92; mass, 227; Wundtian, 87, 100n54
psychosis, 191, 194, 202, 209, 210; cybernetics invocations of, 204–5; as rationality, 198–200
Puckle, James: design by, 137, *138*
Pugin, A. W. N., 164

Quatremère de Quincy, Antoine-Chrysostôme, 14, 49

Rabinow, Jacob, 74
Radiation Lab, 195
radiosity, 27, 30–31
railroad stations, 166, 175, 189nn43–44
Ramsey, Charles George, 133
RAND Corporation, 172, 174, 192, 193
rationality, xii, 194, 195, 203, 212; algorithmic, 208; psychosis as, 198–200; redefinition of, 201
ray-tracing, 27, 30
reading machine, 71, *72*, *73*
real time, 184, 188n32, 191, 194, 226, 231; immediacy and, 170–75; media of, 170–75; technical conditions of, 236
reason, 203, 208, 209, 215n32; calculative/computational, 199. *See also* rationality
reasoning: architectural, 219, 220, 235, 238; historical, 239; neonaturalistic, 238; orthographic, 228; probabilistic, 236–37; restructuring of, 236; statistical, 236
redundancy, 172–73
reflection, historical/philosophical, 220, 222, 237
Reiselius, Salomon, 112
Reizen, 79, 81; telegraphic notation by, *80*
relationships, 211; causal, 236; cybernetic, 195; historical, xii; space-time, 171
rendement, 12, 39n40
Rendered Account (Compte Rendu), 12
rendering, 2, 4, 5–6, 8, 9, 10; Arts and Crafts–inspired definition of, 32; classical, 24; computer, 27; day of, 15; digital, 1, *2*, 25–28, 30–31; experiential basis of, 26; experiment, *29*; hand, 36n14; instruments, 33; machine, 28; mechanical, 22, 24–25; tools, 26, 31; as working drawing, 12, 14–15, 18, 20, 22
rendu, 12, 14, 15
representation, 206, 220; computational, 209; crisis of, 219, 238; graphic, 133, 141; logical, 201, 209; mathematical, 209; neonatural, 238–39; theories of, 57, 61

repressilator, learning from, 56–62
restitutors, 24, 25
Restor House, 22
REX, 32; design by, 2
Reynolds, Joshua, 49, 50, 53, 54, 61; Hodges and, 47, 48
Ringer, Fritz, 90
Riskin, Jessica, 111
Robert-Houdin, Églantine Lemaître, 113, 122, 123
Robert-Houdin, Émile, 113
Robert-Houdin, Jean-Eugène, 123–24, 125n21, 125n24; automata and, 111, 112; as *escamoteur*, 123; family drama and, 109–14; hospitality of, 122; memoir of, 103, 105, 115, 124; monitoring by, 119; performance by, 113, 114; Priory and, 115, 116–17, 120, 121; Soirées Fantastiques and, 113, 115–16; stage sets of, 109; theater of, 108
Robert-Houdin, Paul, 123
Robinson, Solon, 147, 151
Rockefeller Center, 181
Romain du roi (King's roman), oblique letters for, 229
Roman, Gretta Tritch, 181
Rome Prize, 15, 18
Rondelet, Jean-Baptiste, 9
roof plan, 8
Rookery Building, 153
Root, John Wellborn, 182; schematic plan by, 183
Rosen, Paul: work of, 34
Rosenblatt, Frank, 77
Rosenblueth, Arturo, 195
Rotman, Brian, 174
Rowe, Colin, 87
Royal Academy of Arts, 47
Rural Architecture (Upjohn), 141, 144, 146
Ruskin, John, 163, 169, 177, 184nn3–4, 185n6, 185n8, 186n14; architecture and, 164, 165, 166
Russell, Bertrand, 201

Saint-Gervais, 103, 105, 115
salon, Louis XV–style, 108, *108*
Salon of 1763: 106–7
Santner, Eric, 205
scanning, 74, 76, 77, 82, 84, 88, 91, 92, 95, 99n43, 208, 220, 239
Schaeffer, Simon, 9, 31
schizophrenia, 192, 210, 213n2, 217n53
"science and spectacle," culture of, 11
Science in Action (Latour), 55
sciences, 91–92, 200; architectural, 4–5; building, 220; computer, xvi, 27; concepts of, 54; critique of, 56; history of, 36n14; human, 90, 200, 204, 207, 209, 213n6; information, 194; make-believe and, 61–62; natural, xvi, 45–46, 50, 51, 90; operating procedures of, 61; philosophy of, 65n36; physical, 169; puzzle solving and, 61; social, 90, 203, 204, 213n6; subjective, 198; tabletop, 6–12
Sears, Roebuck and Company, 131, 139
Select Views in India (Hodges), 47
self-referential systems, 194, 206
semantic situations, 56, 68n59, 70n94, 71, 74
Semper, Gottfried, xiii, xxn19, xxinn23–24
shadow-casting, 8, 28
shadows: lines and, 4–5, 27, 36n14; naturalist artifice and, 7; photographic, 22; science of, 8, *8*; shades and, 6; trigonometry and, 31
Shakespeare, William, 166
Shanken, Andrew M., 155
Shapin, Steven, 9, 31
Shaw, Edward, 144, 146; frontispiece for, *145*
Shepard, David H., 75, 77, 95n3; reading machine of, 71, *73*, 74, 76, 84
Siegert, Bernhard, x, xi, 188n34
SIGGRAPH '87, 28, 30
signalization, 224, 234, 237, 241n8; electrical, 238; mechanization and, 236; signification and, 238

signals, 224, 234; sending/receiving, 79, 81
signification, 205, 227, 238
Simmel, Georg, 81
Simon, Herbert, 203
simulation, 45, 111, 173, 230, 231, 234
"Six Platonic Solids" (Arvo and Kirk), 30
Sketchpad, 27
Sleeper, Harold Reeve, 134, 155
software, 31, 158; digital, 20, 26, 27, 129; drafting, 28; modeling, 44n98; rendering, 32
Soufflot, Jacques-Germain, 9
space, 15, 163, 211, 185n5, 241n14; administering, x–xi; geometricization of, 5; surveying, x–xi
specification, 29, 141, 157, 158; architectural, 130, 131, 136
"Specification Desk, The," 155
Sprague, Frank J., 177, 189n46; third rail by, *179*
Staffordshire pottery works, 50
stage set, Louis XV–style, *108*, 113, 122
standard, 132, 136; custom and, 130; internal, 134
standardization, 133, 134, 146, 158
static theory, 192
statistical thinking, 45, 237, 238
Stendhal, 111
Stevens, Alfred, 177
Steyerl, Hito, 32
Stiegler, Bernard: on technics, 172, 241n6
Stil, Der (Semper), xiii
stimulus, 78, 198, 200, 209; response and, 77
Stones of Venice, The (Ruskin), 163, 164, 165
storage, 201, 212, 224, 227; memory and, 211
St. Paul's Cathedral: Great Model of, 49, *50*; rebuilding, 49
Stratton, G. M., 84
Stroud, John, 208, 209

Study of Architectural Design, The (Harbeson), 20
subjectivity, 194, 198, 204, 212
Sullivan, Louis, xiii
surveying, x, 7, 31, 36n14, 41n70; architectural, 22, 24
Sutherland, Ivan Edward, 27
"Sweet's" (Architectural Record Company), 153, 155–56
switching system, 173, 174, 189n38
switching theory, 77
synchronization, 45, 55, 158, 223
systems theory, 169, 173, 187n23
Syzchowski, Janek: experiment by, *58*

table volante, 107
Tafuri, Manfredo, 22, 181
Tauschek, Gustav, 75, 77, 92, 95n3, 97n17; career of, 97n16; reading machine of, 71, *72*, 74, 76, 84
technical, 204, 220, 221–22, 232
technical systems, xvii, 222, 230
technics, 76, 172, 188n32, 221, 222, 230, 241n6; architecture and, x, xv; artifactual, xi, xv; engagement with, xviii; instrumentalizing knowledge and, xv; modernism and, xiv; presignalized, 239; technology and, xii–xiii; term, xii; understanding, xvi. See also *Technik*; technique; technology
Technik, x, xii, xxn13. *See also* technics; technique; technology
technique, 237; architectural, xixn9; biological philosophy of, 236; formalist, 95; instrumentalizable, 239; representational, 188n30; technology and, xii
technology, xxn14, 56, 71, 88, 133, 194; architecture and, xxiiin44; artifactual, xi; communication, 174; development of, 76, 174; digital, xv; domestic, xviii; explicit, 198; gendering, xxn14; hazardous concept of, xii; media, 195, 204, 212; nonarchitectural, 33; print, 166;

recognition, 96n3; scanning, 76; statistical, 207; tactile, 25; technics and, xii–xiii; telegraphic, 79; viewing, 77
technoscience, 219, 220
tectonics, xiii, xiv, xvii, 170
telegraphic notations, *80*
telegraphy, 78, 79, 81, 224
telemasis, 237–39
telematics, 226, 233, 239, 241n8
Temple of Minerva, 144
Temple of Paestum, 15; restoration of, 18, *18*, 22
Temple of Theseus, *142*
temporality, 45, 175, 191, 194, 195, 206, 211; deterministic, 193; historical, 200; mechanical, 193; probabilistic/predictive, 198; self-referential, 208; system-generated, 208; teleological/functional, 205; vitalist, 193
termini, 171, 175, 189n43
Théâtre des Soirées Fantastiques, 103, 110, 115–16; automata and, 112–13; showbill for, *115*; stage set for, *108*
Théâtre Robert-Houdin, 122, 123
theorization, 233; logistics and, 165, 169
third rail, section and plan of, *179*
Thomas, Katie Lloyd, 136
Thompson, Edward G., 152
Thorpe, George C., 169, 171
thought: architectural, 165; forms of, 220–21; probabilistic, 193–94; self-referential, 193
"3D Modeling Software for Urban Environments" (Esri CityEngine), *234*
time, 192, 204–8; conception of, 222, 230; fragmentation of, 188n32; indeterminant, 198
Toon, Adam, 60, 69n83
track levels, schematic plans for, *180*
Trevelyan, G. M., xvii
triangulations, 10–11, 24
trigonometric operations, plan of, *11*
trigonometry, shadows and, 31

Turing, Alan, 201
Turing machine, 196, 198, 200, 201, 205
typology, 170, 175

Ulysses (Joyce), 166
unconscious, 206, 209; computational methods of, 207; Freudian, 193; scanning, 92, 95; tectonic, xiii, xv, xxin21
Unmasking of Robert-Houdin (Houdini), 109–10
Upjohn, Richard, 141, 146; framing by, *143*; publication by, 143–44
Upton, Dell, 141
Urban Apparatus (Martin), 181
urbanism, 10, 11, 165, 233
U.S. Capitol building, 28
U.S. Department of Defense, 172
U.S. National Laboratory System, 181
U.S. Railroad Administration, 171
Utah teapot, 28, *30*
Utopia's Ghost (Martin), 181

Valade, Jean, 106–7
Van Creveld, Martin, 168
Van Santen, David, 15
Vaucanson, Jacques de, 111–12, 113
Veblen, Thornstein, xxn13
Verniquet, Edme, 12, 38n31; demonstrations sheet and, 11; plan by, *11*, 38n30, 38n35, 38n39; triangulation and, 24; trigonometry/shadows and, 31; urban survey by, 10; workshop of, 38n37
Vers une architecture (Le Corbusier), 170
View from the Window at Le Gras (Nièpce), 226, *226*
"View of Part of the City of Benares, upon the Ganges" (Hodges), *48*
violence, 192, 194, 210; self-referential, 209
Viollet-le-Duc, Eugène-Emmanuel, xiii, 41n69, 166, 167
Virgilio, Paul, 181; doxology and, 171, 188n30

vision, 88, 92, 222; epistemic, 227; mechanization of, 20
visualization, 14, 27, 190n54, 191, 208, 212, 220; architectural, 1, 5, 33; conscious, 92; data, 207; technoscientific, 238
Vom Krieg (On War) (Clausewitz), 167
von Neumann, John, 199, 200, 208, 215n24
Vorkurs, 90

Wachsmann, Konrad, 131, 132, 133, 139, 157, 159n3; diagrams by, 134; wood-frame system of, *132*
Walton, Kendall, 60, 69n83, 70n89; pretense theory and, 60–61
Warren & Wetmore, section diagram by, *180*
Watson Library, 28
Wedgwood, Josiah, 50, 51, *53*
Weisberg, Michael, 57
Wertheimer, Max, 87
western frame, 134, *135*
Western Union, 81
Whitehead, Alfred North, 201

Wiener, Norbert, 191, 193, 194, 195, 196, 208
Wild A8 analog photogrammetry restitution machine, *24*
Wilgus, William J., 189n46; Grand Central Terminal and, 177; schematic plan by, *180*; third rail by, *179*
Williams, Raymond, 9
Wittgenstein, Ludwig, 61, 70n91, 210
Wölfflin, Heinrich, xviii, 82, 99n46
wood-frame system, illustrations of, *132*
Woods, Mary, 141
Woodward, George E., 147, 151, 152
Woodward's Country Homes (Woodward), 151
Woodward's National Architect (Woodward and Thompson), 152
World Trade Center, rendering of, 33
Wren, Christopher, 49–50
Wundt, Wilhelm, 84, 86
Wundtians, 86–87, 100n54
Wyatt, Matthew Digby, 177

Zola, Émile, 163, 167